OSCAR S. STRAUS
© BY PIRIE MAC DONALD, N.Y.

Under Four Administrations

Oscar S. Straus

Under Four Administrations

FROM CLEVELAND TO TAFT

RECOLLECTIONS OF

OSCAR S. STRAUS, Litt.D., LL.D.

Member of the Permanent Court of Arbitration at The Hague
Three Times Minister and Ambassador to Turkey
Former Secretary of Commerce and Labor

WITH ILLUSTRATIONS

Boston and New York
HOUGHTON MIFFLIN COMPANY
The Riverside Press Cambridge
1922

The Riverside Press
CAMBRIDGE · MASSACHUSETTS
PRINTED IN THE U·S·A

DEDICATED TO
MY GRANDCHILDREN
AND THEIR CONTEMPORARIES
OF EVERY RACE AND CREED

PREFACE

I AM drawing these memories to a close in my log cabin in the primitive Maine woods, where my wife and I have been coming for rest and for fishing for the past twenty years. Here we renew our youth, and far from tumult and crowds, near to nature, we realize anew how little is required in order to be contented and happy. Here I am taken back to the memories of my childhood in the little town in Georgia where too our home was a log house, but for appearances had the luxurious outer and inner dressing of clap-boarding painted white. The logs of the upper story where we children played and slept had no covering, which pleased us all the more.

In a highly organized society, we are often attracted by pomp and circumstance, rather than by qualities of heart and mind, which after all are the true measure of enlightenment. Here in these woods, fair dealings and human relations are not regulated by statutes, but by the golden rule of conduct. We need not hide our possessions behind locked doors, honesty is the accepted rule of life; there are no treasures to hide and no bars to break.

It has been permitted me to do useful work and to have interesting experiences. Privileged opportunities have been afforded me for public service. Of these I write.

Perhaps in chronicling the experiences of a life which at many points touched vital affairs and the most interesting personalities, I may be able to add something to the record of men, movements, and events during those decades still absorbing to us because they are so near.

The story is one of service at home and abroad, of personal relations with six of our Presidents, with diplomats, labor leaders, foreign rulers, leaders of industry, and some plain unticketed citizens who were the salt of the earth and certainly not the least of those whom it was a pleasure to know.

To write of one's self requires a certain amount of egotism. The autobiographer usually tries to justify this vanity by explaining it as a desire to gratify his children and kinsmen, or as a yielding to the urgent request of his friends. Benjamin Franklin, whose autobiography, incomplete though it be, is one of the most human in our language, frankly conceded that he was prompted by the weakness of praise. He says: "I may as well confess it, since my denial of it will be believed by nobody, perhaps I shall a good deal gratify my own vanity."

I do not wish to conceal from those who may from interest or curiosity read what I write, that I am not entirely free from that vanity, even though it be my chief aim and purpose to cast some additional light upon our country's development and upon events in which, in public and private life, I have been permitted to take part. Having held official positions at home and abroad under four administrations, and having come in close relationship with many of the statesmen and others of distinction in this and foreign countries, perhaps my narrative will serve to give more intimate knowledge and truer appreciation of their personal traits and their exceptional qualities.

I have also been influenced by a desire to bring a message of encouragement to the youth of our country, especially to those who may be conscious of handicaps in the race, not to lose heart, but to be patient, considerate, and tactful, and not to withhold the saving extra ounce of effort which often spells the difference between failure and success.

So long as our democracy remains true to its basic principles and jealously guards the highways of opportunity, the golden age will not be in the past, but ever in the future. In externals the age in which we live has changed, but the qualities of effort, of industry, and the will to succeed which were required when I was a boy, have not changed; they lead to the same goals now as then, with this difference: that the boy of to-day has greater advantages, better educational facilities, and more avenues of advancement than the boy of two generations ago. There never was a time in our history when more men of humble origin have attained commanding positions in industry, in commerce, and in public affairs than now. While our American system is not without fault, the fact that an enlightened public is ever watchful to maintain our democratic principles and to correct abuses is convincing proof of our country's wholesome development in conformity with the changing conditions of modern life.

I desire to make acknowledgment to my long-time and esteemed friend, Mr. Lawrence Abbott, the President of "The Outlook," who encouraged and advised me to write these memoirs and even outlined the chapter plan which I have largely followed.

CONTENTS

ILLUSTRATIONS

Under Four Administrations

. .

CHAPTER I

ANCESTRY AND EARLY YEARS

Napoleonic Era: the Sanhedrin — A forefather in Napoleon's councils — My father and the German Revolution of 1848 — My father emigrates to America — My father starts business in Talbotton, Georgia — My mother and her children arrive, 1854 — We attend the Baptist Church — My early schooling — Deacons duel with knives — Household slaves — Life in a small Southern town — Frugal and ingenious housekeeping — Outbreak of the Civil War — Our family moves to Columbus, Georgia — First lessons in oratory — General Wilson's capture of the city — The town is looted — Our family moves North — My father surprises Northern creditor by insisting upon paying his debts in full — I attend Columbia Grammar School in New York City — My accidental schoolroom glory before Morse, the inventor — I enter Columbia College in 1867 with Brander Matthews, Stuyvesant Fish, and other distinguished classmates — My classroom début in diplomacy — Poetic ambitions — Military aspirations and an interview with President Grant — Choosing law as a career.

MY ancestors, on both my father's and my mother's side, were natives of the Palatinate of Bavaria, of the town of Otterberg and immediate vicinity. Up to the time of Napoleon's taking possession of that part of the country the Jews of the Palatinate had not adopted family names. This they did later, beginning in 1808, when, under Napoleon, the Palatinate became the Department of Mont Tennérre and part of France. My great-grandfather, for instance, before adopting the family name of Straus, was known as Jacob Lazar, from Jacob ben Lazarus, or Jacob son of Lazarus, as in biblical times.

Jacob Lazar, afterwards Jacob Straus, had three sons: Jacob, Lazarus, and Salomon. My father, Lazarus Straus, born April 25, 1809, was the son of the eldest,

Jacob; and my mother, Sara Straus, born January 14, 1823, was the daughter of the youngest, Salomon. My paternal grandfather died when my father was a young man, but my grandfather Salomon Straus and his brother Lazarus were known to us as children, particularly to my eldest brother, Isidor, who knew them quite well. They were men of culture and education, landowners who sent their crops — mainly wheat, oats, clover and clover seed — and those of their neighbors to the markets of Kaiserslautern and Mannheim, the chief commercial towns of the section. They spoke German and French fluently, and had also, of course, been thoroughly educated in the Hebrew language and literature.

The name of Straus was well known among the Jews of Bavaria, and both my great-grandfather and my father contributed to its prominence. During 1806 a spirit of reaction, political and religious, swept over France, making itself especially troublesome in Alsace and in the German departments of the upper and lower Rhine. Exceptionable and restrictive laws were advocated to deprive the Jews there of rights they were enjoying throughout France. As had happened often before, and not unknown since, the reactionaries fanned the hatred against Jews, making them the scapegoats in their campaign against the advancing spirit of liberalism. Thus the cause of the Jews was linked with the cause of liberty itself.

Napoleon himself was at first prejudiced against the Jews, regarding them as usurers and extortioners. He soon realized, however, that the characteristics which confronted him could not be imputed to Judaism, but were due rather to the restricted civil and industrial rights of the Jews and to their general unhappy condition. It was made manifest to him that in Bordeaux,

MOTHER AND FATHER OF OSCAR S. STRAUS

Marseilles, and the Italian cities of France, as well as in Holland, some of the most useful and patriotic citizens were Jews. Napoleon always had an eye on his historical reputation, and desiring to do nothing that would obscure his fame, he decided to convene a council of representative Jews from the various provinces. Accordingly, on May 30, 1806, he issued his decree, famous in the annals of the Jews in modern times, summoning the Assembly of Notables of the Jewish nation to meet in Paris the following July. The prefects in the various provinces were required to aid in the selection of the most distinguished men from among the rabbis and the laity.

The deputies came to Paris from all parts of the French Empire. They numbered one hundred and eleven in all, and spoke French, German, and Italian. Many of them were themselves well known, others achieved a posthumous glamour in the deeds of descendants who have since won distinction in European history and in the annals of Jewry. There were Joseph Sinzheim, first rabbi of Strasbourg, foremost Talmudist and considered the most scholarly member of the Assembly, who was made president of the Assembly and later chairman of the Great Sanhedrin; Michel Berr, afterwards the first French Jew to practice at the bar; Abraham Furtado, son of a marano or crypto-Jewish Portugese family from which was also descended the wife of the first Benjamin D'Israeli and Sir John Simon; Isaac Samuel d'Avigdor of Nice, grandfather of Jules d'Avigdor who was a member of the Piedmont Parliament; Israel Ottolenghi, an ancestor of Italy's late Minister of War; Abraham de Cologna, rabbi of Mantua, a great political leader and reformer; and many others of equal rank and caliber. Their task was a monumental one, for it was nothing less than to justify Judaism and Jewry to the world; and they assembled with a full consciousness of their responsibility.

At this Assembly my great-grandfather represented the Department of Mont Tennérre. He evidently played an important part in the diplomacy which this unprecedented council involved, for he was a member of the sub-committee of fifteen delegated to meet the commissioners appointed by Napoleon, also a member of the committee to which the Assembly gave the delicate work of preparing the groundwork for discussion with the commissioners. Subsequently he was appointed to the committee of nine of the Great Sanhedrin which the following year presented to Napoleon's committee the conclusions formulated and agreed upon by the Assembly, and which helped to bring about their adoption.

My father, in turn, was active in the revolutionary movement in 1848. This was an heroic effort on the part of the liberal forces of Europe to achieve constitutional government, and when it failed many of those who had borne a conspicuous part fled to other countries. Thus it was that Generals Sigel, Schurz, Stahl, and others, who later were prominent in our Civil War, came to America. These men and their immediate followers constitute one of the most valuable groups of immigrants that have come to these shores since our government was organized. In the land of their birth they had already made sacrifices for constitutionalism and democracy, and basically they had made them for American principles. They were Americans in spirit, therefore, even before they arrived.

Having been active only locally in the revolutionary movement, my father was not prosecuted. He was made aware, however, of the suspicions of the authorities and was subjected to all those petty annoyances and discriminations which a reactionary government never fails to lay upon people who have revolted, and revolted in vain. My father decided, in consequence, to emigrate. This purpose he did not carry into effect until the spring of 1852. He had many ties, which it was difficult to break at once. He had been in comfortable circumstances, like his father and grandfather a landowner and dealer on a large scale in farm products, principally grains. The revolution left him reduced in circumstances and even to some extent in debt. He had four children, of whom I was the youngest, being then less than a year and a half old. Therefore, like the prudent man he was, he waited, and then came to America alone with the purpose of establishing himself in some small way before allowing his family to exchange the comparative security of their familiar surroundings for the insecurity of an unknown land.

He landed at Philadelphia, where he met a number of former acquaintances who had preceded him to America, some of whom were already established in business. They advised him to go South. Acting on this suggestion he went on to Oglethorpe, Georgia, where he met some more acquaintances from the old country. Through them he made a connection with two brothers Kaufman, who plied the peddler's trade. They owned a peddler's wagon with which they dispensed through the several counties of the State an assortment of dry goods and what was known as "Yankee notions."

For my father this was indeed a pioneer business in a pioneer country, yet it was not like the peddling of to-day. In the fifties the population of the whole State of Georgia was only about nine hundred thousand. Because of the existence of slavery there were on the large planta-

tions often more colored people than there were whites
living in the near-by villages. The itinerant merchant,
therefore, filled a real want, and his vocation was looked
upon as quite dignified. Indeed, he was treated by the
owners of the plantations with a spirit of equality that it
is hard to appreciate to-day. Then, too, the existence of
slavery drew a distinct line of demarcation between the
white and black races. This gave to the white visitor a
status of equality that probably otherwise he would not
have enjoyed to such a degree.

Provided only, therefore, that the peddler proved himself an honorable, upright man, who conscientiously
treated his customers with fairness and made no mis-
representations regarding his wares, he was treated as an
honored guest by the plantation owners — certainly a
spirit of true democracy. The visits were made periodi-
cally and were quite looked forward to by the plantation
owners. The peddler usually stayed one night at the
house of his customer and took his meals with the family.
Another ideally democratic feature about these sojourns
was that spirit of Southern hospitality which, even in the
relationship between the wealthiest, most aristocratic
family and the humble peddler, permitted no pay for
board and lodging, and only a small charge for feed for
the horses. The peddler in turn usually made a gift to
either the lady or her daughter. Often he provided himself with articles for this purpose, but usually on one
visit he would find out what might be welcome and on the
next visit bring it. The bonds of friendship thus made
are, I venture to say, hardly understandable in our day.

In the course of these wanderings my father came to
Talbotton, a town of some eight or nine hundred inhabitants, the county seat of Talbot County, and about

forty miles east of the Alabama boundary. Talbotton immediately impressed him so favorably that he selected it as the next home for his family. It had an air of refinement that pleased him; there were gardens with nicely cultivated flowers and shrubbery, and houses that were neat, well kept, and properly painted. Upon inquiry he found further that there were splendid schools for both boys and girls.

There was another factor which doubtless caused father to be favorably impressed with Talbotton; it was court week when he arrived, at which time a town has a more or less festive appearance and is at its best so far as activity is concerned. Then there was a third factor that influenced him to settle there. Before doing business in any county, peddlers were required to go to the county seat to buy a license. At Talbotton this license was very high, and my father doubted that his business in Talbot County would warrant the expense. The idea occurred to him to utilize the presence of the many strangers in town to test the possibilities of the place by unpacking and displaying his goods in a store. An interview with Captain Curley, the only tailor in the town, developed the fact that the store he occupied was too large for his needs and he would be willing to share it with my father. So this arrangement was promptly made, and at a cost less than the expense of the county license for itinerant merchandising.

The experiment proved most satisfactory. In a few weeks the stock was so depleted that my father proposed to his partner that they rent a store and settle in Talbotton. This they did. My father then prepared to go to Philadelphia to get a stock of goods. His partner counseled against this. There was a merchant in Oglethorpe who, up to this point, had supplied them with all their merchandise; they would need to refer to him for credit, and they were still indebted to him for the stock in hand; also, he would probably not approve of their settling down in a store instead of peddling. The new store offered large display space in comparison with the wagon, and the partner doubted my father's ability to get enough credit in Philadelphia to make a proper display. Still another obstacle. The line of merchandise that was to constitute most of their stock was what was then known as dry goods and domestics. This business was entirely in the hands of the Yankees and the most difficult one in which to gain a foothold, especially for a German immigrant without capital.

However, in the end my father did go to Philadelphia. He had found several acquaintances in that city, as I have already said, who had been resident in his neighborhood in the old country. These people were established in several of the wholesale houses in the different lines of merchandise he required, except the dry goods. And solely on the strength of his character and the reputation he had had in Europe he was able to establish with them the necessary credit, which neither his capital nor his business experience in a new field and a strange country warranted. In fact, their faith in him was so strong that one of them gladly introduced him to the wholesale dry goods merchants, and he was able to accomplish the full purpose of his mission, to the great amazement of his partner.

That was in 1853, and marked the beginning of my family's history in this country. This bit of success encouraged my father to write home that he might be able to have us join him the following year. Accordingly, on August 24, 1854, our little party left Otterberg. It

BIRTHPLACE OF OSCAR S. STRAUS
OTTERBERG, RHENISH BAVARIA

CHAPEL AND SCHOOLHOUSE
COLLINSWORTH INSTITUTE, TALBOTTON, GEORGIA

was a journey that required no little courage and resourcefulness. My mother had three years before suffered a paralytic stroke, and of her four children the eldest, my brother Isidor, was only nine years old. My sister Hermina was a year and a half younger, Nathan was six, and I was only three and a half. My mother's father accompanied us from Otterberg to Kaiserslautern, he on horseback and the rest of us with our nursemaid in a carriage; we then took the train to Forbach, a French frontier town, where we remained overnight. The next morning we left for Paris. There we stayed until August 29th, when we started for Havre to board the steamer St. Louis on her maiden voyage. As our boat was being docked in New York on September 12th, my mother recognized my father energetically pacing the wharf. Minutes seemed like hours.

We did not go directly to Talbotton. Yellow fever was raging in Savannah, and as we had to go through that port *en route* to Talbotton, we waited in Philadelphia for a few weeks, until the danger was considered over. Even then we avoided entering the city until it was time to board the train for Geneva, where we were to take the stage-coach for the remaining seven miles to Talbotton. The boat docked at Savannah in the morning, and we spent the day until evening in the small shanty that was called the station. When finally we reached Talbotton we found a very comfortable home ready for us. My precocious brother Isidor immediately inspected the whole and thought it odd to be in a house built on stilts, as he called it. The house, typical of that locality, had no cellar, but was supported by an open foundation of wooden pillars about twenty-five feet apart.

Our family was received with kindness and hospitality,

so that in a very few years our parents were made to feel
much at home. My mother, who had considerable experience in the cultivation of flowers and vegetables, soon
had a garden which was very helpful and instructive to
her circle of neighbors and friends. My father, always a
student and well versed in biblical literature and the
Bible, which he read in the original, was much sought by
the ministers of the various denominations, several of
whom habitually dined at our house when in Talbotton
on their circuit. At such times the discussion usually ran
along theological lines. One of my earliest recollections is
hearing my father take passages from the Old Testament
and translate them literally for the information of these
ministers.

We were the only Jewish family in the town. This at
first aroused some curiosity among those who had never
met persons of our race or religion before. I remember
hearing some one doubt that we were Jews and remarking
to my father, who had very blond hair and blue eyes,
that he thought all Jews had black hair and dark complexion.

My brother Isidor and my sister were immediately
sent to school, and my second brother and I were sent as
soon as we arrived at school age. I was seven years old
when I began learning my letters.

My main religious instruction came from conversations
with my father and from the discussions the ministers
of various denominations had with him, which I always
followed with great interest. When my brother Nathan
and I were respectively about eleven and eight and a half
years old, we were sent to the Baptist Sunday school
upon the persuasion of the Baptist minister, who had
become an intimate friend of my father's. There we heard

the Bible read and were taught principally from the Old Testament. Our teacher was a gunsmith who had more piety than knowledge, and what he lacked in erudition he made up by good intentions which, after all, had a cultural value. We continued our attendance some two years.

At eleven I entered Collinsworth Institute, a higher school for boys, about a mile outside of Talbotton. Isidor had been there, and Nathan was there then. It was not a large school, though it was the best of its kind in our vicinity. The recitation hall or chapel was a little frame building standing in a square, and around that were eight or ten one-story frame houses where boys coming from a distance lived. The pupils ranged in age from about ten to eighteen, and there were three teachers. We were taught the three R's, and the advanced pupils studied the classics.

In our small town, being the county seat, we had gala days each month when the court convened and people came from the surrounding districts as for a holiday. There was much drinking of gin and whiskey by the young country squires, which frequently ended up in some fighting where pistols and knives were freely used. This all left a deep impression on my young mind and made me a prohibitionist long before I knew the meaning of the word. In the North when boys got to fighting they used their fists; in the South they used, besides their fists, sticks and stones, and consequently it was a more serious and dangerous affair. If in the North one boy cursed another or called him a liar, it would not necessarily lead to a fist fight; in fact, it usually stopped at recrimination. In the South that kind of quarreling meant a serious fight. I think because of these facts the Southern boys were much more guarded and polite to each other in speech than was customary among Northern boys. Per-

haps much of the so-called Southern politeness had its
roots in the use, in boyhood, of milder terms in case of
disagreement. I recall one fight between two of the leading men of Talbotton, both deacons in the same church.
One took out his pocket knife and cut the other's throat,
and he died. After considerable delay the murderer was
tried, but because of his high standing in the community
he was acquitted, doubtless on the plea of self-defense,
and he got off scot-free.

As a boy brought up in the South I never questioned
the rights or wrongs of slavery. Its existence I regarded
as matter of course, as most other customs or institutions.
The grown people of the South, whatever they thought
about it, would not, except in rare instances, speak
against it; and even then in the most private and guarded
manner. To do otherwise would subject one to social
ostracism. We heard it defended in the pulpit and justified on biblical grounds by leading ministers. With my
father it was different. I frequently heard him discuss
the subject with the ministers who came to our house,
and he would point out to them that the Bible must be
read with discrimination and in relation to the period to
which the chapters refer; and it must not be forgotten
that it is the history of a people covering more than a
thousand years; and that even then there had been no
such thing as perpetual bondage, as all slaves were declared free in the year of jubilee.

Looking backward and making comparisons between
my observations as a boy in the South and later in the
North, I find there was much more freedom of expression
in the North than in the South. Few people in the South
would venture to express themselves against the current
of dominant opinion upon matters of sectional importance. The institution of slavery with all that it implied

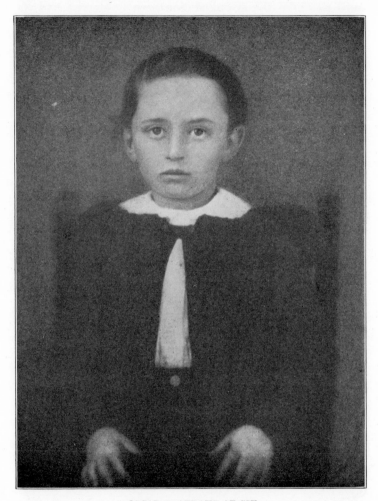

OSCAR S. STRAUS AT SIX

seemed to have had the effect of enslaving, or, to use a milder term, checking, freedom of expression on the part of the master class only in lesser degree than among the slaves themselves.

In our town, as in all Southern communities, the better families were kind, especially to their household slaves, whom they regarded as members of the family requiring guardianship and protection, in a degree as if they were children. And the slaves addressed their masters by their first names and their mistresses as "miss." My mother, for instance, was "Miss Sara." I recall one of our servants pleading with my mother: "Miss Sara, won't you buy me, I want to stay here. I love you and the white folks here, and I am afraid my master will hire me out or sell me to some one else." At that time we hired our servants from their masters, whom we paid an agreed price. But as the result of such constant pleadings my father purchased household slaves one by one from their masters, although neither he nor my mother believed in slavery. If we children spoke to the slaves harshly or disregarded their feelings, we were promptly checked and reprimanded by our parents. My father also saw to it that our two men servants learned a trade; the one learned tailoring and the other how to make shoes, though it was regarded disloyal, at any rate looked upon with suspicion, if a master permitted a slave boy or girl to be taught even reading and writing. When later we came North we took with us the two youngest servants, one a boy about my age, and the other a girl a little older. They were too young to look out for themselves, and so far as they knew they had no relatives. We kept them with us until they grew up and could look out for themselves.

The people throughout the South, with the exception of the richer plantation owners, lived simply. In our household, for instance, we always lived well, but economically. My mother was very systematic and frugal. She had an allowance of twenty dollars a month, and my brother Isidor has well said that she would have managed to save something even if it had been smaller. It was her pleasure to be her own financier, and small as her allowance sounds now, she was able in the course of two or three years to save enough to buy a piano for my sister. This she felt to be an expense with which my father's exchequer should not be taxed.

We raised our own vegetables and chickens. Fresh meat, except pork, might have been termed a luxury. Many of the families had their own smokehouses, as we did, which were filled once a year, at the hog-killing season. There was no such thing as a butcher in our little town. When a farmer in the country round wanted to slaughter an ox or a sheep, he would do so and bring it to town, exhibit it in the public square in a shanty called the market (used for that particular occasion and at other times empty), toll the bell that was there, and in that way announce that some fresh meat was on sale. This procedure never occurred oftener than once in two or three weeks during the cold weather.

Ice was another luxury in that community. It had to be shipped many miles and was therefore brought in only occasionally, mainly for a confectioner who at times offered ice cream to the people.

There was no gas lighting. Oil lamps were used, but to a larger extent candles, which were manufactured in each household, of fat and bees' wax. In that process we children all helped.

Indeed, with a small business in a small town in those

days it was possible for a man to accumulate a surplus only through the practice of the strictest economy by his family as well as by himself, an economy almost bordering parsimony. There were no public or free schools in that part of the South; every textbook had to be bought and tuition paid for; and there were four of us.

When the war broke out new economies were called for. A simple life has its advantages; it is conducive to self-help, also to the ability to do without things and meet emergencies without unhappiness. My father's partner joined the Fourth Georgia Regiment, and my brother Isidor, then sixteen, was withdrawn from Collinsworth Institute to take up work with my father. He had gained some experience in carrying on the business by helping father evenings, for our store was open until nine-thirty. It was closed during the supper hour, but reopened thereafter.

In that part of the country coffee became unobtainable except when now and then a few bags arrived on a ship that had run the blockade. Our mothers learned to give us an acceptable substitute by cutting sweet potatoes into little cubes, drying them in the sun, then roasting and grinding them, together with grains of wheat, like the ordinary bean. This made a hot and palatable drink having the color of coffee without the harmful stimulus of its caffeine.

Salt also became scarce. It was difficult and at times impossible to obtain enough to cure our pork. Some one discovered that the earthen floors of the smokehouses were impregnated with considerable salt from previous curings, so a method was invented for recovering it from that source.

In the later years of the war, when railway transportation was very poor and in many localities interrupted, we did not suffer for food, because, as I have said,
most households in the small towns and in the country
raised the major part of their food supplies; they had their
own chickens, eggs, milk, butter, garden provisions.
Children of my age lived largely on corn bread and
molasses, of which there was an ever-plentiful amount.

During the second year of the war my father's partner
was discharged from his regiment for physical disability.
My father, always insistent upon the best possible education for us all, therefore urged my brother Isidor to continue his studies. Most of the high schools and colleges,
however, had been suspended because the teachers, as
well as many of the senior scholars, had joined the army.
On the other hand, the war had fired the whole South
with the military spirit, and as was natural for a young
man barely seventeen, my brother chose to attend the
Georgia Military Academy at Marietta, which was running full blast. Earlier in the war, when the Fourth
Georgia Regiment, taking practically all the able-bodied
men of the town, had left for the front, the boys of Talbotton organized a company of which Isidor was elected
first lieutenant. They had offered their services to the
governor of the State, but he replied that there were not
enough arms to equip all the men, so that equipping boys
was out of the question. All these incidents had influenced my brother in his choice, and he left quite enthusiastically for the Georgia Military Academy to take his
entrance examinations. When he returned, however, his
mood was much different. Upon his arrival at Marietta
he had about an hour's waiting before he could see the
proper person. Some acquaintances whom he met on the
campus invited him to visit their living quarters mean-

while. As he entered one of the rooms the door stood ajar. Without noticing this he gave the door a push, resulting in his being drenched to the skin by a bucket of water that had been balanced over the door and held there by the position of the door when ajar. He had to return to the hotel to change his entire apparel. He had not heard of hazing before, and the incident disgusted him so that he never returned to the academy. He embarked upon his career as a merchant the very next morning.

In 1863 our family moved to Columbus, Georgia. It was a much larger place than Talbotton, having a population of about twelve thousand, offered more opportunities, and, too, my brother Isidor had already found employment there. With its broad main street and brick residences it looked like a great city to me.

As in Talbotton, there were no public schools in Columbus, so I was sent to a private school kept by an Irish master named Flynn, who did not act on the pedagogical principle, "Spare the rod and spoil the child." By him I was taught the three R's and began Latin. I also experienced my first stage-fright at Master Flynn's, when my turn came to speak a piece before the entire school. In all Southern schools much emphasis was placed upon elocution. I well remember practicing before a mirror and reciting under the trees in stentorian voice with dramatic gesture the great oration put into John Adams's mouth by Daniel Webster, beginning: "Sink or swim, live or die, survive or perish, I give my hand and my heart to this vote."

After another year this school was discontinued and I was sent to one kept by a Dr. Dews. He was a teacher trained in the classics and far less severe than Flynn, more sympathetic and cultured. Under him I began Virgil and afterwards Horace. It was not customary to teach English grammar; we derived that from our laborious drilling in Latin grammar.

There were no public libraries, and few families, other than those of professional men, had many books. The standard assortment consisted of the Bible, Josephus, Burns; some had Shakespeare's works. I do not recall at this period reading any book outside of those we had for study at school. Boys of my age led an outdoor life, indulging in seasonable sports which rotated from top-spinning to marbles, to ball-playing, principally a game called town-ball. We all had shot-guns, so that in season and out we went bird-hunting and rabbit-hunting.

We went barefooted nine months of the year, both for comfort and economy. As in Talbotton we lived most economically. We were not poor in the sense of being needy; we never felt in any way dependent. Our home was comfortable, wholesome, full of sunshine and good cheer, and always hospitable to friends. Our wants were few and simple, so we had plenty, and I felt as independent as any child of the rich.

We were now in the midst of the Civil War, and money, measured in gold, was worth about five cents per dollar. My brother Nathan seemed to be affected by this into constant scheming for making pocket money. He was fifteen years old, and out of school hours helped father in the store; but he seemed to be in need of more pin-money. He finally hit on a plan that proved quite lucrative. He collected or bought up pieces of hemp rope and sold them to a manufacturer. Hemp was very scarce and much needed. With the proceeds he bought a beautiful bay pony, which he and I prized more than any possession we have ever had, before or since.

On the 16th of April, 1865, after a feeble skirmish on the part of the citizen soldiers, mainly superannuated men and schoolboys, Columbus was captured by General James H. Wilson at the head of a cavalry corps of fifteen thousand men. The war had practically ended seven days before, as Lee surrendered on the 9th at Appomattox Court House in Virginia; but as telegraph and railroad communication had been disrupted, this fact was not yet known in our part of Georgia. As soon as Wilson's army took possession of our debilitated city general confusion reigned. Looting began by the town rabble, led by several drunken Federal soldiers; cotton warehouses were burned, the contents of which represented the savings of many, including most of my father's; all horses were seized, and among them our little pony, which I never saw again, though I still retain a vivid picture of him in my mind's eye. Frequently since, when I have met that fine and accomplished old veteran, General Wilson, who is still among the living, hale and hearty, I have jestingly reproached him for taking from me the most treasured possession I ever had.

This incident and others served to give me a most vivid impression of the closing years of the Civil War. Another very vivid impression that occurred shortly before the beginning of the war clings to my memory. Robert Toombs, one of Georgia's most conspicuous United States Senators, was making a speech at the Masonic Temple in Columbus, Georgia. It was a hot summer day. Toombs was a short, thick, heavy-set man of the Websterian type, and one of the South's most picturesque orators. After the election of Lincoln, however, Toombs advocated secession and resigned from the Senate, was talked of for the Confederate presidency, did become Confederate Secretary of State, and was later commissioned a brigadier-general, and commanded with distinction in numerous battles of the Civil War. During the speech I heard him make, he drew a large white handkerchief from his pocket with a flourish, and pausing before mopping his perspiring forehead, he exclaimed:

"The Yankees will not and can not fight! I will guarantee to wipe up with this handkerchief every drop of blood that is spilt!"

Neither he nor the audience foresaw what was coming. The Civil War was a family affair, yet the hostility it engendered and the misconception it brought in its train regarding the valor, and even the standards of civilization, of the enemy, were as extreme and virulent as in a war between nations of different continents and races. Such are the brutalizing passions war arouses in banishing from the individual mind the most elementary ideas of brotherhood.

When the war ended my father had to begin life anew, and because of the discouraging prospects and conditions of the South he decided to move North. In the North, too, he could more readily dispose of the remainder of his cotton, his chief asset, to pay off debts which he owed in New York and Philadelphia for goods purchased before the war. With the few thousand dollars remaining after paying these debts, and with good credit, he thought he could begin some new business in a small way.

Simultaneously with our arrival in Philadelphia my brother Isidor arrived in New York from Europe, where he had gone two years before as secretary of a commission to buy supplies for the State of Georgia. The blockade of the Southern ports became so effective that ships could not get through, so that he did not succeed in getting over the supplies; but he made several thousand dollars in the sale of Confederate bonds. Upon learning in New York that we were in Philadelphia, he immediately came there to find out my father's plans. He persuaded father that New York, as the chief market, was preferable to Philadelphia as a secondary one. Consequently we moved to New York, and father and Isidor, together with Nathan, planned to establish themselves in the wholesale crockery business. Isidor, twenty years old, first used part of his fortune to buy for my mother a high-stoop, three-story brick house at 220 West Forty-Ninth Street, now long since torn down, but which we occupied for over eighteen years.

It was fully six months before the new business venture was launched. My father depended for his part of the capital upon the sale of the remainder of his cotton, which had been shipped to Liverpool, and this was not effected until early in 1866. In the intervening months he visited his creditors in New York to arrange for paying his debts. In this connection I remember one significant incident: His principal New York creditor was the dry goods house of George Bliss & Co., to whom he owed an amount between four and five thousand dollars. (Bliss afterward became a member of the banking firm of Morton, Bliss & Co.) When he called regarding the payment of this, Mr. Bliss asked how old he was, what family he had, and what he intended doing. My father answered that he was fifty-seven, that he had a wife and four children, and that he hoped to make a new start in the wholesale crockery business. "I don't think you are fair to your family and yourself," said Mr. Bliss, "to deprive yourself of the slender means you tell me you possess by paying out your available resources. I will compromise with you for less than the full amount in view of the hardships of the war and your family obligations."

My father had a very high sense of honor and was

always more concerned in maintaining it beyond possible reproach than in making money. Some parents forget that they cannot successfully live by one standard outside and another inside the home, and many never realize that children are influenced not so much by the preaching as by the true and real spirit of their parents. My father believed that "a good name is better than riches," and within the home or without he lived up to that standard. I clearly remember the impression I received of his integrity at the time of this Bliss incident, and of a certain feeling of compunction on the part of his creditor, as though he had expected something different. Most Southern merchants regarded themselves morally freed from paying Northern creditors because the Confederate government had confiscated such debts and compelled the debtors to pay the amounts to the government. But my father held true to his standard, and I well remember his parting words to Bliss that day: "I propose to pay my debts in full and leave to my children a good name even if I should leave them nothing else."

My brother Isidor, always my guide, philosopher, and friend, now arranged for my schooling. In my geography textbook was a picture of Columbia College, and I had the fixed idea that when we came to New York I wanted to go there. On inquiry we learned that I was too young, for I was only fourteen and a half, and that I had not the requirements for admission. So in the autumn of 1865 Isidor had me enter Columbia Grammar School, then one of the best schools in the city. It was my first experience in a really first-rate school, and the teaching was so much more thorough and exact than my previous training had been that it seemed to me I had to learn everything anew. The tuition fee and the cost of books was considerable, in view of the modest income of the family; but my father, economical in all other respects, was liberal beyond his means where the education of his children was concerned. My brother, moreover, was desirous that I should have the advantages of the college training which circumstances, notably the war, had withheld from him.

I appreciated to the full the privileges I was permitted to enjoy and studied with all my might. The school regulations required that parents fill out a blank each week stating, among other things, the number of hours we studied at home. The average number of hours daily reported were three or four, and as my record was fully double that, I felt rather ashamed to give the true number, so I always gave less. The school was on Fourth Avenue and Twenty-Seventh Street, and our home on Forty-Ninth Street was near Eighth Avenue. I invariably walked both ways, saving car fares and at the same time conserving my health, for aside from a half-hour of gymnastics twice a week in school I had neither time nor opportunity otherwise to get the exercise my body required.

Owing to the careless preparation I had received at the schools in the South, I made a poor showing in spite of my hard work now, though on one occasion I shone with accidental glory. It was the custom for the instructor to put the same question to pupil after pupil, and to elevate the one who gave the correct answer to the head of the class. In this instance, it so happened that I gave the fortunate answer and thus qualified for the seat of scholastic eminence. As I sat there enjoying a near view of the teacher's countenance, I wondered how long I should remain thus distinguished, and was unable to resist the impulse to cast an occasional backward glance at the rows of seats in the rear.

At about this time, an elderly gentleman of distinguished appearance entered the classroom. He was S. F. B. Morse, inventor of the telegraph. Morse, whose grandson was in my class, knowing the custom and observing me in the seat of honor, complimented me. He observed that I, like himself, had a large head in comparison with the body, and remarked that I must be a bright boy. But I felt embarrassed rather than gratified at the praise, for I knew, and so did the rest, that I did not deserve it. I still recall that scene, and see the venerable old man, then seventy-five years old, with the long white beard that made him look even older.

When the time came, in the spring of 1867, for our class to go up for college examination, the Rev. Dr. Bacon, successor as principal of the school to Charles Anthon, the distinguished classical scholar and editor of classical works, called the boys of our class before him and gave us each a blessing with some encouraging words. When my turn came he was very kind, telling me he knew I had tried hard, but because of my early training, or lack of it, he feared I might not pass. I saw my chances of a college education go glimmering. There were, however, still two weeks before the examinations, and I determined to use those for all they were worth. I worked night and day, cramming with a vengeance. I felt I could not expect my father to keep me in school another year when after two years of preparation I had shown myself so deficient. That thought was my spur, though in point of fact I am sure both my brother Isidor and my father, realizing I had done the best I could, would have insisted upon my taking another year for preparation.

The result of my entrance examinations was more favorable than I could have hoped. It turned out that

I was the only one from our grammar school class to pass in all subjects without a single condition. It was luck rather than brilliancy. The professor who examined my classmates in ancient geography, being the author of the book upon which the examination was held, was so meticulous that unless the student gave the answer exactly as in the book he was marked deficient. By the time it came my turn to be examined another and more generous-minded professor had taken his place and passed me with the highest mark. The others, who had all flunked, regarded me, in their own language, as "the lucky dog."

My college course began on October 7, 1867. Here I did not find the studies hard. I had ample leisure for reading and took full advantage of the college library, from which we were free to select and take home whatever books we desired. Then, as now, I cared little for fiction. To me the literature of facts was more interesting and therefore lighter reading, and I read much biography and history.

Our class matriculated fifty-two, but dwindled down to thirty-one by graduation. In the class were Brander Matthews, now professor of literature at Columbia as well as literary and dramatic critic; Robert Fulton Cutting, financier and ideal citizen, descendant of an old and famous New York family, as his name indicates; Stuyvesant Fish, banker, also of a well-known New York family, whose father, Hamilton Fish, was Secretary of State in the Grant Cabinet, and whose grandfather and father both were among Columbia alumni; and Henry Van Rensselaer, who became a Jesuit father and is now no longer among the living.

At the commemoration of the one hundred and fiftieth

anniversary of the founding of the college three of us —
Robert Fulton Cutting, Brander Matthews, and myself
— received the honorary degree of LL.D. At this writing, fifty years after graduation, there are but ten of us
remaining.

The most coveted honors in those days were to be had
for literary achievement and class rank. Among the
few prizes was one known as the Alumni Prize, awarded
to the most deserving student in the graduating class.
The college board nominated for that honor William
Henry Sage, now our class historian, Joseph Fenelon
Vermilye, and myself; and the class elected Vermilye for
the prize.

Athletics had not attained the vogue it has in American
universities to-day, and was particularly absent in our
college, confined then to a city block. Doubtless due to
this lack the boys of our class, on the whole a spirited and
boisterous lot, found self-expression in a disregard for
proper decorum in the lecture rooms. There was one period where this was conspicuously the case. The subject
was Evidences of Christianity. It was compulsory and
along denominational lines. It did not interest many of
the boys, and some of those who were not Episcopalians
even resented it; to boot, the professor, Rev. Dr. Mc-
Vickar, was a mild-mannered man, entirely unable to
maintain discipline. The result was frequent and various
disturbances during the sessions of his class, which often
put the good-natured and unsophisticated man at his
wits' end. He complained to the college board, and
President Barnard took the matter up with some seriousness, but no real appeasement.

I felt great sympathy for Dr. McVickar, for he was
earnest and gentle, and took much to heart the conduct
of the men in his class. Of course, in common with most

of my classmates I strongly favored that the subject be elective instead of compulsory; yet I realized that, as colleges were then constituted, the original Columbia being largely an Episcopalian foundation, there was a legal right, as distinguished from reason, for the requirement that the course in Evidences of Christianity be compulsory.

One day when the disturbances became most flagrant, and the poor professor was really quite helpless, I ventured to point out to him how he might bring about order. He received my suggestion most favorably, so I asked him to let me take his chair for a few moments. I made a brief appeal to the class, reminding them that we were now seniors, and that there were some, especially those intending to study for the ministry, who were interested in the subject and prevented from following it by the boisterous behavior of the rest. I was jeeringly dubbed Professor Straus, but I went right on. I said I knew there were a number who were opposed to the study of Evidences of Christianity, and I proposed that they rise. To those who got up I gave permission to leave the room, and as I recall it, there were some eight or ten left. Then I turned to Dr. McVickar and said, "Here is a class you can teach." And the session went on smoothly enough. Subsequently a petition was drawn up and signed by a large majority of the class, asking that we be excused from examinations in this particular subject; but President Barnard replied that the request could not be entertained.

On the whole my four years at college were full of serious effort and not altogether free from anxiety. I had a restless ambition to have a useful career and it seemed difficult to discover for what I was best fitted. For a while, in those dreamy days, I even believed I might achieve some measure of success as a poet. I recall with a smile that the choice for class poet at commencement lay between Brander Matthews, whom we then knew as James Brander Matthews, and myself. And for some reason, which posterity will doubtless find even more difficult to fathom than I have, I was chosen. Matthews had already given evidence of his literary talents; he contributed much to the college papers, and wrote humorous poems. However, at our graduation exercises held in the Academy of Music, Fourteenth Street and Irving Place, the city's largest auditorium then, my class poem was well received by a capacity audience of proud parents and sympathetic friends. I had gravely entitled it "Truth and Error."

A more fervent aspiration held by me in those years was to devote my life to the nation, and I could conceive no better way of doing so than to enter the army. One day I saw an item in the press that President Grant had several appointments to make to the United States Military Academy. I consulted with Dr. F. A. P. Barnard, president of Columbia, and he gave me a letter of introduction to Grant, highly commending me for an appointment. When President Grant came to New York I called on him. He received me very kindly, but informed me that he had only something like eight appointments allowed him by law, and he had decided to give them where possible to the sons of officers who had been killed in the war; if, however, there were not enough such candidates he would be glad to give me a chance. I told him I thoroughly agreed that his decision was so appropriate that I would not even ask to be appointed under the circumstances.

During the second half of my senior year I finally

OSCAR S. STRAUS

At the time of his graduation

chose the law as my vocation. I preferred it to a business career because I disliked the idea of devoting my life to mere money-making, as business appeared to me then. My outlook was idealistic rather than practical, and to harmonize it with the workaday world caused me much mental anguish and struggle, as it does many a young man, even where affluent fortune has smiled. However, my father and brother had begun to prosper and had no need for my coöperation unless on my own account I chose to join them. Besides, I was the youngest and had the benefit of the brotherly interest and economic protection of Isidor and Nathan, should I need it. This gave me a feeling of security, and encouraged me to put forth my best efforts not only to succeed for myself, but to show my appreciation to them. Where, under moderate circumstances, a family puts forth coöperative effort in making its way forward, closer family ties result, with the advantages of stimulating unselfishness and common devotion, which in turn promote a happiness that members of richer families often miss because of their more independent relations.

So I prepared to enter Columbia Law School in the fall of 1871. Meanwhile that summer I took my first vacation since coming to New York. I went to Wyoming Valley, near Wilkes-Barre, Pennsylvania, where I had a good time despite the farmer with whom I boarded. Perhaps I had no right to expect much for the five dollars a week I paid him; but whatever I expected I know I got less. However, there were fish in the brooks and I do not recall that I starved. I had spent other summers assisting in some branch of my father's business, not because I relished work unduly, but because I regarded it less as labor than as diversion. It was interesting and useful activity which gave me an understanding of business that was valuable later in following my chosen profession.

CHAPTER II

LAW, BUSINESS, AND LETTERS

Columbia Law School — Impressions of the faculty — I begin law practice — Early partnerships — A $10,000 fee — Founding of the Young Men's Hebrew Association in 1874 — The "dissipations" of a law partner — The Hepburn Committee on railway rates; my partner Simon Sterne represents the Chamber of Commerce — On the bridle-path with Joseph H. Choate — I become a member of L. Straus & Sons, manufacturers and importers — My marriage to Miss Sarah Lavanburg — My début in politics — The Cleveland-Blaine campaign — The "rum, Romanism, and rebellion" episode — "Origin of the Republican Form of Government," my first book — Recommended as minister to Turkey; Henry Ward Beecher writes the President — Cleveland nominates me minister to Turkey.

COLUMBIA LAW SCHOOL in 1871 was at Lafayette Place. The course covered two years, at the end of which a successful examination entitled a student to admission to the bar without a further State examination, and for those who gave serious attention to the course it was an easy matter to pass this finishing examination.

Particularly worthy of mention with regard to the school are Professors Theodore W. Dwight and Francis Lieber. Professor Dwight, the able director of the school at that time, well deserved his great reputation as the most distinguished teacher of law in the country. He was not only a master of his subject, but had a marvelous gift for imparting his great knowledge.

Professor Lieber, whose lectures we attended once a week, taught us political science. He was a Prussian veteran who fought in the Battle of Waterloo. At the close of the Napoleonic Wars he had returned to his studies in Berlin, and thereafter was arrested several times for his outspoken liberal views. After frequent persecution and even imprisonment, he fled to England, and in 1827 came to America.

He was author of many books on legal and political matters, among them "Civil Liberty and Self-Government," which was adopted as a textbook in several of our universities. In 1863 he prepared "Instructions for the Government of Armies of the United States, in the Field," which Lincoln promulgated as Order No. 100 of the War Department. It was a masterly piece of work, embodying advanced humanitarian principles, and it later formed the basis of several European codes.

As a rule, egotism and real merit negate one another rather than coördinate; Lieber was the exception. He had both, and combined them to a marked degree, sometimes in a manner that afforded amusement to his students. For instance, he referred continuously to "my Civil Liberty" as a book of extraordinary erudition, new in its field and the last word on the matter. He was so full of his subject that he was apt to lose himself and stray off, with his distinctly German accent, into the vast field of his profound philosophical and historical knowledge. A veritable encyclopædia of information, he was really more of an expounder than a teacher. As his course was optional, those who came to listen came to learn, and we received a larger view of the function of law in civil society than we derived from all our studies of municipal law.

I was graduated from law school in June, 1873, and immediately entered the offices of Ward, Jones & Whitehead, one of New York's prominent firms. John E. Ward, the senior member, who presided over the Democratic National Convention that nominated Buchanan, and later served for two or three years as Minister to China, was a friend of my brother's, and he took me into his office largely out of friendship for Isidor.

I remained with this firm only a few months. Later in 1873 I formed a partnership with James A. Hudson, a man about ten years older than I, who had also been associated with the Ward firm. As Hudson & Straus we opened offices on the fourth floor of 59 Wall Street.

On the same floor in this building was the office of Charles O'Conor, then the acknowledged head of the American Bar. He had practically retired, but retained a small office of one or two rooms, with one clerk. He came in only two or three times a week. Often when he felt fatigued he would rest on a lounge in a room set apart as library in our office. For a young lawyer like myself it was an unusual privilege to have such pleasant personal relations with so able and wise a leader in the profession. Incidentally I think O'Conor was instrumental in sending us our first important case, the collection of an old debt of considerable size. We were so successful for our client that, of his own accord, he sent us a check for ten thousand dollars, saying he would make it larger if we regarded it insufficient. The fact was, the amount was larger than we had thought of charging, and we frankly told him so. With five thousand dollars in reserve I felt rich and independent. My wants were naturally simple and our general practice was encouraging.

At about this time I first became active in public-spirited undertakings. The Young Men's Christian Association a few years before had opened its Twenty-Third Street Branch at the corner of Fourth Avenue and Twenty-Third Street, and the movement on the whole was getting much publicity and proving very successful in its work among young men. But it was an institution for Christians, and it occurred to several of us — as I remember it, there were two of my fellow members of the bar, Meyer S. Isaacs and Isaac S. Isaacs; Dr. Simeon N. Leo, Solomon B. Solomon, and myself — that it would be a useful undertaking if we organized a Young Men's Hebrew Association for the cultural and intellectual advancement of Jewish young men. After a few preliminary meetings we launched our project early in 1874. We rented a house in the vicinity of Nineteenth or Twentieth Street and began in a very modest way. Our first entertainment was of a purely literary nature, and I recollect on that occasion addressing the members of the infant enterprise on the subject of literary clubs, ancient and modern, from the time of Socrates and Plato to the days of the coffee houses of Addison, Steele, and Goldsmith. The Y.M.H.A. subsequently had its years of struggle for existence, but to-day its place in our cities as an influence for the development of culture and patriotism is assured, as well as that of its sister organization of later birth, the Young Women's Hebrew Association.

I had chosen the law as my profession, but I still wrote verse, and in the decade following my graduation published several pieces. At one memorable event I was invited to deliver an original poem. It was in 1875, at a large fair in Gilmore's Garden, the predecessor of the present Madison Square Garden. The fair was held to raise funds toward the erection of a new building for the Mount Sinai Hospital, and the immense auditorium was crowded. Samuel J. Tilden, then Governor of New York and also prospective Democratic nominee for President, made the opening address. My poetic possibilities, however, rested more upon aspiration than inspiration, and my craving for versification was but a passing phase of my literary activities.

About 1876 we removed our office to the New York Life Building, then, as now, at 346 Broadway, corner of

Leonard Street. Our clientèle was mostly commercial and this neighborhood seemed more convenient. Our neighbors at the new location were Chamberlain, Carter & Eaton, a prominent commercial law firm of which Charles E. Hughes subsequently became a member.

A few years later we took into our firm Simon Sterne, then one of the brilliant younger members of the bar, and our firm became Sterne, Hudson & Straus. But Hudson wanted to devote himself to patent law, in which he had specialized somewhat, so the firm soon changed again to Sterne, Straus & Thompson. Daniel G. Thompson had been our managing clerk. He had an attractive personality and a philosophical temperament, but was more a psychologist than a lawyer. He was author of several works on the science and history of psychology which were favorably received and commended by such men as Herbert Spencer and other high authorities in both Europe and America. These qualities made him a target for the sarcasm of Sterne, who, on the other hand, was thoroughly the lawyer. On one occasion I remember Sterne asking me whether I knew Thompson was dissipating. I expressed surprise, and Sterne went on: "Certainly he is, for when he goes home he works till all hours of the night writing psychology, and naturally next day he comes with an exhausted brain to his legal work. He might better go on a spree, for one gets over that. But when one buries one's self in such an exacting science he is lost for the law, which is a jealous mistress and will not bear a rival."

Under the name of Sterne, Straus & Thompson we had a practice that ranged all the way from the collection of debts to questions affecting street railways and public utilities. Our old firm had a business like that of most young lawyers, but Sterne's practice was much more important, his field being mainly banking and railroads. Sterne, in fact, was rapidly achieving a reputation as an authority in the State on railways and railway legislation. At that time there was no Interstate Commerce Commission. Many New York merchants were complaining, through the New York Chamber of Commerce and the New York Board of Trade and Transportation, that the railroads were discriminating and giving to certain shippers much lower rates than to others, also giving preference to some in the moving of freight. In 1879 the Legislature finally appointed a committee of eight men to investigate these charges. A. Barton Hepburn, member of the Assembly from St. Lawrence County, was made chairman, causing the committee always thereafter to be referred to as the Hepburn Committee. Sterne represented the Chamber of Commerce and the Board of Trade in this investigation.

The committee sat intermittently for about nine months. The railroads had a brilliant array of legal talent, but Sterne elicited testimony from them which proved the charges of the merchants. Sterne then drafted the report of the committee, which included several recommendations for legislation. It was the first impressive and well-directed attempt to deal with the regulation of transportation companies, and resulted in the passage, in 1880, of the bill creating the first Board of Railroad Commissioners. Later, in 1887, the influence of this work was still alive in connection with legislation for the creation of the Federal Interstate Commerce Commission. The business of our firm did not exactly benefit by this public service of Sterne. As a result of his public activities and settlement of litigation, such railway clients as we had were lost to us at about this time.

At this point in my career I have the fond recollection of a dear and intimate friendship, which continued for several years, with Joseph H. Choate, of the firm of Evarts, Southmayd & Choate. We used to ride horseback together in the park before breakfast. This intimacy naturally was very valuable to me. We discussed all manner of topics, not only affecting our profession, but touching many public matters and the philosophy of life and living in general. In these morning hours, with the exhilaration of our ride, Mr. Choate was always full of fun and good humor. He was the most sought after person for addressing all important public functions, and frequently he would outline the substance of his addresses. Speaking one day of the many demands upon him as a speaker, he remarked that he appeared to be in the fashion just then, but, like wall-paper, fashions change, and it was not likely to last long. In his case, however, the fashion lasted, even increased, until his death in 1917.

My major law work was in the most exacting and nerve-racking branch, the trying of cases. My general physical condition, though never robust, was none the less good, but I had not learned what one is more apt to acquire later in life: to conserve my energies. The result was that the wear and tear of court work reduced my weight to one hundred and five pounds. My physician strongly advised me to do less exacting work, and especially to stop trying cases. As this branch of the law appealed to me most, it was a grave disappointment to have to abandon it. Rather than continue in the profession with such an inhibition, therefore, I yielded to the advice of my father and brother to join their firm.

I took a vacation of several months, and upon my

return early in 1881 I became a member of L. Straus & Sons, who had become large manufacturers and importers of china and glassware. On account of the growing business they really needed my services, and my transition from professional to business man was made as acceptable and agreeable as possible. As was to be expected, I continued for some time to long for "the fleshpots of Egypt," for I was much attached to my profession. As a compensation, and to satisfy my intellectual longings, I devoted my evenings and spare time to historical reading and study.

Having embarked on a business career, I reversed a decision that I made while practicing law. As a lawyer I had taken very seriously and literally the saying that "the law is a jealous mistress." I was her devoted slave, quite willingly so, and I determined never to marry. I was economically independent as a single man and could devote my time to the law for its own sake. This I preferred to do, as the idealist that I was, rather than pursue the law for economic reasons first and for its own sake as much as possible secondarily, which I felt would have to be the case if I married. But as a business man things were different, and I decided now to marry.

On January 22, 1882, I became engaged to Sarah, only daughter of Louis and Hannah Seller Lavanburg, and we were married on the 19th of April following, at the home of her parents on West Forty-Sixth Street, near Fifth Avenue. At the wedding dinner, to which had come hosts of our friends and acquaintances, Joaquin Miller, poet of the Sierras, as he was called, read a poem which he composed for the event. The manuscript I think is still in my possession.

In the year of my marriage I also made my début in

politics. I was secretary of the Executive Committee of an independent group organized for the reëlection of William R. Grace as mayor of New York. The distinguished lawyer, Frederick R. Coudert, was chairman of that committee. Grace had been a Tammany mayor and given the city a good business administration — so good and so independent that Tammany refused to nominate him for a second term. On the independent ticket Grace had a large Republican as well as the independent Democratic support, and was duly elected.

I next took part in the Cleveland-Blaine campaign. In 1884 we formed in New York City the Cleveland and Hendricks Merchants' and Business Men's Association, of which I was secretary of the executive committee, and we coöperated with the Democratic National Committee, Senator Arthur P. Gorman, chairman, whose headquarters were at the old Fifth Avenue Hotel, corner of Fifth Avenue and Twenty-Third Street. We organized a parade and marched forty thousand strong from lower Broadway to Thirty-Fourth Street. It was the first time business men had ever been organized along political lines.

All who remember this campaign know what an exciting and close battle it was. The dramatic event which doubtless put the balance in Cleveland's favor was the speech of the Rev. Dr. Samuel D. Burchard, a Presbyterian minister of New York, at Republican headquarters. A few days before the election the Republican managers had called what they termed a ministers' meeting, to which came some six hundred clergymen of all denominations to meet Mr. Blaine. Dr. Burchard, noted as an orator, was to speak, followed by Mr. Blaine. In concluding his address, Dr. Burchard evidently lost control of his dignity, for he stigmatized the Democratic Party as the party of "rum, Romanism, and rebellion." In the face of the great efforts the Republican Party had made, with some measure of success, to secure the Roman Catholic vote, this denunciation gave a big opportunity to the Democrats. Furthermore, Blaine, keen a politician as he was, failed immediately to repudiate the remark.

I was present at Democratic headquarters when the reporter who had been sent to this meeting returned. Senator Gorman asked him to read from his shorthand notes, and when he came to the expression, "rum, Romanism, and rebellion," Gorman at once said, "Write that out." The Democratic managers saw their chance. Quickly the whole country was placarded with posters headed "R.R.R.," with all sorts of variations and additions of the original phrase. In the end it was the New York vote that determined the victory for the Democrats, and doubtless because of the influence the words of Dr. Burchard had had upon Roman Catholic voters.

When the election returns were in, Cleveland had won by only 1047 votes. Because of the closeness of the vote in New York the Republicans did not at first concede the victory. Among the Democrats, on the other hand, there was a great feeling of bitterness and nervous apprehension lest an effort be made to make it a Republican victory, as was the case in 1876 when the uncertain returns were decided by an electoral commission, which, to the disappointment of many, made its decision on party lines. Jay Gould, who controlled the telegraph lines, was accused by the Democrats of holding back returns.

The Merchants' and Business Men's Association promptly organized a large meeting in the Academy of Music, to proclaim and celebrate Cleveland's election.

August Belmont, Sr., as chairman, presided, and I, as secretary, presented the resolutions. We had invited the most prominent speakers we could get, and there were Henry Ward Beecher, Daniel Dougherty of Philadelphia, Algernon S. Sullivan, among others. I distinctly recall a humorous and cryptic remark of Beecher's address that day: "If the chair is too small, make it larger" — referring to Cleveland's avoirdupois and the claim that he did not fit in the presidential chair. The note of victory, and the determination to stand by that victory at all costs, had a reassuring effect throughout the country.

When the campaign was over I was told by a member of the National Committee that if there was any political office to which I aspired, the Committee would be glad to further any ambition I might have; but I replied my only wish was that Cleveland live up to the political principles which had brought him the support of so many independent or "mugwump" voters and so made possible his election.

During the winter of 1883-84 the Young Men's Hebrew Association invited me to speak in their course of lectures. I was to choose my own subject. They had hired Chickering Hall, at Fifth Avenue and Fifteenth Street, a large lecture hall in those days, and as great importance was being attached to the occasion I naturally put my best foot forward in the preparation of my material. I chose as my theme "The Origin of the Republican Form of Government." In it I traced the rise of democracy, in contradistinction to monarchy, from the Hebrew Commonwealth as expounded in the Old Testament and interpreted by the early Puritans of New England, especially in their "election sermons," which were of a politico-religious character and were delivered annually before the legislatures of the various New England colonies.

There was a huge audience, and the next morning the press gave very generous reports of the address. It attracted the attention of various ministers in Brooklyn, and subsequently I was asked to repeat it before the Long Island Historical Society, in that city. There I had an amusing experience. In the course of the talk I quoted ideas similar to mine that had been advanced over a hundred years before by Thomas Paine in his "Common Sense," and I referred to the high estimates of Paine held by Washington, Monroe, Dr. Rush, and others of the time. I refrained from expressing opinions of my own, contenting myself with a reference to those of the fathers of the Republic. Suddenly, however, several ministers left the hall, protesting that they had not come to hear a eulogy on Paine.

Later I developed this address, under its original title, and published it in book form. The first edition came out in 1885. The appearance of a first book is quite an event in cne's life, especially when it is well received among critics and by the press. At any rate, it seemed like a landmark in my own life. Historical writers referred to it as a distinct contribution to our historical literature, and I felt that so far as the pen was concerned I had discovered this branch of writing to be my forte rather than poetry. After all, historical writing is no less imaginative than poetry. Without the use of imagination history is lifeless and a dry record of facts instead of literature.

A second impression of the book was issued in 1887, and in 1901 a second and revised edition was published. A French edition had appeared simultaneously in Paris and Brussels, 1890, translated by M. Emile de Laveleye, eminent Belgian publicist and professor at the University of Liége, and containing an introductory essay by him. This essay was translated into English and embodied in the 1901 American edition. Since then additional impressions of this revised edition have appeared. I might mention that on the strength of this book I was admitted to membership in the Authors' Club, in 1888.

In the fall of the year following the original publication of my first book I chanced to meet Senator Gorman of Maryland in the Palmer House, Chicago, where we both happened to be stopping — he on his return from a trip to the Far West, and I on an important business errand. He told me he and his son had read my book on their trip, and that he had not in a long time read a book with so much valuable information in it and giving such a clear view of the sources and early growth of our form of government. We naturally talked of matters political, and he reminded me of an earlier conversation he had had with me since Cleveland's election, stating that Mr. Cox — S. S. Cox — our minister to Turkey, had or was about to resign, and that he would like to recommend me to President Cleveland for appointment in Cox's place. He thought at the same time it might enable me to make further studies along the lines of my book.

The idea was a complete surprise to me. As I have mentioned, I had no thought of entering public life. My political activities had been limited to the part I took in the reëlection of Mayor Grace and the Cleveland-Blaine campaign. Even had I been ambitious for a political position I should never have ventured application for a diplomatic post, for I had never given much attention to our foreign relations. Besides, I had been in business only a few years, I was married and had two small daughters;

everything considered, I felt I could not afford to leave my affairs to go abroad.

Upon returning to New York I conferred with my father and brothers, and their attitude changed my views somewhat. They generously offered to see that my interests should not suffer, and gave me every encouragement to entertain Senator Gorman's suggestion. I could not possibly have further considered the subject without this generosity on their part. My obligations to my family did not permit the expenditure of several times my salary, required in a position of this kind. The salary of minister to Turkey had been reduced to seven thousand five hundred dollars, though it was subsequently restored to ten thousand; and in order to live properly he had to rent a winter house in the capital and a summer house outside, or live in hotels as Mr. Cox, and his predecessor, General Lew Wallace, did. General Wallace was restricted to his salary and felt compelled to decline the invitations of his colleagues because he was not in position to reciprocate. (His "Ben Hur," by the way, he had written before his sojourn in the East, and not afterward as is often supposed.)

Senator Gorman was not finally able to make the recommendation he had proposed. His relations with the President became strained, so that recommendations for appointments coming from him were not regarded with favor by Cleveland. Gorman told me as much when we met subsequently, but advised me to use such influence as I might command in other directions.

I presently spoke of it to an old friend of my days in the law, B. Franklin Einstein, who was counsel for the "New York Times" and the personal adviser of George Jones, its proprietor. Einstein suggested that I speak with Jones about it, and this I did. Jones encouraged me and said he would be glad to help. He said he had read my book and felt sure I would give a good account of myself and be a credit to the administration; that he had never asked any favor of the administration and felt justified in asking Cleveland to make the appointment. The "Times" had been an independent Republican paper, but in the campaign of 1884 it came out for Cleveland.

I also conferred with Carl Schurz, with whom I stood on intimate terms, and with John Foord, another friend. In the early eighties we used to have a lunch club that met about once in two weeks at a little French restaurant, August Sieghortner's, at 32 Lafayette Place, now Lafayette Street, in a house that had been a former residence of one of the Astors. We used to discuss various political and reform matters — the "mugwump" movement, the Cleveland campaigns, or what not. There were ten or twelve of us, and Carl Schurz was one; the late Charles R. Miller, who was for many years the leading editorial writer of the "Times," was another; and John Foord, whose death by accident occurred in Washington only a few days ago as I write, was another. Foord was then editor-in-chief of the "Times." He took up my appointment with both President Cleveland and Secretary of State Bayard. Schurz encouraged me and said he would speak to Oswald Ottendorfer about having me appointed. Ottendorfer, proprietor of the "New Yorker Staatszeitung," was a client of our law firm and knew me well. Subsequently I saw him and he wrote to Cleveland strongly recommending the appointment.

Cleveland was favorably enough impressed, but he hesitated. He said our chief concern in Turkey was the protection of American missionary interests, and he would not like to appoint any one to this particular mission who might be objected to by the two principal missionary bodies — the American Board of Commissioners for Foreign Missions and the Presbyterian Board of Missions.

It happened that on a return trip from Washington about this time my brother Isidor met A. S. Barnes, prominent textbook publisher and a member of the American Board of Commissioners for Foreign Missions, to whom also I was quite well known. He had been in frequent consultation with our law firm when we represented the City of Brooklyn in its suit against the Atlantic Avenue Railroad to compel the road to sink its tracks, in which suit, as one of Brooklyn's public-spirited citizens, he was much interested. He was sympathetic toward me and brought the subject of my appointment before his missionary board, with the result that its Prudential Committee wrote a letter to the President expressing fullest approval of my appointment, suggesting only that I be asked not to hold receptions on the Sabbath, as one of my predecessors had done to the great disapproval of the missionaries and all Protestant Christians in Constantinople. Even without this intimation I would quite naturally have refrained from offending the religious sensibilities of my nationals at that post.

The representatives of all the Protestant churches who had interests in Turkey were most generous in favoring the appointment when they learned that I was being considered for that mission. The most admired and best beloved American preacher of his time, Henry Ward Beecher, of Plymouth Church, Brooklyn, heard of it through Mr. O. A. Gager, one of the trustees of his church; also that there was some diffidence about my actual selection because of my religion. He immediately wrote the President a beautiful and characteristic letter, urging my appointment. The original of this letter, now in my possession, was given to me by Governor Porter, first assistant Secretary of State.

With my wife I had gone to Atlantic City for a few days, to recuperate from a cold, when on March 24, 1887, I received telegrams from friends all over the country congratulating me on my appointment as minister to Turkey. The papers of the day announced it, and the "New York Times" published the Beecher letter just referred to.

To the press of the country my appointment was of added interest because of the Keiley incident of two years before. A. M. Keiley, of Virginia, was nominated by Cleveland as minister to Austria-Hungary, but objected to by that country because Mrs. Keiley, being of Jewish parentage, was *persona non grata*. As a matter of fact this excuse for the rejection of Keiley was supposedly made because the Austro-Hungarian Government thought it might be acceptable to us in lieu of the truth.

The real reason lay much deeper. Keiley had earlier been nominated as minister to Italy. The Italian Government, through its representative at Washington, made known to our Department of State that Keiley would be *persona non grata* because it was remembered that in 1870 he had made a public speech in Richmond violently denouncing King Victor Emmanuel for his treatment of the Pope. The nomination was therefore withdrawn. And when a few months later Keiley was appointed minister to Austria-Hungary, that country, being a member with Italy in the Triple Alliance, did not want to run the risk of displeasing Italy by accepting a representative not satisfactory to her; but not wishing to admit this, based its excuse on religious grounds.

State
rec'd Feby 17/6/

Feby 12. 1887
Brooklyn
N.Y.

Grover Cleveland

Dear Mr. President

Some of our best
Citizens are Solicitous
for the appointment of
Oscar Straus, as Minister
To Turkey. — Of his fitness
there is a general consent
that he is personally, and
in attainments, eminently
Excellent. —

But I am interested in
another Quality — the fact
that he is a Hebrew

The bitter prejudice against Jews, which obtain in many parts of Europe, ought not to receive any Confederate Countenance in America. It is because he is a Jew that I would urge his appointment and a fit recognition of this remarkable people, who are becoming large contributors to American prosperity & whose intelligence, Morality, and large liberality in all public measures for the welfare of society, deserve & should receive from the hands of our government some such recognition—

Is it not, also, a duty to

Set forth, in this quiet, but effectual method, the Genius of American Government?. which has under its fostering care people of all civilized Nations, and which ~~regards~~ treats them without regard. to civil, religious, or race peculiarities as Common Citizens? - We send Danes to Denmark, Germans to Germany, We reject no man because he is a Frenchman, Why should we not make a Crowning testimony to the Genius of our people, by sending a Hebrew to Mr. Key?

The ignorance & superstition of mediæval Europe may account for the prejudices of the dark age. But how a Christian in our day, can turn from a Jew, I cannot imagine. Christianity itself sucked at the bosom of Judaism. Our roots are in the Old Testament — We are Jews ourselves gone to blossom & fruit, Christianity is Judaism in Evolution. and it would seem strange for the lead to turn against the Stock on which it was grown

Henry Ward Beecher

This so incensed our Administration that Secretary Bayard rebuked the Austro-Hungarian Government with the statement:

It is not within the power of the President nor of the Congress, nor of any judicial tribunal in the United States, to take or even hear testimony, or in any mode to inquire into or decide upon the religious belief of any official, and the proposition to allow this to be done by any foreign Government is necessarily and *a fortiori* inadmissible.

And Mr. Cleveland made reference to the episode in his First Annual Message to Congress:

The reasons advanced were such as could not be acquiesced in, without violation of my oath of office and the precepts of the Constitution, since they necessarily involved a limitation in favor of a foreign government upon the right of selection by the Executive, and required such an application of a religious test as a qualification for office under the United States as would have resulted in the practical disfranchisement of a large class of our citizens and the abandonment of a vital principle of our Government.

These statements contain a clear exposition of one of the fundamental principles of our laws and system of government; they form one of the most illuminating and inspiring chapters of our diplomatic literature. Following the Keiley incident, my appointment was a silent but effective protest against such illiberal views as those expressed by Austria-Hungary; and to me personally it meant something to be sent as the representative of my country to the power whose dominion extended over the land that cradled my race, Palestine.

Leaving Atlantic City, we soon proceeded to Washington, where I called on Secretary Bayard, who received me with characteristic cordiality and referred me to John Bassett Moore, now our famous authority on international law, compiler of the International Law Digest,

American judge of the Court of International Justice by vote of the Council and Assembly of the League of Nations. At the time I met him, thirty-five years ago, he was third assistant Secretary of State, and I could not have wished for a better instructor in the intricate matters that involved our relations with the Ottoman Empire.

Alvey A. Adee, veteran of our Foreign Office, then as now the second assistant Secretary of State, was another man who gave me most helpful advice. His encyclopædic knowledge of our foreign relations for more than forty years is remarkable, and our diplomatic appointees for years have been indebted to him for much helpful guidance.

Later in the day we called on the President. Our conversation during this call was purely of a general nature, and as I was leaving Mr. Cleveland expressed pleasure at my promptness in calling and hoped that I would start for Turkey as soon as personal convenience permitted. When I told him I hoped to sail at the end of a week, he answered, "That is businesslike; I like that," and he asked me to call again before leaving Washington.

Two days later, by appointment of Colonel Lamont, the President's secretary, Mrs. Straus and I, accompanied by brother Isidor and E. G. Dunnell, "New York Times" correspondent, called on Mrs. Cleveland in the Green Room of the White House. I vividly recall this visit. Mrs. Cleveland came into the room with a sprightly and unceremonious walk, very friendly, with charm of manner and a sufficient familiarity to put us entirely at our ease. She was a very handsome woman, with remarkable sweetness of expression, and her appearance symbolized beauty and simplicity.

What most impressed me about the Clevelands, after

these two visits, was the simple, unassuming manner that was so in keeping with the spirit of our laws and the democracy of our institutions. Verily, I thought in the words of Cleveland himself, "a public office is a public trust," and while administering office we are indeed servants of the people.

Before leaving Washington we again called on the President as agreed. His entire conversation and attitude showed satisfaction with my appointment. He said he understood the missionaries were doing good work, and he felt sure from what he had learned of me that they would receive impartial and just treatment at my hands. He commented on the fact that the press of the country had been so unanimously in favor of my appointment. "I wished they would go for you a little; I have something to give them," he said. From Mr. Dunnell later I learned the meaning of this remark. He had received a letter from the Prudential Committee of the American Board of Commissioners for Foreign Missions, highly approving of his appointing me as minister to Turkey and endorsing me of their own accord in unqualified terms. This letter he was holding to give to the press should any unfavorable comment be made because a member of the Hebrew race was being sent to a post where the Christian mission interests were so large. Mr. Cleveland's parting remark to me was: "I know you will do well; I have no trepidation — none at all."

On Saturday, April 9th, at 6 A.M., we — my wife, Aline, the younger of our little daughters, and myself — sailed out of the harbor on the S.S. Aurania. My one prayer in bidding farewell to my home was that I might find no vacant seat at my table upon my return, and that I might discharge my high trust with credit and honor. For this no sacrifice would be too great.

CHAPTER III

ENTERING DIPLOMACY

At sea — Our arrival in London — Concerning George Eliot and Lewes —
At the banking house of Baron de Rothschild — In Paris — Boulanger's
Napoleonic dreams; his suicide — Josef Hofmann as a boy pianist — The
artist who painted "Christ before Pilate"; an extraordinary wife — Distinguished hosts and rich cooking — Vienna and the Balkans — Thoughts on
passing through the Bosphorus — Constantinople, the city of picturesque
dirt — Many delays obstruct my audience with the Sultan — The fast of
Ramazan — Diplomatic garden parties — An ambassador's £300 Circassian
slave-wife — The Sultan says his prayers — Advice from a seasoned diplomat
— My address at Robert College commencement — In the Sultan's Palace.

OUR voyage was not altogether a light one. We had
found it expedient to leave Mildred, our elder daughter,
then four years old, with her Grandma Lavanburg; and
while she was in excellent hands my wife was naturally
heavy-hearted at the thought of traveling so far and for
so long without her. The weather on board ship was for
the most part stormy. Our little Aline and her nurse
were so seasick that the child resented being on board
with all the force of age three. "Mama, this ship is nobody's home; why did you bring me here? I shall write
sister Milly never to go on the ocean," she declared re-
belliously.

Having reached London, however, things went more
pleasantly. Our minister there at the time — we did not
yet appoint ambassadors — was Edward J. Phelps, for
many years Professor of International Law at Yale, a
scholarly gentleman. I called on him almost immediately
on my arrival, and subsequently Mrs. Straus and I dined
at the legation to meet Rustem Pasha, Turkish ambassador, veteran diplomat who had been in the service for
thirty-three years and was about twice as old. He was
leading Turkish representative at the Congress of Berlin

in 1878, following the Russo-Turkish War. He referred
to the various questions pending between his Government
and mine — the interpretation of Article 4 of the Treaty
of 1830, signed only in Turkish; the proposed treaty of
1874, negotiated by Minister Boker and not confirmed
by the Senate, concerning naturalized citizens of the
United States returning to Turkey; missionary matters;
our refusal to negotiate a treaty for the extradition of
criminals. I had informed myself regarding all of these,
but I deemed it wise not to discuss them in detail; rather
I chose to be the listener and draw him out, assuring him
that when I arrived at my post all these subjects would
have my very best attention. He was particularly concerned with the treaty for the extradition of criminals,
but the so-called criminals that came to the United States
at that period, especially from Russia and Turkey, were
with rare exception political refugees, and it is provided
in most of our extradition treaties that political offenders
are not to be delivered up.

We remained in London about ten days, calling on a
number of interesting people. We spent one pleasant
evening with Dr. and Mrs. John Chapman, of the "Westminster Review." My article on "The Development of
Religious Liberty in America" was appearing in a current
number of the "Review." The Chapmans were good
friends of George Eliot and Professor Lewes. In fact, the
novelist and the professor first met at the Chapman
home. Dr. Chapman also told me he was the one who
first employed George Eliot in literary work. He became
editor of the "Review" in 1851 and engaged her as associate editor. When George Eliot resigned, Mrs. Chapman became the associate editor. With us that evening,
too, was Harold Frederic, London correspondent of the
"New York Times" and a novelist of some promise.

From Messrs. J. & W. Seligman of New York I had received a letter to the Seligman banking house in London, at 3 Angel Court. Mr. Isaac Seligman invited us to dine *en famille*, and arranged for me to call at Messrs. N. M. Rothschild & Sons', where I was very pleasantly received by Baron Alfred Charles de Rothschild, who showed me through his magnificent banking establishment and offered to send me a letter to the Paris Rothschild firm. The Baron was then about forty-four years old, very agreeable, a polished gentleman of the best Jewish type.

In Paris, our next stopping-place, we also had a very interesting time. Of course we called on our minister, Robert M. McLane, then seventy-four years old, but looking sixty. He was distinctly of the old school, with all the grace of manner, combined with ability and wide experience in public service — an excellent representative who was esteemed by the French people quite as highly as by our own citizens in France. I speak of this especially because in capitals like Paris it is not an easy task to please both elements.

At dinner one evening in the home of my friend Adolphe Salmon, an American merchant residing in Paris, we met Count Dillon and his wife, most affable people to whom we felt ourselves immediately attracted. The Count was a thorough Royalist, had been for many years in the army. At this time he was managing director of the Mackay-Bennett Cable Company and the leader of a movement, really anti-Republican intrigue, designed to put General Boulanger, Minister of War, at the head of the State. The Count was a close personal friend and schoolmate of Boulanger, then the most extolled man in all France. The Count suggested that he arrange a luncheon or dinner to have us meet the General, if that was agreeable to us, for he felt sure the General would be pleased.

Consequently a few days later we lunched at Count Dillon's beautiful villa some thirty minutes outside of Paris. It was an intimate two-hour luncheon party, just Mr. and Mrs. Adolphe Salmon, the Count and Countess Dillon, General Boulanger, Mrs. Straus, and myself. Boulanger was a young-looking man for his fifty years, of medium height and weight, wearing a closely trimmed beard; rather Anglo-American than French in appearance, unassuming, of pleasant expression, and probably at the height of his power. Five years before he had been Director of Infantry in the War Office and made himself very popular as a military reformer. In 1886, under the ægis of Clemenceau and the Radical Party which brought Freycinet into power, Boulanger was made Minister of War. He was noted for his fire-eating attitude toward Germany in connection with the Schnaebele frontier incident, and because of this was hailed as the man destined to give France her revenge for the disasters of 1870. In fact, the masses looked upon him as a second Napoleon, "the man on horseback," and his picture on horseback was displayed in countless shop windows.

At our luncheon party he entertained us with many an interesting anecdote, and I particularly recall his telling of coming to the Yorktown Centennial Celebration and traveling as far as the Pacific Coast in company with General Sherman to see our fortifications. "I was asked what I thought of your American fortifications ["You know what antiquated and insignificant things they are," in an aside to Mrs. Straus], and I praised them and said I thought they were splendid, that I had never seen any better ones because" — and here his eyes twinkled — "no

country has such nice ditches in front of its fortifications."
He meant, of course, the Atlantic and the Pacific.

When the champagne was being drunk and toasts were
in order I turned to the General, after drinking to the
health of the company, and said: "May you administer
the War Department so successfully that posterity will
know you as the great preserver of peace." To this he
responded that for fifteen years France had always been
on the defensive and permitted insults rather than take
offense, but that the time had come when she could no
longer do so and must be ready for the offensive. He
evidently had in mind that war was imminent. At a later
meeting he asked me whether, in case of war, I would be
willing to take charge of French interests in Turkey. I
told him that while of course it would be agreeable to
me personally, such action could be taken only under the
authority of my government, which authority I would
have to obtain before giving an official answer.

The subsequent meteoric career of Boulanger is a
matter of history. For two years more his personality
was one of the dominating factors of French politics. I
remember writing from Constantinople early in 1889:
"The most menacing condition exists in France, where, I
am of opinion, Boulanger will gain the presidency before
many months and from that time perhaps try to tread
in the footprints of his Napoleonic ideal. If so — alas,
poor France, and alas the peace of Europe!" He had
become an open menace to the republic; and when Con-
stans was Minister of the Interior a prosecution was
instituted against Boulanger and a warrant signed for his
arrest. He fled from Paris and was afterward tried and
condemned *in absentia* for treason. In 1891 he committed
suicide on the grave of his mistress in a cemetery at
Brussels.

We dined, on another evening in Paris, with Mr. and Mrs. William Seligman, of the banking firm of Seligman Frères, the Paris branch of J. & W. Seligman of New York and of the London Seligman establishment. This dinner was a very large and elaborate affair, with many distinguished guests present. After dinner we were entertained by the budding genius of Josef Hofmann, then ten or eleven years old.

The noted Hungarian, Munkacsy, painter of "Last Day of a Condemned Man," "Christ before Pilate," "Christ on Calvary," and other celebrated works, was also there with his wife. As a couple they presented a striking contrast indeed. He was a silent man, talking very little and haltingly; he impressed one as a refined artisan of some sort, perhaps a carpenter. He was a large man of about five feet ten in height, with bushy hair combed up, bushy beard and mustache, and small eyes which he screwed up to almost nothing when observing something. His wife, on the other hand, was as coarse-looking a woman as one might discover, with a loud, raucous, almost masculine voice which, like a saw in action, rose above every other sound. However, I have observed that these contraries in personality in couples often make for happiness.

The artist seemed to take a keen interest in Mrs. Straus. He quite embarrassed her by his constant staring, and after dinner sought an introduction and sat next to her. Her plain hair-dress, smoothly brushed back and rolled in a coil behind, fascinated him. He remarked how natural and becoming it was and wanted to know whether she always wore it that way; he wondered whether it would be as becoming any other way. He wanted to know how long we should remain in Paris and expressed regret when told we were leaving in three or four days.

Mrs. Straus felt he had studied her head long enough to paint it from memory. And who knows, perhaps he has used it in some painting that we have not yet discovered!

Another memorable dinner was at the home of Eli Lazard, of Lazard Frères, bankers, where we met Judge Wilson and daughters, of Cincinnati. All of these hospitalities were very pleasant, but personally I should have been glad to escape them, for the late hours, together with the rich cooking of Paris, were not in accord with my quiet habits and simple tastes in food and drink.

In Vienna I called on our consul-general, Edmund Jussen, whose wife was the sister of my esteemed friend Carl Schurz, which fact really prompted me to make the call. Jussen himself was not very admirable. He had much of the arrogance of a German official, so out of place in an American representative. However, during our sojourn in the city he and his wife exchanged several visits with us. Mrs. Jussen did not much resemble her distinguished brother, except for an expression about the eyes. She was a very amiable woman with a good face. She told me much of her brother's childhood and school years — how he had to struggle hard for his education. Their father was a small shopkeeper, but no business man, and was never able to make money. Carl did not earn money, but always applied himself diligently. This and much more that has since been published about Schurz interested me greatly, of course.

We continued our journey to Varna on the Black Sea, there to take the steamer for Constantinople. In those days there was no railway connection with Constantinople. The Oriental Express went only to Varna, by way of Bucharest. On that particular part of our journey we got our first glimpses of the picturesque costumes of the

Balkan district, especially those of the men with their
bare legs and flying shirts.

The trip from Varna to Constantinople was beautiful
and inspiring. We boarded the boat at about four in the
afternoon and retired early so as to be up by five or six
next morning, when we passed through the Bosphorus,
round which clusters so much of classical memory. I
suddenly realized how much of my Homer I had forgotten — the Homer on whom I had spent years of hard
study. However, most of us meet so many new subjects
that have a more direct relation to our surroundings that
it is next to impossible to get that "elegant leisure"
necessary for a continued interest in the classics.

The effect of the trip through the Bosphorus is quite
like a dream. The high coast on both sides is covered
with green, with here and there a house or some large
huts; on one side is Europe and on the other side Asia,
looking very much alike, bathed by the same sunshine,
peaceful.

We sailed past Buyukdereh, Therapia, the summer
residence of most of the diplomats, about twelve miles
from Constantinople, where the English, French, Austrian, and Russian embassies had magnificent palaces and
the Germans were engaged in building; on past the lovely
old towers of Roumeli-Hissar, built eight hundred years
before, when first the Turks set foot in Europe, and back
of this the tower of Robert College.

Suddenly my ever-smiling and happy wife spied a
launch flying a large United States flag at the stern. "It's
our launch!" And sure enough, when we waved our
handkerchiefs we discovered the members of my official
family, who had come in the legation launch to meet us.
There were Pendleton King, acting chargé d'affaires;
Mr. Gargiulo, dragoman; J. Lynch Pringle, consul-

general; Mehmet, the *cavass;* and several clerks of the consulate and legation.

The *cavass*, by the way, is a sort of bodyguard. He walks before the minister, or rides on the box beside the driver, and serves the purpose of designating that the minister or ambassador follows. He carries two huge pistols and a sword suspended from a gold belt, and his coat, sometimes red and sometimes blue, is much be-braided and embroidered. The natives know each minister or ambassador by his *cavass*.

Our first impression from the windows of the Royal Hotel in Constantinople was of picturesque dirt. As Mrs. Straus said at the time, dirt not only on the hard earth roads and the people, but even on the dogs. In time, however, one is less impressed by the dirt than by the picturesqueness — the venders calling out their wares of fish, fruit, meat, vegetables, all carried on the edges of baskets covered with leaves; the water-carriers with their urns carried on yokes; and the veiled women.

Immediately upon my arrival, of course, I communicated with His Excellency, Saïd Pasha, Minister of Foreign Affairs, to present my credentials and arrange for an audience with His Majesty the Sultan, Abdul Hamid. The Pasha replied at once, appointing a time two days later, and accordingly I went to the Sublime Porte, as the Turkish Government seat is called, in company with the chargé and the dragoman or interpreter. That was about May 26th. Not until June 6th, however, did I receive a communication from Munir Pasha, Grand Master of Ceremonies, that His Majesty had named June 8th for my audience. The next evening I received a telegram postponing the audience to the 10th. On the 9th I received another communication, postponing it *sine die.* On the 15th a new appointment was made for the 17th; then, between midnight and one o'clock on the night of June 16th–17th, the personal secretary of the Sultan came knocking at the door of my apartment, and, after apologizing for his arrival at that untimely hour, informed me that he had come at the Sultan's special request to say that word had come from the Porte that June 17th was a most sacred day, a fact just determined by the phases of the moon, and the Sultan therefore was constrained to postpone the audience again. The date was later set for July 1st, when I finally had my audience.

It was a peculiarity of Abdul Hamid to delay audiences to new representatives for weeks and sometimes months by these successive appointments and postponements, to no other purpose than to impress the agents of foreign governments with the importance of His Majesty. In my case there was some added cause: it was the month of Ramazan, during which only the most pressing official functions take place.

Ramazan, ninth month of the Turkish calendar, is a period of fasting. For twenty-nine days every Mussulman abstains from food and water, and even smoking, from sunrise to sunset; which the rich arrange conveniently by sleeping all day and eating all night, while the poor who have to work all day eat at sundown, at midnight, and very early in the morning. The first meal after the fasting, at sunset, is called *iltar*. The fast is broken with Ramazan bread, a cakelike bread, circular in shape, which we saw much in evidence at a bazaar in the courtyard of a mosque at Stamboul, the more Oriental part of Constantinople, where the costumes of Greeks, Armenians, Turks, and Arabs form a strange mixture indeed.

During Beiram, a three days' feasting following

Ramazan, the mosques are all illuminated at night, and the view over the water, with the moving lights of boats in the foreground and the dimly lighted houses beyond, interspersed with brightly illumined mosques, is quite like a picture of some enchanted land.

Because of the Sultan's peculiarities in receiving foreign representatives, the custom in regard to official calls at Constantinople is different from that at most capitals. Elsewhere calls on colleagues are not made until after a minister or ambassador has had his audience; but here usage dictated calling on one's colleagues as soon as possible. Therefore I called first on Baron de Calice, ambassador from Austria-Hungary and *doyen* of the diplomatic corps. He received me with great cordiality and kindness, and advised me fully regarding diplomatic practices at Constantinople. And we were welcomed by each and all of my colleagues in turn, so that I found these calls very much less disagreeable than I had anticipated; I even enjoyed many of them. At each visit coffee or tea was served, and generally cigarettes too, as is customary with the Turks, which is wonderfully effective in taking off the chill of diplomatic formalities. One soon gets to expect these refreshments; it is a delightful custom that might be adopted in other places to advantage.

Another reason why these formal calls were less formidable than they might have been was that three days after our arrival at the capital we were invited to a garden party given by Lady White, wife of the British ambassador, Sir William A. White. This served to give us a prompt introduction to all my colleagues. In fact, in the five weeks intervening between our arrival and my audience, we had attended so many garden parties and dinners given to us, that I found myself heartily long-

ing for respite. My natural inclination was to regard
these social gatherings in the light of idle frivolities,
especially in the summer, when one is supposed to be
relatively free from functions of this kind; and I was not
alone among my colleagues in preferring more evenings
at home to the occasional headaches that it cost to continue the very late hours these many engagements forced
us to keep. Yet I could not consistently decline invitations; such a course might have been interpreted as a
desire on my part to withdraw from the diplomatic circle
and would have interfered with the pleasant social relations it was incumbent on me to cultivate. Attendance
was really part of my duty, and in time I found these
functions distinctly advantageous.

We looked forward with more than usual interest to the
evening of our dinner at the Persian embassy. The Persian ambassador's wife had been a Circassian slave, whom
he was said to have bought for £300 with a horse thrown
into the bargain. The ambassador's wife was, of course,
typically Circassian; chalky white skin, soft black eyes,
small features, an unattractive figure unattractively
dressed, with whom conversation was almost nil because
she knew only Persian.

The streets of Pera, the European part of Constantinople, are exceedingly narrow and very hilly, for the
city is built on several hills, like ancient Rome; in addition they are poorly paved and dirty. This makes driving
dangerous and, as in mediæval times, sedan chairs were
quite generally in use as a means of conveyance for the
ladies of the diplomatic corps and the wives of the higher
Turkish officials, especially at night to dinners and other
official functions. Two sinewy porters carry these chairs,
one in front and the other behind, and they shuffle along
with considerable rapidity. Usually the lady is carried

while the gentleman, preceded by his *cavass* in the case of a diplomat, walks alongside, except in inclement weather when he follows also in a chair. I am reminded of the wife of the German ambassador at the time, a large, heavy woman, whom the porters quite justly charged double. She, however, was entirely oblivious of her extra avoirdupois and always complained of the injustice of these porters! The Austrian and Russian embassies were particularly difficult of approach by conveyance other than the sedan.

We certainly were living in a new sphere of life, in a strange land among strange people, with customs and habits that brought to mind the age of the patriarchs. There was much to see where some thirty nationalities lived and did business as if in their own homes — much to wonder at, much to deplore, much to praise and admire. The natives are a peculiar people, with many admirable characteristics; they are kind and hospitable, comparatively honest and reliable, especially the lower classes, and they manifest a most sincere devotion to their religion. The lower classes are poor, very poor; yet they are content and reasonably happy because their wants are few. Their poverty is not a suffering condition and they seemed to be better off than the poor elsewhere. Their religion strictly interdicts the use of alcoholic drinks, and as they are true to it and live faithfully up to its principles, they are spared all the evils that fall in the train of drunkenness.

During the weeks that I waited for my audience with the Sultan I devoted my time to studying in detail the various questions in regard to our diplomatic relations, so that I might be better informed when they came up. This study was very interesting from an historical point of view, for some of the questions were related to capitula-

MRS. STRAUS IN TURKEY

tions that dated as far back as the fall of Constantinople in 1453. My legal training also proved valuable in enabling me to understand and handle matters.

On our first Friday in Constantinople we witnessed Selamlik, the picturesque ceremony held with great pomp every Friday, attending the Sultan's going to the mosque. The Sultan's mosque is on the top of a hill commanding the most beautiful view of the city, from which can be seen the Bosphorus and, farther on, the Sea of Marmora. On the roads surrounding the mosque as far as the eye could see were ranged ten or more regiments of infantry and cavalry, each dressed in glittering uniforms according to the section of the empire from which they came, the most resplendent being the Nubian and the Arabian. The Sultan arrived in an open landau, and opposite him Osman Pasha, distinguished soldier, hero of the Battle of Plevna in the Russo-Turkish War, and Grand Marshal of the Palace. The coachman was magnificently dressed in scarlet and gold, and following were the aides-de-camp, also beautifully dressed, one, an Armenian, all in white and gold. As the Sultan entered the mosque a priest chanted a call to prayer which sounded not unlike the old Hebrew chants in some of our synagogues. The mosque was so crowded that we could see many Moslems kneeling and salaaming on the streets outside the doors. The service lasted about twenty minutes, whereupon the bands played and the Sultan reviewed his troops from one of the windows of the mosque. He then returned to the Palace in a beautiful top phaëton drawn by two horses, which he drove himself, again with Osman Pasha opposite, followed by his aides and the carriage that had brought him. Usually several carriages, open and closed, also several saddle horses, are brought

from the royal stables to the mosque, that the Sultan
may take his choice for his return to the Palace.

It is expected as a display of good will that the ministers
and ambassadors occasionally attend this ceremony. It
was practically the only occasion on which Abdul Hamid
appeared in public, for he constantly feared assassination, and his expression showed his timidity. Following
Selamlik he quite frequently arranged to receive in
audience. In the kiosque or small house beside the
mosque, there is a special suite of rooms reserved for
the diplomatic corps. An aide informs the Sultan what
diplomatic representatives or other persons of distinction
are at the kiosque, to each of whom His Majesty then
sends some gracious message. While prayers are being
said in the mosque, the guests at the kiosque are served
coffee and cigarettes.

One of the persons whom I met shortly after my
arrival in the city was Sir Henry Drummond Wolff, who
was in Constantinople as Britain's special envoy to
negotiate a convention regarding the withdrawal of
British troops from Egypt. He had a suite at our hotel
where we saw each other frequently and became very
good friends. Drummond Wolff, as he was usually
spoken of to distinguish him from the several other
prominent Wolffs, was certainly a remarkable and clever
man, and a great *raconteur*. He was then in his late
fifties, had had wide experience as a diplomat, and was
thoroughly familiar with the Turkish temperament. In
fact, he was at home in all that part of the world. He
was born in Malta, the son of the famous missionary,
Rev. Joseph Wolff, a Jew who became a convert first to
Catholicism and then to Episcopalianism, being ordained
as priest in the Church of England. While in America

he received the degree of Doctor of Theology from the College of St. John's, Annapolis, Maryland.

Sir Henry advised me in dealing with the Turkish authorities always to be patient, pleasant, persistent. He also impressed upon me the importance of maintaining the most cordial relations with my colleagues and of returning all hospitalities; that a well-disposed colleague can often be of incalculable assistance in inducing the authorities to accede to any proper demand one might have to make. However, his own relations with the British ambassador, Sir William White, were not so friendly. The estrangement between them was quite evident, caused no doubt by personal jealousy, which is so likely to result between a special envoy and the regularly accredited representative of the same country in a given territory.

We stayed at the Royal only about ten days, and then moved to summer quarters in a hotel at Therapia, a name given to the district some three thousand years ago by the Greeks because of its healthful and balmy climate. Here, too, Drummond Wolff had a neighboring suite, and later, when by reason of a longer stay than anticipated he was obliged to give up his apartment before he was ready, we put a portion of ours at his disposal, which he much appreciated. It was a very pleasant arrangement, and diplomatically no less profitable. We dined together every evening, and often in our party were also Prince Ghika, Roumanian chargé, and the Princess; Baron Van Tetz, Dutch minister, and the Baroness. The Baron was later accredited to Berlin, and then made Minister of Foreign Affairs in his own country. He has now retired and at this writing he and the Baroness still live at The Hague. They are charming people.

On June 21, 1887, the entire diplomatic corps was

present in official dress at services in the English chapel, in honor of the Queen's Jubilee. The chaplain of the English embassy, the Reverend George Washington, officiated. He said he was of the same family as our own George Washington.

The day before my audience I presided at the commencement exercises of Robert College at Roumeli-Hissar, by invitation of the venerable president, Dr. George Washburn. The college in 1887 had about one hundred and eighty students, mainly Bulgarians, Greeks, and Armenians, with two or three Turks. The commencement was quite similar to those at home, except that the orations were delivered in the various languages of the East as well as in French and English.

I took this first occasion to refer in a larger way to the aims and purposes of Robert College and similar American institutions. The Turks had not been able to understand the benevolence that prompted the establishment of schools and colleges by Americans throughout the empire. They were suspicious, and their attitude was founded on experiences with various institutions and societies of several of the other nations, notably the Greeks, who, under guise of scientific and benevolent activity, had fostered political design. The Turks believed that behind our institutions lay a purpose inimical to the sovereignty of Turkey, a belief stimulated by Russia and by some of the French Catholics, who were opposed to the extended use of the English language and the influence of Protestant English and American ideas in the East. This gave rise to many of the vexatious questions that the legation had to solve. By way of throwing some oil upon these troubled waters, therefore, I said, during my address:

For centuries the tide of progress and civilization has been making its way toward the West. Its course has been marked by blood and carnage. The history of the Middle Ages and of modern times chronicles the nations and empires that have sunk in this mighty current, and the new life and new civilization that have sprung up over the ruins of the old. That flood tide, pushing its irresistible course onward, still swept on, until in our day it mingled its waters with the Great Pacific Ocean. The Ultima Thule having at last been reached, the great ebb-tide began to course its way backward; and America, the youngest of nations, in gratitude for all the past, as a token of her amity and her friendship, has sent back on the advance current of this return tide not ships of war nor armed troops, but her most cherished institutions, a fully equipped American college.

So that here, to-day, on the beautiful and picturesque shores of the classic Bosphorus, on the very spot where the nations of the East four and a half centuries ago erected and left the well-preserved monument of their passage to the West, stands Robert College. What a tale and what a history! Robert College here and the Towers of Roumeli-Hissar there! The one the fortified remains of bygone wars, the other the tranquil emblem of returning peace. What a double tale do these two institutions speak to one another! The tie that unites them is one of love and peace, a league more puissant than army or navy for the welfare and happiness of nations. When centuries shall have rolled by and another Gibbon shall come to write of empires, may it be his privilege to record no longer the decline and fall, but the rise and rejuvenation of this Orient to which we look with affection.

And now that I had been received and entertained by about everybody in Constantinople, it was time for my audience with the Sultan, who came last like the prima donna. Official functions at Yildis Palace, as the Sultan's residence is called (Yildis meaning star), were always most dignified and punctilious. Royal carriages were sent from the Palace with escorts for myself and staff. At the entrance to the Palace we were met by the Introducer of Ambassadors; then we proceeded to the salon of the Grand Master of Ceremonies, where I was met by the Minister of Foreign Affairs and conducted by Osman Pasha, Grand Marshal, into the presence of His Majesty.

The Sultan was standing ready to receive me. He was a small man, of rather spare frame, sallow complexion, dark eyes that sparkled with a furtive expression, prominent aquiline nose, and short full black beard which later, when it turned gray, he dyed reddish with henna. He had on a black frock coat that buttoned to the neck.

According to custom I handed him the letters of recall of my predecessor, then presented my credentials, and made a brief address, a copy of which in writing I left with him. It read as follows:

The President of the United States has been pleased to charge me with the distinguished honor and agreeable duty of cultivating to the fullest extent the friendship which has so happily subsisted between the two Governments, and of conveying to Your Imperial Majesty the assurances of his best wishes for the welfare of Your Imperial Majesty and for the prosperity of Turkey.

As the faithful representative of my Government, charged with the duty of protecting the interests of her citizens, permit me to express the hope that Your Imperial Majesty's Government will lend me its kindly aid in the efforts I shall at all times make to maintain and further cement a good understanding for the development of the relations of amity and friendship between the two Governments, and that the same courtesy and cordiality may be shown me which were so generously accorded to my honored predecessors.

The time has at last come, through the progress of science, when all nations by reason of the facility and rapidity of communication have been brought nearer together, so that their mutual interests and relations verily entitle them to be called one great family.

In the spirit of that relationship I have come to dwell near the Government of Your Imperial Majesty, and to greet you in behalf of and in the words of our Chief Magistrate as his "Great and Good Friend," with the hope "that God may have Your Imperial Majesty in His wise keeping.

Which is the customary language of such documents, with the exception of the third paragraph. His Majesty replied in a brief address, expressing his pleasure in receiving me. He then sat down and bade me do likewise, whereupon we were served with cigarettes and Turkish coffee, the latter in egg-shaped cups resting in jewel-studded holders. The Sultan speaks only Turkish, and I spoke English, so we understood one another by means of the dragoman, Mr. Gargiulo, who had been for twenty years the very able Turkish adviser and interpreter of the legation and remained at that post for ten years thereafter.

The audience concluded, we returned to the legation in the same stately fashion we had come, following which we gave a reception to the American colony, composed almost exclusively of the missionaries resident in Constantinople, together with the president and faculty of Robert College and of the Home School for Girls, then located at Scutari, across the Bosphorus. I was now ready for the official business of my mission.

CHAPTER IV

FIRST TURKISH MISSION

Turkey's jealousy of foreigners — My protest against the closing of American mission schools — Diplomacy prevents drastic regulations proposed by Turkey — The schools are reopened — Defending the sale of the Bible — A cargo of missionaries and rum — Robert College — A visit to Cairo — "Bombe à la Lincoln" — Governmental reforms in Egypt — My protest against persecution of Jews in flight from Russia and Roumania — At Jerusalem — Huge delegation of Jews pleads with me for release of imprisoned relatives — I make drastic demands, and prisoners are promptly released — Their grateful memorial to me — Rights of American citizens on Turkish soil — Disputes regarding our Treaty of 1830 — Uncle Sam gives $10,800 worth of presents to Turkish officials, on conclusion of a treaty — Diplomatic tangles; United States left without Treaty of Naturalization with Turkey — Baron de Hirsch, international celebrity — I am invited to arbitrate his dispute with the Sultan, and am offered an honorarium of 1,000,000 francs — I decline honorarium, but offer to mediate — Baroness de Hirsch's philanthropies — American capitalists consider Turkish railway concessions — Sultan grants permission for American excavation in Babylon — My resignation in 1888 — The Sultan's farewell.

FOR several years the Turks had been very jealous of foreigners, especially in Asia Minor, and the result was many restrictions which manifested themselves in a variety of relations. The growth of the mission schools and their increase in number quite naturally enhanced the suspicion of the authorities, with the help, as I have mentioned, of those whose interests were served in helping the Turks to see danger in this growth of our institutions.

At the legation the interests of the American missionaries with regard to their schools and their printed matter formed the major portion of the affairs requiring my immediate attention. About four hundred schools had been established in Turkey by the Presbyterian and Congregational missionary boards. Beginning with the winter of 1885, upon one pretext or another, thirty of

these schools in Syria were closed, many of the teachers
arrested and forbidden ever to teach in the country
again, while the parents were threatened with fine and
imprisonment if they continued to send their children to
American schools. With few exceptions all the teachers
and parents were natives and Turkish subjects. The
official reason given for the closing of these schools was
that their boards had not complied with the Turkish law
requiring that textbooks, curriculums, and certificates of
the teachers be submitted to the authorities for examination; although the missionary representatives gave
assurance that these requirements had been met.

Soon after my audience with the Sultan I took up the
subject of these schools with the Grand Vizier, Kiamil
Pasha, who was perhaps the most enlightened statesman
of the Turkish Empire. Mr. King, while acting chargé,
had made an agreement with the Minister of Public
Instruction whereby the missionaries at these schools
were to submit the textbooks and other documentary
equipment to the local authorities. I protested to the
Grand Vizier against the closing of the schools, and after
some weeks we reached an understanding: he was to telegraph the vali or governor-general at Syria that the
schools were to be allowed to reopen upon their compliance with the law, according to an arrangement between
himself and myself. The outcome looked hopeful, though
months dragged along without further result.

Meanwhile, and quite by accident, I learned that the
Porte had formulated proposed additional regulations
concerning all foreign schools, and that these regulations
were about to be submitted to the Council of Ministers
to be made law. I immediately requested a copy from
the Grand Vizier. I found, to my surprise, that the
regulations were calculated to place insuperable obstacles

in the way of every foreign school in the empire. Among other things, in addition to the requirement that text-books, curriculums, and teachers' certificates be submitted for examination, all schools were to obtain an iradé or express sanction of the Sultan in order to function. Failing to receive that iradé within six months from the date of the law embodying the new regulations, the authorities in the several provinces were commanded to close such schools.

I communicated my discovery to those of my colleagues who were interested with me in this dispute: Count de Montebello, French ambassador; Baron Blanc, Italian ambassador; and Sir William White, British ambassador. At the same time I submitted copies of the proposed regulations to the Reverend Doctor Isaac Bliss and the Reverend Henry O. Dwight, of the American Board of Commissioners for Foreign Missions in Western Turkey. They all viewed the matter as I did.

The following day I again called on the Grand Vizier, informing him that I looked upon these regulations as seriously infringing upon the rights of American citizens in Turkey, and pointing out my objections in detail. The three colleagues just referred to did the same on behalf of their respective subjects who had mission or other schools in the empire. We succeeded in impressing the Grand Vizier with the force and validity of our objections, for he requested us to put them in writing and forward them to the Porte. With the aid of Drs. Bliss and Dwight I prepared such a document, and I am glad to be able to say that our protests came in time and were sufficiently forceful to prove effective in preventing this new legislation.

As I had now been negotiating for several months with reference to the Syrian schools, I decided that the most efficient way of translating into concrete result the repeated promises in regard to them was to visit some of our missionary schools throughout the empire. I obtained the necessary permission from Washington and took a journey to Cairo, Jaffa, Jerusalem, Beirut, Mersina, and Smyrna, where I conferred with our missionaries, with our several consuls, as well as with the respective governors and governor-generals. I found the relations between the local authorities and our consuls, and between the authorities and the missionary representatives, quite friendly, in some places indifferent, but nowhere hostile.

I had instructed the missionaries to get ready for the opening of the schools, and I planned the trip so as to be in Beirut about the time my order for the reopening was to be put in force. My plan had the desired effect. In anticipation of my arrival at Beirut, fifteen of the schools were reopened; and while I was there five or six more. That was about as many of the total thirty as the missionaries cared to or were in a position to reopen then. For the time being I felt satisfied that I had sufficiently reversed the Government policy to check the progressive closing of the schools which, if continued, would seriously have threatened the existence of all American schools in Turkey.

I must here express my appreciation of the assistance given me by Erhard Bissinger, our consul at Beirut. He was an earnest, sincere man, formerly a New York merchant. Although his health was frail he worked with unremitting zeal and efficiency, discharging his official duties with rare judgment and tact. I could always rely on the correctness of his reports respecting the many difficulties as they arose, and I could always feel assured that in each instance he would apply every effort to bring about an adjustment with the local authorities, by whom he was as highly esteemed as by the missionaries.

Another expression of the Government's enmity toward the activities of our missionaries was the treatment being accorded the colporteurs, or persons who went about selling Bible tracts. The agents of the American as well as the British Bible Society were constantly and arbitrarily being arrested. They were charged with plying their trade without license, yet when they made application they were never able to get license. From time to time I protested against these arrests and secured the release of one after another of the agents; but the thing to be done was to prevent arrests.

The fact was they were being made without real cause. Before these tracts or any other material could be printed a permit had to be obtained from the Ottoman Government. The material had to pass censorship before it was allowed to be printed, so that the very fact of its appearing in print was proof of the authorization of the censors. I held that, once printed, to prohibit the sale of these tracts was in restraint of commerce; that there was no reason why book hawkers should be under different regulations from hawkers of any other wares.

I prepared an argument along these lines, which I presented to the Grand Vizier, and he agreed with my conclusions. He forthwith gave orders for the release of all colporteurs and that no further arrests were to be made. The British Bible Society, of course, benefited equally with our own by these orders, and I received their grateful appreciation through my colleague, Sir William White.

All this hostility toward the missionaries and their work might be construed to be founded upon an objection

by the Government to having its subjects converted to
Christianity. But it was rather foreign influence as a
whole that was being fought, and religion was simply the
convenient peg. Conversions from Mohammedanism
were few and far between, and for the number of Mohammedans turned Christian in the course of a year there
were as many Christians turned Mohammedan. The
Mohammedans are intensely and sincerely devoted to
their faith. On the whole they are convinced that their
religion is the only true one and that Christianity is
inferior and less rational. Such converts as the missionaries do make come almost exclusively from among
the Armenians, Syrians, Greeks, Maronites, and other
Christian sects whose form of Christianity is of a mediæval character. The chief missionary work in Turkey is
educational, carried forward in a religious spirit. At the
time of my visit to the various vilayets, the Presbyterian
Board alone had over one hundred schools throughout
Syria, all located in places where previously there had
been no schools at all.

Many of the men who carried forward missionary
work had consecrated their whole lives to it. Chief among
these were Rev. Henry H. Jessup, venerable patriarch of
the Presbyterian missionaries; Rev. Daniel Bliss, president of the Syrian Protestant College; and Dr. George
Washburn, president of Robert College.

Dr. Jessup and Dr. Bliss had started for the field together in 1856, when, in bleak December, they both left
Boston in the sailing vessel Sultana, which, according
to Dr. Jessup's autobiography. "Fifty-Three Years in
Syria," carried in addition to nine or ten missionaries a
cargo of New England rum to Smyrna — a cargo spirited
no less than spiritual.

Dr. Bliss was succeeded in 1902 by his distinguished son, Rev. Howard S. Bliss, who conducted with renewed vigor the work of his father, enlarging the scope and curriculum of the college so that through its thousands of graduates in the arts, in science, and in medicine it became a potent force throughout the whole Near East. During my subsequent missions to Turkey I became very intimate with the younger Bliss, and during the Peace Conference in 1919, when he was in Paris in behalf of Syria, I was able to continue this intimacy. Unfortunately in Paris he was already suffering from a serious malady which resulted in his death in America the year following. He was honored, respected, and beloved in both the old world and the new.

Dr. Washburn was a man of statesmanship as well as erudition. His book of recollections, "Fifty Years in Constantinople," is valuable for the light it throws on political issues in Turkey no less than on questions educational and religious. He was recognized as an authority on Turkish and Balkan affairs, and the influence of the college was by no means limited to the Turkish Empire; it was felt quite as much throughout the Balkan States. Bulgaria at one period was largely governed by officials who had been graduated from Robert College, and they looked to Dr. Washburn as their chief adviser. The British ambassador at Constantinople frequently consulted him and was swayed by his advice, for Dr. Washburn understood the Turks and spoke their language. He was the second president of the college, having succeeded his father-in-law, the Reverend Cyrus Hamlin, D.D.

On the faculty of Robert College were a number of other very able men: Dr. Albert L. Long, Professor of Natural Science, distinguished as an archæologist as well, was a man of engaging personality. He had a large acquaintance among the learned Turks, whose estimate of our country was materially influenced for the good by their association with him. Then there was Dr. Edwin A. Grosvenor, Professor of Latin and History, who resigned shortly afterward to accept a professorship at Amherst. He was then at work on his scholarly "History of Constantinople," which I consider the best and most reliable work on that subject.

In 1888 I secured for Robert College, after arduous negotiation, permission for the erection of two new buildings, one a house for the president and the other an addition to the college itself. When the permits came through there was no mention of the addition to the college, and as work on it meanwhile had been begun, no little anxiety ensued. It developed that some one on the staff of the Grand Vizier had been bribed by an enemy of the college to tamper with the permits. However, because of the good relationship between Kiamil Pasha and myself, he acknowledged this bit of chicanery and duly rectified it.

I might add that in numerous instances I was able to arrange unofficially with the Grand Vizier matters which threatened to become more or less troublesome. This method of negotiating was peculiarly advantageous at the Porte, where delays were proverbial and so frequently defeated official action. Again, some of the difficulty experienced by my colleagues in getting proper redress for violations, even gross violations, was due to the fact that the Porte was not always able to control the governor-generals of the provinces.

I have said that my trip among our missionary schools included a visit to Cairo. At that time Egypt was still under Turkish sovereignty and questions of larger importance had to be taken up with the Sublime Porte. Thus American questions came under my jurisdiction as envoy extraordinary and minister plenipotentiary to the empire. Our representative at Cairo, John Cardwell, had the title of consul-general and diplomatic agent, and had to receive his exequatur from the Sublime Porte. He was a conscientious and capable official who had been there since the beginning of the first Cleveland Administration.

On this trip also I saw much of Anthony M. Keiley and his charming wife; I have spoken of him in a previous chapter as having been rejected for the post of United States minister by Austria-Hungary. Keiley was serving as one of the American judges of the Mixed or Reform Tribunal at Cairo and was highly respected for his ability at this international court.

Mohammed Tewfik, son of the extravagant Ismail of Suez Canal fame, whom he succeeded, was Khedive of Egypt and entertained us during our visit. He was only thirty-six years old, and without his fez might have been taken for an Englishman. He spoke fluent English and his conversation showed him to be well informed regarding the governments and peoples of Europe. Within an hour after my first call upon him he called with his aide-de-camp upon me at the Hotel Shepheard. He wanted to decorate me, but I informed his aide that under our system we did not permit diplomatic representatives to accept such distinctions; so the next day he sent a lesser decoration to the manager of the hotel, which, it was said, he did in my honor.

A few days later we were invited to lunch with him, and there were also present a number of higher officials. The menu consisted of dishes with such improvised names as "crevettes à l'Américaine," "bombe à la Lincoln," etc. One dish that made a deep impression upon my none-too-keen gastronomic memory was the delicious Egyptian quail, which is larger and plumper than our own. In season the birds migrate from the north and are trapped in great numbers. They could be bought in the markets for a piaster, or less than five cents.

I had frequent conferences with Nubar Pasha, Egypt's foremost statesman. He was an Armenian educated by Jesuits in France. His knowledge was extensive, and he combined the enlightened viewpoint of a European statesman of the first rank with all the subtlety of an Oriental. It was he who conceived the plan of introducing a legal system and good government in Egypt, and creating the mixed tribunals or international law courts. In the reorganization of Egypt he acted in sympathy with Lord Dufferin's programme and consequently was highly regarded by the British.

With Sir Evelyn Baring, British agent and consul-general in Egypt, afterwards Lord Cromer, I had a pleasant conversation. He was then at the height of his power in the reconstruction of Egypt. Major-General Sir Francis Grenfell, sirdar or commanding general of the Egyptian army, is another memory in connection with that visit.

I regretted that time did not permit my going up the Nile; but like every one with an historical imagination I was immensely impressed with the grandeur and massive beauty of the pyramids and the classic ruins of ancient Egypt, which with their five thousand or more years of existence have outdistanced all other relics in bringing the handiwork of man down through ages of devastating time.

There was a matter pending at Jerusalem regarding which our Secretary of State had instructed me, and which I thought best to look into personally while on this trip. Foreign Jews were being expelled simply because of their race, and American Jews were being discriminated against along with those of other nations. In the background of this action by Turkey were Russia and Roumania, for since the days of the Spanish Inquisition the Ottoman authorities, with rare exceptions, had been not only tolerant but hospitable to Jewish immigrants. Roumania, contrary to express provisions of the Treaty of Berlin guaranteeing equal political and civil rights to all subjects in this newly created principality, placed restrictions upon her Jewish subjects, causing a large number to emigrate. And from Russia, following the enforcement of the Ignatieff laws of 1882 (some of them laws that had been on the statute books unenforced for years), there was also a wholesale exodus of persecuted Jews. Most of these people went to America, but some to other countries, including Palestine.

It was the irony of persecution that the Russians who came to Turkey were claimed as subjects by Russia, which entered a protest at the Porte against making them Ottoman subjects. On the other hand, the Russian Patriarch in Turkey and the dignitaries of the Roman Church objected to the settlement of foreign Jews in Palestine. This pressure from powers that Turkey wished to please brought forth the promulgation of a law interdicting all Jews from coming to Palestine for permanent residence. Besides those from Russia and Roumania, there were a few Jews coming from England and France. And there were a very few coming from America — naturalized citizens.

At the Porte I had taken this matter up with the Grand Vizier. He told me that a regulation was communicated to the Imperial authorities at Jerusalem limiting the stay of foreign Jews there to one month. Later he told me that the Council of Ministers was about to change this limit to three months. He gave as reasons for the existence of any such regulations, first, that at certain times of the year, Easter, for example, religious fanaticism was at so high a pitch that Jews had to remain in their houses to escape attack and perhaps murder at the hands of the Christians. In the second place, it had been reported that the Jews of all the world were planning to strengthen themselves in and around Jerusalem with a view to reestablishing their ancient kingdom at some future time.

I answered that of course the first reason could be done away with by a strong force of police. As for the second, if the Porte would make inquiry it could satisfy itself that there was no such plan among the Jews of the world, that the immigration was caused by the persecution in Russia and Roumania. (This was nine years before the publication of the pamphlet, in 1896, by Dr. Hertzl, from which generated modern Zionism. I shall speak of Dr. Hertzl later.) So far as the American Jews were concerned, I informed the Grand Vizier that it was a fundamental principle of our Government to make no distinction of race or creed among our citizens, and that we had consistently denied to foreign nations that right over our citizens, as the provisions in our treaties with the Ottoman Empire showed. To all of this the Grand Vizier replied simply that should any American be expelled he would carefully consider my arguments and give instructions accordingly.

On communicating with our consul-general at Jerusalem, Henry Gillman, I learned that he had taken the same position, and that to date no American citizen had been expelled; also that the American consulate was the only one which had refused aid to the authorities in the expulsion of foreign Jews, and our representative was not

being made very comfortable for this non-coöperation
with the local government. Here the matter stood when
I left Constantinople.

There were a number of other vexatious questions
pending between the vali at Jerusalem and Mr. Gillman,
and I deemed it good policy to show my resentment to
the vali for his arbitrary methods. I declined the courtesy
of the official conveyance with which he sent one of his
aides to Jaffa to meet me and my family and take us to
Jerusalem. We took a Cook's conveyance, stopped overnight at Ramleh, and next day drove over the hills of
Judea to Jerusalem, where Mr. Gillman conducted us to
comfortable quarters at a hotel outside the walls.

Scarcely had I arrived at the hotel when a huge delegation of Jews, men and women, some with infants in their
arms, came to plead with me to obtain the release of relatives and friends who had been put in prison by the vali
or governor because they had come to settle there. I had
known of the troubled conditions in Jerusalem because
of the immigration of the Jews; but until my arrival there
I was not aware of the imprisonment of these people.
More than four hundred of them were being held in prison
awaiting deportation.

Instead of calling on the vali as ordinarily would have
been proper, I sent a note to him through the consul demanding the immediate release of the immigrants who,
I claimed, were being imprisoned contrary to our treaty
as well as the treaties of Great Britain, France, and other
powers; I said that I should decline to call upon him
until this injustice was righted by such release; and that,
further, unless my request was promptly complied with I
should appeal to the Sublime Porte for his removal.

I felt authorized to take so drastic a step by reason of

the negotiations I had had with the Grand Vizier and in view of our treaty and the treaties of several of the powers I have referred to. I obtained the desired result. The vali communicated my message to the Porte, and the Grand Vizier instructed him to comply with my request. Within twenty-four hours all the prisoners were released.

The following morning there was a delegation of several thousand people outside my hotel, who had come to express their gratitude. They presented me with a beautifully embossed memorial, the text of which, translated, reads:

With delight of soul we bring to thee, O Sir, glory of our people, the blessing of our community, the congregations of Israel dwelling in Zion and in all the cities of the Holy Land,

THE BLESSING OF MAZZOL TOV
(good fortune)

because the Lord God of Israel has raised thee to fame and glory and has given to thee a seat of honor among the mighty of the earth. And we lift our hands to the Holy Sanctuary (praying) that thy horn be exalted with honor and splendor, and that thou be given the strength and the power to exalt the horn of Israel, thy people, to speak in their favor before the throne of the Government — may its glory increase! — and that thou continue in thy honored office for many days, until he (the messiah) shall come unto Shiloh "and unto him shall the obedience of the people be" — soon, in our days, amen!

Such is the blessing of those who respect and honor thee in accordance with thy high and exalted station.

The leaders of the Jews in Jerusalem — may it be built and established in our days!

It is signed with the seals and signatures of Rafail Meir Panisel (Haham Bashi), chief rabbi of the Spanish and Portuguese Jews in Jerusalem, and Samuel Salant, chief rabbi of the Ashkenazim, Perushim, and Hasidim in Jerusalem.

Now I called upon the vali, who received me very graciously and with great courtesy. I thanked him for his prompt compliance with my request, and expressed the hope that, inasmuch as I had an understanding with the Porte that no discrimination was to be made against Jewish immigrants to Jerusalem, I should not in future have to complain of any infringement upon this understanding, otherwise I should again be compelled to take drastic action. I called his attention to the treaties referred to, of which he had had no previous knowledge.

I stopped to make some official calls, accompanied by the consul and his staff. As is customary when high officials go through the streets of the Holy City, several halberdiers of the vali preceded, to give distinction to the party as well as protection and a clear passage through the crowds. I could remain in Jerusalem only three or four days, however, for I had to catch the steamer that stopped at Alexandretta and Smyrna, where I wanted to confer with our consuls.

Upon my return to Constantinople my French and British colleagues were much pleased at my having secured the release of the Jewish immigrants in Palestine. They had received, through their foreign offices, expressions of appreciation and grateful acknowledgment from such organizations as the Anglo-Jewish Association of London, and the Alliance Israélite of Paris.

The next step in the development of this question was a communication received by our State Department from Mavroyeni Bey, Turkish minister at Washington, informing the Department of a change, indeed, of the time limit from one month to three for the sojourn of Jews in Jerusalem, with the proviso, however, "that they are going to Jerusalem in the performance of a pilgrimage,

אסקאר שטרויס

TESTIMONIAL GIVEN TO MR. STRAUS IN JERUSALEM
IN APPRECIATION OF THE RELEASE OF
SEVERAL HUNDRED PRISONERS

and not for the purpose of engaging in commerce or taking up their residence there."

This communication was received while I was on my trip, and Secretary Bayard forwarded it to me with the instruction that I take up the subject with the Ottoman Government as follows:

To require of applicants for passports, which under our laws are issued to all citizens upon the sole evidence of their citizenship, any announcement of their religious faith or declaration of their personal motives in seeking such passports, would be utterly repugnant to the spirit of our institutions and to the intent of the solemn proscription forever by the Constitution of any religious test as a qualification of the relations of the citizen to the Government, and would, moreover, assume an inquisitorial function in respect of the personal affairs of the individual, which this Government can not exert for its own purposes, and could still less assume to exercise with the object of aiding a foreign Government in the enforcement of an objectionable and arbitrary discrimination against certain of our citizens.

Our adherence to these principles has been unwavering since the foundation of our Government, and you will be at no loss to cite pertinent examples of our consistent defense of religious liberty, which, as I said in my note to Baron Schaeffer of May 18, 1885, in relation to the Keiley episode at Vienna, "is the chief corner-stone of the American system of Government, and provisions for its security are embedded in the written charter and interwoven in the moral fabric of its laws."

I received this upon my return. Secretary Bayard asked me also to ascertain the views of my colleagues respecting this iradé, and I found them willing and ready to take it up with the Porte in a manner similar to the instructions I had received.

I called on Saïd Pasha and left with him a note in accordance with my instructions, and I sent a copy of this note to the French and British ambassadors. They in

turn each advised the Ministry that they could not admit
of regulations prejudicial to the existing rights of their
subjects as secured by treaties. And here for a time the
matter rested.

Several months later three American Jews were expelled from Jerusalem because they had not left the city
at the expiration of three months, and again the question
had to be taken up with the Porte. This time Saïd Pasha
replied that the restrictions with regard to the three
Americans had been ordered withdrawn, "the Sublime
Porte having lately decided that the measure concerning
the Israelites going to Palestine shall not be applied but
to those who emigrate in number (*en nombre*), and that no
obstacle shall be opposed to the sojourn of those who are
not in this class."

This, like most other questions that arose between the
Ottoman Government and our own, could not be settled
for any length of time by principle, law, or treaty. Such
documents might be used as reminders of agreements
once reached, but in Turkey they do not of themselves
direct policies or action. Drummond Wolff had advised
being "patient, pleasant, persistent," to which I would
add: eternally vigilant.

On the whole, the interests of the United States
throughout the Ottoman Empire were peculiar, in that
the majority of the complaints related to personal, as
distinct from commercial, rights. I have said in an earlier
chapter that some of the questions at issue, especially
those involving extraterritoriality, grew out of capitulations dating back over four hundred years, to the conquest of Constantinople by the Moslems in 1453. The
terms of these capitulations or "privileges" were made
originally between the Greeks and the various Italian

city republics — Pisa, Genoa, Venice. The Moslems later embodied them in revised capitulations with France in 1535, 1604, 1673, and 1740; with England in 1583 and 1675; with Holland in 1680; with Austria in 1718; and with Russia in 1783. On these later European capitulations was based our own first treaty with the Sublime Porte in 1830. Practically speaking, therefore, consular jurisdiction in Turkey was then not very different from what it was in the fifteenth century.

When I took office one of the vexatious questions to be settled was the interpretation of Clause IV of the Treaty of 1830. This treaty was negotiated by Charles Rhind, as American commissioner, with Reis Effendi, Turkish representative. Rhind had prepared it, with the help of dragoman Navoni, in French and in Turkish, and when it was finally drawn up, according to Rhind's own report, Reis Effendi "signed and sealed the treaty in Turkish and I did the same with the French translation, and we exchanged them." Thereupon the original Turkish version, together with a copy of the French translation as signed by the American commissioners — President Jackson had appointed Captain James Biddle and David Offley together with Rhind — and several English translations were transmitted to Washington. The treaty actually approved by the Senate was one of the English versions.

Before the ratifications were exchanged the American chargé d'affaires at Constantinople, David Porter, received word that the French version was not exactly in agreement with the Turkish. Porter's simple method of correcting this discrepancy was to sign a document, also in the Turkish language, accepting the Turkish version of the treaty without reserve; and when the translation of this document reached Washington nothing further was said.

Indeed, the treaty rested in peace until 1868, when the American minister, acting according to the English version, clashed with the Turkish authorities in the interpretation of Clause IV, regarding jurisdiction over American citizens — in this case two who had been arrested and imprisoned for alleged offenses against the Turkish Government. The English version read:

Citizens of the United States of America, quietly pursuing their commerce, and not being charged or convicted of any crime or offence, shall not be molested; and even when they may have committed some offence they shall not be arrested and put in prison, by the local authorities, but they shall be tried by their Minister or Consul, and punished according to their offence, following, in this respect, the usage observed towards other Franks.

When our Government proceeded to obtain exact translations of this clause, it was found that the Turkish version did not contain the words "arrested" or "tried," although the phraseology made clear that American citizens were not to be imprisoned in Turkish prisons, but punished through their minister or consul. Consequently, the Turkish authorities could arrest but not imprison, could try but not inflict punishment.

The Turkish Government would not recognize as accurate any of the translations the United States presented. When asked to present a translation of its own, however, the matter was gradually put in abeyance.

In 1862 our minister, E. J. Morris, concluded another treaty with the Porte, entitled, as was the first one, "A Treaty of Commerce and Navigation," which, by its Article XX, was to remain in force twenty-eight years unless either party saw fit to abrogate at the end of fourteen or twenty-one years. In January, 1874, the Turkish

Government gave notice to our Department of State of its desire to' terminate the treaty, following this notice up with another communication to the same effect in September, 1875. Although by the terms of the treaty such notice was to be permissible not earlier than June, 1876, nothing was said in Washington regarding the untimeliness of these communications, and in his Annual Message of December, 1876, President Grant announced: "Under this notice the treaty terminated upon the fifth day of June 1876." President Cleveland, on the other hand, in his first Annual Message nine years later, questioned the official termination, but added: "As the commercial rights of our citizens in Turkey come under the favored-nation guarantee of the prior treaty of 1830 . . . no inconvenience can result" from our agreeing to the abrogation. Thus questions of jurisdiction and commercial rights were thrown back for settlement under the Treaty of 1830, the translation of which was and has remained in dispute.

Much of this confusion was due, again, to the slight actual regard, on the part of the Ottoman Empire, for the terms of treaties. In this attitude they had been encouraged by some of the European nations — most of all Russia in its more powerful days — who, in return for other advantages, were not insistent upon their claims under the capitulations, especially the claims of jurisdiction over nationals. So far as concerned the United States, this loose effectiveness of treaties caused constant misunderstanding with regard to the handling of cases arising under them.

With every question that came up under the disputed Clause IV, for instance, the Turks would controvert the right of our consuls to try, and we would insist on that right. The battle then would be won after a fashion by

the side with the most persistence. During my administration I happened to be the winner much of the time,
although my winning merely released a possibly innocent
person; for while we argued about a trial for the suspect
he lingered in jail, and after I got his release the Turks
would refuse to acknowledge our jurisdiction and not
prosecute. Innocent and guilty alike were made to suffer
in jail, and alike were set scot-free upon release. Not only
that, but whenever an American citizen committed, or
was alleged to have committed, a crime and was arrested
by the Turkish authorities, it created irritation and a
strain of our relationship.

The only other treaty then negotiated between the
Ottoman Government and our own — the Treaty of Naturalization and Extradition — had also been a subject for
discussion and dispute ever since it was signed by Minister George H. Boker in 1874. When it was concluded,
the Senate refused to confirm it because under it American citizenship was forfeited *ipso facto* by the return of
the naturalized citizen to his native land and his remaining there two years; but the Senate amended this treaty
by changing the phraseology of the clause containing
the two-year reference. The Sublime Porte accepted the
amendment by a declaration of what it understood to
be its intent and significance, which interpretation our
Government, in turn, would not accept.

And there that treaty was hung in 1875, although our
Government that year made an appropriation of ten
thousand eight hundred dollars for presents to Turkish
officials, which was then customary on concluding a
treaty with the Porte.

As the conditions which had called forth the treaty
continued to exist, I was instructed to renew negotiations

in the matter. A number of Christian subjects of the Porte — some Greeks and some Syrians, but principally Armenians — in order to free themselves from Turkish jurisdiction had fled to the United States. Here they remained long enough to become citizens, and from time to time they came back to Turkey, where they were charged with being involved in alleged conspiracies against the Turkish Government. Such cases arose frequently, and it was felt that the Treaty of Naturalization and Extradition with the two-year clause, similar to the one we have with many other nations, would prevent citizens of the Porte from using naturalization in America as a means of escaping liability as subjects of Turkey upon their return there.

I addressed myself to bringing about an adjustment of these difficulties, either by securing a new treaty or having the one of 1874 accepted as amended. A long and tedious exchange of notes on the subject ensued. Finally the Porte agreed to accept the Treaty of 1874 as amended.

Of course I was elated, and the State Department was pleased. That the treaty was one very much desired by our Government was clear. I received a long, flattering cable of congratulation from Mr. Bayard, and a letter in similar vein from Mr. Adee, saying in part:

Whatever may be the outcome of these negotiations, you are to be congratulated without stint on having achieved a decided diplomatic success by causing the Government of the Porte to recede from the position which it took in 1875, with respect to the Senate amendments, and to which it has so pertinaciously adhered ever since, until you wrought a change of heart and induced it to take a more rational view of the subject. This makes it far easier for us to deal with the question now as justice and equity and due respect for the rights and privileges attaching to American nationality may demand.

Then the bubble burst! Under my instructions I had assured the Turkish authorities that with their acceptance of the amendments of our Senate the negotiations in the matter would be concluded, and all that would be necessary to give effect to the treaty was the proclamation of the President. Instead, however, it was thought best again to submit the terms to the Senate, as fourteen years had elapsed since the negotiation of the original treaty. Thereupon some of our leading missionaries, at the instigation of prominent Armenians who had been naturalized in America and returned to Turkey, opposed ratification, and no further action was taken. It was a very discouraging situation, for many annoying cases constantly came up, some of a rather serious nature.

I might add that ten years later, when I was again minister to Turkey, I was instructed to renew negotiations, but the Ottoman Government was now unwilling to negotiate at all on this subject, and we were left without any treaty of naturalization.

There were one or two interesting special matters that came up during this mission. Toward the end of 1887 Baron Maurice de Hirsch came to Constantinople to adjust some financial differences with the Turkish Government. His railway, connecting Constantinople with European cities, was about completed. The Turkish Government claimed that he owed it 132,000,000 francs, a claim growing out of kilometric guarantees and other concessions.

One day while I was calling on the Grand Vizier, Kiamil Pasha, he asked to introduce some one to me, and forthwith I met a tall and slender man in his fifties, dark eyes sparkling with spirit and energy, clean-shaven except for a full black mustache, dressed rather dudishly in a cutaway coat, white vest and white spats — Baron de Hirsch. I was glad of this opportunity, for I had often heard of him and his great philanthropic activities. We had a pleasant conversation about things in general.

A few days later I took dinner with the Sultan. He spoke to me about Baron de Hirsch and the claim of Turkey against him. The Turkish Government was hard-pressed for funds — its chronic condition. The Sultan explained that for some time efforts had been made to arrive at some settlement, and that it was now proposed to arbitrate. The Baron had suggested first the French and then the Austrian ambassador as arbitrator, but neither was satisfactory to His Majesty; he, however, had much confidence in my judgment and impartiality, so that he had counter-suggested my name to the Baron, which was satisfactory to the latter; and they had agreed to pay me an honorarium of one million francs.

I assured the Sultan that I was much complimented by his request, but I would have to consult the Secretary of State. He told me he had already requested the Turk-ish minister at Washington to inquire the views of the Department, and that Mr. Bayard had said there was no objection to my acting as arbitrator. But I said I would have to communicate with Mr. Bayard personally and would let His Majesty hear from me in the course of a few days.

I cabled Mr. Bayard and learned, as the Sultan had said, that there was no objection to my acceding to the latter's wishes and accepting the honorarium if it ap-peared to me advisable. Upon giving the proposal careful consideration, however, I felt it would not be wise for me to comply with the Sultan's request, much as I should have liked to please him. Any transaction with the Turk-ish Government involving money was open to suspicion

of improper methods and bribery. Had I as arbitrator
made a decision disappointing to the Turkish Government, I should certainly have fallen under such suspicion,
and I deemed it improper to assume an obligation which
might throw the American legation into a false light.

I advised Secretary Bayard accordingly and frankly
told the Sultan I could not accept. I added, however,
that while I would not accept an honorarium, I should be
glad to act as mediator to see whether a satisfactory adjustment could not be brought about between the Baron
and the Grand Vizier, which offer the Sultan accepted.

As the negotiations went forward, the Baron and the
Grand Vizier had frequent disagreements and alterca-
tions. Each of them would come to me with his grievance,
and I would give my opinion and bring them together
again. Finally there arose a legal question, and this was
submitted to Professor Gneist, the famous German
authority on international law. Upon his decision the
Baron finally paid the Turkish Government 22,000,000
francs.

During these negotiations, which lasted several months,
an intimate friendship developed between the Baron and
his wife and Mrs. Straus and myself. They often took
family dinner with us. They were declining official invitations because of the recent death of their only child,
Lucien. The Baroness was an exceptionally fine woman,
learned and able, whose principal aim in life seemed to
be to find ways of being most helpful to others. In the
quarters of the poor, both Jew and Gentile, her short,
trim figure, dressed in deep mourning, was familiar. Her
face had an attractively benign expression. A story regarding her activities in connection with the construction of her husband's railroad was characteristic of her.

In a village near Constantinople a number of houses belonging to the poor had to be torn down to make way for the railway station. The work was to be done with the understanding that the Turkish Government would compensate these people, but evidently no such consideration was forthcoming. A number of those thus dispossessed came to the Baron to complain, but he answered that it was the Government's responsibility, not his. On hearing of this the Baroness informed her husband that she did not propose to let the railroad cause unhappiness to people, that it would probably be a long time before the Government paid the compensation, if ever, and that she insisted on paying these people out of her own private fortune so they could at once build new houses and be happy. Then and there she carried out that programme.

The Baron spoke to me of his own benefactions and said he purposed during his lifetime to devote his fortune to benevolent causes. His philanthropy up to that time had been bestowed mainly in Russia, but he was desirous of doing something for the Russians who, because of the oppression resultant from the Ignatieff laws, were emigrating to America. They had been persecuted and were poor, and he wanted to enable them to reëstablish themselves.

I was familiar with the conditions of these Russian immigrants, because prior to my coming to Turkey I had been in close relationship for several years with Michael Heilprin, author of a number of scholarly works and one of the chief editors of Appleton's Encyclopædia. He worked untiringly on behalf of these new arrivals, collecting money for them and aiding them personally in numerous ways. I think his untimely death was due primarily to his generous expenditure of energy in this way. I mentioned Heilprin to the Baron and said I would write him for suggestions how best the immigrants might be helped.

When I heard from Heilprin I forwarded the letter to the Baron, together with a list of men who had done most in the way of benevolent work for the Jews of New York. Prominent on that list were Meyer S. Isaacs, president of the United Hebrew Congregations; Jesse Seligman, president of the Hebrew Orphan Asylum; Jacob H. Schiff, who was connected with a number of our charitable enterprises; and my brother Isidor. The Baron subsequently communicated with Mr. Isaacs and some others, and out of their arrangements grew the Baron de Hirsch Fund and the Baron de Hirsch Trade School. Later the Baroness, upon conferring with Mrs. Straus, endowed the Clara de Hirsch Home for Working Girls.

Neither my wife nor I wish to claim any credit for the founding of the de Hirsch benevolent institutions. We were simply the medium through which these came into being. We never even suggested the nature of them. We only gave the requested information regarding the need for such institutions.

But to come back to Constantinople and its railroads. During 1888 the question of a railroad from Constantinople to the Persian Gulf was much agitated, especially by the Germans. The Grand Vizier several times brought up the subject in conversation with me, asking me to help him get in communication with some reliable American railroad builders. He assured me that the Turkish Government would give more favorable terms to a group of Americans because the project would then be free from the political complications that might ensue if a road

OSCAR S. STRAUS
Constantinople, 1888

through the heart of the empire were controlled by
Germany or any other European power.

William K. Vanderbilt was in Constantinople at the
time. He had arrived in his yacht, which was larger than
most yachts that came through the Dardanelles, so it was
stopped until I could procure for him a special permit
from the Sultan to proceed. At the Sultan's request, I
spoke to Vanderbilt about the railroad and introduced
him to the Grand Vizier. But he was on pleasure bent
and not inclined to take up the cares and burdens involved
in such an undertaking.

Of course it was apparent that if American capitalists
and railroad builders with their vast experience would
take up the construction of this road it would put tremendous power and prestige into American hands. I
suggested that Carl Schurz and Henry Villard might be
the proper persons to undertake this gigantic work. Villard's name had figured prominently in the completion of
the Northern Pacific; he was close to Schurz, and they
each enjoyed a high reputation. Soon thereafter the
Porte submitted the matter to a syndicate of German,
British, and French bankers, and the famous Bagdad
Railroad was not built by Americans.

Early in 1888 I received a letter from an old friend, the
Reverend William Hayes Ward, eminent Assyriologist
and scholarly editor of the "Independent," respecting an
expedition for excavating in Babylonia which the Reverend John P. Peters, of the University of Pennsylvania,
contemplated. Under Dr. William Pepper, provost of the
university, Dr. Peters was organizing the Babylon Exploration Fund, which would base its work on the recommendations made in 1884–85 by the Wolfe expedition
headed by Dr. Ward himself. The Wolfe expedition,
financed by Miss Catherine L. Wolfe, of New York City,

had been limited to reconnoissance and exploration. Shortly thereafter the subject was brought to my attention officially by Mr. Adee, of the Department of State, who wrote me:

We find ourselves between two fires, — on one hand is the Philadelphia organization under the lead of Dr. Peters, which has the money, and on the other is the Johns Hopkins enterprise, which has the most solid ballasting of Assyriological talent, but, unfortunately, its dollars are limited. As the Johns Hopkins people deposit all their collections in the National Museum, Professor Langley feels kindly disposed towards them. . . . We shall probably have to look to you as the *deus ex machina* to prescribe a solution.

I conferred unofficially with Hamdy Bey, director of the Imperial Museum at Stamboul, himself a very competent scientist and in charge of all excavations in Turkey, who informed me fully regarding the Turkish law governing excavations, among other things that a permit for making them had to be obtained from the Ministry of Public Instruction (and these permits were not easily obtained); and that all objects discovered were the property of the Turkish Government, the excavator being permitted only moulds or drawings thereof, except possibly in the case of certain duplicates.

To save time in the matter, I brought it before the Grand Vizier, who promised support in laying the project before His Majesty the Sultan, with the view possibly of getting an iradé to export at least a portion, if not half, of the objects discovered. I suggested to our State Department that the University of Pennsylvania and Johns Hopkins work together and operate as one body, so that an iradé, should it be obtainable, might serve for the benefit of all concerned.

While *en route* to the United States on a short leave of

absence I met Dr. Peters in London. He handed me a letter of introduction from President Cleveland asking my good offices. The proposed excavations interested me very much, and I promised Dr. Peters I would give the subject immediate attention upon returning to my post. Meanwhile I instructed the chargé, Mr. King, how to proceed in my absence.

Early in November when I got back to Constantinople I asked for an audience with the Sultan to explain the purposes of the exploration fund, the interest of the various universities and scientific societies in it, adding that I had received a personal letter from the President in regard to it, and that if he would give the permit to excavate it would meet with high appreciation in my country.

It was the custom for ministers, as distinct from ambassadors, to dismount at the Palace gate and proceed to the Palace on foot. For this occasion, however, orders had been given for our coming in at the Palace door. Here I was met by His Highness, the Grand Vizier; the Minister of Foreign Affairs; and the Grand Master of Ceremonies. After some fifteen minutes the Grand Vizier and the Grand Master of Ceremonies ushered me into the presence of His Majesty. A private audience took place, wherein the Sultan seemed very affable indeed. He said he was happy to welcome me back to my post and hoped that Mrs. Straus and I had had a pleasant trip.

His Majesty then led the way to the brilliantly illuminated dining-hall, where a military orchestra of about thirty members was playing. I was seated at His Majesty's right, with the dragoman next to me, and the Grand Vizier was at the left; down both sides sat the pashas, their breasts sparkling with diamond orders. The dinner was served on gold and silver plates, and the menu was excellent and not overburdened. The Sultan conversed freely, cheerfully, and apparently without reserve.

After dinner we went with him to a play in the little theater on the Palace grounds. At an opportune moment between the acts, while His Majesty questioned me regarding some matters in the United States, I referred to the excavations, and to the fact that several representatives of the universities were awaiting his decision. He graciously stated that permission would be granted, and it was given a very few days thereafter.

Though we were all somewhat disappointed because the permit was more restricted than we had been led to expect, it enabled Dr. Peters and his party to go ahead with their work. Dr. Peters has left a full account of the explorations and the objects discovered, some of them dating back earlier than 4000 B.C., in his two volumes entitled "Nippur," which form a lasting memorial to his services in the cause of archæology.

Unfavorable as we thought the permit was, I was accused by Theodore Bent, British archæologist, writing in the "Contemporary Review," of bribing Hamdy Bey to obtain a favorable firman. He himself had dug at Thasos the previous year and had run into difficulties with the Turkish authorities, resulting in the seizure of his findings. He still felt revengeful toward Hamdy Bey, and the knowledge of our negotiations for a permit afforded him ground for a scurrilous attack on the director of the museum, who was, nevertheless, a man of fine character and high repute.

The fact really was that the Sultan felt somewhat under obligations to me because of my services in another matter. There were in the Ottoman Empire a million or more Persians, mainly rug dealers. Many of them had married Turkish women. The Sultan claimed that when a Persian in Turkey married a Turkish subject his nationality followed that of his wife. The controversy had gone so far that the Shah of Persia was about to recall his ambassador, and they finally agreed to submit the matter to me for decision.

I took the subject under advisement and wrote an opinion in accordance with the universally accepted doctrine of nationality under such conditions, namely, that upon marriage nationality followed that of the husband. But instead of rendering my decision, I advised the Sultan what it would be and suggested that it would probably make for better relationship if he would anticipate my decision by agreeing with the Shah's contention. This he appreciated. At the same time it relieved me from the necessity of deciding against the sovereign to whom I was accredited.

Of course the Shah's ambassador, Mohsin Khan, who was practically viceroy in the Ottoman Empire, desired to confer upon me Persia's decoration, the Lion and the Sun, set in costly brilliants, and once more I had to explain our custom in regard to such things. It is indeed a wise provision of our Constitution which prohibits American officials from accepting "any present, emolument, office or title of any kind whatever" without the consent of Congress.

The election of 1888 having resulted in a Republican victory, I tendered my resignation to the new President upon his taking office, as is customary for heads of missions when there has been a change in the administration. I was unofficially informed that numerous letters and memorials had been received in Washington from individuals and missionary and church bodies, asking that I be retained at my post; Dr. Pepper, of the University of

Pennsylvania, and several other university heads also joined in urging my retention. But I wrote Dr. Pepper not to push the request, as I could no longer absent myself from my private affairs. The main matters of difference between the two Governments had been settled, and I felt justified in resigning, even had Cleveland been reëlected, for I could not afford to stay on except under pressure of patriotic necessity.

The salary at the Porte barely covered my house rent. I had secured the best available house with facilities for entertaining and the returning of hospitalities, and, as I have mentioned before, such functions are essential for the proper relations with one's colleagues and the government to which one is accredited. Besides, it is important to be able to show to one's nationals the hospitality they expect from their diplomatic representatives, especially in the case of prominent visitors who bring letters from high officials at home.

Again, "noblesse oblige" has its widest and most emphatic application in diplomacy. Americans are supposed to be rich, and if an American diplomat does not show the usual hospitalities he is charged with penuriousness, for it is understood that a man who is not able to live according to his station would not be chosen to head a mission. That his pay may be inadequate for the discharge of his social duties is not generally known. When I was in Washington during my leave of absence Mr. Cleveland asked me how I got along on my salary, and I told him then that I could have got along fairly well on four times the amount, for I had spent between thirty-five and forty thousand dollars a year.

A few days prior to leaving my post in June, 1889, I again dined with the Sultan. I had often done so during my stay, but this time he was especially gracious and unreserved. He expressed great regret at my going, saying that at no time during his reign had the relations of our countries been more agreeable, and that he and his minister had had every confidence in my candor and fairness. What seemed to have impressed him most was my handling of a large claim by an American which was being urged through the legation. I carefully examined this claim and found it to be justified neither in morals nor in law, and I informed the Turkish Government accordingly that I had withdrawn it. The Porte was not accustomed to such fair treatment! Of course, ever afterward when I presented a matter it was believed to be justified.

The Sultan held the government pretty firmly in his own hands — too much so in fact — and kept himself very well informed regarding all manner of things. On this evening he said he had heard of the great disaster and loss of lives caused by the Johnstown flood and he desired to transmit through me two hundred pounds to be used for relief work. I cabled the amount to the Secretary of State on the following day and communicated to His Majesty our Government's acknowledgment:

Express grateful appreciation of the President and the Government of the United States for the Sultan's generous relief for flood sufferers.

When it became known that I was about to leave my post I received many communications expressing regret. These were a great satisfaction, especially one beautiful letter from the missionaries of Constantinople, signed by Edwin E. Bliss, I. F. Pettibone, Joseph K. Greene, H. S. Barnum, Charles A. S. Dwight, Henry O. Dwight, and William G. Bliss.

After we had boarded the steamer to Varna, homeward bound, a royal caïque — a rowboat of the graceful lines of a Venetian gondola and manned by six oarsmen — came alongside our ship and one of the Sultan's aides came aboard to present to Mrs. Straus the highest order of the Shefekat decoration, a star set in brilliants, with the special request of His Majesty that she accept it as a token of his esteem and regard. As the regulations prohibiting me from accepting such honors did not apply to my wife, she graciously accepted this parting gift from Abdul Hamid.

And so farewell to Pera and the beautiful Bosphorus!

CHAPTER V

HARRISON, CLEVELAND, AND McKINLEY

One function of ex-diplomats — Russian refugees in flight to America — President Harrison remonstrates with Czar against persecutions — "A decree to leave one country is an order to enter another" — Grover Cleveland's fight for sound money — His letters to me — "The Little White House" — Cleveland under fire for Van Alen appointment — Cleveland's theatrical tastes — A midnight supper of delicatessen and beer — Cleveland's first meeting with Charles F. Murphy, of Tammany Hall — The final confidences of an ex-President — A pilgrimage in England to the school attended by Roger Williams — I join the fight for election reforms — President McKinley summons me to Washington to discuss plan to avert war with Spain — A proposal to "rattle the Sultan's windows" — McKinley urges me to again accept the Turkish post — "Secretary of State for Turkey."

HAD diplomacy been a career, nothing would have pleased me more than to continue in such service of my country. On the whole I cannot say that I advocate changing our system as to a more permanent service for the heads of missions. Our President is now unhampered to select men who are best qualified to deal with the problems in hand at the various posts. This is an advantage over a system that tends to keep in office ministers and ambassadors who are ill equipped to bring statesmanlike qualities to their work, though they may be past-masters in routine and social requirements. But it would be well if, on a change of administration, removals of heads of missions were the exception rather than the rule. Of course, after four or eight years, the return of our diplomatic chiefs from foreign fields to the various parts of our country has the advantage of enabling these men, by reason of their experience and standing, to inform and in a measure guide public opinion on questions concerning international affairs.

On my return to New York I reëntered business, but

continued to take a deep and active interest in public affairs. I spent much of my spare time lecturing on public questions and historical matters.

Waves of Russian-Jewish immigrants were pounding our shores in the spring of 1891. In Russia, pogroms and other forms of mob persecution had become so persistent that refugees were arriving in pitiful droves at our ports. Sinister circumstance had hurled them from one country into another. Many had been compelled to abandon their employment or even their own established businesses in Russia, owing to the enforcement of the Ignatieff laws and the consequent prohibitions, restrictions, and persecutions.

Determined to make a strenuous protest, a small committee was formed of prominent Jews from New York, Cincinnati, and Chicago, to lay before President Harrison the pitiable conditions day by day presented by the arriving refugees, many of whom had been stripped of all their possessions.

Our committee was headed by Jesse Seligman, and among the others I recall Jacob H. Schiff, of New York, and General Lewis Seasongood, of Cincinnati, besides myself. The President listened to our story with sympathetic interest, and then turned to me and asked what, in the light of my international and diplomatic experience, I thought should be done. I told him that we had a right to remonstrate with any nation with which we were on friendly terms, as we were with Russia, for committing an unfriendly act if that nation by special laws forced groups of its people, in pitiable condition, to seek refuge in another country and that country our own.

The President agreed, but suggested that our Government ought to have before it an official report or statement of facts. I replied that this could easily be obtained by sending a competent commission to Russia to make inquiry. Promptly Colonel John B. Weber, immigration commissioner at Ellis Island, admirably qualified because of his experience in office and his sympathetic interest, together with Dr. Walter Kempster, a physician known for his studies of the pathology of insanity, were sent abroad to make an investigation and report. Their investigation was thorough, and they embodied their findings in a report that is a model of its kind. It was the first authentic and official report on these Russian restrictions and persecutions, and when published it aroused great interest in all enlightened parts of Europe as well as at home. The distinguished English historian, Lecky, refers to it in his own work, "Democracy and Liberty."

George Jones, of the "New York Times," also had an investigation and report made by his London correspondent, Harold Frederic. These findings the "Times" published as articles and syndicated them to several other papers of the country, and later Frederic brought them out in book form under the title "The New Exodus.',

President Harrison was much impressed with the report of the commission, and through diplomatic channels brought the matter to the attention of the Russian Government. His reference to this action in the Annual Message of December, 1891, is such a clear and convincing recognition of humanitarian diplomacy, that I quote it:

This Government has found occasion to express, in a friendly spirit, but with much earnestness, to the Government of the Czar, its serious concern because of the harsh measures now being enforced against the Hebrews in Russia. . . . It is estimated that over one million will be forced from Russia within a few years. . . .

The banishment, whether by direct decree or by not less certain indirect methods, of so large a number of men and women is not a local question. A decree to leave one country is, in the nature of things, an order to enter another — some other. This consideration, as well as the suggestions of humanity, furnishes ample ground for the remonstrances which we have presented to Russia, while our historic friendship for that Government can not fail to give the assurance that our representations are those of a sincere wellwisher.

The President's Message was largely quoted and favorably commented upon in this and many European countries. All of this had a reaction in Russia itself. No matter how autocratic a government may be, as Russia then was, it cannot free itself from "a decent respect to the opinions of mankind." For the time being conditions in Russia for the Jews were ameliorated.

In the fall of 1891 I was a delegate to the Democratic State Convention at Saratoga and was a member of the platform committee. One of the questions to be solved was: What should be our position regarding silver? Cleveland's statement of his position during his first term had lost him the Presidency.

Quite purposely Cleveland had boldly accentuated, while in office, the outstanding issues then before the country — the tariff and sound money — without any regard to political consequences. His friend, Richard Watson Gilder, has said of him in this connection:[1]

Every once in a while Cleveland "threw away the Presidency," and I never saw him so happy as when he had done it; as, for instance, after the tariff message, and now again after the silver letter.

Cleveland, while not a scholar, was ultra-conscientious and had an honest and logical mind that dealt with fundamentals. He would "mull over" (that is the very phrase

[1] *Grover Cleveland, A Record of Friendship*, p. 33.

I have heard him use) a question until he got to the bottom, and there he would start to build up his premises and arrive at his decisions. Because of the surplus accumulating in the Treasury he had been impressed more and more with the fact that the taxes and the tariff should be reduced. He realized, during the spring and summer of 1887, that the rapid increase of this surplus was becoming a menace to the stability of our financial system, and he felt it his duty to provide some means for averting commercial disaster. At the opening of Congress that year, instead of a message covering all of the Government activities as was the invariable custom, he prepared one devoted exclusively to the revenue system and to the necessity of reducing the tariff. He gave much care and deliberation to this message, but none to the political consequences.

Again later, when the free coinage of silver became a topic of prominence, the Reform Club of New York invited him to attend a banquet at which this question was to be discussed. Many of his friends advised that he remain silent on the subject, in order not to mar his chances for reëlection. Cleveland, however, accepted the invitation and boldly announced his position regarding "the dangerous and reckless experiment of free, unlimited and independent silver coinage." That was too much for the machine men of the party; the note of Cleveland's doom was sounded from one end of the country to the other.

After his retirement partisan bitterness largely disappeared, and it soon became a foregone conclusion that he would again have to stand for the Presidency. Although he had occupied the President's chair only one term, I doubt whether any ex-President of our time, with the exception of Roosevelt, carried with him into private life a deeper interest or a higher esteem on the part of the great body of the people. His rugged honesty of purpose and determined stand for the best principles in our public life were more and more appreciated and valued. During the entire period between his defeat and his reëlection he was the most distinguished representative of his party.

When the silver question came up in the State Convention at Saratoga, a few others and myself contended for a sound money plank. We met with opposition from a majority of the platform committee. Richard Croker, boss of Tammany Hall, had not up to that time bothered much about the subject. I laid before him the reasons underlying the question and got him to throw his powerful influence and help on our side, and we succeeded in the end in incorporating a strong sound money plank.

Cleveland expressed his satisfaction with that accomplishment in the following note to me:

816 Madison Avenue
Sept. 27, 1891

My dear Mr. Straus:

I have a suspicion that you had much to do with the formation of the silver plank in the platform adopted at Saratoga. I am so well satisfied indeed that you thus merit my thanks as a citizen who loves the honor of his country and as a Democrat who loves the integrity of his party, that I desire to tender them in this frank informal manner.

Yours very truly
Grover Cleveland

I may add here that upon his retirement in 1889 Cleveland came to New York to live, and the pleasant relations I had had with him in office became close and intimate.

Early in July, 1892, I wrote Cleveland regarding his position on the tariff, and after the Chicago convention which nominated him for the Presidency, I received the following communication from him:

GRAY GABLES
BUZZARDS BAY, MASS.
July 25, 1892

MY DEAR SIR:

I wish to thank you for your letter of July 12, and to express my disappointment that while in New York last week I did not have the opportunity to converse with you on the suggestions which your letter contained. You cannot fail to see by some expressions in my address in reply to the notification committee, that thoughts quite similar to yours have occupied my mind in regard to the tariff plank in our platform. I am exceedingly anxious that there should be no misrepresentation of our true position, and I regret exceedingly that there should have been any form of expression adopted which makes us liable to that danger.

I shall continue to give the subject earnest thought and when I write my letter of acceptance if it should then seem to be necessary I shall not hesitate to pursue the subject further. I have heard of your labors at Chicago and of your constant and earnest devotion to my cause, and while your previous conduct and our relations have been such as to lead me to expect such things of you, I am none the less gratified and beg to thank you from the bottom of my heart.

With the kind remembrances of Mrs. Cleveland to you and Mrs. Straus, in which I heartily join, I am

Very truly yours

GROVER CLEVELAND

In 1888 his position on these two questions caused his defeat; in 1892, his position still the same, these very issues were the dominant factors that brought about his renomination and election.

During the winter before his second term of office, in order to get some rest and be freer than was possible in New York from the constant stream of visitors and place-hunters, he and his family accepted the invitation of my brother Nathan to occupy a little frame house which my brother had bought from a New Jersey farmer in connection with the property on which stands the Lakewood Hotel. The little two-story house, surrounded by pines, simple as could be, was renovated and painted white, and became known as "the little White House." To it from time to time Cleveland summoned the people with whom he wished to confer — the leaders of his party with regard to policies and the make-up of his Cabinet, and personal friends. He had no secretary and wrote all letters with his own hand.

During his stay at "the little White House" he sent for me several times to talk over things with him. On one of these occasions he proposed connecting me with the Administration in some way that might be agreeable to me. While I appreciated highly his intention, I told him I felt I owed it to my brothers to stick to business for the next few years. He answered that he would have to have one of the brothers in his Administration. I learned later that in his mind he had reserved the ministership to Holland for Isidor. At about this time Isidor had been nominated, and was subsequently elected, to fill a vacancy in Congress, and Cleveland purposely did not fill the Dutch post until after that special election. He afterwards remarked to a friend he and Isidor had in common, William L. Wilson, of West Virginia, chairman of the Ways and Means Committee and responsible for the Wilson Tariff Bill, that he much preferred Isidor in Congress where he could have the benefit of his wisdom and knowledge in financial and tariff matters. Indeed, my brother was largely responsible for Cleveland's calling the extra session of Congress for the repeal of the Sherman Silver Coinage Act.

Among my letters from Cleveland at this period I have one concerning a subject that caused a great deal of stir

and unfavorable comment: the appointment of James J.
Van Alen, of Newport, Rhode Island, as ambassador to
Italy. Van Alen was a very rich man. He was the son-in-
law of William Astor and the personal friend of William
C. Whitney, the real manager of the Cleveland campaign,
whose appointment as Secretary of the Navy was not
liked by the "mugwump" wing of the party, headed by
Carl Schurz and others. When Van Alen was appointed
a hue and cry arose from the idealists, and Cleveland's
enemies alleged that the appointment was nothing more
than a reward for the very large contribution Van Alen
had made to Whitney for the campaign, for which Whitney had promised this position. Schurz, as editor of
"Harper's Weekly," wrote a savage editorial against
Cleveland on this subject, and in a letter to me he stated
that he felt Cleveland's prestige would never recover
from the blow he had struck against himself in making
that appointment. I wrote to Cleveland about the matter
and how it was regarded by some of his friends, mentioning Schurz among others. The President sent me the following reply:

Executive Mansion, Washington
Oct. 29, 1893

My dear Mr. Straus:
 Your letter was received to-day.
 I need not tell you how much I value your friendship; and I
hardly need confess how touched I am by the manifestation of
affection afforded by the solicitude you evince in the Van
Alen matter. I am amazed by the course pursued by some
good people in dealing with this subject. No one has yet presented to me a single charge of unfitness or incompetency. They
have chosen to eagerly act upon the frivolous statements of a
much mendacious and mischievous newspaper, as an attempt to
injure a man who in no way has been guilty of wrong. I leave
out of the account the allegation that his nomination was in
acknowledgment of a large campaign contribution. No one

will accuse me of such a trade and Mr. Whitney's and Mr. Van Alen's denial that any such thing existed in the minds of any one concerned, I believe to be the truth. I think it would be a cowardly thing in me to disgrace a man because the New York World had doomed him to disgrace. Since the nomination was sent in I have left the matter entirely to the Senate, and I hear that the nomination was confirmed to-day. This ends the matter. I am entirely content to wait for a complete justification of my part in the proceeding.

I am sorry you regard this matter as so unfortunate, and if anything could have induced me to turn away from a course which seems to me so plainly just and right, it would be my desire to satisfy just such good friends as you have always proved yourself to be.

I shall be glad to see you at all times.

Yours very sincerely

GROVER CLEVELAND

Van Alen was confirmed by the Senate, but on November 20th he sent in his resignation, which Cleveland reluctantly accepted, but urged Van Alen to reconsider his decision, as his (the President's) preference was emphatically that Van Alen accept the post and by the discharge of his duties vindicate the wisdom and propriety of his selection.

During the second term I saw little of the President. I was very much tied to business and went to Washington only when summoned there to discuss a few international questions as they arose. But while I am reminiscing about my relations with Mr. Cleveland, I shall jump ahead about ten years and speak of a visit he paid me for three days during March, 1903. He was to deliver an address at the Henry Ward Beecher Memorial in the Brooklyn Academy of Music on Sunday evening, and he arrived from Princeton on Saturday. He was like a boy out of school.

We were going to the theater on Saturday evening and I suggested Justin McCarthy's "If I Were King," played by Sothern.

"I hope it is not sad," Cleveland said. "I want to see it from start to finish"; and with a smirk he added, "for I am a hayseed." I discerned afterward that he would rather have seen a comedy or vaudeville.

When we arrived at the theater, many in the audience recognized Cleveland and heads were constantly turning in the direction of our box. I mentioned it to him, but he said: "Oh, no, they don't know me any more." After the theater we had a supper of delicatessen and beer at home, which I knew he would like, and he amused us with several funny stories and mimicry. My wife remarked that he might have made a success on the stage, and he replied that his friend Joe Jefferson had often deplored his having missed that profession.

Cleveland gave an imitation of the humorous Congressman Campbell, of New York, who used to come to the White House and, pointing to the room occupied by Cleveland, ask the clerk: "Is His Royal Nibs in?" And sometimes Tim Campbell made requests that Cleveland had to deny as unconstitutional; then Tim would come back with "Oh, I would n't let the Constitution stand between friends!"

At dinner on Sunday we were joined by Mr. and Mrs. John G. Carlisle, my brother Isidor, his wife, and his business associate, Charles B. Webster. Carlisle had been one of the most distinguished Senators in Congress, former Secretary of the Treasury, and a close friend of Cleveland. When the champagne was served my wife said to the ex-President:

"Does Mrs. Cleveland let you drink this? You know it is bad for your rheumatism!"

"No, but I won't tell her," answered Cleveland.

They compromised on one glass.

After dinner the conversation turned to the bond loans during Cleveland's second Administration — the first made through J. P. Morgan & Company and the subsequent popular loans — to keep the gold in the United States Treasury. The ex-President referred to his fight against the silver craze and said he had been compelled to abandon the fundamental issue, the tariff reform, to combat that dangerous heresy.

When the guests had gone, Cleveland wanted to know whether we would like to hear the speech he was to deliver that evening, and of course we assured him we should be delighted. This led to conversation about Beecher, and I showed him the original letter that Beecher wrote him in 1887 recommending my appointment to Turkey. He said he remembered it perfectly, and it was the thing that turned the scale while he was considering whether or not he could properly appoint a person of my race to a post largely concerned with the protection of Christian missions. I made bold to request the manuscript of his Memorial Address to file with my Beecher letter, and he kindly consented with the words: "Yes, certainly; they are kind of cousins."

After a light supper we drove to Brooklyn. Cleveland liked to be punctual and I took care that we should arrive at the appointed hour, 7.45. It was pouring rain, and Cleveland anticipated that most people would be kept away; but when we entered the hall it was packed from pit to dome and several thousand persons were turned away. At the close of the meeting hundreds crowded onto the stage to greet the ex-President, showing that the love and admiration of the people had in no degree waned.

The next morning we prevailed upon him to stay an-

other day. He said he knew I had a speech to make at
Brown University and that its preparation would engage
my time. But I assured him the speech was all prepared
and the subject was "Brown in Diplomacy." He asked
me to read it to him, and I did. He pronounced it appropriate and fine, which gave me some confidence in the
success of the occasion, for I knew he was not given to
flattery and would not have praised the speech without
meaning it; that was not his habit.

He had to go to Rockwood, the photographer, at
Thirty-Ninth Street and Broadway, so I went with him.
He said he had hundreds of requests for pictures and
wanted a new one taken so that when people wrote for
them he could refer such requests to Rockwood; similarly
he had had some pictures made by a Philadelphia photographer. These arrangements would save him much
trouble. I asked Rockwood to take a special, large picture
for me. He brought forward his larger camera and took
one of the best photographs of Cleveland I have ever
seen. I had two finished: one for Mrs. Cleveland and the
other for myself, and it now hangs in my library.

For luncheon we met Isidor at Delmonico's. At the
next table sat Charles F. Murphy, successor to Croker as
boss of Tammany Hall, who requested me to introduce
him to Cleveland. They had quite a chat, after which
Cleveland remarked: "He looks like a pretty clean fellow."

During the meal our guest told us, with language, voice,
and manner befitting the tale, how, when he was being
spoken of for reëlection before his second term, he met a
farmer who said to him: "Now if you will go on sawin'
wood and don't say nothin', they will give you back that
job in Washington." No actor could have given a more
vivid characterization of that farmer.

That evening we went to Weber and Field's Music Hall, on Twenty-Ninth Street near Broadway. Cleveland suggested this himself. He said he liked to be amused at the theater and not saddened or instructed.

At about this period Cleveland from time to time showed evidences of illness. He called them stomach attacks. Whether or not his personal friend and physician, Dr. Joseph D. Bryant, had diagnosed the malady as more serious I do not know; but at times I rather inferred that he had. Dr. Bryant made it a point to accompany Cleveland on several of his hunting and fishing expeditions, which were taken not alone for pleasure, but as health measures, for a change of air and the outdoor recreation.

On and off during those years also, when the family wanted a little change, they occupied "the little White House" at Lakewood. Cleveland liked it for its simplicity and because it was not unlike the parsonage at Caldwell, New Jersey, where he was born. Early in June, 1908, while the Clevelands were at Lakewood, the ex-President sent for my brother Isidor; he desired to have a talk with him. He seemed to wish to unburden his mind.

This proved to be the last time he spoke to any one outside of his immediate family while still in the possession of all his faculties. That very night he had another attack of his malady, after which, as I was told, his faculties seemed to go under a cloud. Two weeks later, on June 24th, the country was shocked, though it was not unprepared, to learn that the ex-President had died that morning at his Princeton home.

On June 26th Grover Cleveland was laid to rest. The funeral was private; my brothers and I had received a note from Mrs. Cleveland asking us to be present. At his home we met about one hundred of his personal friends. It had been his express wish that there be no eulogy or funeral oration, and his friend Dr. Henry van Dyke conducted a simple service at which he read passages from Wordsworth's poem, "The Happy Warrior." In a carriage with Chief Justice Fuller, Judge George Gray, of Delaware, and Governor Fort, of New Jersey, I accompanied the body to the cemetery.

For Grover Cleveland there were no longer enemies to traduce and vilify. Perhaps no President had ever been so reviled by a hostile press throughout the country as this great man, and, strong as he was, these attacks quite naturally pained him. Public appreciation of men who struggle against the tide for righteous things is often deferred, sometimes until after death. In his case, happily, it came while he was yet among us in the constantly increasing manifestations of admiration, love, and esteem by the people of the country.

I have mentioned that during Cleveland's second Administration I seldom went to Washington. At that time I was occupied also with the writing of two books. I was not, of course, relying upon my pen for a living. I should not have survived long if I had! Historical writing has fittingly been called the aristocracy of literature; it requires long and patient investigation and yields meager returns. For me it made a fascinating avocation. My "Roger Williams, the Pioneer of Religious Liberty," was published by the Century Company in 1894, and "The Development of Religious Liberty in the United States" appeared in a limited edition, published by Philip Cowen, New York, in 1896.

The latter was a slim volume, an amplification of an

address I had delivered in New Haven before the Yale College Kent Club, and elsewhere; the former grew out of studies I had made in preparing my first book, "The Origin of Republican Form of Government." "Roger Williams" was well received and had a generous circulation, being several times reprinted. Brown University, under the presidency of that eminent historian and scholar, E. Benjamin Andrews, conferred upon me the honorary degree of Litt.D.

When I was again in London in 1898 I carried out a purpose I had long had, to visit Charterhouse School, earlier known as Sutton's Hospital School, where Roger Williams received his early education. I met the Reverend Doctor William Haig Brown, master, who showed me the register of the school for 1624 containing the inscription of Roger Williams. When he saw I was much interested in Roger Williams he told me of a recent life of him that had been written, which he considered very fine and with which he wanted to acquaint me. He went to his library on the floor above, and when he returned he handed me my own work! (I had not previously told him my name.)

I observed in the main hall of the school a number of tablets commemorating distinguished scholars who had attended there. There were represented Thackeray, General Shakespeare, Archdeacon Hale, Sir Henry Havelock, and several who were sacrificed in the Crimean War and the Indian Mutiny. I asked Dr. Brown whether he did not think it fitting that a tablet should be added in memory of Roger Williams, and said that I should be glad to defray the expense thereof. He agreed, and I authorized him to have the tablet made. He employed Howard Ince, a well-known architect, to design the tablet, which contains the following inscription:

In Memory of Roger Williams
Formerly a Scholar of Charterhouse
Founder of the State of Rhode Island, and the
Pioneer of Religious Liberty in America. Placed here by
Oscar S. Straus, United States Minister to Turkey, 1899

I did not wish my name on it, but Dr. Brown quite
definitely preferred it so.

Of all my books, the Life of Roger Williams " contains
the greatest amount of work in the way of research and
study; but the amount of pleasure it gave me in the doing
was commensurate.

In politics I had become more impressed year by year
with the importance of a reform in our electoral system,
especially in our large cities. The bosses in the two big
parties were the "invisible powers" who dictated the
nominations. Primaries were primaries in name only,
and were so conducted as to strengthen the power of the
bosses. In Chicago a campaign to purify the primaries
had been carried on by the political committee of the
Civic Federation. The Federation, of which its organizer,
Ralph M. Easley, was the secretary, now enlarged its
scope in the political field and issued a "Call for a National Conference n Practical Primary Election Reform,"
in the name of some two hundred and fifty of the leading men of New York, Chicago, San Francisco, and
thirty-five cities in between. Prominent in this list I
remember Mayor William L. Strong, of New York; ex-
Mayor Abram S. Hewitt, of New York; Darwin R. James,
president of the New York Board of Trade; Andrew B.
Humphreys, of the Allied Political Clubs of New York;
Mayor Josiah Quincy, of Boston; Mayor James D.
Phelan, of San Francisco; ex-Mayor George W. Ochs, of
Chattanooga; Albert Shaw; Nicholas Murray Butler;

Carl Schurz; Lyman Abbott; Lyman J. Gage; Melville
E. Stone; Myron T. Herrick; Albert J. Beveridge; Robert
M. La Follette.

The meeting was held in the rooms of the New York
Board of Trade on January 20, 1898, and we organized
the National Primary Election League. I was elected
president; Josiah Quincy, first vice-president; Charles
Emory Smith, of Philadelphia, second vice-president;
Walter C. Flower, of New Orleans, third vice-president;
Ralph M. Easley, secretary; and Darwin R. James,
treasurer. The conference gave a distinct impetus to
primary reform all over the country, and in many of the
States led to the passage of laws providing for such reforms.

In the presidential election of 1896 I voted for McKinley, despite my former political affiliations. The outstanding issue between the Republican and Democratic
Parties was the money question, and I was an advocate
of sound money.

Early in the new Administration our relations with
Spain were rapidly drifting to a crisis over conditions in
Cuba. My friend General Stewart L. Woodford was
appointed minister to Spain. I gave him a letter of introduction to Sir Henry Drummond Wolff, who was now
British ambassador at Madrid. Wolff was very sympathetic toward America. Woodford later informed me
that the letter had been very serviceable, especially as
his audience had been delayed for several weeks on account of the Queen's absence from the capital. He very
frankly laid before Wolff the American position and
attitude with regard to Cuba, which Wolff asked permission to detail to his Government. Based on that information the British diplomatic representatives were advised

by Lord Salisbury: "The American cause is absolutely impregnable; govern yourselves accordingly."

President McKinley frequently invited me to Washington and encouraged my writing to him, especially on international matters; and my letters always received prompt reply over his own signature. Accordingly on March 12, 1898, I wrote him at length stating that perhaps the impending war with Spain could be averted if we proposed to Spain a plan of suzerainty. I quote from my letter:

We have no need for Cuba; our destinies point to the Continent; to leave it to make conquests will weaken our rights, . . . and will place us against our will on the world's chessboard, from which we have happily kept clear. The Cuban insurgents are imbued with a spirit of belligerency, but have neither past training nor the knowledge to maintain freedom and to accord to each other individual liberty.

The great problems, I take it, are, first: to stop the war; secondly, to find a solution which will bring independence to Cuba, and at the same time preserve the *amour propre* to Spain. . . . The proposition to which I have given considerable thought . . . is the following:

That we insist that Spain accord and Cuba accept the position of suzerainty such as are the relations between Turkey and Egypt. This will give Cuba self-government, and will at the same time preserve the *amour propre* of Spain by retaining a semblance of a claim of sovereignty without power to interfere with self-government on the part of the Cubans. . . . We could much better afford to help Cuba with a number of millions which would after all be a small fraction of what a war would cost us, . . . especially when the end attained is the independence of Cuba, and attained in such a way as not to entail upon us unending responsibilities full of care and entangling obligations.

Immediately upon receipt of this the President asked me to come to Washington for a conference. He was very much interested in the idea and requested me to write

out the plan in more detail. This I did. I discussed with
him the suzerainty plan as developed in Europe and as
it was working in Egypt. I expressed the opinion that as
the leading nations of Europe were familiar with the idea
it was not likely to meet with any serious objections.
McKinley was impressed with the feasibility of my proposal and was in favor of some such arrangement. He
said he was having difficulty because of the jingo agitation in Congress and the storming for war of the American
press. He felt when the report of the Board of Inquiry on
the destruction of the Maine was made public, as it would
be in a few days, nothing could hold back Congress and
the press, and the Cuban controversy would be pushed to
an issue.

However, he immediately communicated the plan to
Minister Woodford, who brought it to the attention of
the Spanish Government. General Woodford reported
that he had every reason to believe it would be acceptable
to Spain. But meantime things moved with lightning
speed and war was declared.

Matters in Turkey at this time were also not going very
smoothly. At a conference with McKinley one day he
showed me a communication from Dr. James B. Angell,
minister at the Porte, suggesting that the only way to
bring Turkey to terms was to send warships up there and
"rattle the Sultan's windows." The President was much
disturbed. He felt the sending of warships might result
in another incident like the blowing up of the Maine. He
said the situation had worried him so that it interfered
with his sleep, and he begged me to accept again the appointment of minister to Turkey, declaring with conviction that he regarded me as the only man who could adjust the situation. I explained to him frankly how I was

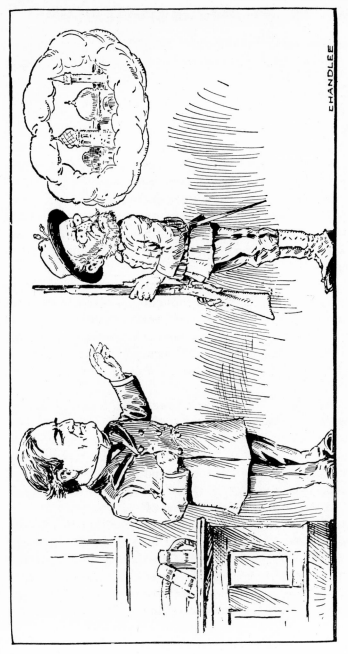

PRESIDENT McKINLEY SENDING THE AUTHOR TO TURKEY ON HIS SECOND MISSION, 1898

situated in regard to my business obligations and that it was very difficult for me to drop them at this time; but under the circumstances as he had stated them to me I felt I had no right to interpose my personal affairs as a reason for refusing, for I certainly regarded no sacrifice too great to make in the service of the country when it was needed, as in this instance. I said I had been too young to shoulder a gun in the Civil War as he had done, but with a full understanding of my situation if he should feel it necessary to call upon me I should be at his service.

Dr. Angell was a distinguished scholar and not lacking in diplomatic experience. He was president of the University of Michigan at Ann Arbor, and had been special envoy to China. He was also an adviser and one of the trustees of the American Board of Commissioners for Foreign Missions. However, in some public utterance he had criticized Turkey unfavorably, and the Porte was having its revenge. Every request Dr. Angell made was declined; exequaturs were refused to our consuls appointed at Erzerum and Harpoot. Dr. Angell was discouraged and incensed. He was about to resign.

Finally one day I received a telegram:

EXECUTIVE MANSION
WASHINGTON, D.C.
May 27, 1898

HONORABLE OSCAR S. STRAUS
    New York

Remembering our talk of a few months ago I would be glad to have you accept the post of Minister to Turkey. Dr. Angell has resigned to take effect 15 of August. I would be pleased to nominate you before Senate adjourns.

WILLIAM McKINLEY

And I telegraphed back that same day:

PRESIDENT McKINLEY
    Executive Mansion
       Washington
Your request that I should accept the post of Minister to
Turkey, with which you honor me, I regard as a command, and
deem it my patriotic duty to you and to the country to accept.
                                        OSCAR S. STRAUS

Among the telegrams and letters of congratulation I
received was one from William L. Wilson, then the president of Washington and Lee University at Lexington,
Virginia, reading: "Washington and Lee greets you as
Doctor of Laws."

The National Civic Club of Brooklyn gave me a dinner
and reception, presided over by my friend and college
mate, Frederic W. Hinrichs, at which the leading speaker
was Dr. St. Clair McKelway, editor of the "Brooklyn
Eagle." During the evening a letter was received from
my former chief and Secretary of State, Thomas F.
Bayard, saying:

It was my good fortune to be associated with Mr. Straus
when he first took up the tangled web of Turkish diplomacy, so
that few persons can so well attest as I, his possession of those
talents and high personal characteristics which give him
weight everywhere.

Ex-President Cleveland, who was prevented from being
present by another engagement, wrote:

I would be glad to join those who will do honor to Mr. Straus
. . . and thus show my appreciation of his usefulness and the
worth of his good example in recognizing the demands of good
citizenship and responding to the call of public duty.

And there were also messages from many others, including President McKinley.

I did not leave for my post for several months. Meanwhile I had more conferences with the President re-

garding the Spanish situation. Early in August, in discussing pending Spanish peace negotiations, he wanted
my ideas regarding them and as to how much of the Philippines we should take. I strongly advised that we take
as little as possible — nothing more than a naval and
coaling station; otherwise to appropriate the Philippines
would in the long run entail endless obligations without
commensurate benefits. I told him I believed these to be
the views also of many of the more thoughtful citizens,
and that I had spoken with a number of prominent men,
such as ex-Postmaster-General Wilson, ex-Secretary of
the Treasury Carlisle, and Clifton R. Breckinridge, formerly of the Ways and Means Committee, all of whom
were of like opinion. The President seemed to appreciate
my view, but again feared the jingo spirit of Congress.
He complained also of the attitude of the Cuban insurgents, who were exaggerating their numbers as well as
their demands.

Turning for a moment to my appointment, he said:
"I don't know whether you know it, but your nomination
has been received with more praise by all parties throughout the country than any nomination to office I have
made since I am President." I assured him I was gratified, but realized the emphasis this put upon my responsibilities.

Because I had been a Cleveland Democrat my appointment by a Republican President had, of course, created a
great sensation in the press; it was heralded as a step
toward the merit system in our foreign service.

John Bassett Moore was now assistant Secretary of
State, and with him I spent several days in the preparation of my instructions. I considered him even then the
best equipped authority on international law in the
country, and I thought it was a pity his services could

not be retained in the Department of State; but his salary there was five hundred dollars a year less than as professor, and he had a family to support. He told me that the President and Secretary Day wished him to accompany the Peace Commission to Paris, and subsequently he went as secretary and counsel.

While I was with the President for a final conference a week before sailing, Attorney-General Griggs came in all aglow and announced with much enthusiasm that he had just had a telephone message from Justice White (Associate Justice of the United States Supreme Court, later Chief Justice) that he would consent to be one of the members of the Spanish American Peace Commission. That specially pleased the President because White was a man of great ability, and because the fact that White was a Catholic might make a more favorable impression upon Catholic Spain. The President immediately directed that the names be given to the press. Shortly thereafter, however, White reconsidered his acceptance, for reasons which were not made public, and Senator George Gray, who was serving as a member of the Quebec Commission, and who like White was a Democrat, was prevailed upon by the President to accept in his stead. The other members were all Republicans. The commission as finally constituted was: Secretary of State William R. Day, Senator Cushman K. Davis (chairman of the Foreign Relations Committee of the Senate), Senator William P. Frye, Senator George Gray, and Whitelaw Reid.

There was considerable clamor, from missionaries and others, that we send warships to Turkey. Of this I entirely disapproved and so told the President. He answered me: "I shall be guided by you; I shall support you; I have confidence in your ability and foresight. No vessels will be sent to Turkey unless you demand them, and then, only then, will they be sent. And when you get to London I wish you to see Ambassador Hay" — Hay was about to return to take up the post of Secretary of State — "and tell him that I have not only constituted you Minister to Turkey, but Secretary of State for Turkey, and that both he and I will be guided entirely by your judgment and advice."

CHAPTER VI

MY SECOND MISSION TO TURKEY

Conferences with Ambassador Hay and Dr. Angell in London regarding Turkish matters — I make suggestions for coördinating work in our diplomatic service — With Baroness de Hirsch in Vienna — Arrival at Constantinople; audience with the Sultan — The visit of the Emperor and Empress of Germany — Breaking Turkish passport regulations — The Porte refuses to negotiate a treaty of naturalization — The indemnities for missionaries at Harpoot and Marash; the Sultan admits claim and promises to pay; I obtain iradé for rebuilding college at Harpoot — The Philippine Mohammedans; a diplomatic romance — American flour cheapens bread in Turkey — Aid to the British ambassador in the protection of Armenian orphanages — A renegade Roman priest — Lord Rosebery — Dr. S. Weir Mitchell — The Sultan entertains American tourists — His Majesty's only smile — A visit to Athens — Happy days on the Bosphorus — The Sultan's gift of vases — Dr. Theodor Hertzl — A visit to Rome — I return to Washington and conduct negotiations from there — LL.D. from Pennsylvania University — I end my mission.

In London I had several conferences with Ambassador John Hay, who was shortly to return to Washington as Secretary of State in the place of William R. Day, chosen to head the Spanish-American Peace Commission at Paris. Mr. Day a few years afterward was made associate justice of the United States Supreme Court, and the duties of that post he still discharges with distinction.

Mr. Hay and I went over in detail the questions at issue in Turkey and the plans I proposed for their adjustment. I told him of the pressure being brought upon the President to send warships to the Bosphorus, and said I regarded such a course as mixing up in the Eastern question, that traditional tinder box of Europe, aside from the possible danger of another incident like the blowing-up of the Maine. Mr. Hay agreed and promised to support me to the fullest extent in settling matters with Turkey.

I also met Dr. Angell in London on his way back from Constantinople, and went over matters with him. He told me what a fruitless year and a half he had had there and how he was made to feel he was *persona non grata.* He had not been invited to dine at the Palace once during his entire stay.

Before I left London I had a call from William E. Dodge, of Phelps, Dodge, & Company, New York, and president of the Evangelical Alliance of America. He came to express his appreciation for my making the personal and business sacrifice to go to Turkey again. He was one of our most benevolent citizens, prominently connected with the missionary bodies and therefore deeply interested in the American colleges and schools in the Ottoman Empire.

When I left for Constantinople this time, there were with me, besides my wife, my daughters, Aline and Mildred, respectively fourteen and fifteen years old; my little son Roger, six and a half years old, and his nurse; my niece Sissy, daughter of my brother Nathan; and my nephew Percy, second son of my brother Isidor, who was to be my private secretary. Mildred we allowed to return from Paris to continue her studies at Barnard, as we were unable to find a suitable school for her in either England or France. We had sailed for Liverpool on the S.S. Lusitania on September 3d.

My friend General Horace Porter had been appointed ambassador to France, and while in Paris I dined with him several times. He was a man of means and had located the embassy in a magnificent residence in one of the most fashionable parts of Paris. There we met among others Ferdinand W. Peck, United States Commissioner to the Paris Exposition, and Mrs. Peck; also William F.

Draper, ambassador to Italy, who with Mrs. Draper was in Paris on a leave of absence.

To Messrs. Porter and Draper I proposed what I had felt the need for during my earlier mission: some sort of coördination and coöperation among our various diplomatic representatives throughout Europe. I suggested we might have conferences from time to time, or prevail upon the State Department to keep each of us informed respecting negotiations between the Department and all the others. Much of this material would be of interest and value to us in connection with our respective embassies or missions. It was being done by other foreign offices. The British Foreign Office, for instance, issues confidential communications in the form of blueprints, which are sent to the heads of all British missions. During my previous sojourn at Constantinople my colleague, Sir William White, frequently gave me the benefit of extracts from these blueprints referring to American matters. They were very informing and helpful.

Porter and Draper said they would coöperate with me in urging the State Department to adopt some such scheme, and when I wrote to our colleague at Berlin, Andrew D. White, he gave similar support. However, when I suggested the idea to the State Department nothing came of it. Since then some further effort has been made in that direction, but I have not learned to what extent this desired system has been effected.

We went on to Vienna to meet Baroness de Hirsch, who was coming from her estate at Eichhorn. She had put her beautiful Paris residence on the rue d'Elysée at our disposal, but unfortunately my appointments made it impossible for us to avail ourselves of her hospitality. The Baroness looked ill to me, and I warned her against allowing her intense occupation with benevolent activities to wear upon her. She said she had had the grippe, and later told my wife that her physicians feared her ailment might be more serious. In spite of this, however, she went right on, while at the Hotel Bristol in Vienna, with conferences with her almoners, among others Ritter von Gutmann and Baron Günzburg, who were associated with her in her endowed enterprises in Austria and elsewhere. Alas, her malady was more serious than grippe, for it was only a short time after our reaching Constantinople that her family informed us of her death.

We met some of the leading Jewish scholars, artists, and literary men while in Vienna: the architect, Wilhelm Stiassny; the actor, Adolf von Sonnenthal; Dr. Adam Politzer; the Hungarian artists, Leopold Horowitz and Isidor Kaufmann; Professor David Heinrich Miller, of the Vienna University; and the attorney, Dr. Adolph Stein. Herr Stiassny was president of the Jewish Historical Society, and at a meeting of that body at which I was present he referred in glowing terms to my appointment, saying that, amid the anti-Semitic spirit that was taking hold of Austria and other European countries, America had shown by my appointment that no race or religious distinction existed here, which could not fail to have an influence in Austria and in several other European states.

On arriving at Constantinople we were welcomed by the secretary of the legation and acting chargé, John W. Riddle, together with other members of the legation and consulate and several of the missionaries. Mr. Riddle, by the way, had conducted the affairs of the legation in the interim with discretion and ability. He has since filled several other posts most creditably; he was ambassador to Russia under Roosevelt, and at the present writing is ambassador to Argentina.

The Minister of Foreign Affairs at the Porte now was Tewfik Pasha, who had been ambassador to Germany. He spoke German better than French, so I conversed with him in the former language. As was customary, I left with him the letters of recall of my predecessor and a copy of my presentation address. I was informed that the Sultan and all the officials at the Porte were pleased at my return, because they knew me and had every confidence in me both personally and officially. Of course, these remarks may have been diplomatic polite-ness, but events seemed to show some sincerity in them. My audience, for instance, instead of being delayed for weeks, was granted within one week of my arrival; and in-stead of being accorded the lesser formalities of a minister, I was received with all the ceremony accorded an am-bassador: four state carriages were placed at my disposal, preceded by four postilions and outriders; a detachment of guards rendered military honors as I arrived at the Palace; the Sultan was attended by Osman Pasha, Fouad Pasha, general-in-chief of the Turkish armies, and some thirty other high civil and military officers.

After the formality of presenting my credentials and making my address, the Sultan reiterated three times that he felt great pleasure in welcoming me back, as my former mission had given him much satisfaction. He said that he knew I was a "gentleman"; and that is the only English word I had ever heard him use.

President McKinley had authorized me to arrange for the elevation of the mission at Constantinople to an em-bassy, as by the Act of March 3, 1893, provision was made for the appointment of ambassadors. Up to that time, based on the idea that ambassadors represented the person of a monarch and that republics should not thus be represented, we had had only ministers. The act reads:

Whenever the President shall be advised that any foreign government is represented, or is about to be represented, in the United States by an ambassador, envoy extraordinary, minister plenipotentiary, minister resident, special envoy, or chargé d'affaires, he is authorized, in his discretion, to direct that the representative of the United States to such government shall bear the same designation.

The initiative for sending an ambassador, therefore, rested with the foreign power, and we could not send an ambassador to Turkey until that Government accredited an ambassador to us.

During my audience I informed the Sultan that the President had said he would be pleased to raise our mission to an embassy, but I observed that His Majesty did not take kindly to the suggestion. He replied politely that he would take it under consideration.

Among my colleagues, Baron Calice still represented Austria-Hungary. Germany was represented by Baron Marschall von Bieberstein, former Prussian minister, a large man of the von Moltke physique; he died later in London (1912) after a short service as ambassador to Britain. From France there was Paul Cambon, brother of Jules Cambon, who was ambassador at Washington at the time of the Spanish-American War and continued the Spanish negotiations after our rupture with Spain; a little while after my arrival in Constantinople Paul Cambon was transferred to London. From Great Britain there was Nicholas R. O'Conor, whom I met during my former mission when he was consul-general and chargé at Sophia; he had meanwhile been ambassador to Russia. And from Italy there was Signor Pansa. Severally they informed me that since my first mission, ten years before, the power of the Ottoman Government had been more and more concentrated in the Palace, that the Sultan himself was the "whole show" and very little power was left at the Porte.

Constantinople was all agog with preparation and excitement, for the Emperor and Empress of Germany were expected on October 17th! (As a matter of fact, rough weather on the Ægean caused them to arrive a day late.) The main streets of Pera were paved anew, and the walls surrounding Yildis were newly whitewashed. All business at the Porte was suspended. A Government official told me that the visit would probably cost the Ottoman Empire not less than five hundred thousand pounds! One of the residences at Yildis, near the Palace, was placed at the Emperor's disposal.

As is customary on such visits, all the heads of missions left their cards at the German embassy and inscribed their names in the Emperor's visiting register. Each visit was promptly returned the next day by von Bülow, Minister of Foreign Affairs, who left his card.

The Emperor and Empress drove through Pera in state, preceded by a company of Turkish lancers and followed by numerous officers on horses and in carriages. They rode in the royal victoria, drawn by four horses, accompanied by numerous outriders in gala uniforms and on caparisoned horses. The whole procession was gorgeous, and the royal pair bowed to left and right as the crowds in the streets greeted them.

Some time after midnight on October 20–21 the doorbell rang and my portier brought me a communication, just received from the Grand Master of Ceremonies at the Palace, inviting Mrs. Straus, myself, and our first dragoman to the banquet to the German Emperor and Empress

at 7.15 o'clock on the evening of the 21st. The doyen of
the diplomatic corps had sent suggestions that the ladies
wear high neck and long sleeves, as the Sultan objected to
the regulation European evening dress. The ladies accordingly contrived to cover their necks and arms with
chiffons, laces, and long gloves. It proved unnecessary,
however, because the Empress and her ladies-in-waiting
wore the usual décolleté.

In the recollection of the oldest diplomats present,
this banquet was the most brilliant in its appointments
that had ever been given at the Palace. More than one
hundred persons were there, all the heads of missions and
the leading officials of the empire. The approach to the
Palace for quite a distance was illuminated and lined on
both sides of the way with rows of soldiers. At the Palace
entrance, where we were met by the court officials, we
passed between rows of magnificently uniformed Turkish
and German officers, each wearing his full regalia of
numerous decorations.

At the proper time we were ushered into the audience
room, where the diplomats and their wives were arranged
in a circle, the ladies on one side and the gentlemen on the
other. When the Emperor and Empress with the Sultan
entered, every one made a court bow. The Sultan and
the Emperor then engaged in conversation through an
interpreter in the center of the circle, while the Empress
greeted each lady individually. Each person, as was the
custom, bowed before and after being spoken to. When
the Empress had greeted all the ladies and started with
the gentlemen, the Emperor started with the ladies.

When he came to Mrs. Straus, he made some mention
of having seen her queen lately and that she was as beautiful as ever. Mrs. Straus, by way of indicating that she
was from the United States, said, "I suppose Your Maj-

esty refers to Mrs. McKinley"; but the Emperor, evidently without stopping to listen to what was being said, clicked his heels, made his courtesy, and greeted the next person. It seems on being introduced he had misunderstood "Roumanie" for "Etats-Unis," especially since Mrs. Straus was next to the Serbian minister's wife. Count Eulenburg later explained to Mrs. Straus that the Emperor's hearing was a little defective.

When the Emperor reached me, he at once expressed a keen desire that it might be possible for him to visit my country, and especially our great shipyards, such as those of Cramp, which he had heard were wonderful. He then asked me whether I knew our ambassador at Berlin, Andrew D. White; and when I informed him that Mr. White had been a friend of mine for a number of years, he said a few complimentary words about him.

The dinner service included gold plates and gold knives and forks. The waiters wore brilliant red and gold uniforms. Between courses the Sultan and the Emperor conversed by means of the interpreter who stood behind them, and until they had finished talking the waiters were patiently holding the next course up in the air for a cooling.

After the dinner we again formed a circle, made more courtesies at the proper time, while the Sultan himself went round and greeted and shook hands with each one. That ended the royal dinner.

During the meal I sat next to the Emperor's personal physician, Dr. Lidhold. He had held the same position under the late Frederick III, whom he characterized as a most lovable man. He said William II was active and fond of amusing himself, and enjoyed constantly traveling about, which was not so pleasant for his physician and other members of his train. He admitted that the

Emperor's left arm was quite lame, but it did not interfere much with his movements because he had acquired such dexterity with the other. He added that the magnificent attentions of the Sultan could not fail to have a great influence upon Germany's attitude toward the Ottoman Empire.

The visit of the Emperor at this time, following as it did the dreadful massacre of Armenians only a few years before at Harpoot and then at Constantinople itself, was very much resented by the Christians throughout Europe. It was interpreted as an effort on the part of the Emperor, for his own gain, to reinstate the "bloody Sultan" in the esteem of the world. It was stated that the Sultan presented the Empress with a very costly string of pearls.

One of the four outstanding questions included in my instructions concerned the right of our citizens to travel in the interior of Turkey. Following the Armenian massacres of 1896 the Turkish Government made new passport regulations, and all foreigners were required to get a tezkirah, or special local passport, from the Sultan before traveling into the interior. As usual in Turkey, asking for a permit of any kind was one thing; getting it was quite another. This regulation proved most obstructive to our missionaries and those of Great Britain who had missions in the interior. They would go home or to Europe on a leave of absence, and upon returning to Constantinople would be held up, sometimes for weeks, on account of these tezkirahs, which were not definitely refused, but not given, which practically amounted to the same thing.

When I arrived at Constantinople eight Americans, bound for Erzerum and Harpoot, were being held up in this way. One of them was Dr. C. F. Gates, president of the Euphrates College at Harpoot. After exhaustive negotiations with the authorities, in which I pointed out the fact that refusal of the tezkirah was in violation of treaty rights, I myself gave Dr. Gates a permit, signed by me, with the seal of the legation on it. I then informed the Porte of my action and said that if any injury befell the party *en route* I should hold the Turkish Government responsible. I also sent an open cable to our State Department informing Secretary Hay what I had done. My British colleague was a bit disturbed when he heard of it, because there were several British missionaries in the party.

That same night I got another of those Turkish midnight messages. After apologizing for disturbing me, the messenger brought me the intelligence that my cable had been held back, and that the Minister of Foreign Affairs sent word that instructions had been given for the full protection of the missionaries *en route* to their posts. That broke down the passport regulations, and a very few days thereafter I received notice that the Council of Ministers had taken up the matter and ruled that the regulations for traveling into the interior should be restored to what they were before the Armenian troubles.

At about the same time I was enabled to cable to our Department of State that I had obtained the Sultan's iradé granting the exequatur for our consul at Erzerum.

The third item in my instructions, the Treaty of Naturalization, I had to drop. The Porte refused to negotiate this question because of the failure of our Government to accept the terms I had obtained during my previous mission, and for this I could not blame them. As during my earlier mission, when matters involving questions of naturalization arose I succeeded in securing the rights of the persons concerned on the merits of each individual case.

Lastly there was the question of indemnities due missionaries at Harpoot and Marash for property, real and personal, plundered and destroyed during the massacres. This was a delicate matter, because the Americans were not alone in making claims for such damage; also the Government was very poor. At first the Porte denied all liability and refused to pay. I started the negotiations in November, 1898, and the process proved a long and tedious one, lasting over a year. But step by step progress was made. By December the Sultan admitted the claims and promised to pay as soon as the amount was fixed. By February, with the amount still unfixed, he had decided how payment was to be made: he would buy a cruiser in America, to the cost of which the indemnities could be added, enabling him to make payment "behind a screen," which he preferred. He said arrangements were being made for loans through a bank in Paris to begin installments on such a contract. By early September the iradé for the purchase of a ship from some American builder had been given, and plans were being studied to determine the type of ship. By the end of the month the Sultan again assured me that the subject was receiving his attention and would be settled in a month or two.

The state of the Turkish finances was, of course, deplorable, and the Minister of Foreign Affairs told me that the Government was planning to apply to the purchase of the ship, money coming due in two months upon the conversion of some loans. And there were claims from England, France, Germany, and Italy, none of which the Sultan had recognized or promised to pay.

Even so, I planned that if His Majesty showed a
disposition to deny his promise I should offer to arbitrate
and thus bring matters to a head. That would put him
upon one of two horns of a dilemma: if he accepted, it
definitely and authoritatively exposed to all the world
the horrible details of the massacre; if he refused, it put
him in the position of having declined the only peaceful
method of adjustment. Tewfik Pasha, however, in the
name of the Sultan continued to make promises of payment, and the matter dragged along a few months more.

Having settled all other problems that were irritating
the relations of the two Governments, I asked for leave
to visit the United States. I planned this trip so as to
accentuate our displeasure at the procrastination of the
Ottoman Government in settling the indemnities, and
notified the Minister of Foreign Affairs that as my Government had been patient for over a year I should now return
home for consultation regarding the delay.

Upon my return to the United States I carried on the
negotiations through the Turkish minister at Washington and prepared the instructions for our chargé at Constantinople through the State Department. This finally
resulted in a contract with the Cramp Shipbuilding Corporation, with an additional amount of ninety-five thousand dollars to pay the indemnity claims, though actual
payment was not made until June, 1901, under the incumbency of John G. Leishman, my successor.

During the course of the indemnity negotiations I
succeeded in obtaining the Sultan's iradé for the rebuilding of college and missionary buildings at Harpoot which
had been injured or destroyed during the massacres.

Among the interesting episodes during these fifteen
months at Constantinople was what might be termed a

diplomatic romance. In the spring of 1899 I received a letter from Secretary Hay enclosing a communication from William E. Curtis, Washington correspondent of the "Chicago Record," and one of the best-known syndicate writers of the time, who was well informed regarding what was going on in both official and unofficial circles at Washington. Curtis reported a conversation with an important official of the Turkish legation wherein he learned that since the Turko-Greek War the Sultan had regained authority and respect among Mussulmans throughout the world, and his advisers thought the time propitious for him, as the religious head of Islam, to make known his authority to the Mohammedans of the Philippines, Java, and neighboring islands. The official had gone on to say that our victories over Spain had surprised the Sultan beyond description, and he was anxious to cultivate the friendship of a government whose navy could sink the enemy's fleet and go round the world without the loss of a man.

Curtis thought that, in view of our present minister's influence and our good relations with the Turkish Government, the Sultan under the circumstances might be prevailed upon to instruct the Mohammedans of the Philippines, who had always resisted Spain, to come willingly under our control. Secretary Hay said he would give me no advice or instructions, but would leave to my judgment what, if any, action I might deem it wise to take; that if I could succeed in getting the Sultan of Turkey to send a message to the Sultan of the Sulu Islands which would result in peaceful and harmonious relations between the Sulu Sultan and our officers, it would of course be a great accomplishment. The subject interested me greatly. I saw the possibility of rendering an effective service, and I was fascinated by the romance of the suggestion.

When I went to Turkey on my first mission, my father placed his hands upon my head, gave me his blessing, and a parting advice which sank deep into my consciousness: "When you have an important matter coming before you, don't act promptly, but sleep over it." My father's death in January, 1898, accentuated this advice in my memory, and when I received the Hay-Curtis letters I followed it. I knew very little about the Philippines. I doubt that our State Department knew much more. The library at Constantinople had nothing on the subject. I had a copy of the testimony taken by our commissioners at the Paris peace negotiations, but it contained only vaguest references. But one of my colleagues had the works of Jean Jacques Reclus, the French geographer. From this I learned that the Mohammedans of the Philippines were not Shiites, like those of Persia, but Sunnites, and therefore recognized the Sultan of Turkey as their spiritual head.

I thought about the problem for a few days, and then I sent a note to the Palace that I should like to have an audience with His Majesty, as I had some private communication to make to him that I believed might interest him, for it would enable him to render a great service to a section of his co-religionists. The audience was promptly arranged, and I gathered that the Sultan knew very little about the Sulu Mohammedans. He asked regarding their sect. I told him they were Sunnites. He asked whether they made pilgrimages to Mecca. I told him I thought they did, the same as those of Borneo.

Then a curious incident occurred. In order to be able to take up the matter very fully with the Sultan, I had anticipated all kinds of questions and armed myself with pertinent information. Among them I thought he might seek some assurance as to our Government's attitude toward Mohammedanism, and to reassure him I had come prepared with a translation into Turkish of Article XI of an early treaty between the United States and Tripoli, negotiated by Joel Barlow in 1796. It read:

As the Government of the United States of America is not in any sense founded on the Christian Religion; as it has in itself no character of enmity against the laws, religion, or tranquility of Musselman; and as the said States never have entered into any war or act of hostility against any Mehomitan nation, it is declared by the parties, that no pretext arising from religious opinions shall ever produce an interruption of the harmony existing between the two countries.

When the Sultan had read this, his face lighted up. It would give him pleasure, he said, to act in accordance with my suggestions, for two reasons: for the sake of humanity, and to be helpful to the United States. He added that he hoped his services would be appreciated, and that when occasion presented itself a like friendly spirit would be shown to him. He knew I was a "gentleman" and would make known to my Government the spirit in which he met my suggestions. The Mohammedans in question recognized him as khalif of the Moslems and he felt sure they would follow his advice.

We discussed means of conveying his message to them, and finally decided to send a telegram to Mecca, where the Moslem pilgrims were then gathered, to ascertain if any Sulu chiefs were there. Before transmitting it, His Majesty's secretary read the telegram to me in translation.

Two days later the Sultan invited me to the Palace to inform me that he had received a reply that two Sulu chiefs were at Mecca. Another telegram was then formulated instructing the chiefs in the name of the Sultan that a definite understanding had been reached with

the American Elchi Bey (American minister) that they
would not be disturbed in the practice of their religion if
they would promptly place themselves under the control
of the American army; that because of the Sultan's deep
concern for their welfare he advised and instructed them
to return at once to their people to prevent any blood-
shed.

Immediately I cabled Secretary Hay, that he might
be able to advise General Bates, one of our commanders
in the Philippines. The negotiation proved to be very
important and valuable to us. Some three months later
our Government received word from the Philippines that
an insurrectionist leader, Aguinaldo, had sent emissaries
among these Sulu Mohammedans, but they had refused
to join the insurrectionists and had placed themselves
under the control of our army, thereby recognizing
American sovereignty.

Lieutenant-Colonel John P. Finley, who had been
governor of the District of Zamboanga, Moro Province,
of the Philippine Islands for ten years, wrote an article
for the April, 1915, issue of "The Journal of Race Development" in which he refers to this incident:

At the beginning of the war with Spain the United States
Government was not aware of the existence of any Mohammedans in the Philippines. When this fact was discovered and
communicated to our ambassador in Turkey, Oscar S. Straus,
of New York, he at once saw the possibilities which lay before
us of a holy war. . . . He sought and gained an audience with
the Sultan, Abdul Hamid, and requested him as Caliph of the
Moslem religion to act in behalf of the followers of Islam in the
Philippines. . . . A telegram to Mecca elicited the fact that
they not only visited Mecca in considerable numbers, but that
at that very time there were Moros from Sulu in the Sacred
City. . . . The Sultan as Caliph caused a message to be sent to
the Mohammedans of the Philippine Islands forbidding them

to enter into any hostilities against the Americans, inasmuch as no interference with their religion would be allowed under American rule.

President McKinley sent a personal letter of thanks to Mr. Straus for the excellent work he had done, and said its accomplishment had saved the United States at least twenty thousand troops in the field. If the reader will pause to consider what this means in men and also the millions in money, he will appreciate this wonderful piece of diplomacy in averting a holy war.

There was one commercial trouble to be attended to, in the settlement of which I nevertheless emphasized the human aspect. Bread was, of course, one of the main staples of the people, and it was rising in price. There was a shortage of flour, yet a shipment of twenty thousand bags from the Pillsbury-Washburn Flour Company of Minneapolis had been rejected. The reason given was that it did not contain a sufficient percentage of gluten and elasticity.

As a matter of fact, a shipment received six months before had had the effect of reducing the retail price of bread about thirty-three per cent. Such shipments competed with the local flour mills, whose owners, chiefly Greeks, thereafter paid liberal baksheesh (tips, or bribe money) to have the flour rejected.

I secured expert testimony to show that the flour, instead of being inferior, was far superior to the local flour. I made the issue urgent and sent an open telegram to our State Department that the flour was being refused admission in distinct violation of our treaty rights. This had the effect I anticipated. The flour was admitted.

The result of this negotiation was reflected in every household, and was significant especially for the poorer people, who were grateful to the American legation and the American people for further reducing the price of their bread. After this, other large shipménts of flour arrived from time to time and were admitted without difficulty.

The British ambassador came to me one day to ask whether, in view of the success I had had in opening and protecting American schools, I could give him some assistance in the protection of the orphanages which British benevolent societies had established following the Armenian massacres. The Duke of Westminster had called the attention of Her Majesty's Government to the Porte's ruthless closing of a number of these orphanages.

Although it was not a matter that came officially under my jurisdiction, I told my colleague I should be glad to aid in every way possible. I called on the Grand Vizier and explained to him that if the Government persisted in destroying these institutions for the protection of orphan children, it would have a prejudicial effect in aggravating the justified horror produced in America as well as in England by those massacres. I stated frankly that while this was not an American question, it would, none the less, from a humanitarian standpoint, create a disastrous impression to the further disadvantage of the Turkish Government.

We got the desired result. It so pleased my colleague that in reporting to Lord Salisbury he expressed great appreciation for the valuable help I had given him. This recognition was widely published, in the London "Times" and other British papers, as well as throughout America. The Germans also reaped some benefit, for several of the orphanages, as at Palu and Diarbekir, were under the supervision of their nationals.

Occasionally in the City of the Sultan there arose

strange and peculiar incidents. I had a call one day from Monsignor Bonetti, the papal delegate, who had a summer residence near mine. He said it had been reported to him that a Roman priest named Brann, who had left his position in America about a year before because of some moral delinquencies, had arrived in Turkey within a few days. He was doubtless under an assumed name, but Bonetti had heard that the renegade priest was among our missionaries, and requested that I make inquiry. I asked him what he proposed doing should the priest be found. He said he wanted to counsel him to return to the church. The missionaries with whom I spoke gave me every assistance, but the priest had evidently not come among them, for he could not be found.

A number of distinguished people, European and American, visited Constantinople during the winter of 1898–99. Lord Rosebery arrived in his mother's yacht and was the guest of the British ambassador, Sir Nicholas O'Conor. We had the pleasure of meeting him several times at dinner. In a conversation I had with him he expressed great admiration for America and said that at one time he was on the point of becoming an American. I remember particularly his remark to the effect that he believed America and England, by coöperating, would control the world for the interests of the world, without having to fight a battle; that the peace and welfare of the world were in their hands, and sooner or later it must come.

We talked about our respective forms of government, parliamentary and congressional. He thought McKinley wise in referring all questions, during and since the Spanish-American War, to Congress. To quote his own words: "He is sailing on unknown seas, and it is wise to let the representative body do the steering."

He asked whether I was an ambassador or a minister. I explained to him that the President desired to raise the mission to an embassy, but as the law stood we were dependent upon the initiative of the Sultan. He said that during his incumbency as prime minister he had much to do with having the United States name an ambassador to London; he took special care that Great Britain should be the first nation to send an ambassador to Washington and to receive an American ambassador.

He spoke in a complimentary manner of Secretary Hay and said he should have remained in London, especially as it seemed to be his preference. He spoke of the ambassadorship of Edward J. Phelps and said he had heard him make some of the ablest public speeches he ever listened to; they were effective not only in what they expressed, but in their reserve. He thought public speaking in America was more finished than in England, of a higher order or better grounded from the standpoint of oratory: "We can't speak as you do."

I replied that one had only to point to him as an example to disprove that complimentary comparison. But he thought hardly anybody ever read his speeches.

Dr. S. Weir Mitchell, of Philadelphia, and his wife, together with the great-grandson of Alexander Hamilton, Philip Schuyler, and his wife, came to Constantinople. We saw much of them. The Mitchells had just lost their daughter.

Dr. Mitchell, who was regarded as the leading authority on nervous diseases — if I mistake not it was he who first introduced the rest cure, at any rate so far as America is concerned — was very anxious to see something of a Turkish household, which was not easily possible by reason of the seclusion of Turkish women. It happened that Tewfik Pasha, Minister of Foreign Affairs, had often spoken to me about the illness of his wife, who seemed to be suffering from some nervous ailment. She was a German-Swiss whom he had married while ambassador at Berlin, but their *ménage* was kept purely Turkish. Here, then, was my opportunity to kill two birds with one stone: I should satisfy Dr. Mitchell's curiosity by rendering Tewfik Pasha a service. In speaking to the Pasha I explained, of course, that Dr. Mitchell would accept no fee, that he would give his services as a favor to me and an act of courtesy to him. Dr. Mitchell was able to prescribe with excellent effect for Mme. Tewfik, and the Pasha was very grateful indeed.

Dr. Mitchell and I went to the museum one afternoon to see two famous marble tombs that had recently been unearthed at Sidon, upon discovery by Hamdy Bey, director of the museum. Both these tombs were supposed to be of the best period of ancient Greece. One was known as the Alexander tomb because it portrayed in high bas-relief the battle of Issus and also a hunting scene, in each of which one of the figures was identified as portraying Alexander. At first some scholars believed it to be the tomb of the monarch himself, but that seemed not to be correct, and it was doubtless the tomb of one of his generals. The other tomb was of equal size and proportions, about five feet high and ten feet long. Round its four sides it had a number of figures of a woman in various phases of mourning, the same figure with varying expressions. This ancient work of art appealed to the bereaved heart of Dr. Mitchell and he sat before it for quite a while. Later he wrote an "Ode to a Lycian Tomb," one of the best, if not the best, of his poems. He sent me a copy when it was privately printed, and subsequently it appeared in the "Century Magazine."

The inauguration of trips to the Orient by the Hamburg-American and the North German Lloyd Steamship Companies frequently brought hundreds of Americans to Constantinople at a time. In March the S.S. Augusta-Victoria arrived with three hundred and fifty American visitors. The Sultan was most gracious to them. Through one of his aides he asked me to invite them to Selamlik, after which he arranged a luncheon for them on the grounds of the ambassadorial kiosque, and had them visit the royal stables. When they left, the Sultan's aide carried on board the ship for them a large assortment of delicious Turkish candies and cigarettes, which they appropriately acknowledged in a letter that I transmitted to the Palace for them.

From time to time, especially when the weather was fine, I attended Selamlik, as was customary among the diplomats. On one very beautiful Friday I took with me my little son Roger, then seven years old. It was the Sultan's birthday and the pageant was exceptionally fine. From the window of the ambassadorial kiosque Roger leaned out as far as he possibly could to get a good view of the Sultan as he passed beneath in his victoria. The Sultan bowed in acknowledgment of our greeting, when suddenly Roger realized that he had not taken off his cap and pulled it off rather comically. This made the Sultan smile, and it was the only time I ever saw his habitually sad face wreathed in a smile.

After a strenuous winter, replete with difficult and trying negotiations, I took advantage of the invitation of M. Paul Stefanovich-Schilizzi, a philanthropist of Greece, to visit him in Athens in May. He was a man of great wealth and beloved throughout the Near East by reason of his benevolence. It is his niece, who was a frequent guest at our home, who recently married Eleutherios Venizelos, the famous Greek statesman.

En route to Athens we stopped for several days at Smyrna, where we met Kiamil Pasha, the Grand Vizier with whom I had so satisfactorily carried on a number of important negotiations during my first mission. He was now vali at Smyrna, highly regarded, and justly called the "grand old man" of Turkey, being about seventy-five years old. Amid the corruption of his time no one ever questioned his honesty. He had been grand vizier several times. He spoke English fluently, doubtless acquired in his youth at Cyprus, where he was born.

He deplored the hopeless condition of affairs at Constantinople, where all the power had gradually been concentrated at the Palace. Thus the grand vizierate became a post without power, which, he explained, did not interest him any longer. Besides, he did not agree with the Sultan's methods, though he was thoroughly loyal to Turkey. His sympathies, as between the contending powers, were with Great Britain; he believed good relationship with her was the surest guarantee for the welfare of his country.

From Smyrna we took a ship for Piræus, a sixteen-hour trip. There we took a carriage, instead of the train, to Athens. We stayed at the Hotel Grande Bretagne, which was owned by our friend Stefanovich. It was, and doubtless still is, the leading hotel on the square near the King's palace, and from the balcony of our rooms we had a clear view of the Acropolis.

This was our second visit to Athens. We had been there ten years before as guests at the beautiful residence of Dmitri Stefanovich-Schilizzi, brother of Paul, where we were sumptuously entertained; we dined at the palace, attended several functions there, and met, at various social gatherings, the leading people of the city. This time, however, we came for rest and recreation; we made no official calls, but spent the six days or so visiting places of interest, chiefly the excavations that were being made, and the museum.

Returning we took a steamer direct for Constantinople. We had learned that the Montenegrin portier in charge of our house at Pera had a slight case of smallpox, so we went directly to our summer home at Yenikeui on the Bosphorus, about a mile distant from Therapia where most of my colleagues had their summer residences. We had succeeded in securing a house that was a veritable palace and admirably arranged for entertaining, so that we were well able to reciprocate the attentions of our colleagues and extend proper hospitalities. A wealthy Greek had constructed and owned this mansion, but on account of some questionable dealings with the Palace involving large sums of money, he was a fugitive from Turkey.

The house was surrounded by a park of its own, fronting on the Bosphorus. There were pomegranate and magnolia trees in bloom, under which we took our lunch. We had a launch that I named the Franklin, and it was one of the fastest on the Bosphorus, so that within an hour I could readily be at the Porte to transact the business of the legation, although things are more quiet during the summer.

Altogether that summer was thoroughly delightful. My brother Isidor and his devoted wife had both joined us. My brother had had an attack of influenza and his health was not very good, so they had come to Europe to consult a distinguished specialist, Professor Erb, at

Heidelberg. After completing the cure my brother came to Constantinople for rest and quiet with us. The climate on the Bosphorus is ideal, never very hot because of the constant cool breezes from the Black Sea. During that summer there were only three days when the thermometer rose to ninety.

Everything seemed to prosper with me. I had brought several important issues to a successful termination; our whole immediate family was together, for Mildred had come to spend her vacation with us; and I had the pleasure of a visit from my dear brother and his wife. I recall no period of my life that was such a happy one.

Toward the end of the year I telegraphed to Washington for leave to return home. I had adjusted all the matters at issue between the two Governments except the indemnity, so that I felt justified in leaving my post. I knew that I could rely on Lloyd C. Griscom, the secretary who would be in charge, for a tactful and efficient handling of the affairs of the legation. The indemnity required only steady pressure and patience. As I have already stated I timed my return so as to make it effective in adding a little more pressure.

When I was about to depart, the Sultan sent to my residence a pair of beautiful vases, each several feet high, and artistically ornamented. They were manufactured at the royal pottery which the Sultan had had established on the Palace grounds, and the workmanship was French. As the question of cost did not enter into the manufacture, some wonderful productions were turned out at this pottery, and the vases sent to me were exceptionally fine specimens. I was very much embarrassed, yet I did not want to give offense by refusing them. I sent Mr. Gargiulo, our veteran dragoman, to explain to the Sultan's secretary how much I appreciated this attention, but as I was not permitted to accept the vases for myself I would accept them for our National Museum at Washington. That pleased the Sultan, and the vases now have a place in our museum at the national capital.

As there was no need for hurrying home, we made a few stops on the way, first at Vienna. The papers announced our arrival at the Austrian capital, and I received a note from Dr. Theodor Hertzl asking for an appointment. I was glad of the opportunity to meet him, for I had read much about him. I found him a man of attractive appearance: a little above medium height, coal-black beard and hair, very dark, expressive, bright eyes. He was about forty years old, seemed full of energy, beaming with idealism, but a man of the world. He did not at all impress one as a religious fanatic.

He said the idea of Zionism, or, rather, the colonization of oppressed Jews, had been developing in his mind for ten or twelve years. I told him I was not a Zionist, though I did not want him to understand that I was in any way opposed to the movement, or disposed carelessly to ignore the solemn aspirations which the deeply religious members of my race had prayerfully nurtured in sorrow and suffering through the ages. In answer to his question whether the Sultan had ever spoken with me about the subject, I told him he had not, as he probably understood it was not an American question and did not in any way come under my jurisdiction. But I told Hertzl of my negotiations regarding the immigration of the Jews to Palestine during my first mission to Turkey, when I visited Jerusalem.

We spoke of the condition brought about through the agitation of Zionism, the immigration of hundreds of Jews without means into Palestine, where there was as yet no industry to enable them to make a livelihood. He said he appreciated that and was doing everything in his power to prevent such immigration until a permit for a "chartered company" with sufficient capital had been obtained from the Sultan, and that he was in correspondence with an official of the Porte for the securing of such a permit. I suggested that it might be best for him to go to Constantinople and personally take up such negotiations; that I had been shown a letter from him to Artin Effendi, the under-Secretary of State, and this man was one of the biggest rogues in the empire, an Armenian kept nominally in office by the Sultan to mislead and hold in check his oppressed co-religionists. Dr. Hertzl thought he might take my advice.

He informed me that some months before, he had taken the matter up with the German Emperor and was led to believe that the Emperor was not in any way opposed to Zionism, nor to the returning of the Jews to Palestine, but Dr. Hertzl feared the opposition of the Catholics. He gathered also, from what he had heard, that Russia did not oppose the plan.

I mentioned Mesopotamia to him as a better place for the colonization of the Jews than Palestine; it was the original home of Abraham and his progenitors, was sparsely settled, and if the ancient canals were reopened that country could support several million people. He said he was somewhat familiar with this idea, as well as with Professor Haupt's pamphlet, and a scheme for the colonization of Cyprus, and that it was perhaps well to have more than one plan; if one did not serve as an outlet for emigration another might.

It seemed to me that Hertzl was one of those men who, having capacity and idealism, attach themselves to a cause that appeals to their intellect or their sympathies, and grow in spirit and effectiveness through the intensity of their devotion. Such men often develop extraordinary qualities of true greatness under conditions that impose weighty responsibilities, to an extent which they themselves did not realize.

We next went to Rome. All my life I had looked forward to visiting "Imperial Rome" on her seven hills, the old Rome that inspired some of the leading chapters of the world's history. And my imagination was fired the more because in my mind's eye I carried for comparison a picture of Athens, city of Pallas Athene, once proud intellectual mistress of the world; Jerusalem, from whence emanated the spiritual endowment of civilization; and the new Rome to which Constantine brought the scepter of the world.

While in Rome we were entertained by our ambassador and Mrs. Draper. They were occupying Palazzo Piombino, one of the most magnificent of the newer palaces, where they entertained in a manner befitting their station. We met there several of my former colleagues at Constantinople who were now representing their governments in Rome. Moses Ezekiel, our distinguished American sculptor, was also in Rome at this time, and with him and Mr. Bonney, in charge of the excavations of the Forum then in process, we went through the recently excavated chambers of the vestal virgins.

Before leaving the city we were received by the beautiful and charming Queen Margherita. She was a remarkably well-informed woman, even about events in our country. She spoke about the American press, and said one of our papers had a correspondent in Rome who was an ardent supporter of papal rule and could see no virtue in the Italian Government. She referred to the invention of the flying machine by Professor Langley, of the Smithsonian Institution, which, if it proved a success, would ultimately change the life of all peoples, which she hoped would bring the nations nearer to one another and into closer spiritual contact.

We visited Pompeii, and then went to Naples, where we boarded a steamer for New York, arriving home on February 8, 1900.

Immediately I went to Washington for a conference with Secretary Hay and to give him the details of the various negotiations. He was especially interested in the communication of the Sultan to the Sulu Mohammedans, for the friendly relations that this established between the Sulus and our Government had already prevented the shedding of blood.

I told Secretary Hay that I desired to resign. The matters for which I had been sent to Turkey were adjusted, the payment of the indemnity being only a question of time and patience; on the other hand, it was important, so far as concerned my personal affairs, that I be relieved from further duty abroad, especially as I could not in Turkey properly give to my children the education I felt they should have. The secretary thought my request reasonable and just, but he thought the President would regret it and would have difficulty in replacing me.

I took the subject up with the President next day. He said he realized I had made sacrifices enough and was entitled to have my wishes respected; he did not, however, wish me to send in my resignation just yet, but to continue, for a time at least, to direct matters in Turkey in consultation with Secretary Hay. He expressed great

satisfaction with the result of my mission and said if he
had n't sent me, some hostile demonstration in Turkish
waters would have been inevitable, with possib'e serious
complications as a result; but that the clamoring for a
warship to Turkey subsided with my going over because
of the general belief that I would succeed in handling
matters. "No one else could have done so well; you have
done better than I thought it possible for any one to do,"
he graciously added.

He indicated that there might develop some important
post in the United States which he should like to feel free
to ask me to accept should the occasion arise, but he
made no further explanation. I later learned from St.
Clair McKelway to what this had reference. McKelway
was on intimate terms with the President and at the
same time was a close friend of mine. The President
mentioned to him that he feared Secretary Hay, whose
health was failing, might have to relinquish his post, in
which event McKinley had in mind to offer it to me.

Within a week after my return I received a letter from
Charles C. Harrison, provost of the University of Pennsylvania, informing me that the trustees had unanimously
voted to confer upon me the honorary degree of Doctor
of Laws, and he would be glad if it were convenient for me
to receive the degree at a convocation of unusual importance on Washington's Birthday. This ceremony took
place at the Academy of Music, Philadelphia, and similar
degrees were conferred also upon Justice Harlan, of the
United States Supreme Court; Professor Ames, of the
Harvard Law School; Minister Wu, of China; President
Diaz, of Mexico; and two delegates from the Universities
of Oxford and Cambridge.

From time to time during the next few months I went
to Washington both to direct Turkish matters through

the State Department and to confer with the President on matters in general. On one of these occasions, in August, he mentioned his forthcoming letter of acceptance of re-nomination and spoke about the efforts of the Democrats to fasten the charge of imperialism on the administration, but said he would make it plain that we proposed to give as much freedom of government and independence to the Philippines as they showed themselves able to receive. I read to him from a memorandum I had drawn up regarding our purpose to withdraw our troops as fast and in proportion as the conditions of peace in the islands permitted. He said I had expressed his ideas exactly, and as I was about to replace the memorandum in my pocket he said he wished I would let him have it, which of course I did.

He asked what I thought of conditions in China, and I told him I was convinced our true course was to oppose the partition of that country and to stand firm for the open-door policy; that if Germany, or any other Power, endeavored to bring about a division, we could doubtless prevent it by insisting upon the open door, especially as the nations could not agree among themselves.

Early in December I received a letter from Secretary Hay, asking whether I still preferred to be relieved or whether for any reason I would consent to continue as minister to Turkey. I definitely answered in the negative and my second mission terminated with the following letter:

DEPARTMENT OF STATE
WASHINGTON, *December* 18, 1900

OSCAR S. STRAUS, ESQUIRE
42 Warren Street
New York City

MY DEAR MR. STRAUS:

I have laid before the President your letter of the 12th instant, in which you express your preference not to return to

Constantinople, and offer your resignation of the mission you have honorably and faithfully filled for the past few years.

Deferring to your wish, the President has accepted your resignation. In charging me to inform you of this acceptance, the President desires me to make known in fitting words his high appreciation of the valuable services you have rendered to your country, and his sense of the ability and intelligence you have brought to bear in the performance of a task of more than usual delicacy and difficulty. Called, as you were, a second time to the Ottoman mission and confronted by the problems and entanglements that seem to especially environ that post, you have shown rare aptness in dealing with its perplexities and have notably strengthened the hands of the government in leading the long pending questions toward a settlement. While deeply regretting your retirement and while averse to losing your helpful counsels, the President has felt that he could not rightfully impose fresh personal sacrifices upon you by disregarding your wish. You take with you into honored private life the esteem of those who have known and understood your conscientious worth in the paths of official duty.

I share the President's regrets and equally share his appreciation of the good services you have rendered. My sincere regards and personal friendship are with you always.

Very cordially yours

JOHN HAY

CHAPTER VII

THEODORE ROOSEVELT

Roosevelt appoints me member of the Hague Tribunal — Trouble with Philippine Mohammedans averted — Humanitarian diplomacy under Roosevelt; Hay's Roumanian note; Roosevelt's Russian cable — The Alaska boundary — Panama and the "covenant running with the land" — White House luncheons; Carnegie suggests to Roosevelt a legacy for my grandchildren — Roosevelt and organized labor — Roosevelt's definition of Americanism — Overnight at the White House; conference regarding the President's Message — Roosevelt and the Portsmouth peace negotiations; Count Witte invites a committee to discuss the Russian Jewish question; Roosevelt writes to Witte — Roosevelt's prophetic characterization of Germany — Some essential qualities of Roosevelt.

I BEGAN the year 1901 as a private citizen once more. I devoted much of my time, however, to public activities, giving close attention particularly to the international questions that arose.

The doctrine of citizenship and the rights of naturalized American citizens in foreign countries had for many years formed the major subject in our foreign relations, and it had been one for constant controversy between our own and foreign countries, especially Germany, Austria, and Turkey. In the spring I read a paper at a meeting of the American Social Science Association, of which I was the president, entitled "The United States Doctrine of Citizenship and Expatriation." Later in the year I received, in consequence, a letter from Senator S. M. Cullom of Illinois, chairman of the Senate Committee on Foreign Relations, asking me to prepare materia for amendments to legislation on this subject, which I did.

When Theodore Roosevelt became President of the United States through the lamentable death of William McKinley, one of my earliest relations with him was my being appointed by him as a member of the Permanent

Court of Arbitration at The Hague. Whether or not he acted herein in conformity with McKinley's intention, I cannot say. When McKinley was selecting the original members, he conferred with me and indicated that if agreeable to me, he would be pleased to appoint me as a member. Shortly afterward when the appointments were announced, my name was not among them. It was some time before I saw him again, and while I should never have mentioned it, he did. He said he was very sorry that through the pressure of duties he had quite forgotten his intention to name me when the time came to announce the appointments. I told him I thought perhaps I had been mistaken in understanding that he had offered me one of the appointments. He said I had not misunderstood, but that he would make amends should a vacancy occur while he was still President; he had wanted me as a member of the Court, not alone in recognition of the great services I had rendered, but because he regarded me exceptionally qualfied. He added that when he became ex-President he would like to be a member of that Court himself; it appealed to him more than any other office he could think of.

The vacancy in the membership of the Court occurred sooner than any one anticipated, by the death, in March, 1901, of ex-President Harrison; but by the decree of the gods McKinley himself was no longer with us when the time came to fill President Harrison's place. In fact I think the day we talked about the Court marked my last conference with him. He was always simple in manner and of charming personality. Together we enjoyed a good smoke that afternoon; he was fond of smoking and knew I enjoyed a good cigar, and he was wont to have me take one of his brand. I begged him not to concern himself further with the omission of my appointment at The

Hague, that I was satisfied to know he thought me worthy of the selection.

It is poss ble that Roosevelt knew the circumstance and McKinley's intention, for he was Vice-President at the time it happened. At any rate, when the successor to President Harrison was chosen, I received the following appointment, somewhat different in form from most documents of the kind:

WHITE HOUSE
WASHINGTON, <i>January</i> 8, 1902</div>

MY DEAR SIR:

Article XX of the Convention for the Pacific Settlement of International Disputes, signed July 29, 1899, by the Plenipotentiaries to the Hague Peace Conference, provides for the organization of a permanent Court of Arbitration, and Article XXIII of the same Convention provides for the selection by each of the signatory Powers of four persons at the most, as members of the Court, who are to be appointed for a term of six years.

It will give me pleasure to designate you as one of the four United States members if you will advise me that such action is agreeable to you.

Very Truly Yours,
THEODORE ROOSEVELT

HONORABLE OSCAR S. STRAUS
    New York, N.Y.

Since then I have been reappointed three times: in 1908, again by Roosevelt, in 1912 and 1920, by Wilson.

In April, 1902, there appeared in the press a dispatch to the effect that an expedition of twelve hundred men was to be sent to the southern Philippines to punish the Mohammedans there for killing one of our soldiers and wounding several others. I immediately wrote the President that I believed such a step would be unwise and would probably bring on a general uprising in that province. I called his attention to the negotiation I had had with the Sultan of Turkey regarding these people, and suggested that instead of the expedition a commission be sent to treat with them. The President asked me to come to Washington to confer with him in the matter, and after the Cabinet meeting I met him in his study. There were present also Mr. Taft, who had been appointed governor of the Philippines, Adjutant-General Corbin, and Mr. Sanger, acting Secretary of War. I presented my arguments more fully. The President had already telegraphed General Chaffee regarding the sending of a diplomatic mission, in accordance with my letter.

The result of our conference was that General Corbin was directed to advise General Chaffee to use the office of the friendly datos to obtain the desired redress. It developed later that the soldier killed was laying a telegraph line, which procedure, not being understood by the Moros, was regarded by them as a device for their destruction. The slayers were surrendered and punished and the incident was satisfactorily adjusted.

At about this time disturbances in Roumania were being reflected in our country. Eleven years before, a committee of prominent Jews had brought before President Harrison the pitiable condition of the large number of Jews arriving in New York from Russia, and it was now necessary to take similar steps with regard to the Jews from Roumania.

In Chapter IV I mentioned that Roumania disregarded the provisions of the Treaty of Berlin and placed restrictions upon her Jewish subjects. Into that treaty, by which Roumania was made an independent kingdom following the Russo-Turkish War, Article XLIV was inserted specially for the protection of the Jews, of whom there were about four hundred thousand in the new state. It provided that difference of religion should not be ground for exclusion in the participation of civil, political, or economic rights. In spite of this, however, the Jews in Roumania were being oppressed and discriminated against on the specious claim that they were foreigners, though they and their ancestors had been living in the land for generations. They were compelled to serve in the army, but not permitted to become officers; they were made subject to exceptional taxes; they were excluded from the professions and from owning and cultivating land. In every direction they were being throttled, and new laws were being promulgated to shut off every avenue of self-support.

The result was what had doubtless been the intention in putting into force these drastic measures: the Jews who could emigrated, and they left Roumania *en masse*. The obstacles in the way of their gaining admission into the countries of Western Europe were so great that few of them could settle there. The leading Jewish organizations of Great Britain and France, namely, the Jewish Colonization Association in London and the Alliance Israélite Universelle in Paris, laid the matter before their respective governments, but, on account of the disturbed conditions in the Balkans and the cross-currents of European politics, no pressure could be exerted through these governments.

The main stream of the Roumanian exodus was thus directed to America, and they arrived here in increasing numbers. The leading Jewish agencies of the country, particularly the B'nai B'rith Order under the presidency of Leo N. Levi, used their best efforts to distribute the immigrants over the country and to places where they were most likely to find employment. Later our very able commissioner of immigration at Ellis Island, Robert Watchorn, went over to Roumania for the special purpose of studying the situation and made a graphic report of what he learned. But to alleviate the situation action of a more official character was needed.

Jacob H. Schiff and I prepared a careful brief on conditions and presented it to President Roosevelt. The President said he was willing to take the matter in hand provided something could be done by our Government. Congressman Lucius N. Littauer also extended helpful coöperation. He had recently returned from Roumania and had first-hand knowledge of the question, which he took up in conferences with the President and with Secretary Hay.

Finally, in September, 1902, the President directed Secretary Hay to prepare his now famous Roumanian Note to the Powers signatory to the Treaty of Berlin. The note was sent to our diplomatic representatives in those countries with instructions to present it to the governments to which they were accredited. The occasion for sending it was found in connection with negotiations initiated by Roumania for the concluding of a naturalization treaty with our country. The note gave the reasons why, under the circumstances, we were unwilling to conclude such a treaty. After referring to the Treaty of Berlin and the obligations assumed by Roumania under it regarding the treatment of subject nationalities, the Secretary said:

The United States offers asylum to the oppressed of all lands. But its sympathy with them in no wise impairs its just liberty and right to weigh the acts of the oppressor in the light of their effects upon this country, and to judge accordingly.

Putting together the facts, now painfully brought home to this Government, during the past few years, that many of the inhabitants of Roumania are being forced by artificially adverse discriminations to quit their native country; that the hospitable asylum offered by this country is almost the only refuge left to them; that they come hither unfitted by the conditions of their exile to take part in the new life of this land under circumstances either profitable to themselves or beneficial to the community, and that they are objects of charity from the outset and for a long time — the right of remonstrance against the acts of the Roumanian Government is clearly established in favor of this Government. Whether consciously and of purpose or not, these helpless people, burdened and spurned by their native land, are forced by the sovereign power of Roumania upon the charity of the United States. This Government can not be a tacit party to such an international wrong. It is constrained to protest against the treatment to which the Jews of Roumania are subjected, not alone because it has unimpeachable ground to remonstrate against the resultant injury to itself, but in the name of humanity. The United States may not authoritatively appeal to the stipulations of the treaty of Berlin, to which it was not and can not become a signatory, but it does earnestly appeal to the principles consigned therein, because they are the principles of international law and eternal justice, advocating the broad toleration which that solemn compact enjoins and standing ready to lend its moral support to the fulfillment thereof by its cosignatories, for the act of Roumania itself has effectively joined the United States to them as an interested party in this regard.

One of the most valuable by-products of the Congress of Berlin was to bring into closer relations the autocratic with the liberal governments of Europe and cause the former to become more amenable to the enlightened conscience of the world. Hay's dispatch, while not pleasing to the Government of Roumania, yet, because of the worldwide publicity it received, had a measure of influence in modifying Roumania's indefensible proscriptions.

Another need for humanitarian diplomacy arose the following year. The attitude and proscriptions of the

Roumanian authorities had doubtless encouraged anti-Semitic activity in Russia, and the latter Government, no longer contenting itself with the application of restrictions in the book of laws which compelled Jews to live in the Pale settlements, officially encouraged mobs to massacre and loot, culminating on April 19–20, 1903, with the outbreak in Kishineff, where forty-seven Jews were killed, ninety-two severely wounded, and some five hundred more slightly injured. In addition great material losses were inflicted: seven hundred houses were destroyed, six hundred stores pillaged, and thousands of families utterly ruined.

When these facts became known, they called forth an expression of indignation throughout the civilized world. In New York a mass meeting was called at Carnegie Hall by hundreds of the foremost New York Christians, in protest against the outrages upon the Jews in Russia and particularly against the Kishineff affair. The meeting was presided over by Paul D. Cravath, eminent lawyer, and the speakers were ex-President Cleveland, Mayor Seth Low, Jacob G. Schurman, president of Cornell, and Edward M. Shepard, well known for his unselfish devotion to the interests of the public. I have in my possession the manuscript of Cleveland's address on this occasion, which concludes:

In the meantime, let the people of the United States, gathered together in such assemblages as this in every part of the land, fearlessly speak to the civilized world — protesting against every pretence of civilization that permits mediæval persecution, against every bigoted creed that forbids religious toleration and freedom of conscience, against all false enlightenment that excuses hatred and cruelty towards any race of men, and against all spurious forms of government protection, that withhold from any human being the right to live in safety, and toil in peace.

I will also quote part of the resolutions adopted that evening:

Resolved, that the people of the United States should exercise such influence with the Government of Russia as the ancient and unbroken friendship between the two nations may justify to stay the spirit of persecution, to redress the injuries inflicted upon the Jews of Kishineff, and to prevent the recurrence of outbreaks such as have amazed the civilized world.

A few weeks later a committee from the B'nai B'rith Order, consisting of Simon Wolf, Adolf Moses, Julius Bien, Jacob Furth, Solomon Sulzberger, and Joseph D. Coons, and headed by their president, Leo N. Levi, called upon Secretary Hay and presented to him a statement regarding the massacres in Russia together with a proposed petition which they wished forwarded to the Government of the Czar. The Secretary expressed great sympathy and the desire to do what might be possible in the matter. His reply to the committee, taken down in shorthand at the time, was published in full in the press, and from it I quote the concluding sentence:

All we know of the state of things in Russia tends to justify the hope that even out of the present terrible situation some good results may come; that He who watches over Israel does not slumber, and that the wrath of man now, as so often in the past, shall be made to praise Him.

The Secretary then accompanied the committee to the White House, where they met the President and presented to him an outline of the oppression of their coreligionists in Russia.

Early in July I received a telegram from the President's secretary to the effect that the President would like to have me lunch with him the day following at Oyster Bay, and that Simon Wolf of Washington, and Leo N. Levi also had been invited. When I arrived at Sagamore Hill there were present besides those named Dr. Albert Shaw of the "Review of Reviews," and an English friend of his, Mr. Morris Sheldon Amos.

We discussed the Russian situation throughout lunch. The President suggested that a note be sent by the Secretary of State to John W. Riddle, our chargé at St. Petersburg, and that this note should embody the entire petition which Mr. Levi and his committee had drafted. Dr. Shaw observed that the embodying of the petition to the Czar and giving publicity to the note would have all the effects of a presentation even if the Czar should refuse to receive it, which was exactly what the President had in mind.

After luncheon we adjourned to the study, and Roosevelt said: "Now let's finish this thing up." Hay had been to see him the day before and had left a memorandum. Roosevelt at once drafted the note with his own pen, using part of Hay's memorandum. The note was to be sent as an open cable. It read as follows:

RIDDLE
    St. Petersburg
You are instructed to ask an audience of the Minister of Foreign Affairs and to make to him the following communication:

Excellency: The Secretary of State instructs me to inform you that the President has received from a large number of prominent citizens of the United States of all religious affiliations, and occupying the highest positions in both public and private life, a respectful petition addressed to his Majesty the Emperor relating to the condition of the Jews in Russia and running as follows:

[Here is set out the petition.]

I am instructed to ask whether the petition will be received by your Excellency to be submitted to the gracious consideration of his Majesty. In that case the petition will be at once forwarded to St. Petersburg.

Roosevelt wanted the cable to be sent at once and was in a hurry to get it to Washington. One of his reasons was that the late Russian ambassador, Cassini, had been dismissed and was on his way back to Russia, and he wanted the note to reach the Russian Government before Cassini arrived in St. Petersburg. Mr. Wolf, who lived in Washington, was to take the drafted cable to Secretary Hay; but as he could not return that night the President asked whether I could take it so that it might be dispatched next morning. By ten o'clock the following morning I placed the draft in the Secretary's hands and it was immediately put on the wire.

In planning the cable as he did, the President was right in his anticipation. Duly the American chargé at St. Petersburg informed the State Department that the Russian Government, through its Minister of Foreign Affairs, had declined to receive or consider the petition. Nevertheless, its purpose was accomplished. Official Russia was made to realize the aroused indignation and the public protests of the civilized world. This in turn had a decided influence in checking, for the time being at least, similar outbreaks threatened throughout the empire, besides bringing to trial and punishment some of the leaders of the massacres.

That afternoon at Sagamore Hill, after the Russian matter had been disposed of, the President was talking to Dr. Shaw and me about the Alaskan boundary question. He pulled out a map showing the disputed boundary, and explained that three commissioners from the United States and three from Great Britain and Canada would take up the dispute for investigation. He argued that they were not arbiters and he refused to sign an arbitral agreement; if they did not agree, he would take the matter into

his own hands; that the whole trouble arose from the fact
that the Canadians had shoved down the boundary line
after the discovery of gold. "Suppose a man pitches a
tent on my grounds and claims them, and I want him to
get off; and he says he won't get off, but will arbitrate
the matter!" Roosevelt exclaimed. Then, turning to me,
he added: "Straus, you are a member of the Hague Tribunal; don't you think I'm right?"

I calmly replied that as a member of the Hague Tribunal I should first have to hear what the other side had
to say and therefore must reserve my judgment. And we
all had a good laugh.

During the Venezuela controversy in 1902, Venezuela
on the one side and Great Britain and Germany on the
other, Roosevelt was very much incensed that Germany,
with the feeble backing of England, should undertake a
blockade against Venezuela to make the latter carry out
certain agreements, and he promptly took steps to prevent it. Thereupon there was a disposition on the part of
Germany to ask Roosevelt to arbitrate. Secretary Hay,
it seems, favored such a course, but I strongly advised
against it.

At a luncheon to which I was invited by the President
early in November, 1903, the conditions in Panama came
up as the principal topic of conversation. There were
present on this occasion, besides Mr. and Mrs. Roosevelt,
Cornelius N. Bliss, former Secretary of the Interior;
John Clark Davis, of the "Philadelphia Ledger"; H. H.
Kohlsaat, of Chicago; Lawrence F. Abbott, of "The Outlook"; and the President's brother-in-law, Lieutenant-
Commander Cowles, of the Navy. News had been received that Panama had separated from Colombia and
we were about to recognize Panama. In his informal way,

as was his custom at luncheons, the President began to discuss the situation, referring to the fact that our treaty of 1846 was with New Granada, which afterwards became the United States of Colombia and then the Republic of Colombia, and that in that treaty we had guaranteed to protect the transit route. One of the questions raised was whether the treaty still held us to that obligation, notwithstanding these several changes of sovereignty.

The President was directing his remarks toward me, which was his way of signifying the particular person from whom he wanted to draw comment. I answered that it seemed to me, as I recollected the terms of the treaty, which I had recently read, that the change of sovereignty did not affect either our obligations or our rights; that I regarded them in the nature of a "covenant running with the land."

"That's fine! Just the idea!" Roosevelt replied, and as soon as luncheon was over, he requested me to express that idea to Hay. He scratched a few lines on a correspondence card asking Secretary Hay to go over with me the suggestion I had made and to work into the treaty the "covenant running with the land" idea.

That evening I called on the Secretary. He seized the idea at once and said he would make use of it in a statement he was just preparing for the press detailing the whole situation. The following day there was reported in the papers of the country the fact that the President, following a meeting of the Cabinet, had decided to recognize the *de facto* government of Panama; and then the detailed statement by Secretary Hay regarding the terms of the treaty, the history of the negotiations, and the subsequent development, covered several newspaper columns. It contained this paragraph:

It must not be lost sight of that this treaty is not dependent for its efficacy on the personnel of the signers or the name of the territory it affects. It is a covenant, as lawyers say, that runs with the land. The name of New Granada has passed away; its territory has been divided. But as long as the isthmus endures, the great geographical fact keeps alive the solemn compact which binds the holders of the territory to grant us freedom of transit, and binds us in return to safeguard for the isthmus and the world the exercise of that inestimable privilege.

A few days thereafter I received a short note from the President reading: "Your 'covenant running with the land' idea worked admirably. I congratulate you on it." And from my friend John Bassett Moore I received an amusing letter:

So you had a finger in the pie! I find a good deal of amusement in reflecting on the end reached from the premise of my memorandum; and almost as much on the conclusion reached from your suggestion. Perhaps, however, it is only a question of words — that is to say, it is, indifferently, a question of the "covenant running with the land" or a question of the "covenant running (*away!*) with the land"!!

Those luncheons at the White House were always pleasant and interesting occasions. One met there all kinds of people, of every station in life, but always people who stood for something and who interested the President. At the table Roosevelt would speak without apparent reserve and free from all official restraint, and I doubt whether these confidences were ever abused. By this means, too, he received the frank, unreserved statements and criticisms of his guests.

As an illustration of the range of personalities one would meet at the Roosevelt luncheons, I remember one day when Seth Bullock, a former sheriff of the Black Hills district and an intimate friend of Roosevelt during his cowboy days, sat next to Seth Low at the table. And in his "Autobiography" Roosevelt himself says:

No guests were ever more welcome at the White House than these old friends of the cattle ranches and the cow camps — the men with whom I had ridden the long circle and eaten at the tail-board of a chuck-wagon — whenever they turned up at Washington during my Presidency. I remember one of them who appeared at Washington one day just before lunch, a huge, powerful man who, when I knew him, had been distinctly a fighting character. It happened that on that day another old friend, the British Ambassador, Mr. Bryce, was among those coming to lunch. Just before we went in I turned to my cow-puncher friend and said to him with great solemnity, "Remember, Jim, that if you shot at the feet of the British Ambassador to make him dance, it would be likely to cause international complications"; to which Jim responded, with unaffected horror, "Why, Colonel, I should n't think of it, I should n't think of it!"

Mrs. Roosevelt is a most charming and cultured woman, typically the wife and mother. Literary and intellectual matters appeal to her, though her dominant note is the domestic one. I am sure she would have been just as happy as the mistress of a private household as the leading lady of the land in the White House, despite her great tact, sweetness, and simple dignity in filling the latter position.

The President was an omnivorous reader. He could read faster and remember better than any one I have ever known. On one occasion he recommended to me Ferrero's "Greatness and Decline of Rome," which he had just finished in the original Italian, and which had been brought out in English by the Putnam house. Subsequently, too, I met this author at the White House, where he and his wife were the guests of the President for several days.

In January, 1904, a large conference was held in Washington of representatives of the various peace societies and other persons prominently interested in the calling of an international peace congress. George F. Seward, of New York, was chairman, and others connected with it were the Reverend Edward Everett Hale and Robert Treat Paine, of Boston; Henry St. George Tucker, of Virginia, Andrew Carnegie, and myself. Resolutions were adopted recommending the negotiation of a treaty with Great Britain whereby all differences between us which might fail of adjustment through diplomatic channels were to be submitted for arbitration to the Permanent Court at The Hague. It was further recommended that we enter into like treaties with other powers as soon as practicable. We called on the President and the resolutions were presented by Mr. Tucker; Mr. Carnegie and I each made a few remarks, which the President in turn answered with a brief address. When he had finished and we were all standing around him, Mr. Carnegie said to him, "I have just been congratulating Mr. Straus on the compliments you paid him, and suggested that he get a copy of that portion of your remarks to preserve for his children and grandchildren." Roosevelt immediately turned to Mr. Loeb, his secretary, and instructed him to send to me that portion of his remarks, adding: "And I meant every word I said." I trust I may be pardoned for the egotism which prompts me to incorporate it in these memoirs:

I have had from Mr. Straus aid that I can not over-estimate, for which I can not too much express my gratitude, in so much of the diplomatic work that has arisen in this administration — aid by suggestion, aid by actual work in helping me to carry out the suggestions; and Mr. Straus was one of the two or three men who first set my mind, after I came in as President, in the direction of doing everything that could be done for the Hague Tribunal, as that seemed to be the best way to turn for arbitration.

At another pleasant luncheon there was present Alice, now the wife of Congressman Longworth, of Ohio, Roosevelt's daughter by his first wife. In the course of our discussion about the reciprocity treaty with Cuba and the making of more favorable tariff arrangements, I said: "We went to war with Spain for the liberation of Cuba, and now if we treat her step-motherly and starve her to death, what would the world say?" There was hearty laughter all round the table, and Miss Alice turned to me and said, in her naïve way and with a mischievous sparkle in her eyes: "Do I look starved?" The President had fairly exploded with laughter, and when I remarked that I had "put my foot into it," he added, amid another outburst, "Yes, both of them!"

The President did not smoke, but always served cigars and cigarettes to his guests. When I did not take one, he said, "Straus, you smoke."

"Yes," I answered, "but I certainly want to pay as much respect to you as I always did to the Sultan of Turkey. He did not drink, and I never took any when it was served."

"You go right ahead and smoke. If Root were here he would smoke and always does," replied Roosevelt.

After lunch that day, when the other guests had gone, he and I went into an adjoining room and had a general discussion — labor matters, the National Civic Federation, the Republican Party, etc., etc. He said he had received a number of requests to put into the Republican platform a plank protesting against the discrimination made by Russia against Americans of the Jewish faith. "You know," he said, "I am prepared to do anything that I can for all of our citizens regardless of race or creed, but unless we mean to do something further than simply protest it would look like an effort to catch votes, for such statements in the platform could not be regarded for any other purpose." He added he had in mind a different and more effective way of handling the subject when the time came. He said he remembered that I had never asked him to take action in this or any other question that was not justified on broad American principles, but that if anything arose which specially reflected upon the Jews he looked to me to bring it to his attention, and I was to regard that just as much my duty as the protection of American Christian interests in Turkey.

We spoke about the Russo-Japanese War, and I told him that some one had said that the Japs were yellow-skinned, but the Russians were yellow all the way through. This called forth a hearty laugh. Humor of any kind, provided it was clean, he always appreciated, and his own sense of it continually served, as it did for Lincoln, to lighten the seriousness of his duties.

Like Lincoln, too, Roosevelt combined with that balancing sense of humor an innate and always active sense of justice. Time and again in my relationship with him I have observed and admired it. I recall in this regard the case of an employee named Miller in the Government Printing Office, who was discharged because he did not belong to the union, and Roosevelt reinstated him. Mr. Gompers and several members of the Executive Committee of the American Federation of Labor thereupon called upon the President to protest against this reinstatement. They said his discharge was based on two points: that he was a non-union man, and also that he was an incapable worker. Roosevelt's answer was: "The question of his personal fitness is one to be settled in the routine of administrative detail, and cannot be allowed to conflict with or to complicate the larger question of governmental discrimination for or against him or any other man because he is or is not a member of a union. This is the only question now before me for decision; and as to this my decision is final."

As I was in constant touch with the President by correspondence and conferences, I wrote him telling of my gratification to find in his decision anent the Miller case such consonance in principle with his position regarding the anthracite coal strike, to which I received the following reply that brings out the point I have just made about his sense of justice:

WHITE HOUSE, WASHINGTON
October 1, 1903

MY DEAR MR. STRAUS:

I thank you heartily for your letter. When you can get on here I should like to tell you for your own information some of my experiences in connection with this Miller case. I feel exactly as you do — that my action was a complement to my action, for instance, in the anthracite coal strike, and that I could no more hesitate in the teeth of opposition from the labor unions in one case, than I could when the opposition came from the big monied men in the other case.

Sincerely yours
THEODORE ROOSEVELT

Perhaps no President has had a policy, with regard to labor, so wise and far-seeing as that of Roosevelt. Invariably he sought the counsel of labor leaders in matters affecting their interests, and always they were made to feel that redress for their just grievances, and their rights generally, were as much a concern of his and of his administration as any rights of the rich. In this connection I recall a remark of P. H. Morrissey, then head of the railroad train-men. We were seated in the Red Room of the White House for conference after dinner. There were present some thirty or more men prominently identified with labor, whom the President had invited to discuss labor legislation. Morrissey recalled one time several years before when he sat in front of the great fireplace in the Red Room waiting for the President; and he said he could not help reflecting what a long way it was from the cab of the locomotive engine to this stately room in the official residence of the President of the United States, an honor and a privilege that Roosevelt was the first President to give to men of labor.

On the same evening I saw in clear relief Roosevelt's wonderful tact, judgment, and understanding of men as I had never seen it displayed before. One or two of the labor leaders showed some bitterness in their criticism of certain legislation. Roosevelt showed frank approval of just complaints and allayed irritation in a most tactful way where the demand was unjust or unreasonable.

In the election of 1904 I took an active part and kept in close touch with Roosevelt. An unusual amount of bitterness characterized this campaign, though it was foreseen that Roosevelt would win by a large majority. In this connection I received a characteristic letter from him, dated at the White House October 15th:

I notice that various Democratic papers, including the Evening Post, have endeavored to show that I have appealed to the Jew vote, the Catholic vote, etc. Now the fact is that I have not appealed to any man as Jew, as Protestant, or as Catholic, but that I have as strongly as in me lies endeavored to make it evident that each is to have a square deal, no more and no less, without regard to his creed. I hope that this country will continue in substantially its present form of government for many centuries. If this is so it is reasonable to suppose that during that time there will be Presidents of Jewish faith, Presidents of Catholic faith. Now, my aim as President is to behave toward the Jew and the Catholic just as I should wish a Jewish or Catholic President to behave towards Protestants — in other words, to behave as a good American should behave toward all his fellow Americans, without regard to the several creeds they profess or the several lands from which their ancestors have sprung. Moreover, I am pleased at what Lebowich says at my not having a spirit of condescension or patronizing. I have enough of the old Adam in me to object almost as strongly to being patronized as to being wronged; and I do not intend knowingly to behave toward others in a manner which I should resent if it were adopted toward me.

These sentences bring to mind another and public statement of Roosevelt's in which he characterized Americanism; the occasion was an address at the unveiling of the Sheridan equestrian statue in Washington:

We should keep steadily before our minds the fact that Americanism is a question of principle, of purpose, of idealism, of character; that it is not a matter of birthplace, or creed, or line of descent.

Here in this country the representatives of many old-world races are being fused together into a new type, a type the main features of which are already determined, and were determined at the time of the Revolutionary War; for the crucible in which all the new types are melted into one was shaped from 1776 to 1789, and our nationality was definitely fixed in all its essentials by the men of Washington's day.

Soon after the election he invited me to come to the White House for dinner one evening and to spend the night; there were a number of things he wanted to talk over with me. When I arrived I found Dr. Lyman Abbott and his son Ernest had been similarly invited, and there were additional guests for dinner: Attorney-General Moody, Senator Knox, Secretary of War Taft, and James

R. Garfield, chief of the Bureau of Corporations in the Department of Commerce and Labor.

At dinner the President announced that we had come together to do some business, and he produced from his pocket a slip of paper on which were noted the several subjects he wished to consider with us, mainly things to be incorporated in his forthcoming Message to Congress. First there was the negro question. The South had vilified him because he entertained Booker Washington and appointed Crum Collector of the Port at Charleston. When Congress assembled, one of the things he intended doing was to send in again the name of Crum for confirmation. "The Southerners either do not or do not wish to understand it," he said; adding that his position plainly was that he would do everything in his power for the white man South without, however, doing a wrong or an injustice to the colored man. He was sympathetic with the South, for he was half Southerner himself, his mother having come from Roswell, Georgia. His remarks on this topic were directed mainly to Dr. Abbott.

The conversation then turned to the recent election and became very general, every one joining and relating instances or experiences in connection with it. Mr. Taft, who had waged a vigorous campaign for the Administration, told a joke on himself: he had received a letter from Wayne MacVeagh saying that so far as he (MacVeagh) could see, Taft's speeches did not do any harm.

When the talk had gone along these general lines for a while, Roosevelt interjected with "Now we must get back to business," and proceeded to discuss the diplomatic service in relation to his Message. He thought civil service too strictly applied would be detrimental, as we had a great deal of old timber there that should be gotten rid of.

Next he took up a discussion of Panama. Mr. Taft with several others was to leave next day on a mission there to look into the difficulties between the native army and the President of Panama, and some one humorously suggested that he had better go down and take away the weapons from the army and let them muster as much as they wanted to without weapons.

After dinner we adjourned to the President's study on the floor above. He sat down at his desk and pulled open a drawer as he said: "I want to read to you incomplete drafts of portions of my Message which I should like to have you criticize, as on some of the subjects I have not yet fully made up my mind." The Message was in separate parts, each dealing with an important subject. He took up the part dealing with our foreign relations, in regard to Russia and Roumania, and addressed me, saying he would like me to pay special attention to that as he had consulted me all along concerning the action to be taken. He said our Government had been criticized as interfering with the internal affairs of other nations, and the statement had been repeatedly made that we should not like it if other nations took us to task for our negro lynchings in the South; but he argued that the lynchings were comparatively few, and, though bad enough, were nothing compared to the wholesale murder in cold blood under official sanction and perhaps instigation, as in Kishineff. "My answer to all these criticisms is this," he said; "only a short time ago I received a remonstrance or petition from a society in Great Britain regarding the lynchings in this country. I did not reject it; on the contrary, I answered it most politely and expressed my great regret for these unlawful, unjustifiable acts, with which neither I nor the Government had any sympathy. On the contrary the Government does everything in its power to

prevent these outrages and unlawful acts. And I author-
ize any one to make use of this information whenever the
occasion presents itself."

To the labor question also he wanted me to pay special
attention because of my experience with such matters
and in the arbitration of labor disputes. He began with
the statement that he was in favor of organized capital
and organized labor. I asked him whether right at that
point I might make a suggestion, which was that he begin
with the general subject of capital and labor, because
organized labor did not comprise more than fifteen per
cent of the wage-earners of the country. This suggestion
he accepted.

Roosevelt then expressed himself in favor of the eight-
hour law. Messrs. Moody, Knox, Taft, and myself did
not agree with his statement in the form he had it. We
explained that there were several bills before Congress
on the subject, some of which had passed the lower house,
but were defeated in the Senate; that it was all right for
the Government in its own yards to adopt an eight-hour
day, but when it gave out contracts to other shops, while
it had a right to say that the work upon that contract
should be done by eight-hour days, it had no right to require work on other contracts to be done in eight-hour
days. When we had discussed the subject quite thoroughly, it was agreed to omit it from the Message.

Next he took up the trust question. He said Mr. Garfield had several suggestions to offer for making the interstate commerce law effective. It was generally agreed
that the law as originally passed fully provided the remedy that was intended, but it had been emasculated by
the decisions of the Supreme Court. Messrs. Knox, Taft,
and Moody referred to several of these decisions and
pointed out that the railroads, under subterfuge of

switches and free cars — cars that were furnished by such shippers as the beef trust — got completely around the law. They allowed a mileage charge for the supply of these cars in excess of what should be allowed, and under such cover it amounted to a rebate to those shippers and was a complete circumvention of the law. Garfield's suggestion was that the interstate commerce corporations be compelled to obtain a license or charter from the National Government to do business. We thoroughly discussed this, but it was disapproved as being an interference with the legal rights of States, and that therefore no such law could be passed by Congress. The President then turned to the legal members of our group and said, "Now here is a great wrong and you lawyers have always got a way of preventing us from reaching a remedy."

Knox created a laugh by replying, "The President wants us as usual to jump over the Supreme Court."

The work on the Message done, Roosevelt said it was his intention to go South and make a few speeches. He would begin at San Antonio and would visit Tuskegee and Sewanee Colleges, for he wanted his views in regard to the South and the negro question fully understood. He read us a draft along the lines of thought he wanted to present, quoting much from Lincoln, which seemed highly to the point. When some one mentioned the curtailing of suffrage so as to have it based upon educational qualifications and property ownership, the President said it would not be wise to agitate that subject, and that herein Booker Washington agreed with him; but, he added, "There is something inherently wrong about a Southern member representing in some instances only a quarter of the number of votes that an Eastern member represents, and having an equal vote with him in Congress."

It was half after midnight when our little company

separated. The President then suggested to Dr. Abbott and me that we meet at 8.15 breakfast, if we did not object to having this meal with him and the children. In the absence of Mrs. Roosevelt, who had gone to New York, the President next morning took the head of the table, and with the coffee urn before him served us each with our coffee, cream, and sugar. There were Teddy, Ethel, Kermit, Archie, and Quentin, the governess, the tutor, besides Dr. Abbott, his son, and myself. After the meal we strolled in the park back of the White House until 9.30, when the President left for his work-room in the new office building west of the White House.

I did not see Roosevelt again for several months. One day in May I took lunch with him upon his return from Chicago where he had had a conference with the representatives of the labor unions who were carrying on the teamster's strike that paralyzed the commerce of the city. He said he had received through his secretary my memorandum regarding an adjustment of the trouble, and that it was of great assistance to him in discussing the situation and coming to some equitable arrangement. He was preparing a Message for an extra session of Congress in October, and said he would send me parts of it, especially those referring to immigration and the Far East, for my advice and suggestion.

In 1905, when Roosevelt was busy with negotiations to bring peace between Russia and Japan, I received a letter from him stating that he had endeavored to get these two nations to go to The Hague, but Russia was most reluctant and Japan positively refused; nor would they go to either Paris or Chefoo, but they were both willing to come to Washington. In his own "Autobiography," which I never tire of reading, Roosevelt gives an interesting sketch of his mediation between these two countries which finally brought about the conference and treaty at Portsmouth, New Hampshire.

Count Sergius Witte, head of the Russian mission to Portsmouth, was desirous of meeting some of the representative Jews of our country with a view to seeking what might practicably be done to improve the condition of the Jews in the Russian Empire. While it was said that his wife was a Jewess, his interest in the Jewish question was perhaps primarily to improve the relations between Russia and the United States. The Russian massacres, with the resultant enforced emigration, the public meetings of protest in this country and the press comments, had seriously prejudiced public opinion here against Russia.

The Count therefore invited a committee to confer with him and Baron Rosen at Portsmouth. There were Jacob H. Schiff, Isaac N. Seligman, Adolph Kraus, Adolf Lewisohn, and myself. The Count admitted with much frankness the condition of the Jewish population of Russia, and that it was an injustice. He expressed his purpose to exert his best influence to remedy the just grievances of the oppressed Jews. We assured him that we asked for no special privileges for our co-religionists, but the same, and no greater, rights for them than were accorded other Russian subjects; that the granting of such rights would relieve Russia of the Jewish question and of the international ill-will to which this question naturally and rightly gave rise. Both the Count and Baron Rosen agreed with us, but argued that it was not practicable to grant such complete emancipation, but that it should come about gradually. We told them, of course, that with that premise we could not and would not agree.

The Count was very much impressed with our pres-

entation of the subject, and our statements were cor-
roborated by his own observations later when he made a
visit to the lower East Side of New York where he spoke
with a number of the Russian-Jewish immigrants. He
said that upon his return to Russia he would at once take
up the problem with a view ultimately to secure equal
rights for the Jewish subjects, that he realized the necessity for this not only from a humanitarian standpoint,
but from the standpoint of Russia's best interests and
of her relations with the leading nations of the world,
particularly with the United States.

Before going to Portsmouth on Count Witte's invitation, I conferred with Roosevelt. He wanted me in an
unofficial capacity to observe carefully the progress of
the negotiations and keep him advised. Just at that time
it looked as if the conference might break up, and before
that stage was actually reached he wanted to be notified,
for he would probably have a communication to make
to the commissioners. On arriving at Portsmouth I had
a confidential talk with Fedor Fedorovich Martens, the
great Russian international jurist, who was one of my
fellow members at the Hague Tribunal, and with whom
I had been in personal touch on several previous occasions. He was legal adviser to the Russian delegation. I
apprised him of what I knew to be the desire of the President, and he agreed that if a break became imminent, a
communication such as the President would send would
be likely to have the right influence, and he would see
to it that, should the necessity arise for such a message,
Roosevelt should be promptly informed. I advised the
President of my understanding with Martens, but fortunately no rupture occurred and the terms of peace were
agreed upon.

In his "Autobiography" Roosevelt says, with regard

to these Portsmouth negotiations: "I had certainly tried
my best to be the friend not only of the Japanese people
but of the Russian people, and I believe that what I did
was for the best interests of both and of the world at
large." He refers with characteristic generosity to the
help given him at St. Petersburg by our ambassador,
George von Lengerke Meyer, who "rendered literally
invaluable aid by insisting upon himself seeing the Czar
at critical periods of the transaction, when it was no
longer possible for me to act successfully through the
representatives of the Czar, who were often at cross-
purposes with one another."

And when the Portsmouth Conference was over, the
President further took a deep interest in bringing about
amelioration of the condition of the Jews in Russia.
When Count Witte came to New York, Roosevelt wrote
him the following letter, of which he sent me a copy:

OYSTER BAY, N.Y.
September 10, 1905

MY DEAR MR. WITTE:

. . . In furtherance of our conversation of last evening I beg
you to consider the question of granting passports to reputable
American citizens of Jewish faith. I feel that if this could be
done it would remove the last cause of irritation between the
two nations whose historic friendship for one another I wish to
do my best to maintain. You could always refuse to give a
passport to any American citizen, Jew or Gentile, unless you
were thoroughly satisfied that no detriment would come to
Russia in granting it. But if your Government could only see
its way clear to allowing reputable American citizens of Jewish
faith, as to whose intentions they are satisfied, to come to
Russia, just as you do reputable American Christians, I feel
it would be from every standpoint most fortunate.

Again assuring you of my high regard, and renewing my congratulations to you and to your country upon the peace that has
been obtained, believe me,

Sincerely yours
THEODORE ROOSEVELT

Early in 1906, when the Algeciras Conference regarding Morocco was in session, and the press reported that it was likely to break up without an agreement on account of Germany's attitude, Carl Schurz, knowing of my close relationship with Roosevelt, wrote to me that the President could probably prevail upon the Powers concerned to refer the question to the Hague Tribunal. This letter I forwarded to Roosevelt; but although he was ever ready to vitalize the machinery of the Hague Tribunal, advice coming from Mr. Schurz at this time was not regarded with favor, possibly because of their previous differences. In his reply to me, however, the President showed what a clear and prophetic insight he had into Germany's attitude and purposes:

Modern Germany is alert, aggressive, military and industrial. It thinks it is a match for England and France combined in war, and would probably be less reluctant to fight both those powers together than they would be together to fight it. It despises the Hague Conference and the whole Hague idea. It respects the United States only in so far as it believes that our navy is efficient and that if sufficiently wronged or insulted we would fight. Now I like and respect Germany, but I am not blind to the fact that Germany does not reciprocate the feeling. I want us to do everything we can to stay on good terms with Germany, but I would be a fool if I were blind to the fact that Germany will not stay in with us if we betray weakness. As for this particular case, when I see you next I shall tell you all that I have done and you will see that I have been using my very best efforts for peace.

In all my relations with Roosevelt, even before I became a member of his Cabinet, I was more and more convinced that no consideration of political self-interest or partisan advantage ever entered his mind in determining his attitude or action in upholding the right or dethroning a wrong. He resented nothing more than when some politician or inconsiderate person made an appeal to him for action on the plea that it would be good politics. He was visioned, but not visionary; and withal highly practical, in that he understood the workings and tendencies of human forces. Just as he would read a book by absorbing a page at a glance, so he would instinctively appraise his fellow men; their qualities would impress him just as a brilliant paragraph in a book would arrest his instant attention.

Roosevelt would not make an idle gesture or even imply a threat which he did not purpose to carry into action. He was more abused by those whom he designated as "the interests," and better understood and trusted by the masses, than any President in our history with the exception of Lincoln. So it is always with real leaders, who seek to guide rather than pander to public opinion. The latter course appeals to weak though well-intentioned public men; the former requires not only clear vision but high courage, and these qualities Roosevelt possessed to an extraordinary degree.

CHAPTER VIII

INDUSTRIAL DIPLOMACY

Trade unions and federated unions — Formation of the National Civic Federation — Notable industrial disputes are settled — Andrew Carnegie dines with fighting labor leaders — Marcus Hanna, general of industry — My chairmanship of the Board of Railway Labor Arbitration — Our findings and recommendations — My chairmanship of the New York Public Service Commission — Military necessities impinge upon industrial relations — The President's Industrial Conference of 1919-20.

WHEN our industries were small, a strong human tie bound together employer and worker. Following the expansion which began after the Civil War, our industries resolved themselves into vast organizations and corporations, and the relations between employer and worker became more and more impersonal. The workers first organized into trade unions, which presently expanded into federated unions similar to those which a generation before had begun to be formed in Great Britain.

The rapid growth of our industries and the impersonal relations between employer and employed made it apparent that social justice required that reciprocal rights be recognized in order to bring about a better understanding of a relationship which had already become increasingly strained and often embittered, resulting in serious strikes and lock-outs. One of the first organizations to meet this need was formed in Chicago in 1894, following the Pullman strike. It was called the Civic Federation of Chicago and was under the leadership of a number of prominent men of that city, directed by Ralph M. Easley.

Six years later the scope of this organization was enlarged, and in the name of the National Civic Federation a conference was called in Chicago, in December, 1900, and the debate centered round the proposition that in American industries voluntary conciliation was preferable to compulsory arbitration. At that conference a committee was selected whose duty it was to collect information at home and abroad regarding measures of arbitration, and to advise with employers and workmen in this country whenever and wherever possible.

In the following December, 1901, the National Civic Federation held a conference in New York in the rooms of the New York Board of Trade and Transportation. I was then president of that Board and was asked to preside at the conference. After adjourning the sessions, we organized the industrial department of the Federation, with a committee of twelve men representing the public, twelve men representing employers, and twelve men representing wage-earners. These three groups were headed, respectively, by Grover Cleveland, Marcus A. Hanna, and Samuel Gompers. All of their colleagues were men of national distinction and were recognized leaders in their fields. From this larger committee of thirty-six, an executive committee of five was selected, whose members were as follows: Marcus A. Hanna, chairman; Samuel Gompers, first vice-president; I, second vice-president; Charles A. Moore, treasurer; and Ralph M. Easley, secretary.

The scope and plan of the industrial department was to promote industrial peace in whatever way might seem best. We planned for a large meeting in May, when two public sessions were to be held, one at Cooper Union and one in the rooms of the New York Chamber of Commerce. We issued a statement of our plan and scope and inaugurated a broad educational campaign.

Meanwhile our department proved itself most practical. It actively helped settle several disputes, notably the

Albany street-car strike, the disagreement between the National Metal Trades Association and the International Association of Machinists, and the United States steel strike. And it was instrumental in averting the threatened anthracite coal strike.

The identical ideal that I held up in my opening address at the meeting in January, 1901, I should hold up to-day: namely, that industrial peace, to be permanent, cannot rest upon force, but must rest upon justice, and in essential industries especially, upon a high sense of responsibility to the public by both employer and employed. In no other country are conditions, by nature and by principles of government, better adapted to the equitable adjustment of the reciprocal rights, duties, and privileges of labor and capital than in our own, because we are a democratic people with no fixed class distinctions to separate us. The laborer of to-day may be the capitalist of to-morrow, and *vice versa*. Capital and labor are interdependent, not opponents; and it is on the basis of that dependency that adjustments in the relationship between them must be made. This ideal is, happily, more widely recognized to-day than it was when the National Civic Federation was organized.

I gave considerable attention to the work of the Federation for a number of years. As the offices were in New York and the president and first vice-president were both resident in other cities, the direction of the organization between conferences largely fell upon me as second vice-president, with the important assistance of the secretary, Mr. Easley.

The Federation afforded a neutral forum where, under the chairmanship of one of its officers, the disputants could discuss their grievances and arrive at an understanding. Many times the growing bitterness between them was checked and a strike or lock-out averted. The fact was often borne in upon me how many of these industrial disputes grew out of misunderstandings which were cleared away when men assembled around a table and frankly discussed their differences.

To further the work and interests of the Federation I brought together in social relationship, at several dinners at my home, the representatives of all three groups; namely, the public, the wage-earner, and the employer. One day Andrew Carnegie expressed the desire to meet the labor leaders who had instigated the strike in the Carnegie works which resulted in the Homestead riots. Accordingly I arranged a dinner, to which I invited a number of the men of the labor wing of the Federation, as well as some others of the committee, together with Messrs. Wighe and Schaeffer, of Pittsburgh, officers of the Amalgamated Union, who had led the Homestead strike.

Carnegie knew these leaders well, and they knew him. He called them by their Christian names and they called him "Andy." They said that night that they and their colleagues in the union had always believed that that strike and riot would never have taken place had "Andy" been present. As a matter of fact, Carnegie's relations with his men had always been very friendly. He was unjustly accused of the responsibility for the Homestead riots, which might not have occurred had he, instead of Mr. Frick, been in charge of the employers' side. Mr. Carnegie at the time was in Scotland.

Only a short while before this Carnegie dinner, Marcus Hanna had died, and our executive committee offered to Mr. Carnegie the presidency of the Federation, to succeed Mr. Hanna. Mr. Carnegie was gratified and very much touched, especially by the implied confidence on the part of the twelve labor men of the Federation; but on account of his advanced years he felt that he could not give the position the attention it deserved. He was, however, glad to become a member of the executive committee, and as such revealed himself in a most favorable light. Beneath his Scotch nimbleness of mind there was a broad, tolerant, and lovable heart. He met the laboring men, not as their superior, but as one having a genuine brotherly interest in their welfare. It became very evident to us all why he was so highly regarded by his workmen, and why he had so much influence with them: they trusted to his fairness and had a real affection for him personally. In his Autobiography he makes feeling reference to his connection with the Federation.

Marcus Hanna, who was known to the country chiefly through his political activities, was looked upon as the leader of a group of rich men who had won political power by commercializing our political system; and was regarded by many as an evil influence. But in connection with the great industrial interests that he had built up in Ohio and elsewhere — coal mines, iron works, shipping, street railways — little was known of him. He had shown great capacity as an industrial general in the management of his men, winning their good-will by fair and equitable treatment; and it is said he never had a strike in the industries he administered. He was highly regarded by the labor leaders, who had confidence in his fairness to the wage-earners. He did not oppose, as did so many of the employers of his time, the organization of labor unions. On the contrary, he believed that such organizations were necessary adequately to protect the rights of the workers.

As chairman of the executive committee of the Civic Federation, Hanna displayed this better side of his character and his great ability as an organizer and a leader. Here he was not the cunning politician, but the genial head of an industry who recognized the just demands of the wage-earners and was always generous with them in regard to compensation and labor conditions.

The work we did and the experiences we encountered as officers of the Federation, each group coming into close contact with the others and adjusting with them industrial differences, had a decided educational value for us all. For myself, the study I gave during these years to the relations between capital and labor, and my active part in the conciliation and arbitration of labor disputes, provided me with an intensely practical background and preparation for the secretaryship of the Department of Commerce and Labor, which later fell to my lot. It was this experience and my personal acquaintance with the representatives of capital and labor all over the country that induced me, as head of that Department, to organize the Council of Commerce and to plan the Council of Labor, to both of which I shall refer more specifically later.

The Board of Railway Labor Arbitration of 1912 was perhaps the most important labor arbitration body brought into existence up to that time. Its decisions affected the whole Eastern district: that is, that section of our country lying east of Chicago and East St. Louis, and north of the Ohio River to Parkersburg, West Virginia, and of the Potomac River to its mouth. Fifty-two railroad lines and over thirty-one thousand engineers were involved. The latter negotiated through the Brotherhood of Locomotive Engineers.

The representatives of the Brotherhood and the members of the Conference Committee of Managers of the railroads held several conferences in March, 1912, at which the Brotherhood made certain requests. The conferences ended with the refusal of the roads to grant these requests or any part of them, whereupon ninety-three per cent of the members voted for a strike. Charles P. Neill, United States Commissioner of Labor, and Judge Martin A. Knapp, of the United States Commerce Court, tendered their friendly offices under the Erdman Act, but were unable to mediate, and the contending parties would not agree to arbitrate under the provisions of the Erdman Act. It was then decided to submit the dispute to a board of arbitration composed of seven members, one to be chosen by each side, and those two to agree on the other five within fifteen days of their own appointment.

The roads chose Daniel Willard, president of the Baltimore and Ohio Railroad, and the Brotherhood chose P. H. Morrissey, former grand master of the Brotherhood of Railroad Trainmen. At the end of fifteen days, these two had not succeeded in agreeing upon the other five members of the board, though they had agreed upon a list from which the five might be chosen. A committee consisting of Mr. Neill, Judge Knapp, and Chief Justice White, of the Supreme Court of the United States, then chose five names from that list, and the final personnel of the board was as follows: Dr. Charles R. Van Hise, of Madison, Wisconsin; Frederick N. Judson, of St. Louis; Dr. Albert Shaw, Otto M. Eidlitz, and myself, of New York, in addition to Mr. Morrissey and Mr. Willard.

On July 12th the board met and organized, electing me as chairman. The decisions of the board were to be binding for one year and thereafter could be terminated by either side upon a thirty days' notice. For two weeks we held hearings, morning and afternoon, at the Oriental Hotel, Manhattan Beach, New York. When the hearings were

MEMBERS OF THE RAILWAY BOARD OF ARBITRATION

From left to right: Standing: Daniel Willard, Otto M. Eidlitz, Albert Shaw, P.H. Morrissey
Sitting: Charles R. Van Hise, Oscar S. Straus, Frederick N. Judson

over, the board adjourned until early September, when the work of making the awards was begun. Because of my nomination for Governor by the Progressive Party at the time, I found it advisable to relinquish the chairmanship of the board to Dr. Van Hise, although I continued my membership and active interest to the end.

The hearings were reported and consisted of 1250 pages of testimony. The questions that confronted the board were not alone whether or not the wages in a given case should be raised, but, if it was found that the rate was inadequate, by what margin should it be increased? It was fairly difficu t to arrive at principles of standardization applicable to so many roads, and to fix a basis of differentiation for the many and complicated branches of employment. The whole subject, however, had our most careful and painstaking consideration. We took up the whole intricate problem of the running of railroads, with relation to the several kinds of work performed by the engineers, in passenger service, freight service, in switching, and in yard work, bearing in mind always that railways were public utilities and that the necessities and comfort of the whole people depended upon their functioning; and that therefore the necessity for uninterrupted service far transcended the interests of either the roads on the one side or the employees on the other.

Our decisions as finally printed made a book of one hundred and twenty-three pages. One of our chief recommendations was that National and State wage commissions be created which should function in relation to labor engaged in public utilities as the public service commissions functioned toward capital. I quote from the report:

Especially for the public utilities is it important that labor should have a just wage, and if the existing wages are not adequate, they should be increased. If a just increase in wages places the public utilities in a position that does not enable them to secure a fair return upon capital invested and maintain a proper reserve, they should be allowed to increase their rates until they are in that position.

Another point upon which we laid stress was the limitation of the right to strike:

While it is clear from the public point of view that a concerted strike of railway employees for a great region would be as intolerable as a strike of the postal clerks; on the other hand, the position of the employees is a very natural one. They feel under existing conditions that the power to strike is their only weapon of defense against employers and the only means by which they can enforce a betterment of their conditions of service. They realize, too, that the principle of concerted action, for all the railroads in a great section of the country, gives them a most effective weapon, and they are naturally loath to relinquish or impair it.

While this is the situation under the present conditions, and the railway employees feel that they cannot surrender their right to strike, the necessity would no longer exist for the exercise of this power, if there were a wage commission which would secure them just wages.

Finally, it is the belief of the Board that in the last analysis the only solution — unless we are to rely solely upon the restraining power of public opinion — is to qualify the principle of free contract in the railroad service. A strike in the army or navy is mutiny and universally punished as such. The same principle is applied to seamen because of the public necessity involved. A strike among postal clerks, as among the teachers of our public schools, would be unthinkable. In all these cases, the employment, to borrow a legal phrase, is affected with a public use; and this of necessity qualifies the right of free concerted action which exists in private employments.

However, if the principle be accepted that there are certain classes of service thus affected with a public interest and men who enter them are not free concertedly to quit the service, then these men must be guarded in the matter of wages and conditions by public protection; and this it is believed can best be done through an interstate wage commission.

The report was signed by six members of the board, Mr. Willard adding an explanatory statement. Mr. Morrissey wrote a dissenting opinion. For a number of years the findings of this board, with slight alterations, continued to be effective in adjusting wages for the different kinds of service among the engineers, and in governing conditions and number of working hours of the employees.

The President's Industrial Conference of 1919–20, of which I was a member, was of value chiefly in that it correlated the best ideas in practice throughout the country with regard to the prevention and relief of industrial unrest and the betterment in general of the relationship between employer and employee, and that it published suggestions based on these ideas, of which the main points were the following:

1. The parties to the dispute may voluntarily submit their differences for settlement to a board, known as a Regional Adjustment Conference. This board consists of four representatives selected by the parties, and four others in their industry chosen by them and familiar with their problems. The board is presided over by a trained government official, the regional chairman, who acts as a conciliator. If a unanimous agreement is reached, it results in a collective bargain having the same effect as if reached by joint organization in the shop.

2. If the Regional Conference fails to agree unanimously, the matter, with certain restrictions, goes, under the agreement of submission, to the National Industrial Board, unless the parties prefer the decision of an umpire selected by them.

3. The voluntary submission to a Regional Adjustment Conference carries with it an agreement by both parties that there shall be no interference with production pending the processes of adjustment.

4. If the parties, or either of them, refuse voluntarily to submit the dispute to the processes of the plan of adjustment, a

Regional Board of Inquiry is formed by the regional chairman, of two employers and two employees from the industry, and not parties to the dispute. This Board has the right, under proper safeguards, to subpœna witnesses and records, and the duty to publish its findings as a guide to public opinion.

5. The National Industrial Board in Washington has general oversight of the working of the plan.

6. The plan is applicable also to public utilities, but in such cases, the government agency, having power to regulate the service, has two representatives in the Adjustment Conference. Provision is made for prompt report of its findings to the rate regulating body. The Conference makes no recommendation of a plan to cover steam railroads and other carriers, for which legislation has recently been enacted by Congress. (Esch-Cummins Bill.)

7. The plan provides machinery for prompt and fair adjustment of wages and working conditions of government employees. It is especially necessary for this class of employees, who should not be permitted to strike.

8. The plan involves no penalties other than those imposed by public opinion. It does not impose compulsory arbitration. It does not deny the right to strike. It does not submit to arbitration the policy of the "closed" or "open" shop.

9. The plan is national in scope and operation, yet it is decentralized. It is different from anything in operation elsewhere. It is based upon American experience and is designed to meet American conditions. It employs no legal authority except the right of inquiry. Its basic idea is stimulation to settlement of differences by the parties in conflict, and the enlistment of public opinion toward enforcing that method of settlement.

Unfortunately nothing came of the painstaking work of this conference beyond the publishing of its final report of March 6, 1920.

The chairmanship of the New York Public Service Commission did not at all appeal to me when first Governor Whitman offered it to me. The commission as it

then existed had unfortunately lost public confidence to
a large extent, and I felt that it was not the kind of service
for which I was especially qualified. However, it was
pointed out to me that there was constant danger of
strikes on the part of the thousands of workmen engaged
in the construction of subway and elevated extensions,
and an added appeal was made to me in view of the considerable experience I had had in adjusting labor difficulties. And so, after declining, I was finally prevailed
upon by the Governor and the late George W. Perkins,
in December, 1915, to accept this arduous duty.

As soon as it became known that I had accepted the
chairmanship, the Governor received a communication
from William Henry Hodge, the distinguished engineer,
announcing his willingness to serve on the commission,
although before my selection he had refused such appointment. The other members of the commission were:
Charles E. Hervey, William Hayward, and Traverse H.
Whitney. Messrs. Hayward and Hodge left the commission, when we entered the war, to join the army. Mr.
Hayward was commissioned Colonel, having organized
the 15th New York, afterward the 369th United States
Infantry, a regiment of colored men who performed gal-
lant service in France. Mr. Hodge was commissioned
Major and was promoted to Lieutenant-Colonel, and
gave his splendid talents to the services of his country in
building roads to the battle fronts of France. Due to his
strenuous labors over there, this gifted engineer and
exemplary patriot died shortly after the armistice.

The commission had charge of the building of the sub-
ways and elevated lines then in process, as well as the
regulation of traffic and all public utilities. As the war
progressed, it became clearer that our country would
inevitably be drawn in, and therefore increasingly im-

portant that nothing should prevent the functioning of our public utilities. And accordingly it was not long before my services as adjuster and arbitrator of labor difficulties were needed. The cost of living was rapidly rising, and there was great unrest among laborers; and the demand for skilled and unskilled labor grew day by day. When our country entered the war, it was highly important for the moral effect upon our own people, as well as to avoid giving encouragement to our enemies, that the transportation system of our greatest metropolis should operate without interruption. During the following year and a half I was able to adjust a dozen or more important labor disputes and to prevent a number of strikes. The situation was complicated by the fact that the laborers were not employees of the commission, but of the several contractors to whom contracts had been awarded under conditions of fierce competition, so that every increase in wages materially affected their profits and in the end caused many of them to suffer considerable loss. I had to appeal to the patriotism of both sides, and it is a pleasure to be able to state that in every instance the response was most gratifying.

CHAPTER IX

IN THE CABINET

BEFORE I became a member of President Roosevelt's official family, I was in what he termed his "kitchen cabinet." My experiences in both cabinets are among the treasured recollections of my life.

We were the unofficial advisers who met round the luncheon and dinner table and afterwards in the White House study, where the President spoke without reserve of his executive problems and read for our criticism and counsel his rough drafts of congressional messages, speeches, and notes to foreign governments.

Holding no portfolios of state, these "kitchen cabinet ministers" yet gave of their best; were always prepared to toil to any extent to be of assistance to the President. He had the quality of vitalizing things — a situation or condition coming within his executive ken became so charged with life and imagination that men wanted to put their hands and minds to it. They served Roosevelt as energetically and loyally as if the grave responsibilities of state were upon their own shoulders.

International relations and labor arbitration were the public activities which interested me most. The President had appointed me a member of the permanent board of arbitration at The Hague to succeed the late Benjamin Harrison, and shortly thereafter in his charming manner had designated me as a member of his "kitchen cabinet." Thus there had commenced for me a memorable series of conferences.

There is much misapprehension regarding Roosevelt's so-called impulsiveness. This was evident to those who had an intimate view of the man at work. He was quick. He was a prodigious worker. He was so constituted and so self-trained that he had to do things immediately, get them out of the way. What people called his impulsiveness might have been more aptly termed his preparedness.

I had hundreds of opportunities to observe his methods. When he accepted an invitation to deliver an address or write an article, he would prepare it immediately, even if the occasion were two, three, or six months off. He revised considerably, showed his work freely to friends and associates for criticisms, but completed it at the earliest opportunity. He never waited. This method served to perfect his thought and expression on a given subject. His promptness left him free for other things.

The President never seemed to be hurried, though he always worked with a wonderful driving force. He seemed never to waste any time. It was play or work, and both with his whole heart.

His public addresses were almost invariably the result

of preparation. It was seldom that he spoke extemporaneously. The fire and animation which he imparted in the delivery of his speeches certainly conveyed no impression that they might have been carefully prepared and considered at a desk in a study. The pages of his manuscript were so small and inconspicuous that they did not interfere with his natural gestures. The effect was almost as if he spoke extemporaneously. The written address, printed on sheets about 3 × 6 inches, and held in one hand, was completely lost sight of by the audience in those moments when Colonel Roosevelt became emphatic. In those moments he also interspersed extemporaneous remarks which brought out his arguments more vividly and forcefully.

I stopped in Washington and called on President Roosevelt, early in January of 1906, on my return from a short vacation in the South. He took me into his private room, where we found his personal and political friend, James H. Sheffield, and Senator Spooner. He spoke about the political changes in New York, the defeat of the machine in that State, the election of Herbert Parsons as chairman of the County Committee, and of young Wadsworth (now United States Senator), son-in-law of John Hay, as Speaker of the House. He took a special delight in the election of both of these men; he had a high regard for them personally and for what they stood. He said he had written a letter to Parsons which he hoped would be helpful to him.

The President asked me to come to lunch with him, which was another of those delightful, informal meetings. Besides Mrs. Roosevelt, his daughter Alice, and her fiancé, there were William Dudley Foulke, a former colleague of the President on the Civil Service Commission and friend of mine from my college days; Robert Hitt son of Congressman Hitt; and Lieutenant Fortesque, an officer of the Rough Riders.

After luncheon, the President asked me to wait for him in the Red Room, as he wanted to have a talk with me. When the other guests had departed, he came back to me and with his face beaming with geniality he said: "I don't know whether you know it or not, but I want you to become a member of my Cabinet. I have a very high estimate of your character, your judgment, and your ability, and I want you for personal reasons. There is still a further reason: I want to show Russia and some other countries what we think of the Jews in this country."

Of course I was gratified, very much gratified. I told him I had heard from several persons that he had spoken of this intention, but that I had meant to take no notice of it until he should speak to me about it; that I should certainly esteem it the very highest honor to become a member of the Cabinet, and especially to have the privilege of working alongside of him.

"I knew you would feel just that way; therefore I was anxious to let you know of my intention as long in advance as possible," replied the President. He said all this in such a cordial and affectionate manner that I was profoundly touched with this manifestation of close friendship for me.

He then added that he could not see that it would do any good, and might do harm, to make further protests or utterances regarding the massacres in Russia under the disorganized conditions there; and he did not want to do anything that might sound well here and have just the opposite effect there. He thought it would be much more pointed evidence of our Government's interest if he put a man like me into his Cabinet, and that such a course would doubtless have a greater influence than any words with the countries in which unreasonable discrimination and prejudice prevailed.

He told me that it might be July or even later before he could carry out his purpose. He would prefer to put me at the head of the Department of Commerce and Labor, because of my knowledge in that field, but he could not determine the specific position until later. But at any rate, I was to regard my appointment to one of the Cabinet positions as certain.

He asked whether I knew Senator Platt, and indicated that it might be well for several of my friends to have a talk with the Senator. But he quickly added that it would make no difference to him whether it suited the New York Senator or not, though it might perhaps be a little more agreeable if I did not have the latter's opposition. I preferred to feel that my selection was personal, which it really was, and without even the semblance of political influence; so I did not ask any of my friends to speak to Senator Platt, nor did I think he would oppose me.

My wife and the rest of my family were of course elated at hearing the news, particularly my brother Isidor, whose attitude toward me, his youngest brother, was always more like that of an affectionate father than a brother. I felt no trepidation, especially should I be selected for the Department of Commerce and Labor. My past training and interest in many of the subjects that came up under that department made me conversant with the main questions it had to administer.

Upon my return to New York I began to make arrangements for severing all business connections. This I thought wise, particularly if I became head of the Department of Commerce and Labor. It was not a necessary step, but I wanted it never to be said that I advocated any measure or made any decision that might in the remotest way be of advantage to my private interests. I spoke to Roosevelt about my intention, and he said that while it was not essential, if I could do so it would on the whole be advisable; that situated similarly he would do the same thing himself. Before assuming office, therefore, I had retired from business for good, and I have not since that time been connected with any business for personal profit.

My nomination was officially made in September, but it was not until early December, 1906, that I received a letter from William Loeb, Jr., the President's secretary, notifying me that the President desired me to assume office on December 17th. On that day, accordingly, I appeared at 9 A.M. at the Department of Commerce and Labor, then located in the Willard Building across the street from the Hotel Willard on Fourteenth Street. There I met my predecessor, Victor H. Metcalf, who had been appointed Secretary of the Navy. Mr. Metcalf welcomed me in a brief address and introduced me to the twelve bureau and five division chiefs of the department.

The Department of Commerce and Labor was the youngest of the nine departments of the Government, the bill creating it having been approved by President Roosevelt on February 14, 1903. Roosevelt had done much to establish the department and took great pride in it. The first Secretary of Commerce and Labor was George B. Cortelyou, who had been secretary to the President, and by reason of his intimate relations with the officials of the Government was admirably equipped to organize this department, which he did with great skill and administrative ability. After holding the office for about a year and a half, Secretary Cortelyou became Postmaster-General, and Victor H. Metcalf, Congressman from California, was appointed, thereby becoming the next Secretary of the Department on July 1, 1904; I was therefore the third.

The scope of the Department as constituted then was probably the largest of the nine branches of the Government. It was charged with the work of promoting the commerce, mining, manufacturing, shipping, and fishery industries of the country, as well as its transportation facilities and its labor interests; in addition it had jurisdiction over the entire subject of immigration. It had twelve bureaus: corporations; manufactures; labor; lighthouses; census; coast and geodetic survey; statistics, including foreign commerce; steamboat inspection; immigration and naturalization; and standards.

In order to coördinate the work of these various bureaus I instituted the simple method employed by large business administrators of having the several bureau chiefs come together with me twice a month to discuss and confer regarding the more important administrative subjects. This enabled me to keep better informed and served to make the various heads of bureaus conversant with the whole scope of the Department, preventing overlapping and duplication of functions. I learned that this simple administrative method had never been made use of before in federal departments, but thereafter it was adopted by several of the other department heads.

Thanks to Mr. Cortelyou's admirable organization of the department, I found, almost without exception, a fine and competent set of men in charge of its several branches. Some of them were friends of Roosevelt, members of his "tennis cabinet," and were thoroughly imbued with his spirit and ideals. The assistant secretary was Lawrence O. Murray, a capable and conscientious official. James

R. Garfield, chief of the Bureau of Corporations, devoted himself to the difficult task of exposing the abuses and legal infractions of some of the great corporations, and did it with judgment and ability, and with conspicuous courage. Charles P. Neill, chief of the Bureau of Labor, a laboring man in his early days, and afterwards an instructor at Notre Dame, and professor of economics at the Catholic University, in Washington, D.C., was eminently qualified for his duties and had the confidence alike of labor leaders and employers. Dr. Samuel W. Stratton, a scientist of distinction and a fine administrator, was then chief of the Bureau of Standards, a veritable institution of science.

Fortunately, when the Department of Commerce and Labor was organized, the civil service law applied to all appointments excepting bureau chiefs, so that I was able to devote my time to the duties of my office, free from claims of patronage, which had been the bane of the older departments of the Government before the civil service law became so generally operative.

My wife had so promptly put our household in order that in a week after our arrival, we were comfortably installed in our Washington home, No. 2600 Sixteenth Street, a house known as the "Venetian Palace" from the style of its architecture. It was a new house, built by Mrs. John B. Henderson, and well suited to our needs and for entertaining. The social functions in Washington I found most agreeable. During the season we either gave a dinner or attended a dinner on an average of five evenings a week, but these occasions were not burdensome because they usually ended by ten-thirty o'clock.

According to custom, President Roosevelt at the beginning of the season designated the date on which each Cabinet member was to give a dinner to the President, and the date assigned to me was February 19th. It had been usual for each host to invite to this dinner all the other Cabinet members and their wives, which left little opportunity to invite others. Roosevelt changed this custom so that other friends of the host were invited rather than one's fellow members in the Cabinet. Foreign diplomats also were not invited, the entire purpose being to give these occasions the character of intimate gatherings, not large, usually from eighteen to twenty-five guests.

Our dinner went pleasantly. The President was in his usual good humor. Wines were served liberally, but it was Roosevelt's habit to drink very little. This I had observed on several previous occasions, both at the White House and elsewhere. Roosevelt usually took some white wine with apollinaris, and perhaps a glass of champagne. For this dinner my wife had secured the additional services of a certain colored cook in Washington, a woman famous for preparing terrapin, which was one of Roosevelt's favorite dishes.

Tuesday and Friday mornings, beginning at eleven o'clock, were the regular days for the meetings of the Cabinet, then as now. The day after taking office, therefore, I attended my first meeting, taking the chair assigned to me. It was labeled on the back "Secretary of Commerce and Labor, December 17, 1906."

The Cabinet table is oblong, the President seated at the head, and to his right and his left the secretaries in the order in which their departments were created — Secretary of State first to the President's right, Secretary of the Treasury first to the left, and so on. Being head of the ninth and youngest Department, my seat was at the foot of the table, opposite the President.

The meetings were informal and no minutes were taken or other record made. After some brief preliminary talk, in which the President often had some incident to relate or some amusing caricature or savage attack upon himself to exhibit, the business of the day began. The President calls on every secretary, but in no fixed order. He presents such matters as he may deem important, and upon which he may want discussion and advice.

At this meeting I intended not to bring up anything, preferring to wait, as the saying is, until I got "warm in my seat." But an important matter had come up that very morning upon which I had made a decision, based on the carefully reasoned opinion by the solicitor of the department, Mr. Charles Earl. The State of South Carolina, under one of its recent laws, had authorized its State Commissioner of Immigration to go to Europe and select a number of skilled factory hands for the industrial establishments of the State. There were about four hundred and fifty of these immigrants, and there was some question about admitting them. The Immigration Law of 1903, as well as previous laws, excepted the State from its contract labor clauses, and I therefore decided upon their admission.

Indeed, no subject in the department occupied my daily attention to the extent that immigration did. Fortunately, at the chief port of entry, Ellis Island in the New York Bay, there was a capable, conscientious, efficient commissioner, Robert Watchorn.

The right of the immigrant to land, after his medical examination, was based upon the decision of a board of inquiry. This board often made hurried and ill-considered decisions, especially when the immigration was large. In the case of exclusion, the immigrant has the right to appeal to the Secretary of the Department of

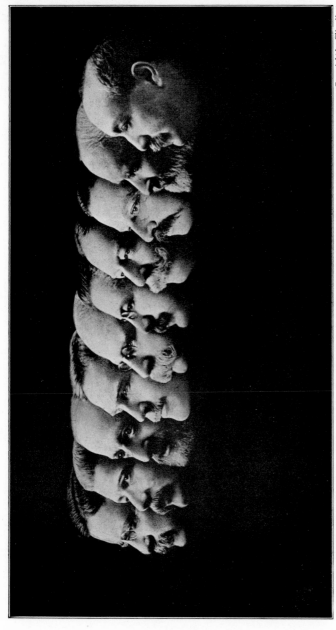

THE ROOSEVELT CABINET

Left to right: The President, Root, Straus, Garfield, Metcalf, Cortelyou, Taft, Meyer, Wilson, Bonaparte

Commerce and Labor. Of course, cases coming under certain portions of the exclusion provisions, such as contract labor, mental deficiency, affliction with loathsome and contagious diseases, were easily enough disposed of; but under the provision "Likely to become a public charge" there was room for the personal attitude of the members of the board, and the fate of the immigrant then depended on whether or not these men were restrictionists. I felt that there was a domestic tragedy involved in every one of these cases, and as the law placed the ultimate decision upon the Secretary, I decided this responsibility was one that should not be delegated; so day by day I took up these decisions myself, frequently taking the papers home with me and carefully reviewing them before retiring.

Important among the immigration subjects were those which presented phases of the Japanese question, the immigration *en masse* of Japanese to the Pacific Coast States, California in particular. The question was brought up by Secretary Root at one of the Cabinet meetings. The city of San Francisco had taken action excluding Japanese from the public schools. It was deemed detrimental for the white children of tender ages to be in the same classes with older and even adult Japanese who came to these schools to learn English. My predecessor, who was a resident of California, had investigated and was conversant with all aspects of the case.

The President insisted that, as it directly affected the relations between the two nations, it was a national concern. Several members of the Cabinet also regarded the subject as one having serious probabilities. Secretary Root asked me whether I could furnish some data as to the use made of Hawaii by Japanese immigrants for circumventing our contract labor law, as many of the Japanese immigrants were coming to the mainland via Hawaii. Upon looking into this question I found during the year previous fully two thirds of the Japanese came via Hawaii. The President took the situation in hand and had the mayor of San Francisco and other leaders of the Japanese agitation come to Washington.

The obnoxious matter was finally adjusted with Japan in a manner to allay irritation by a "Gentlemen's Agreement," by which that country itself was to prevent the emigration of its laboring classes. It was, of course, much better that the Japanese interdict emigration of their own people than that we offend that nation's pride by preventing their entrance, although it was made clear that we should pass an exclusion law if they did not take prompt and effective action.

With some exceptions, this plan worked well. The whole Japanese question, however, was still smouldering. A few months later, during a call at the Department, the Japanese ambassador mentioned to me that in some parts of the Pacific Coast the Japanese were being molested in the streets and that, of course, such things made bad blood and stirred up the people in Japan, with which I had to agree. I admitted that this was an outrage, stating that I was sure our respective governments would do all in their power to maintain good relations, to which he replied that he did not see how those good relations could be disturbed.

Ambassador Aoki then referred to the naturalization of his countrymen in the United States. I told him that on that question I agreed entirely with the President, who in one of his recent speeches had dwelt emphatically on it, advocating laws for the naturalization of Japanese the same as accorded to other aliens. He then mentioned the

Executive Order of the President with reference to Japanese immigration and the regulations for the enforcement of it. I told him I had these regulations in hand and he could rely upon me to make them so as to avoid every possible friction and reflect in every way the broad and liberal spirit of the administration; also that under the immigration act the matter was to a large extent in the control of Japan in issuing limited passports to the special classes affected, namely, skilled and unskilled labor.

After one of the Cabinet meetings I had a conversation with Secretary Root and submitted to him redrafted regulations for any suggestion or amendment that might appear to him desirable, for I was anxious that the Secretary of State should give the regulations critical examination, in view of their affecting our relations with Japan. He returned them to me within a few days with one or two slight changes, which I adopted, and out of them grew the "limited passports" provision of the Immigration Act of 1907.

From time to time I brought up the Japanese situation and emphasized that I regarded it in a most serious light. Meanwhile, whenever the opportunity presented itself I did whatever was possible to promote good-will between the two countries. Japan's great military chief, General Tamemoto Kuroki, paid a visit to the United States, and was given a gala dinner at the Hotel Astor in New York, following ovations to him all the way across the continent from the time he landed at San Francisco. There were over a thousand guests. Admiral Dewey was presiding officer; John H. Finley was toastmaster, and it was felt he was particularly chosen, being president of the College of the City of New York, because of the protest this would imply against the exclusion of Japanese children from the San Francisco public schools. I was invited to deliver an address, in which I said:

The Government and people of Japan, not unmindful of the good-will and early friendship of our country, are too wise to permit the San Francisco school incident, which was fostered by ignorance and propagated by injustice, to cloud their just appreciation of the enlightened spirit of American institutions.

Captain Tanaka, of General Kuroki's staff, had handed me in translation a message that the General had prepared for the American people, which I read in the course of my address. It was as follows:

The Japanese people love peace. They fought for peace. My nation wants peace in which to develop the opportunities that are hers. We have no other desire.

The profession which I have the misfortune to follow is noble only because sometimes it is necessary to establish conditions in which peace may be maintained and in which the arts of peace may flourish.

To this I added that nobler sentiments never fell from the lips of a conquering hero, and they would stand beside those uttered by our hero of the Appomattox: "Let us have peace." This was received with much enthusiasm.

Early in June, 1907, there was another outbreak in San Francisco against the restaurant keepers, and telegrams from Tokyo told of the irritation this caused among the people in Japan. At the Cabinet meeting I took the subject up again with considerable emphasis. I pointed out that these incidents were accumulating and were bristling with grave consequences; that Japan had come into the front rank among nations and could not afford to permit us or any other nation to slap her, as it were, in the face, or to treat her even in small things as a nation of inferior race. I brought up the subject of Japanese nat-

uralization. As the law stood, a Japanese could not be
naturalized, according to the rulings of one or two judges
of the United States courts; but the subject had never
been finally decided. A short time previous to this a
Japanese seaman in Florida had filed a petition for
naturalization which was granted, and I referred the
matter to the Attorney-General to see whether that
would not afford an incident wherewith to test the law.
But no action was taken.

At first the President did not seem to attach to the
subject the importance that I did, but Secretary Root
immediately spoke up that he agreed with my view of it,
and as the discussion went along, the rest of the Cabinet,
as well as the President, gradually came over to my view.
At the end the President remarked: "I am very glad you
brought up that subject."

During the discussion I reviewed the whole legal aspect
of the matter, and referred to the fact that the several
decisions made had been based on Chinese precedents.
I also touched on the ethnological aspect, that it was
doubtful whether the Japanese could be classed as Mon-
golians. This phase appealed to Roosevelt, who seemed
well informed in ethnological studies. I felt rather
gratified with this thorough discussion of the subject. It
had interested me for years, and I had been ruminating
on it for several weeks.

At the last Cabinet meeting before the vacation season,
each member referred to his plans for the summer. I had
decided to combine business with pleasure by taking a
trip along the Canadian border from Montreal to Vancouver to inspect the lighthouse and immigration services, then down the Pacific Coast and to Hawaii, where I
might acquaint myself with regard to immigration as it

affected the Japanese question. The President thought
this would be a useful trip and urged me to take it.

In the administration of a department such as that of
Commerce and Labor, it was important to familiarize
one's self as much as possible with its outlying branches,
to become personally acquainted with the various officers
and the details of their work and surroundings, thereby to
enable one better to do the administrative work than by
remaining at one's desk.

After leaving Vancouver we stopped a few days each
at Seattle, Portland, and San Francisco, where I conferred
with the officials of the Department. From San Francisco
we took a steamer to Hawaii, on board which we met
George R. Carter, Governor of Hawaii, returning from
a vacation in the United States, and Congressman and
Mrs. Nicholas Longworth. It made a very pleasant party.

The authorities and the population gave us a rousing
welcome, cannons saluted, and the militia was out to
escort us. Only once before since the island became
United States territory had a Cabinet official paid a visit,
and that was two years before when Secretary of War
Taft stopped there for a few days *en route* to Japan. We
were comfortably installed in the Hotel Moana, in the
suburb of Waikiki.

The islanders showered upon us bounteous hospitality
in every conceivable form. We participated in rounds of
dinners and receptions. Governor and Mrs. Carter entertained the Longworths and us in the official residence, the
former palace of the Hawaiian rulers, in the throne room
of which hung the portraits of those rulers from earliest
times to the deposed Queen Liliuokalani. The reception
was a brilliant occasion. The leading officials and the
élite of the population were there; the grounds were
beautifully illuminated; and the Royal Hawaiian Band

played the soft, plaintive music so typical of the mild temperament of the people and the luxuriant foliage of the island. My time was much taken up with official and semi-official duties. The island residents impressed me with the great need for better shipping facilities between the mainland and the islands. The coastwise shipping laws applying to them since annexation penalized the carrying of passengers or freight in other than American bottoms. Foreign ships accepting either passengers or freight to American ports on the coast were heavily fined. The result was, not only inconvenience to residents who for one reason or another needed to leave the islands, but the loss of much perishable freight, principally fruit, which rotted on the wharves waiting for American ships. I promised them that I would do everything in my power to help them get the shipping facilities they needed.

A delegation of Japanese editors, representing the four Japanese newspapers of Honolulu, called to ascertain my views regarding Japanese matters in the islands, what my policy was with regard to Japanese immigration, and whether I believed that the preponderance of Japanese people in Hawaii was inimical to the interests of the territory. I answered them:

An ideal condition for the future welfare of these islands would be that there should not be too great a preponderance of any one race, but that an equilibrium be maintained.

I would impress upon you, and upon each of the several races here, to have a care not to exploit these islands and their resources for the benefit of the country from which they come, but to act in the spirit of loyalty to the government under which they live; of loyalty to the interests of the islands which afford such happy and ideal homes for them and their children. I am gratified that the public school system has such a great influence upon the young, who grow up with the American ideals and respect for the liberty of the individual. I would like to see an increasing number of Americans from the mainland come and settle in these islands, if for no other reason than to guarantee for all time to come the continuance of the American spirit for the benefit and welfare of all peoples who have made and will make their homes here.

Unfortunately the time at my disposal did not permit my visiting the various islands. We did, however, see everything to be seen at Oahu, the island upon which Honolulu is situated. Rear-Admiral Very took us on the U.S.S. Iroquois to visit Pearl Harbor, the famous land-locked bay large enough to shelter the battle fleets of several nations. We also visited the Waialua pineapple plantation and cannery, where twenty thousand cans of the large, luscious fruit were put up daily. The processes of paring, coring, slicing, and canning were done by machinery with great speed, and we enjoyed tasting the fruit as much as any school children might.

In Honolulu I met Viscount Ishii, who was then Japanese under-Secretary of State. He has since been ambassador at Washington and at this writing is ambassador at Paris. We had frequent conferences and went over the whole Japanese question. He had fully informed himself upon all phases of the subject, as well as regarding the idiosyncrasies of the Pacific Coast States in opposing the immigration of Japanese laborers. Ishii's thorough understanding of the situation at that time did much to smooth ruffled feelings in Japan. The Viscount returned to the States on the steamer with us.

As we sailed out of the harbor on the Asia, bedecked with Hawaiian flowers, the Royal Hawaiian Band played its farewell music. The last words we heard from the Hawaiian shore were "Aloha Nui," the Hawaiian farewell.

I had satisfied myself that, so far as concerned the carrying out of the President's Executive Order of March 14, 1907, the Japanese officials in both Hawaii and Japan were doing everything in their power. Hawaii at the time had a population of about 160,000, in round figures, of which about 80,000 were Japanese, 20,000 Chinese, and 25,000 native Hawaiians. Of the white element the biggest percentage were Portuguese, who numbered about 22,000, while all other Caucasians together, principally American, British, and German, numbered 14,000. It therefore behooved our officials on the islands, in the Pacific ports, and along the Mexican border, to be especially watchful to carry out the regulations which the Department had formulated with regard to the admission of Japanese or Korean skilled and unskilled labor.

Soon after my return I had a conference with the President at Oyster Bay. The President informed me that Secretary Taft was about to leave for Japan, to go from there to Russia by the Siberian Railroad. He said he had authorized him to see what could be done toward overcoming the difficulties in our relations, and what might be the effect in Japan if we were to endeavor to pass a law giving naturalization to Japanese exclusive of the laboring classes and the small traders who practically belonged to the same class. This subject the President had urged in his last Message to Congress.

On October 25th I brought up in the Cabinet meeting, for the information of the President, statistics regarding Japanese immigration up to October 1, 1907, which showed that the immigration for the twelve months then ended was almost double that of the preceding twelve months, and also that there had been an appreciable increase since April 1, when the President's Executive Order went into effect, compared with the previous months. The statistics regarding the transit of Japanese between Mexico and Canada showed that something like six hundred and seventy registered from April to September, but only about one third that number actually made the transits. It was presumed, therefore, that the rest got off within United States territory.

The President seemed very much annoyed with this condition of things. I recalled to his mind that when the regulations under his Executive Order were originally presented by me, they contained a clause, along the lines of the Chinese regulation on the subject, to prevent the abuse of transit privileges, but that he and the Cabinet had decided it to be unwise to put in that clause. A few months thereafter, when we first suspected the abuse of transit privileges, I directed an accurate account to be taken of these transits, the result of which I now presented.

The first impulse of the President was to direct that all transit be denied, but I pointed out that that would raise considerable objection, as it would place the Japanese in a special class in that respect. He insisted that something must be done. I suggested that the problem needed careful thought and I would take it up and prepare regulations similar to those for the Chinese. This I did, and the Japanese regulations differ only in that we do not require the photographing of the person to make the transit.

I did not propose to drop the matter of Japanese immigration and naturalization. Again and again I brought it up in Cabinet meetings. I believed the best way of adjusting the difficulties was to try to negotiate a treaty with Japan permitting the naturalization of Japanese other than laboring classes, and in return excluding all who came within the category of skilled or unskilled labor. The belief that such a treaty could be negotiated was confirmed by my talks with Ishii both at Honolulu and later when he visited Washington. The right to naturalization would be taken advantage of by only five or six thousand and would not, of course, be granted to the laborers then resident in the United States.

There were about seventy-three thousand Japanese in the United States, and it was fair to assume that two thirds of these were of the laboring class. Of the remainder there was a small percentage of women and children, and then there were those born in America. Japanese eligible for citizenship would therefore not exceed ten or twelve thousand, and it was reasonable to assume that not more than half of them would be willing to throw off their native allegiance. My belief was that such an adjustment of the problem would leave no irritation behind it.

The President did not think such a treaty would be confirmed by the Senate, and to have it rejected would make matters worse. Secretary Metcalf thought the California members would not agree to such an arrangement. Notwithstanding these objections I was of the opinion that such force of argument could be found in favor of the arrangement that even representatives from California would not fail to see its advantage.

The whole question simmered along for a year or more, during which our understanding with Japan in regard to the "Gentlemen's Agreement" and the regulations under it were put into concrete and final shape; that is, a letter was written by the Japanese ambassador to our Secretary of State setting forth the understanding of Japan, to which the Secretary replied accepting that understanding and setting forth the amicable relations existing between the two countries.

In late January, 1909, there was a recrudescence of anti-Japanese legislation in California. There were introduced in the State legislature three bills: (a) to exclude Japanese from ownership of land; (b) to segregate the Japanese in special districts of the city; (c) to prohibit Japanese from attending the public schools. With his usual good judgment the President telegraphed the Governor of California saying he was writing him and asking that he withhold any legislation affecting the Japanese until the receipt of that letter. For the time being this action had the desired effect.

The legislature of California was somewhat under the influence of agitators, like the Japanese and Korean Restriction League and some labor bodies. It was believed that the general sentiment of California was against such legislation, but either to avoid conflict, or from indifference or lack of public spirit, such sentiment did not make its influence felt. I had given out figures from month to month showing the number of immigrants from Japan as compared with previous figures. I then made public statistics which showed that for the calendar year 1907 the number of immigrants was 12,400, whereas for the calendar year 1908, after the Japanese Government had taken the matter in hand in accordance with the "Gentlemen's Agreement," the number of immigrants was 4400. Deducting the figure for the emigration from that 4400 left a total increase of Japanese population of only 185 for the year. The California agitators claimed my figures were erroneous, and that hordes of Japanese were surreptitiously coming from the Canadian and Mexican borders. I gave out several interviews to the press to the effect that the figures were absolutely correct; that it was absurd to deny their correctness as I had proofs in my hands; and that if the Californians still

doubted them a committee might call on me and I should
gladly lay my proofs before them. I had sent a copy of
these figures, certified by me, to the California authorities.

Happily our relations with Japan are now more peaceful than they have been for some time, and to a large
degree this has been accomplished by the Four Power
Treaty negotiated at the Washington Conference on the
Limitation of Armaments in December, 1921. The various vexatious instances that I have referred to were stimulated by German officers stationed in the Far East and
fostered by the sensational press in both Japan and our
own country. By this means these happenings were
exaggerated far beyond their significance. The Anglo-
Japanese Alliance of 1911 came into being because of the
aggression of Germany and Russia in the Far East.
After the World War, of course, this condition no longer
obtained, and as the *raison d'être* of the alliance had
therefore vanished, there was a justified feeling in America
that the continuance of the treaty was a menace to our
country. This fact was not unrecognized in Great Britain
itself. As Mr. Balfour stated at the Washington Conference, it was necessary to "annul, merge, destroy, as it
were, this ancient and outward and unnecessary agreement, and replace it by something new, something effective, which should embrace all the powers concerned
in the vast area of the Pacific." By the Four Power
Treaty the Anglo-Japanese Alliance was automatically
discontinued, and Great Britain, the United States,
France, and Japan became associated in friendly partnership as guardians of the peace in the Far East.

So far as concerns the relationship between our country
and Japan, the transcendent importance of this treaty
has been to supersede and overshadow all these minor

matters that before were continually menacing our good relations. By the reservations prepared by the American delegates, and accepted by the other powers, it is provided that the treaty "shall not be taken to embrace questions which according to principles of international law lie exclusively within the domestic jurisdiction of the respective powers." Verily this treaty stands out as one of the great achievements of the Washington Conference.

To return to immigration problems during my incumbency as Secretary of the Department of Commerce and Labor, a minor though nevertheless annoying matter needing adjustment was the regulation with regard to the head tax. After the passage of the Immigration Law of 1903 a head tax of two dollars was levied upon all alien passengers, including even officials of foreign governments. In 1905 Attorney-General Moody had given an opinion to the effect that the tax applied to all alien passengers, whether officers of foreign governments or not. I thought this contrary to the law of nations and to well-established diplomatic usages recognized throughout the world.

As the subject also came within the province of another department, namely, the Department of State, I naturally brought it up at a Cabinet meeting. The President recommended that I issue orders in accordance with my suggestion, and Secretary Root agreed that it was an outrage to levy such a tax upon the representatives of foreign governments. Informally I took the matter up with Attorney-General Bonaparte, but as the decision against this immunity had been made by his Department he felt himself bound by the decision of his predecessor. He suggested that I issue the order on my own responsibility, but I decided for the time being not to do so. At a later Cabinet meeting I again brought up the matter, this time reading the order as I proposed it. The President and Secretary Root, also Secretary Taft, agreed that it should be issued, and this I did.

At the same time I discussed a provision of the Immigration Act of 1906 requiring masters of all vessels bringing in aliens, without exception, to fill out a blank or manifest giving the age, sex, calling, nationality, race, of each alien, and whether able to read or write, and whether anarchist or not. These blanks then had to be signed by the aliens. I prepared two circulars, one ordering the discontinuance of the head tax and the other discontinuing the filling out of these blanks so far as concerned diplomatic or consular officials and other persons duly accredited from foreign governments to the United States, in service or in transit.

At dinner at the British ambassador's home some weeks thereafter Lady Bryce mentioned having to sign a blank asking whether she believed in the practice of polygamy. Of course, she brought it up in a humorous way, but it was apparent that she had felt humiliated at such questioning. I told her I fully appreciated her feelings and was happy to be able to say that that stupid practice had been discontinued.

The subject of naturalization had occupied my attention for years past. Under the law then existing, as well as under older laws, a person could be naturalized not only in the United States courts, but in any State court having a seal. And the naturalization laws prior to the Act of 1906 were most carelessly administered. In the larger cities of many of the States naturalization applications were hurried through in bunches at the direction of some political boss. In that way many persons were

naturalized who would have been found, had time been
taken to sift the applications, not entitled to citizenship.
The effects of so careless a method I saw in Turkey, and
in my dispatches to the State Department I repeatedly
pointed out the evil.

Largely growing out of my presentation of the subject,
Mr. Gaillard Hunt, chief of the passport division of the
State Department, had taken it up in his thorough
manner and made a report to President McKinley, upon
which the President appointed a commission to study the
subject. The commission was renewed by President
Roosevelt. Its report, known as House Document 326,
59th Congress, 2d Session, and entitled "Citizenship of
the United States, Expatriation, and Protection Abroad,"
was the basis of the Act of 1906. This act went far in
preventing fraudulent naturalization as well as in with-
drawing protection from those who were using United
States citizenship not with the intention of becoming part
of the new country in which they had chosen to reside,
but as a means to escape their duties as subjects of the
country of their origin upon returning there to live, as
had happened so often in Turkey.

For the proper carrying out of this law additional
examiners were needed, and also about eleven additional
assistant district attorneys. I therefore arranged with
Attorney-General Bonaparte to appear with him before
the Appropriations Committee of the House to explain
the necessity of an appropriation to cover the enlargement of the corps for the enforcement and administration of the new law. During my experience abroad much
of the time of our diplomatic representatives was taken
up with questions relating to the protection of our citizens, and often this protection was invoked by persons
who should never have been naturalized.

The exclusion and deportation of criminals and anarchists was another phase of the immigration service to which I had given considerable study. I found the law provided for arrest and deportation of criminal aliens only up to three years of the time of their landing, and that there was gross misconception regarding the scope of the law. There was no coöperation between our immigration officials and the local police departments for the detection of such persons. The police departments of most of our cities were disposed to assume that by virtue of the immigration law the whole subject was under the jurisdiction of the Federal Government; and on the other hand our officials did not confer with municipal officials to make use of the immigration law. It is one thing to provide for the exclusion of criminals and anarchists, but it is quite another to discover, on entry, whether a person belongs to either class. They are usually neither illiterate nor lacking in cunning and deception, but within three years they may be detected, as "birds of a feather flock together."

I decided to issue a circular to all commissioners of immigration and immigration inspectors, with a view to bringing about coöperation with the local officials. I took the subject up in the Cabinet and the President approved. It so happened that while this circular was being prepared, an Italian immigrant, recently arrived, killed a Catholic priest in Denver while the latter was officiating at a mass in his church, and a day or two thereafter another recently arrived immigrant, a Russian, attacked the chief of police of Chicago and his family with a dagger. Both of these men would have come under the deportation provisions of the immigration law had the police been aware of these provisions, as in both instances they had been suspected, by their affiliations and their talk, of being anarchists, as that term is defined in the Immigration Act of February 20, 1907. Under the local criminal laws this suspicion was not enough to justify arrest.

Appearing as it did immediately after these two incidents my circular had much publicity and brought about the deportation of a number of undesirables upon evidence supplied by the police and detective officers.

In a Department which covered so many and such varied subjects, the conflict between human and property interests was often apparent. I recall a remark by the President, as we were speaking about this, that whenever within my jurisdiction there occurred this conflict he was sure I would lean on the human side, and I could always count on his support.

A striking example of this conflict grew out of an order I issued for the inspection of excursion and ferry boats at least three times a year instead of once. The summer before I took office the boiler of the General Slocum, a large excursion boat on the Long Island Sound, blew up and caused the death of over a hundred women and children. As spring approached and the excursion season drew near, I made up my mind that I should make all possible provision to prevent the recurrence of any such disaster.

I accompanied the supervising inspector-general, George Uhler, to witness the inspection of some passenger boats plying between Washington and Norfolk, to get personal knowledge of the details of inspection. I carefully studied a report made to me by Mr. Murray, the assistant secretary of my Department, who had been a member of the board of inquiry into the Slocum disaster and later the Valencia wreck. I called a meeting of the board of supervising inspectors of steamboats and impressed upon them the importance of great care in inspection. I urged that no man be retained in the inspection service who was not thoroughly competent and efficient, since they had to deal with the protection of human life.

My order for more frequent inspection brought forth many objections from the steamboat owners, and, as is usual in such cases, a committee came to Washington and presented their grievances and objections direct to the President, in the hope of inducing him to overrule my instructions. They were patiently heard, but their main objection was that it would cost a little more and be a little more inconvenient to have three inspections instead of one, and the President gave them little more comfort than to make it quite clear that he was thoroughly in accord with my action for the provision of greater safety to human life. He told them he felt he was fortunate in having at the head of the Department of Commerce and Labor a man who was a humanitarian besides having large business experience, for while it was his purpose to harmonize human and business interests, always when they conflicted he would lean toward the human side, as I had done in issuing that order.

The President was deeply interested always in the natural resources of the country and their preservation, and asked me to take up the question of the Alaska salmon fisheries. It was certain that unless some drastic action was taken, the salmon would be destroyed in the Alaskan waters just as they had been in the Columbia River. Roosevelt was familiar with the problem and believed that Wood River ought to be closed. I devoted parts of two days to a hearing on the subject. The cannery interests were represented by their counsel and the

Fishermen's Union by several of its officers. Senator Fulton, of Oregon, as well as the two Alaskan delegates in Congress, pleaded for the closing of the rivers.

After hearing all sides and studying the question I signed an order directing the closing of both the Wood and Nushagak Rivers to trap and net fishing, and if the law had permitted, I should have directed the closing also of Nushagak Bay, where extensive trap fishing was carried on.

When I was president of the New York Board of Trade and Transportation I was impressed with the importance of establishing a closer relationship between the commercial bodies of the country and the Government. Shortly after I became Secretary of Commerce and Labor, therefore, I sought to accomplish that end. I had a study made by Nahum I. Stone, tariff expert of the Bureau of Manufactures, of the relations between the European governments and their commercial bodies, especially in such countries as Great Britain, France, Germany, Italy, and Belgium. I sent invitations to about forty of the leading chambers of commerce, boards of trade, and other commercial organizations throughout the country to send delegates to Washington for a two days' conference, with a view to bringing about an organization of these bodies for the purpose of coöperation between them and the departments of the Government having to do with commerce and manufactures.

Accordingly on December 5th a representative gathering of over one hundred delegates met in my Department, and I put before them a plan for organization. I invited Secretary Root, who took a deep interest in the scheme, and he made a thoughtful address, in which he impressed upon the gathering the things that ought to be done, and could be done only through organization and the power of concerted effort. Andrew D. White, our experienced ambassador at Berlin, had sent to the President a letter containing the proposal that a method of instruction in commerce be applied at the instance of our Government as had been done in agriculture; this interesting proposal I read to the meeting.

I then went with the delegates in a body to the White House where the President addressed them. In the afternoon Gustav H. Schwab, of the New York Chamber of Commerce, was elected temporary chairman and the organization of the council proceeded. A committee on organization and a committee on rules were appointed, and it was decided that an advisory committee of fifteen members was to have headquarters in Washington. The number of meetings to be held per year was fixed, as well as the annual dues. On December 5, 1907, the National Council of Commerce came into being.

A year later the first annual meeting was held in my Department. The Council now had permanent offices in the Adams Building, with William R. Corwine in charge. In my address to the delegates I stressed the importance of the development of our commercial relations with the South American republics, particularly in view of the rapidly approaching completion of the Panama Canal. At that time we had only twenty-three per cent of the foreign trade of South America, and one of the main requirements for increasing our share was the establishment of better shipping and postal facilities. To that end I recommended in my annual report that the Postal Subsidy Act of 1891 be extended to include ships of sixteen knots and over, and my colleagues, the Secretary of State and the Attorney-General, made similar recommendations.

A month after the change of Administration the executive committee of the Council held a meeting, again in the Department of Commerce and Labor, at which they passed the following resolution:

Resolved, by the members of the Executive Committee of the National Council of Commerce in meeting assembled in the office of the Hon. Charles Nagel, the present Secretary of Commerce and Labor, That they tender their heartiest thanks to the Hon. Oscar S. Straus, the former Secretary of Commerce and Labor, for his constant and well-directed efforts in forming and promoting the National Council of Commerce, expressing their appreciation of his far-sightedness, his patriotism, his energy, his fairness, and his friendship, assuring him of the high personal esteem in which he is held by all of them, and asserting that in their judgment he has laid the foundation for a movement which will redound not only to his credit as a Cabinet officer, but one which will ultimately be productive of incalculable benefit to the business interests of our country, the development of which he has so deeply at heart.

Later that year the Council was reorganized and called the Chamber of Commerce of the United States, which to-day is an important institution in the commercial life of our country.

To bring about a similar relationship between the Department and the labor bodies, I called another conference in February, 1909, to which I invited the leading labor representatives throughout the country, and about fifty attended. Unfortunately my term of office was drawing to an end and there was not time to organize this wing, but I urged the men to insist upon the continuance of the conferences and the coöperation with the Department thus established.

The matters discussed at this meeting were mainly how best to lessen unemployment, how the Division of

Information under the Bureau of Immigration might be administered for the greater benefit of labor in general, and how the Nobel Peace Prize, which President Roosevelt had set aside for a foundation for the promotion of industrial peace, could be made most effective. There were addresses by Samuel Gompers, president of the American Federation of Labor; Warren S. Stone, grand chief of the Brotherhood of Locomotive Engineers; William F. Yates, president of the Marine Engineers' Beneficial Association; and Terence V. Powderly, chief of the Division of Information in the Bureau of Immigration. The presiding officer was Daniel J. Keefe, Commissioner-General of Immigration and Naturalization.

During my term of office repeated efforts were made in Congress, backed by organized labor, to divide my Department and make two of it — the Department of Commerce and the Department of Labor. I successfully opposed this plan, my idea being that labor and capital were the two arms of industry, the proper functioning of which could best be secured by coöperation, which in turn could best be promoted by administering their interests together. In this I had the support of President Roosevelt. During the Taft Administration, however, the bill was passed creating the Department of Labor.

I have mentioned Roosevelt's Nobel Peace Prize. As received by the President, it consisted of a medal and diploma, and a draft for $36,734.79. He decided not to keep the money, but to turn it over in trust for a foundation for the promotion of industrial peace. In January, 1907, he called me to the White House and told me that he would forward the draft and the papers to Chief Justice Fuller, with the request that he communicate with the other trustees, of whom there were four: James

Wilson, Secretary of Agriculture; John Mitchell, president of the Anthracite Coal Operators; ex-Mayor Seth Low, of New York, and myself.

Later the Chief Justice came to my Department with the papers to go over them with me and to arrange for their safe-keeping until we could have a meeting and formulate a plan of action. Subsequently he informed me that before preparing the draft of the act granting the foundation it was necessary to write a preamble setting forth its objects and purposes, and this he found it difficult to do. I relieved his mind by offering to prepare the bill with the preamble. I consulted with Dr. Cyrus Adler, of the Smithsonian Institution, who had had considerable experience in drafting documents for the creation of trusts of this nature. With his assistance I prepared the draft of the preamble and the bill, which the Chief Justice approved. I then took them to the President, who also approved them and requested me to call a meeting of the trustees, of whom there were to be nine instead of five as originally.

At the meeting of January 27, 1907, a few slight changes were made and adopted in the bill. Thus redrafted, with a report attached giving a history of the award, it was introduced in the House by Congressman Richard Bartholdt, of Missouri, member of the Committee on Labor; and in the Senate by John W. Daniel, of Virginia. It was promptly passed. The board of trustees as finally constituted included: Archbishop Ireland, Samuel Gompers, Daniel J. Keefe, Seth Low, Marcus M. Marks, Dr. Neill, Warren S. Stone, James Wilson, and myself.

The foundation was in existence for about ten years, and in that time the interest on the money merely accumulated, because the trustees were unable to find a proper means for employing it. In July, 1917, Mr. Roosevelt requested Congress to repeal the bill and return the money to him, that he might distribute it among the different charitable societies in the United States and in Europe which were affording relief to the sufferers from the war. The request was granted, and the sum with its accrued interest, amounting to $45,482.83, was thus distributed by him.

Roosevelt always encouraged the members of his Cabinet to make speeches in various parts of the country on subjects uppermost in the mind of the public, with due regard, of course, to the duties of office. I accepted a number of the many such invitations that came to me. At the banquet of the National Association of Manufacturers, held in the Waldorf Hotel, New York, in May, 1907, I was asked to be the principal speaker. I made careful preparation of an address, part of which I devoted to advocating a moderate tariff reform, with a view to providing a maximum and minimum tariff to meet discrimination against us by some European nations. I consulted with the President about it. While he agreed with my premises, he thought the time not ripe to project that issue, so I redrafted my speech and devoted it to such topics as the development of our manufactures, the work of the Bureau of Corporations, and the relations of employers and workers.

On April 3, 1908, the Savannah Board of Trade celebrated its twenty-fifth anniversary, and I was asked to be one of the speakers. Two others were Governor Hoke Smith and Representative J. Hampton Moore, president of the Atlantic Deep Waterways Commission. It was a special occasion and was widely advertised for several weeks. I prepared an address in which I outlined also some of the activities carried on by my Department for the benefit of the commercial interests of the country. On this trip my wife and younger daughter accompanied me. During our stay at Savannah we were the guests of the Board of Trade, who showed us every possible attention, in true Southern fashion, and we thoroughly enjoyed our stay.

The Mayor and prominent citizens of my former home, Columbus, upon learning of our presence in the South, sent us a pressing invitation to visit that city. A committee met us at the station, and in the evening a dinner was given at the Opera House, at which about a hundred of the leading citizens were present. The dinner was served on the stage, and while the toasts were being responded to, the curtain was raised, disclosing an auditorium crowded with people. I was quite touched by this fine attention by the citizens of my former home, who took great pride in the fact that one of their former townsmen was a member of the Cabinet. In the audience were several of my schoolboy friends and those of my brothers, and I found several friends and companions of my parents still among the living.

In the South at that time it was still rare for a person to change his politics, and one of the questions that was put to me was why had I, a member of a Democratic family, once a Democrat myself, and even having held office under a Democratic President, changed over to the Republican side. In other words, why had I been on both sides of the political fence, though they were too polite to ask the question in that direct form. I told them that perhaps no one had a better right than they to ask the reason for my political affiliations. It was true, I said, that I had been, as it were, on both sides of the fence, but that was not my fault; the fence had been moved. This produced great merriment and applause.

Talbotton, the first American home of my family, also extended an invitation to us, which I accepted with pleasure. A dinner and reception were given in my honor at the public hall known as the Opera House, at which the Mayor of the town made an address, as well as several other prominent citizens. While in Talbotton we were the guests of the Honorable Henry Persons, former member of Congress and an old friend of our family. He gave me my first rubber ball, when I was six years old. I visited all the scenes of my boyhood; it was forty-five years since I had lived there. The population of the town was about the same, equally divided between the whites and the blacks. The little Baptist church where I went to Sunday school was much smaller than it had loomed up in my imagination. Collinsworth Institute was abandoned, and only the recitation hall was left standing. The several houses wherein my family had lived brought back vivid memories of the toils and pleasures of my parents. The little frame cottage with the green blinds especially impressed upon me how little is required for happiness where there is the love and contentment which always blessed our family. All who remembered my father and mother spoke of them in the highest terms. I met a number of my boyhood friends, grown gray and old. On the whole the little town had not changed much, though it had fewer signs of prosperity. Before the Civil War it was the center of a rich slave-holding county. The people, however, seemed contented and happy.

From Talbotton we went to Atlanta, and then made one or two more stops on the way home. At each place we met friends of former years and were given a thoroughly royal welcome. In fact, the reception given us throughout the whole tour was in the nature of an ovation. Wherever we stopped our rooms were decorated with an abundance of the most beautiful flowers. The Southerners have ever been known for their hospitality, and in this respect the New South has lost nothing.

Later in the year the Southern Commercial Congress, representing ten States, assembled in Washington, and I was asked to preside at the opening session in the large ballroom of the New Willard Hotel. There were three or four hundred people present. I devoted my address to a comparison between the old agricultural South and the new industrial South, pointing out that as the economic interests of the South were no longer sectional but national, it must follow that politically there is no longer a reason for "the solid South."

On leaving the Cabinet one day at about this time the President's youngest son, Quentin, came up to me. I had a great affection for this bright, attractive boy. He was eleven years old, and he informed me he weighed one hundred and fourteen pounds. He was full of animal spirits, frank, charming. "You gave my brother Kermit some coins," he said to me.

"Yes; are you interested in them?" I asked.

"I am making a little collection," was his answer.

I invited him into my carriage and to come to lunch with me. He accepted readily, and I reminded him that he had better let his mother know. He did so by hurriedly running into the White House and returning in a very few minutes saying his mother said he might go. He behaved like a perfect little gentleman and showed that under his sparkling vivacity there was serious, intelligent hunger for knowledge. After lunch I took him into my library and showed him my collection of Greek and Roman coins. I told him he might pick out what he liked. To the several he chose I added a gold stater of

Philip. He was overjoyed. From that time onward we became still greater friends, and he came to see me whenever he got a new coin for his collection.

In 1909, when I was going through Paris, I met him there with his mother. During this visit he and I were quite steadily together. We visited the museums and other places of interest. I found him a most sympathetic and delightful companion, notwithstanding the immense difference in our ages. What a record of glory and patriotism this lovable boy has left to his country! And with what fortitude his parents bore their most painful loss! Their example strengthened the anguished hearts of many patriotic fathers and mothers of the land who suffered like affliction.

On Christmas Day Mrs. Straus and I received an invitation by telephone to come to the White House between three and four o'clock to see the Christmas tree. Some thirty or forty guests were there, mainly friends of the family. In one of the side rooms in the basement of the house was assembled a large company of children. The room was darkened, that the lighted tree might stand out. There were presents for all the children, and Mrs. Roosevelt played Lady Bountiful to see that each child got its gift. Upstairs in the Red Room the gentlemen sat smoking. It was a genuinely joyful and memorable day.

The social season in Washington is usually begun with the President's New Year's reception, which lasts from eleven o'clock until half-past two on New Year's Day. At a few minutes before eleven o'clock the officials and their wives assembled upstairs, and promptly at eleven the President and Mrs. Roosevelt led the march to the Blue Room. The procession advanced toward the main stairway, where the line divided, the ladies going to the left and the gentlemen to the right, reuniting at the first landing; then through the main hall where the passageway was roped off through a crowd of specially invited guests.

The order following the President was: the Cabinet officers; the doyen of the diplomatic corps, the Italian ambassador and his staff; the ambassadors and ministers of the other nations, according to rank. After them, grouped in more or less regular order, the justices of the Supreme Court, headed by the Chief Justice; Senators; Representatives; Army and Navy officials; the officers of the Government.

On New Year's Day every one is accorded the right to pay his or her respects to the President. The officials come straight to the White House and the uninvited guests form a line on the grounds. On the particular day of which I speak the line stretched through the grounds, along Pennsylvania Avenue and down by the State Department Building, probably more than half a mile long, and the President received about sixty-five hundred people in all. At two o'clock the iron gates of the White House grounds were closed, and those who had not reached that point by that time were barred out. The reception had to end promptly, as the Cabinet ladies who assisted had to be present at the receptions at their own homes from half-past two until six, in accordance with a custom that has been in vogue probably since the days of Washington. Our buffet in the dining-room was kept well replenished, and there were champagne and punch served. We had in all about four hundred guests.

The official functions at the White House during the Roosevelt Administration were agreeable and in stately form. They were usually followed by an informal supper to which were invited personal friends and visitors.

Our series of official dinners began with the one to the

MRS. OSCAR S. STRAUS

Vice-President and Mrs. Fairbanks and ended with the dinner to the President and Mrs. Roosevelt. In addition we followed the pleasant custom of the President and had guests to informal luncheons three or four times a week. These luncheons we gave in the sun parlor back of our dining-room, which was one of the attractive features of our Venetian palace.

It was my privilege to give the last Cabinet dinner to the President, on March 2d, two days before the close of the Administration. The event had been postponed for a week on account of the death of the President's nephew, Stewart Robinson, whose mother was the President's sister. Governor and Mrs. Hughes, who were among our invited guests, stayed over when it was found that the dinner had to be postponed. Mrs. Roosevelt later informed me that she planned that our dinner be the last, knowing that I had some sentiment about it which she and the President shared.

I have made several references to the wonderfully human touch characteristic of Roosevelt. On February 5th, the day beginning the last month of his Administration, a messenger from the White House brought me a package containing a large folio, a handsomely illustrated memorial volume describing the Castle of Wartburg in Saxony, in which Luther was confined and where he worked on his translation of the Bible. The book had been prepared by official direction, and Roosevelt had received two copies of the royal edition, one from the Kaiser personally and one from the Chancellor, which latter he sent to me with this inscription:

"To Mr. and Mrs. Oscar S. Straus, in memory of our days together in the Administration; days which I have so much enjoyed and appreciated. Theodore Roosevelt. February 5, 1909."

CHAPTER X

THE TAFT CAMPAIGN OF 1908

Roosevelt favors Taft to succeed him — I visit Taft at Cincinnati — Roosevelt plans for his African trip — I take part in the Taft campaign — Roosevelt's method of preparedness — Election evening at the White House — Roosevelt rebukes a bigot; his letter on religious liberty — Taft tells Roosevelt he will retain Wright, Garfield, and me in his Cabinet — Roosevelt's speech at the dinner to Vice-President-elect Sherman — Looking toward the end of my term; the last Cabinet meeting — Closing the administration of Roosevelt and ushering in that of Taft.

EARLY in September, 1907, in a conversation with Roosevelt at Oyster Bay, we touched on matters political and the forthcoming national convention of the Republican Party for the nomination of a President. Roosevelt had again publicly made the statement he gave out at the time of his election, that he would not accept a renomination, and had made known his desire that the party nominate Taft.

I had just returned from Hawaii, and told him that throughout my trip to and from the Pacific Coast I observed an almost universal determination to force the nomination upon him. I had met many people and addressed several merchants' organizations and other bodies, and again and again the sentiment of prominent Republicans was: "We know Roosevelt is sincere in his statement that he would decline the nomination, but what can he do if he is renominated? He is a patriotic man, and how can he refuse to obey the unanimous wish of his party and the people at large?" The President knew of this strong sentiment for him, and that was one of the main reasons why he made the public and definite statement that he favored the nomination of Taft, whom

he regarded as best qualified to carry forward the measures
and policies of his Administration.

Some of Roosevelt's closest friends counseled him not
in any way to interfere with the selection of his successor.
He practically agreed to that, but in order to escape the
nomination himself he felt compelled to throw his influence toward Taft. I think it was Secretary Root at the
time who remarked that it would be impossible for
Roosevelt to let the tail of the tiger go without some such
plan. Notwithstanding his positive statements that he
would not accept a renomination at the end of his term,
and his constant reiteration of this determination, the
pressure throughout the country was overwhelming.

The people naturally resent the selection of a candidate
for them by the President in office, and in the past have
shown their resentment by the defeat of such candidates.
But the conditions surrounding the Taft campaign were
somewhat different. Roosevelt was committed heart and
soul to the moral principles for which his Administration
had stood in face of the mighty opposition of the "interests." How the force and might of this opposition had
grown until Roosevelt took up the "big stick" can perhaps hardly be measured except by those who were with
him in the bitter fight. No one was more conversant with
the principles and policies of the Administration than
Taft, and, all things considered, perhaps none better
qualified than he to carry them forward in a firm and
constructive way.

The logic of the situation was, of course, that Roosevelt
stand again for the Presidency, especially as that would
not in reality have been a third term. But he would not
under any circumstances recede from the decision announced on the night of his election. It required great
firmness not to be swept off his feet by the tremendous

pressure to induce him to consent to be renominated. In the face of these facts the people were less inclined to resent his indicating his preference for the successor whom he regarded as best qualified to carry forward the policies he had inaugurated by such reforms as the rebate law against railroads, the anti-trust laws, and child labor legislation, and other progressive measures.

At the Cabinet meeting just before the summer vacation Taft came in radiantly happy. He had been nominated the day before; it had been understood for some time that he would be nominated on the first ballot. Reflecting at the time upon the qualifications of Mr. Taft as a successor to Roosevelt, I put down among my random notes that I thought he possessed the very qualifications for constructively carrying forward the principles Roosevelt had stood for, and which only Roosevelt could have so courageously vitalized. Taft always appeared to be jovial and kept, at least outwardly, a genially good-natured equilibrium. He possessed to a marked degree a fund of spontaneous laughter — a valuable asset in the armor of a public man. The power to create a good laugh has at times not only the elements of argument, but of avoiding argument; with it a man can either accede to a proposition or avoid acceding; it can be committal or non-committal; it conceals as well as expresses feelings, and acts as a wonderful charm in avoiding sharp and rugged corners, in postponing issues and getting time for reflection. In the practice of the law I was once associated with a very able man who had the ability to laugh his opponent out of court. And his was a jeering laugh where Taft's laugh was contagious and good-natured. Not that he lacked the ability at times to be fearless and outspoken; he had shown himself to be that in a number of speeches prior to his nomination.

Withal I could not help feeling sad that Roosevelt's plan had so well succeeded, and in an intimate chat with the President after the Cabinet meeting I told him so. He would not have been human if, amid the satisfaction he felt in having his choice for the Presidency respected, there was not some feeling of regret in stepping down from the greatest office in the world, which he had administered with so much satisfaction and success, and the duties and responsibilities of which he had enjoyed more than perhaps any one of his predecessors. To use his own words as I so frequently heard them: "I have had a bully time and enjoyed every hour of my Presidency." Another four years in office would doubtless have prolonged that enjoyment.

Early in September I went to Cincinnati to meet Taft at his headquarters in the Hotel Sinton, and Terence V. Powderly, head of the Information Division of the Bureau of Immigration, formerly president of the Knights of Labor, accompanied me. I brought to Taft's attention some correspondence that had been conducted by Louis Marshall, of New York, with Charles P. Taft, his brother, and with the candidate for Vice-President on his ticket, Sherman, regarding some narrow and prejudiced editorials on Russian immigration appearing in the Cincinnati "Times-Star," owned by Charles P. Taft. I pointed out that not only were these editorials untrue and unjust, but they did not reflect his policy and yet were so interpreted. Secretary Taft then asked the editor of the paper, Mr. Joseph Garretson, and his nephew, Hulbert Taft, to call on me. With them I went over the whole subject, and upon my return to Washington young Mr. Taft sent me a double-column article from the front page of the "Times-Star," together with a double-column editorial, forcefully and clearly written, embracing the whole matter as we had covered it during my visit to Cincinnati.

Samuel Gompers had come out strongly in favor of Bryan, and no one could tell what effect that might have on the great labor element of the country. Mr. Powderly, who was very broad-minded and independent in his politics, said it would have little if any effect on the labor vote, as it is not a group vote, and no leader, however powerful, can make it so. This statement later proved to be entirely correct. The Democrats among the labor men went their way, and the Republicans went theirs.

The Cabinet met again after the summer vacation on September 25th. The President wanted to talk with me afterward about several matters, so I waited and sat with him while he was being shaved. He spoke about the arrangements he had made for his African trip, and said several taxidermists of the Smithsonian Institution were to accompany him. I told him that Dr. Adler of the Institution had spoken to me of the matter, and my particular concern was that one of the men in his party on this African expedition should be a physician. He assented, saying that after all he was fifty years old and ought to be more careful about his health than when he was younger. He seemed to know that I had had something to do with enabling the Smithsonian Institution to supply these men, but I did not let it appear that I knew much about it. When his book "African Game Trails" appeared he sent me a copy with the inscription:

To Oscar Straus
from his friend
THEODORE ROOSEVELT
Nov. 1st 1910.

In the Appendix he makes acknowledgment to several

of his friends including myself, "to all of whom lovers of natural history are therefore deeply indebted."

He mentioned that he had had an invitation to give a lecture at Oxford University upon his return, which he felt like accepting because it was a course in which some of the most prominent men of the past, including Gladstone, had lectured, and it appealed to him to speak at this ancient university. I encouraged him to do so. He said he did not intend, however, to accept invitations to other European countries, because he did not wish to be fêted. This lecture would be more in line with his work.

At the request of Roosevelt and the urgent solicitation of Taft, I took an active part in the campaign, making scores of speeches in the leading cities of the East and Middle West. I made the first on September 26th, the day after the first Cabinet meeting of the season, under the auspices of the Interstate Republican League, in Washington. It was one of the largest political meetings ever held there. I addressed myself to a recent speech by ex-Secretary of State Olney, in which he had endorsed Bryan. I pointed out how much more had been done under the Roosevelt Administration than by the Democratic Administration with which Mr. Olney was connected, in bringing suits against the trusts under the Sherman law; that in Mr. Olney's time nearly all such suits were brought against labor combinations, while in Roosevelt's time they were brought against the offending corporations.

I had been in close touch with Roosevelt during his own campaign four years before, but I must say he threw himself with greater energy into Taft's campaign, watching every phase of it with great care and circumspection to counteract every unfavorable tendency and to push promptly every tactical advantage. On Sunday afternoon, September 27th, I received a telephone message to come to the White House. When I arrived I found present Secretaries Cortelyou and Meyer, Lawrence F. Abbott, of "The Outlook," and William Loeb. Roosevelt was dictating a letter to Bryan, in answer to the latter's attack upon the Administration's policies, and invited each of us to make suggestions. Those that seemed good he immediately incorporated. I had brought with me some facts and figures that I prepared for campaign use, and all of this material he embodied. When the dictation was finished, he asked us to return at nine o'clock in the evening to go over the finished product, as it was important that the letter be given to the press for next morning's papers.

When we arrived in the evening, the President was already at his desk correcting the typewritten pages, of which there were about twenty. The duplicates were handed to us, and we passed them from one to another for reading and suggestions. At one point I suggested changing an expression to a more dignified form, which the President vetoed with the characteristic remark: "You must remember this letter is not an etching, but a poster." That was an apt illustration of his purpose, namely, to attract and fix popular attention; and I withdrew my suggestion.

The published letter occupied three and a half newspaper columns. It was powerful and effective and nailed some of the main fallacies that Bryan had been expounding. This was the third such letter by Roosevelt, and some people were inclined to criticize them as having the appearance of overshadowing Taft and other campaign orators. This might have been true to an extent, but it was of little consequence in comparison with the tremendous effect of the letters in enlightening the people with regard to the greater national principles for which Taft stood.

The following week I started on a campaign tour. I made speeches at Baltimore, Pittsburgh, Cleveland, Chicago. In accepting the pressing invitation of the National Republican Committee to make a series of speeches, I made one condition, which was that I would not speak at any meeting gotten up on sectarian or hyphenated political lines. It was, and I regret to say still is, customary, in political campaigns, especially among local managers in smaller cities with large foreign-born populations, to appeal to their former national sympathies. I regarded this method as un-American and inimical to the solidarity of our Americanism. My letter to the chairman of the speakers' bureau, Senator Joseph M. Dixon, was by him given to the press and widely published. It had a very good effect, and through that campaign at least put an end to advertising and meetings based on race or creed appeal. Upon my return to New York I spoke at a number of meetings in Brooklyn and New York with Mr. Taft, the last and largest of these being the one at Madison Square Garden, at which General Horace Porter presided. Charles E. Hughes, who was candidate for Governor, also spoke on that occasion.

The President and Mrs. Roosevelt invited Mrs. Straus and me to return to Washington with them in their private car on election day, after we had voted in our respective districts. *En route* the President again mentioned the arrangements for his African trip and told me he had also accepted an invitation to speak at the Sorbonne, Paris. He was already preparing his Oxford address, the draft of which when ready he wanted me to read. It is generally believed that Roosevelt did things hurriedly and impulsively. But those of us who were acquainted with his methods knew the contrary to be true. Preparedness was one of his outstanding characteristics. He was a most industrious worker, and as soon as he made up his mind to do something, whether it was to deliver an address or to bring forward some reform, he set to work at once making preparations, so as not to leave it until the time for the event was at hand. In the case of his Oxford and Sorbonne addresses, for instance, he prepared them long in advance and gave himself plenty of time to correct and polish them. He told me he pursued this method because it freed his mind and enabled him to be ready for the next thing to come before him. That is certainly not the way an impulsive man works.

Election evening in Washington we were invited to the White House to receive the returns. The twenty-five or thirty other officials who were in the city were also there with their wives. The returns began to come in shortly after eight o'clock and were being tabulated by Secretary Loeb and his assistants. It was soon evident that Taft was elected, so that by eleven-thirty we were able to send congratulations to the successful candidate and Frank H. Hitchcock, chairman of the National Committee.

The greatest strength of Taft proved to be what many supposed would be his weakness, namely, that he was the choice of Roosevelt and stood for his principles. The masses had understood the President and appreciated his policies, though the big interests, the "ledger patriots," had been too blinded by their selfish objects to recognize the permanent value of the principles and policies of America's greatest reformer.

I felt convinced then, as I do now, that the Roosevelt Administration will go down in history as marking the beginning of a new era in our history — an era marking the end of aggression upon our political structure by corporate greed and the beginning of larger opportunities for the individual, in which the moral principles of our public life were rescued from the danger of domination by an unprecedented onrush of commercial power.

At the first Cabinet meeting after the election Roosevelt was buoyant as usual. He made a few preliminary remarks about the approaching end of the Administration: he and his Cabinet, especially the last one, had worked in perfect harmony, and he felt sure we had all had a "bully" time of it; he would retire at the end of his term without any regrets, for he had the satisfaction of knowing that he and his Cabinet had done all in their power for the greatest good of the Nation. I think it is safe to say we all felt a little sad, I know I did, to think that in four months we should separate, and that we should lose the inspiring companionship and guidance of our leader, to whom each of us felt tied by bonds of warm friendship and a sense of profound esteem and highest respect, personally as well as officially.

It seemed to me then that it required no prophet's vision to see that, if Roosevelt kept his health, in four or eight years the people of the country would again demand, with unmistakable and overwhelming voice, that he become President. At the end of eight years, even, he would be only fifty-eight, younger than most Presidents at the time of assuming office.

The President now brought up a question that he had been carrying over from the campaign period. He had received several letters regarding the religion of Mr. Taft.

Some orthodox ministerial organizations had endeavored to use the fact that Mr. Taft was a Unitarian as a reason for prejudicing people against him. Roosevelt had been tempted to answer these letters, but when he presented the matter to the Cabinet it was the general consensus of opinion that he should not do so, that the issue intimately concerned Taft, and information regarding it had better be given out or withheld at Taft's discretion. To this the President agreed, but he was incensed at this un-American attempt to bring religion into politics, especially as Taft was every bit as good a Christian as Washington, and a better one than either Jefferson or Franklin; and his church was the same as that of Adams and Webster.

The election being over, Roosevelt was still desirous of expressing his views in this matter, and he brought with him to the Cabinet meeting the draft of a letter to be sent to one J. C. Martin, of Dayton, Ohio, who had asked for a public statement concerning the faith of Mr. Taft. As usual, he invited criticism and discussion. Several of us made suggestions, and Secretary Root made one which the President asked him to write out so that he might incorporate it. When the corrected version of the letter was read, we all agreed that it was a remarkable document for effectively rebuking the spirit of bigotry and upholding the basic principles of the American Government, and that it should therefore be published. It appeared in the papers of the country three days later.

I made bold to ask the President for the draft of this letter, which he gladly signed and gave to me, and Secretary Root also signed his penciled insert. As I consider this document worthy of a permanent place among American annals, I herewith set it forth from the original in my possession:

THE WHITE HOUSE
WASHINGTON, *November 4,* 1908

MY DEAR SIR:

I have received your letter running in part as follows:

"While it is claimed almost universally that religion should
not enter into politics, yet there is no denying that it does, and
the mass of the voters that are not Catholics will not support
a man for any office, especially for President of the United
States, who is a Roman Catholic.

"Since Taft has been nominated for President by the Republican party, it is being circulated and is constantly urged as
a reason for not voting for Taft that he is an infidel (Unitarian)
and his wife and brother Roman Catholics. . . . If his feelings
are in sympathy with the Roman Catholic church on account
of his wife and brother being Catholics, that would be objectionable to a sufficient number of voters to defeat him. On the
other hand if he is an infidel, that would be sure to mean defeat.
. . . I am writing this letter for the sole purpose of giving Mr.
Taft an opportunity to let the world know what his religious
belief is."

I received many such letters as yours during the campaign,
expressing dissatisfaction with Mr. Taft on religious grounds;
some of them on the ground that he was a Unitarian, and others
on the ground that he was suspected to be in sympathy with
Catholics. I did not answer any of these letters during the
campaign because I regarded it as an outrage even to agitate
such a question as a man's religious convictions, with the purpose of influencing a political election. But now that the campaign is over, when there is opportunity for men calmly to
consider whither such propositions as those you make in your
letter would lead, I wish to invite them to consider them, and I
have selected your letter to answer because you advance both
the objections commonly urged against Mr. Taft, namely:
that he is a Unitarian, and also that he is suspected of improper
sympathy with the Catholics.

You ask that Mr. Taft shall "let the world know what his
religious belief is." This is purely his own private concern; it is
a matter between him and his Maker, a matter for his own
conscience; and to require it to be made public under penalty

of political discrimination is to negative the first principles of our Government, which guarantee complete religious liberty, and the right to each man to act in religious [affairs] as his own conscience dictates. Mr. Taft never asked my advice in the matter, but if he had asked it, I should have emphatically advised him against thus stating publicly his religious belief. The demand for a statement of a candidate's religious belief can have no meaning except that there may be discrimination for or against him because of that belief. Discrimination against the holder of one faith means retaliatory discrimination against men of other faiths. The inevitable result of entering upon such a practice would be an abandonment of our real freedom of conscience and a reversion to the dreadful conditions of religious dissensions which in so many lands have proved fatal to true liberty, to true religion, and to all advance in civilization.

To discriminate against a thoroly upright citizen because he belongs to some particular church, or because, like Abraham Lincoln, he has not avowed his allegiance to any church, is an outrage against that liberty of conscience which is one of the foundations of American life. You are entitled to know whether a man seeking your suffrages is a man of clean and upright life, honorable in all his dealings with his fellows, and fit by qualification and purpose to do well in the great office for which he is a candidate; but you are not entitled to know matters which lie purely between himself and his Maker. If it is proper or legitimate to oppose a man for being a Unitarian, as was John Quincy Adams, for instance, as is the Rev. Edward Everett Hale, at the present moment Chaplain of the Senate, and an American of whose life all good Americans are proud — then it would be equally proper to support or oppose a man because of his views on justification by faith, or the method of administering the sacrament, or the gospel of salvation by works. If you once enter on such a career there is absolutely no limit at which you can legitimately stop.

So much for your objections to Mr. Taft because he is a Unitarian. Now, for your objections to him because you think his wife and brother to be Roman Catholics. As it happens they are not; but if they were, or if he were a Roman Catholic himself, it ought not to affect in the slightest degree any man's

supporting him for the position of President. You say that
"the mass of the voters that are not Catholics will not support
a man for any office, especially for President of the United
States, who is a Roman Catholic." I believe that when you say
this you foully slander your fellow countrymen. I do not for
one moment believe that the mass of our fellow citizens or
that any considerable number of our fellow citizens can be influenced by such narrow bigotry as to refuse to vote for any
thoroly upright and fit man because he happens to have a particular religious creed. Such a consideration should never be
treated as a reason for either supporting or opposing a candidate for political office. Are you aware that there are several
States in this Union where the majority of the people are now
Catholics? I should reprobate in the severest terms the Catholics who in those States (or in any other States) refused to vote
for the most fit man because he happened to be a Protestant;
and my condemnation would be exactly as severe for Protestants who, under reversed circumstances, refused to vote for a
Catholic. In public life I am happy to say that I have known
many men who were elected, and constantly reëlected, to
office in districts where the great majority of their constituents
were of a different religious belief. I know Catholics who have
for many years represented constituencies mainly Protestant,
and Protestants who have for many years represented constituencies mainly Catholic; and among the Congressmen
whom I knew particularly well was one man of Jewish faith
who represented a district in which there were hardly any Jews
at all. All of these men by their very existence in political life
refute the slander you have uttered against your fellow Americans.

I believe that this Republic will endure for many centuries.
If so there will doubtless be among its Presidents Protestants
and Catholics, and very probably at some time Jews. I have
consistently tried while President to act in relation to my
fellow Americans of Catholic faith as I hope that any future
President who happens to be a Catholic will act towards his
fellow Americans of Protestant faith. Had I followed any other
course I should have felt that I was unfit to represent the American people.

In my Cabinet at the present moment there sit side by side

Catholic and Protestant, Christian and Jew, each man chosen because in my belief he is peculiarly fit to exercise on behalf of all our people the duties of the office to wich [sic] I have appointed him. In no case does the man's religious belief in any way influence his discharge of his duties, save as it makes him more eager to act justly and uprightly in his relations to all men. The same principles that have obtained in appointing the members of my Cabinet, the highest officials under me, the officials to whom is entrusted the work of carrying out all the important policies of my administration, are the principles upon which all good Americans should act in choosing, whether by election or appointment, the man to fill any office from the highest to the lowest in the land.

Yours truly
THEODORE ROOSEVELT

It is amusing sometimes to contemplate the matters that occupy the attention of certain zealously inclined religious persons or groups. I recall the flurry caused the year previous by the appearance of the new five, ten, and twenty-dollar gold pieces without the legend, "In God We Trust," which by Roosevelt's direction had been omitted. As a matter of fact that legend was not used on our coins prior to 1866, when a law was passed permitting it subject to the approval of the Secretary of the Treasury. The issuance of these coins, artistically designed by Saint-Gaudens, without the legend was merely a return to the precedents of the fathers of the Republic. I had a small collection of early coins at the time, none of which bore the legend. However, when these new coins appeared several religious bodies passed resolutions disapproving of the President's action. Roosevelt gave out a statement to the effect that he had always regarded that legend as connecting God and mammon, and therefore not as religious, but as sacrilegious. But the opinion against the omission was so strong that in subsequent coinage it was restored. The agitation had been somewhat

anticipated by the President, and he was not the least
perturbed by it. At a dinner one evening he remarked
to me, concerning it, that it was sometimes a good thing
to give people some unimportant subject to discuss, for
it helped put through more important things.

After a Cabinet meeting toward the end of November,
1908, I was talking with the President regarding various
phases of the administration of my Department, and I
mentioned one or two matters that I hoped my successor
would carry to completion. Roosevelt said to me: "Well,
I can tell you one thing that Taft told me; you will be
head of the Department under the next Administration,
if you will accept, and I want you to accept." He had
indicated this once or twice before, but had never stated
it so definitely. I had been perfectly content to finish my
term of office with the close of the Administration, but I
felt if it was the wish of both Roosevelt and Taft that
I continue I should be happy to remain.

Taft had evidently intended retaining several of the
Cabinet officials, but subsequently changed his mind,
which was one of the things that caused the break between Roosevelt and him. Mr. Lawrence F. Abbott has
embodied in his excellent book, "Impressions of Theodore
Roosevelt," an article he contributed in January, 1912,
to the Cornwall, New York, local press, covering the
Roosevelt-Taft relations. Before publication this article
was sent to Roosevelt, and by him annotated and returned to Mr. Abbott. The part regarding the retention
of Cabinet members reads as follows:

Mr. Taft on his election no doubt wished to carry on the
work of his predecessor, and, if not publicly, often privately
said that it was his desire and intention to retain those Cabinet
colleagues of Mr. Roosevelt who had contributed so much to

the re-creation of the Republican Party. [Note by Mr. Roosevelt: *"He told me so, and authorized me to tell the Cabinet, specifically Garfield, Straus and Luke Wright."*] But this intention became gradually modified during the winter of 1908–09.

On December 16th I attended the dinner of the Ohio Society in New York, at which President-elect Taft made his first public address. There was a notable gathering of the leaders of finance and commerce and of the Republican Party, and great expectancy was evident as to what Mr. Taft would say. Ex-Senator Spooner, a brilliant speaker, also made an address, which contained some pointed criticisms of Roosevelt policies. He extolled the Constitution and in a veiled way indicated a deviation from it on the part of Roosevelt. Spooner had made other speeches along these lines, and I confess to some exasperation that this occasion should have been used to attack Roosevelt and his policies.

Taft was the last speaker, and I hoped that when he arose he would resent these attacks, or at any rate uphold the policies of the Administration of which he had been an important member. But I was disappointed. He took no notice of what Spooner or one or two of the other speakers had said. To some of us this was the first evidence that there was a rift in the relationship between Roosevelt and Taft.

Mr. Taft invited me to return to Washington on the train with him next morning. *En route* I spoke of Spooner's speech, and said it appeared to me as an attempt to drive a wedge between him (Taft) and the Roosevelt policies, and that the attack was received by the great financiers who were present, Harriman, Ryan, and others, with great favor. Taft said he had observed it and did not like it. He thought first that he might say something in reply, but on second consideration he decided to let it pass. I told him that usually I enjoyed such an occasion more when I did not have to speak, but on that evening I very much regretted not having the opportunity to answer that attack.

We talked of a number of things, but he said nothing about desiring to have me continue in the Cabinet, though Roosevelt had mentioned the subject to me several times. I then concluded that while in New York a change of mind had come to him in this matter, and what occurred at the dinner seemed to emphasize this conclusion. He was going down to Augusta, Georgia, for a short vacation and asked me to come and see him; but when I reached Washington there was much to be done in my Department, and, as he was besieged by politicians and I had nothing special to bring to his attention, I thought the more considerate thing was not to take up his time needlessly.

In January the New York delegation in Congress gave a dinner to Vice-President-elect Sherman at the Shoreham Hotel in Washington. There were present all the New York Congressmen, Speaker Cannon, the junior Senator from New York, Depew, and Senator-elect Root. Along about ten o'clock the President arrived. As usual on such occasions, there was informal speaking, and of course the President was called upon. His offhand remarks that evening were so inspiring that I regretted they were not taken down that they might have been preserved. In my random notes I have incorporated the substance of some of them; to the effect that our highest purpose should be to perform the duties before us. He said he had been in public life twenty-six years (as I understood), and nearly eight years of that as President, and he had enjoyed it all; adding, humorously, "even the scraps I have had."

Referring to the presidential duties, it was not always possible to spell out from the words of the Constitution what those duties imposed upon the occupant of the office. He instanced the anti-Japanese outbreak in California. There was nothing in the Constitution that either permitted or conflicted with his taking the position he had in his communications to the Governor of California. It was his purpose to call the attention of the people at large in that State and throughout the country to the dangers of the situation if the contemplated legislation were put through. He referred to the impractical attitude of the peace societies and other peace advocates in objecting to all appropriations for naval expenditures. They could render a better service by agitating to prevent a condition of international irritation that had all the possibilities of war; the good effect of the well-considered "Gentlemen's Agreement" with Japan had been negatived by the unreasonable legislation proposed in California.

Making reference in a general way to the work of the Administration, he said it was important to look to the future, but to fix one's eyes on the future and neglect the present was as unwise as to limit one's view entirely to the present. He hoped the people would not trouble themselves as to what to do with the ex-President; so far as he was concerned he was able to take care of himself; upon his return from Africa they would find him working not as an ex-President, but as a private citizen in the ranks, and coöperating with his party representatives for the best interests of the country.

He closed by saying that what may become of one's personal reputation, one's fame as an individual, is of no consequence. The individual disappears. Oblivion will engulf us all. Only results count. In order to achieve results there must be coöperation. He was always ready to coöperate with men whose tendencies were forward, even if such coöperation led only one step forward where he would have liked ten; but he would refuse to coöperate with men whose tendencies were backward.

In my Department I continued to push matters forward without allowing the approaching close of the Administration to influence me. Under date of January 22d I received a letter from President-elect Taft, in answer to my inquiry, indicating that in all probability I should not be retained in the Cabinet. He said he would have written sooner, but had not decided in what capacity he wished me to serve his Administration, though he thought perhaps I might be willing to accept an embassy. However, he had not definitely decided not to retain me in the Cabinet. He found Cabinet-making quite a difficult job.

Three days later I received another note from him mentioning the embassy to Japan. He hoped to suit whatever preference I might have in the matter after he had had a chance to talk it over with me in Washington.

At the last Cabinet meeting there was very little business transacted. The President talked to us informally and very impressively, saying he wished to repeat, what he had said before, that a President usually receives credit for all the good work done in his Administration, but, speaking for himself, his co-workers had an equal share in that credit; no President, he said, had had a more effective, able, and coöperative Cabinet than he. Then he added humorously that he wanted no response to modify that statement. Some of us, however, could not resist expressing in brief the sentiments we felt, and

I answered him: If we have performed our duties to your satisfaction and to the satisfaction of the country, it is due in no small degree to the fact that around this table we have caught the contagion of your fine spirit which has enabled each of us to rise to our highest level of efficiency because we felt we were coöperating in furthering those moral issues which you have vitalized in our economic and national life. I wish to add that our President in his boundless generosity has always given to each one of us not only the fullest credit for what we have done, but a recognition far beyond our individual merits.

On March 4th, at nine-thirty in the morning, the members of the Cabinet assembled in the White House and accompanied the President to the Capitol. We went to the President's room on the Senate side and there awaited the bills to be brought in for the signature of the President. That is usual at the closing of a session, and many bills that had been passed in the last few days came from the engrosser for the signature of the President. Each bill was handed to the Secretary whose department it affected, and upon reading it over the Secretary advised the President whether or not to sign it. There were three bills affecting my Department, two of which I approved, and those he signed. Of the third I had no knowledge and so stated; that one the President passed to become law without his signature.

At eleven o'clock President-elect Taft came into the room, and we all extended our congratulations to him. Precisely at noon President Roosevelt went into the Senate Chamber and we followed. Both he and the President-elect took a seat before the Vice-President's desk, and we were seated in the front row, where were also the ambassadors of the foreign powers. Vice-President Fairbanks opened the proceedings with an appropriate address, whereupon Vice-President-elect Sherman was sworn in and made a brief address. The new Senators were then sworn in in groups of four. President-elect Taft next took the oath of office, which was administered by Chief Justice Fuller.

Roosevelt then left the Senate Chamber to go to the station. In our carriages we followed him, and at either side marched over a thousand Republican delegates from the City of New York. One could observe on all sides evidence of a feeling of depression and regret at the departure of the man who had endeared himself to the country at large as no President had since the days of Lincoln. It was apparent then, as the years have proven, that he had the largest personal following ever attained by any man in this country. By personal following I mean one that is not dependent on office, but persists out of office as well. People were attracted to him because he appealed to their idealism. They had faith in him; they had an affection for him. They believed he would lead them where they ought to go and where, therefore, they wished to go. It was the fact that the mass of the people throughout the land regarded him with love and admiration as the embodiment of their ideals of Americanism which enabled him to exercise such a tremendous power for the welfare of the country and which is destined to enshrine his memory among the greatest men in our history.

When we reached the station, the large room reserved on special occasions for officials was closed, and only such persons admitted as were identified by Secretary Loeb — members of the family, members of the Cabinet, and a few intimate friends. When I bade the President, now ex-President, good-bye, he said we should meet often and should still work together.

Roosevelt at the age of fifty was once more a private citizen, having been the youngest President in our history. I am sure I speak for my colleagues as well as for myself when I say we felt we were parting not only from our official chief, but from one of our nearest and dearest friends.

We returned in our carriages to the White House where we took buffet lunch with President and Mrs. Taft; then to the stand erected in front of the White House to witness the review.

CHAPTER XI

MY THIRD MISSION TO TURKEY

A surgical operation delays my departure — Roosevelt in Africa delighted with my return to Turkey under Taft Administration — Received by another Sultan — A royal weakling — The invisible power of the new régime — Foreign concessions and political intrigues — Turkish funeral customs — The Mohammedan indifference to death — Roosevelt urges me to meet him in Cairo — We visit Salonica and Athens — Received by King George of Greece — Roosevelt's arrival at Cairo — The Kaiser's invitation — Roosevelt condemns assassination of Premier despite warning to avoid subject in his address — Roosevelt declines an audience with the Pope — At tea with Prince and Princess Eitel Friedrich — A distinguished Arab on international relations — Rumblings in the Balkans — The brilliant Venizelos — My objections to "dollar diplomacy" — Former Vice-President and Mrs. Fairbanks visit us — Other distinguished Americans visit the Embassy — We visit the King and Queen of Roumania — How the Queen adopted the pen-name "Carmen Sylva" — The cell-like study of the Queen — Vienna and London — Two Rothschilds express their views of the Triple Entente — "The greatest pleasure of going abroad is returning home" — Reflections of the rift between the Roosevelt policies and the Taft Administration.

MY return to private life in 1909 did not prove a disturbing transition for me, notwithstanding the fact that, on entering the Cabinet in 1906, I had terminated all of my professional and business interests. I had no plans for the future. I had always entered public office not without some trepidation, and had always retired from such an office with a certain sense of relief and satisfaction. But my past training and natural disposition had by no means prepared me to be content with a life of "elegant leisure." I soon found much to occupy my energies, and again took part in numerous semi-public activities, and my coöperation seemed all the more welcome because of my experience in office both at home and abroad.

Soon after my return to New York, I was formally welcomed at a banquet at the Hotel Astor, under the auspices of a number of prominent citizens, led by William McCarroll, who had succeeded me as president of the New York Board of Trade when I had left for Washington. It was, of course, gratifying to me to receive this attention from my fellow citizens, irrespective of party, among whom I expected to pass my remaining years. Among the speakers were John Mitchel, St. Clair McKelway, Richard Watson Gilder, poet and editor of the "Century Magazine"; the Reverend Leander Chamberlain, and Dr. Lyman Abbott. Dr. Abbott, one of America's foremost intellectual and spiritual leaders, is the only surviving member of this group, and I am happy to be able to record that he is still in good health, with his pen, which has lost nothing of its charm and vigor, ever inspiring.

I quite dismissed from my mind any idea of holding office in the Taft Administration, especially after Taft had reconsidered his statement or promise to Roosevelt to retain me in the Cabinet. Shortly after my return from Washington, however, on March 13, 1909, President Taft wrote me that he would be glad to have me accept the embassy at Constantinople, and that in time he would transfer me to some other post that might be more acceptable. He concluded: "I hope this will meet your view, because I should like to have you in my administration."

My personal relations with Mr. Taft had of course always been most cordial and agreeable. I wrote him that, naturally, I had no desire to return to a post which I had occupied twice before, unless extraordinary conditions developed which particularly required my past experience there and made it imperative that I accept as a public duty, and even then I should accept only for a short time.

The President wrote me that he would be glad to have me accept the post at Constantinople (which had been raised to an embassy since my last mission), and that in time he would transfer me either to Japan or to some acceptable post in Europe, and I soon received the following letter from the State Department:

April 29, 1909

MY DEAR MR. STRAUS:

The President now desires me to make to you the formal offer of the post of Ambassador to Turkey. The epoch-making events now occurring in the Turkish Empire bring with them difficulties and opportunities which make that post take on even greater importance, and the President feels that your past service and keen knowledge of the Near East make you peculiarly qualified to take charge at this time of the important Embassy at Constantinople.

Adverting to your previous conversations with the President and with me, relative to your disinclination to accept a post which you have previously held, I would add that the President would be glad to consider your transfer from Constantinople to some other post if an opportune time should arrive when this was practicable and when you wished to relinquish the important mission which is now tendered to you.

I am, my dear Mr. Straus,

Very sincerely yours

P. C. KNOX

In June, while I was getting ready for my departure, I was compelled to undergo an operation for appendicitis. I therefore wrote the President asking him to relieve me of my appointment, as my illness would delay me for another month or more. The President promptly advised me not to be disturbed by the delay, that he would be glad to wait until my health was entirely restored before having me start, and that it was not possible, because of the troubled conditions in Turkey, at that time to find any one to replace me.

At this time I received a letter from Roosevelt, addressed from the heart of British East Africa, expressing pleasure at my again going to Turkey:

SAIGO SOI, LAKE NAIVASHA
16th July, 1909

MY DEAR MR. AMBASSADOR:

Your letter gave me real pleasure. Mrs. Roosevelt had written of you, and your dear wife, and two beautiful daughters, coming out to see her; and she told me how much she enjoyed your visit. As for the address at the dedication of the memorial window, my dear fellow, you said the very things that I would most like to have said about me, especially coming from a man whom I so much respect and who is my close personal friend.

I am delighted that you have accepted the Turkish Embassy. The situation was wholly changed by the revolution, and at this moment I think that Constantinople is the most important and most interesting diplomatic post in the world.

I shan't try to write to you at any length, for I find it simply impossible to keep up with correspondence here in camp, and am able to write my letters at all at the moment only because a friend has turned up with a typewriter.

I can't say how I look forward to seeing you. I know nothing whatever of American politics at the present moment. We have had a very successful and enjoyable trip.

With love to Mrs. Straus and with hearty congratulations not to you but to our country for your having gone to Turkey, I am

Faithfully yours
THEODORE ROOSEVELT

The first paragraph refers to an address I had made in May. The Reverend J. Wesley Hill, of the Metropolitan Temple, had one of the windows of his church dedicated to the Roosevelt Administration and I was asked to deliver the principal address. I took for my subject "The Spirit of the Roosevelt Administration," and reviewed the leading progressive acts of the Administration and pointed out how they were all aimed to secure the rights and enlarge the opportunities of the plain people. I had in mind counteracting the influence then current to belittle the work of the Roosevelt Administration. For with the beginning of the Taft Administration, the reactionaries in and out of Congress had become more bitter and outspoken in their opposition to the Roosevelt policies; it seems that they were encouraged by the report that a break had taken place between Roosevelt and Taft, and by the fact that certain Senators and members of the House who had fallen out with Roosevelt seemed to be specially welcomed at the White House. My address was therefore widely quoted in the press and subsequently circulated in pamphlet form. I quote one of its salient paragraphs:

All the Roosevelt measures and policies were based not only upon moral convictions, but upon a statesman's forethought for the welfare of the country. That he would encounter the powerful opposition of the offending corporate interests was to be foreseen and expected. All reforms and reformers no less in our country than in others have encountered the reactionaries of privilege and power, who persuaded themselves that their so-called vested interests, however acquired and however administered, were their vested rights. These trespassing reactionaries when not checked and made obedient to the legitimate needs and righteous demands of the many produced a spirit of revenge which broke out into revolution at the extreme opposite end of the social system.

On August 18th Mrs. Straus and I left New York on the S.S. Prinz Friedrich Wilhelm for Cherbourg. A week later we were in Paris, where we met Mrs. Roosevelt with three of her children, Ethel, Archie, and Quentin. During the fortnight of our stay we saw a great deal of them and several times we went to the theater or sight-seeing together. Mrs. Roosevelt told me that her husband

had solicitously inquired about us in several of his letters
and suggested that I write him.

When we reached Constantinople on September 18th,
the month of Ramazan had begun, and the Minister of
Foreign Affairs, Rifaat Pasha, informed me that the
Sultan, now Mohammed V, brother of Abdul Hamid,
would probably delay receiving me for a week or ten
days, until the middle of Ramazan, and not at the end,
as was customary with the former Sultan. Accordingly
I was received on Monday, October 4th.

The residence of the new Sultan was in the Palace of
Dolma Bagtché. As my rank now was that of ambassador, this audience was a more ceremonious one than
those of my former missions. Eight royal carriages came
from the Palace to conduct me and my staff to the residence of His Royal Majesty. The first of these, in which
I rode, was a most gorgeous affair, with outriders and
two postilions in uniforms of brilliant colors standing on
a platform in the rear of the carriage. The streets of Pera
were crowded with spectators as these dazzling equipages
went by, in spite of a light rain that was falling. As we
entered the Palace, a large troop of soldiers arranged
along each side of the main gate presented arms. I was
met by the Chief Introducer of Ambassadors and several
other officials, who conducted me to the audience chamber
above. With my dragoman, Mr. Gargiulo, I then proceeded with the Chief Introducer of Ambassadors into
the presence of the Sultan while the rest of my staff were
detained in an anteroom.

The Sultan was a man of about sixty-five, short and
very thick-set. He was dressed in military uniform, but
appeared physically inert and clumsy. During the whole
thirty-three years' reign of his brother, Abdul Hamid, he
had been imprisoned in a palace on the Bosphorus and

kept under constant guard. He grew up in ignorance and his appearance clearly indicated mental backwardness. His eyes were dull and his appearance almost that of an imbecile, except when an occasional spark of animation was noticeable. Withal he seemed kind and good-natured.

When I made my address, I felt as though I were speaking to an image rather than a human being, and I went through it as quickly as possible, omitting some parts for the sake of brevity, realizing that it was simply a form and that the Introducer of Ambassadors would presently read the whole of it in Turkish. The Sultan was then handed the Turkish reply to read, which he did haltingly, even consulting the Introducer at times to decipher a word. That being over, the doors to the ante-room were thrown open and my staff entered, also the consul-general and his staff, and each man was presented to the Sultan. We were then conducted back to the ante-room and served with cigarettes and coffee, even though it was Ramazan, when Mohammedans do not drink or smoke until after sundown. In a few minutes more we were conducted back to our carriages. The whole function was more in the nature of mimicry on the stage than a serious diplomatic performance.

With my dragoman I paid my official calls upon the Grand Vizier and the Minister of Foreign Affairs at the Porte, both of whom received me in full-dress uniform and immediately returned the calls.

The Government of Turkey under the new régime, with a Sultan who was merely a figurehead, was in the hands of the ministry, and the ministers in turn were appointed and controlled by the Young Turks, or so-called party of "Union and Progress" which had brought on the revolution of 1908 and deposed the late Sultan in April, 1909. It required no great insight to see that a government thus

controlled by an invisible power without official responsibility could not be one of either liberty or progress; yet
the leading ministers were men of ability and some of
them men of considerable experience. Rifaat Pasha, for
instance, was formerly ambassador to London, an intelligent and thoroughly enlightened statesman. Hussein
Hilmi Pasha, the Grand Vizier, was the former member
of a joint committee charged with the government of
Macedonia. Talaat Bey, the Minister of the Interior,
had previously held an inferior position. He was one of
the leading representatives of the Young Turk Party and
was believed to be the one mainly responsible for the
terrible slaughter and martyrdom of Armenians during
the World War. After that war he fled to Berlin, where,
in 1920, he was assassinated by a young Armenian.
Djavid Bey, Minister of Finance, was a remarkably
brilliant young man, about thirty-four years old, from
Salonica. It was said he was a Donmeh; that is, a member of a sect of apostate Jews also known as Sabbatians
from the name of its Messiah or prophet, Sabbataï Zevi,
who gave the sect its romantic origin in the middle of the
seventeenth century. Professor Graetz gives a full and
interesting description of this whole movement in his
"History of the Jews."

Among my colleagues were Gerard Lowther, who
represented Great Britain; Marquis Imperiali, Italy; and
Baron Marschall von Bieberstein, Germany. Because of
the lack of general society in Constantinople, the members of the diplomatic corps became very intimate with
one another, and this was so with my colleagues generally
and especially between the German ambassador and
myself, for we were also fellow members of the Hague
Tribunal, and in 1907 he was chairman of the German
delegation at the Conferences. He was by far the ablest

and most forceful diplomat in Constantinople at this period. During his term of office there, German influence in the Ottoman Empire entirely overshadowed the British. This influence started its ascendancy following the visit of the Emperor in 1898, when he obtained the promise of the concession for the building of the Bagdad Railway.

When first the Ottoman Government granted this concession, the financiers of Great Britain, France, and Germany had come to a tentative agreement for the joint construction of the road. The Germans then wanted more than an equal control in the enterprise, and the negotiations fell through. Had the interests of Great Britain and Germany been united in the Near East, there probably would have been quite a different alignment of Powers on the chessboard of Europe, and perhaps the World War would have been prevented. The Bagdad Railway, if jointly constructed, would have contributed to a better understanding between Great Britain and Germany instead of accentuating more and more their differences as the road proceeded toward the Persian Gulf.

I could plainly see evidences, both in social life in the Turkish capital and in the unmistakable trend of diplomatic alignments, of a rapidly developing *entente* between Great Britain, France, and Russia. Since the Russo-Japanese War, and with the coming of the new régime in Turkey, Russia had changed her attitude toward Turkey and had become extremely friendly. Italy maintained a neutral attitude as between Great Britain and Germany. Austria, as always, if not controlled by, was in close sympathy with, Germany.

Abdul Hamid had developed into the most autocratic ruler of modern times. With the overthrow of his régime and its colossal system of secret agents, there was hope for a gradual development of a parliamentary government, especially as some of the officials in the Turkish ministry were forward-looking men, of considerable ability and honesty of purpose. However, just as the jealousy between the Great Powers had prevented the dismemberment of the Ottoman Empire for a hundred years or more, so the same jealousy prevented rehabilitation. Great Britain favored the building up of Turkey; the policy of Russia, Germany, and Austria was to keep Turkey weak and disorganized.

With the establishment of the new régime Germany, England, France, and Italy sought concessions from the Government for the development of mines and the building of railroads, docks, and other public utilities. The country was rich and undeveloped, and the Turks themselves had neither the capacity nor the money for such undertakings. But the effect of these concessions was undermining the sovereignty and was foreshadowing conflict.

With the passing of the old régime and the beginning of the new, an appalling massacre of Armenians had taken place in Cilicia; and it was believed that this massacre, which cost the lives of twenty thousand or more victims, was engineered by the old régime to discredit the new.

The first fall of the new ministry was brought about by what was known as the Lynch affair, which concerned a steamship monopoly of an English company on the Tigris and Euphrates. The Lynch Company had a perpetual concession to navigate two steamers from the Persian Gulf to Bassora, and from there to Bagdad on the Tigris and as far as navigable on the Euphrates. There was also a Turkish company with a similar concession, and the English company undertook negotiations with the Grand Vizier for the consolidation of the two companies, by which the Lynch Company was to pay the Ottoman Government £160,000 in cash. The new company was to have a grant for seventy-two years, with the right given to the Ottoman Government to buy it all out at the end of thirty-six years on a basis to be agreed upon. The new company was to have the monopoly of the navigation, and it was to have an English president with a board of directors composed half of Englishmen and half of Turkish subjects.

The arrangements were made on behalf of the ministry by the Grand Vizier, Hilmi Pasha, and the matter was then brought up under interpellation in the Parliament. The first vote taken was against confirmation of the transaction. This amounted to an expression of lack of confidence in the ministry, whereupon the Grand Vizier stated that unless the transaction was confirmed, he and his colleagues would resign. Two days later, on motion of Djavid Bey, the eloquent Minister of Finance, the whole matter was reconsidered and an equally large vote cast confirming the transaction. Aside from registering confidence or the lack of it in the ministry, the vote against confirmation would also have been interpreted as an act of hostility toward England. For the time being the problem was settled.

Shortly thereafter, however, there arose in the Bagdad vilayet such opposition to this transaction that the deputies from that province threatened to withdraw from Parliament. The negotiations were regarded as a victory for England in the strengthening of her influence along the Persian Gulf, and a defeat for the Germans, whose railway terminus would be at Bassora, at the junction of the two rivers. The Persian Gulf, on the other hand, was of strategic interest to Great Britain because it is the corridor to India. German influence proved the stronger with the Young Turks, and the consolidation of the Lynch Company with the Turkish company was not confirmed.

This vote resulted in the fall of the ministry, for a month later the Young Turks forced the resignation of the Grand Vizier. In giving his resignation to the Sultan, the Grand Vizier stated his reason as poor health, but that was merely for public consumption. Talaat Bey and Djavid Bey were known to be prominent members of the Young Turks, and the Grand Vizier, who had been Minister of the Interior and then Grand Vizier under the former Sultan, was not fully trusted as being in accord with the régime of the Young Turks. To bridge over this ministerial crisis the Young Turks offered to Hakki Pasha, ambassador at Rome, the grand viziership, which he accepted.

Early in the year 1910 the diplomatic circle in Constantinople was thrown, if not into gloom, at least into official mourning. The Grand Duke Nicolaiovich, uncle of Czar Nicholas of Russia, and King Leopold of Belgium, died. At Constantinople, more than at any capital in the world, ceremonies of any kind were exaggerated to make an impression upon the Turkish mind. And so in both these instances elaborate funeral services were held which the diplomatic representatives attended in full uniform, loaded with all decorations. The service for the Grand Duke lasted about two hours, although no one apparently listened to any part but the singing, and there was a general sigh of relief when it was over. The service for the Belgian king was of a similar nature, with the addition of a huge catafalque, surmounted by a crown, erected in the center of the church, which was so cold that most of us kept on our overcoats.

Shortly thereafter I attended a third funeral, this time

a Turkish one. Hamdy Bey, director and organizer of the Imperial Museum, had died on February 24, 1910, at about sixty-eight years of age. I had known him for twenty years; he had always been courteous and obliging to American visitors, and had shown many special favors to me, notably in regard to the permit for the Babylonian excavations. The services took place at eleven in the morning in front of the entrance to the Sophia Mosque. The funeral cortège consisted of about a dozen dervishes clad in long black robes with high conical head-coverings made of rough yellowish-gray woolen material, and about three times the height of an ordinary fez. They chanted in plaintive tones, "Allah! Allah! Allah!" Next came the coffin-bearers, six in number. As is the custom among the Mohammedans, the coffin was of plain boards, covered with shawls, over which was draped a black covering with some phrases from the Koran worked into it. On top of the coffin was the red fez or head-covering of the deceased. Behind the coffin walked many of the leading officials of the Government and other prominent people. The entire ministry was present. I joined the procession shortly before reaching the mosque and was asked to walk beside Rifaat Pasha, the Minister of Foreign Affairs. I was the only representative of a foreign power present, and my attendance was warmly appreciated by the Turkish officials and by the relatives of the deceased.

When the procession reached the mosque, the coffin was placed upon the pediment of a Greek column near the entrance, an appropriate place for it to rest, I thought. All the mourners having gathered round, one of the imans or priests standing by the coffin recited a prayer of about six minutes' duration, in the midst of which he put the following questions in Turkish to the bystanders:

"You all knew Hamdy Bey; what kind of a man was he?"

And the audience replied "Eyi," meaning "good."

"If he has done any wrong to you, do you forgive him?"

Their reply in Turkish signified, "We do."

The body was then borne on the shoulders of the carriers to the museum enclosure which was near by, in front of the Chinili Kiosque. Djavid Bey then mounted the marble portico and from there delivered a funeral oration lasting about twelve minutes, in which he referred to the excellent work accomplished by the deceased under the most trying circumstances during the reign of corruption and oppression, and pointed to the buildings surrounding the enclosure as the most fitting and lasting memorial.

A funeral among the Mohammedans is not regarded as a cause for mourning. Death is looked upon as a matter of course. Every respect is shown the memory of the deceased, but there is neither sanctimony nor suppressed sorrow at the funeral service. This is doubtless due to the spirit of fatalism deeply embedded in their religion, and which colors so deeply the life and philosophy of a Mohammedan.

The attitude of prayer on the part of the bystanders during this ceremony was one I had never observed at the ordinary services in the mosques. They all stood erect, arms horizontally extended forward from the elbow, palms turned upward. The simplicity of the whole service impressed me very much. The entire dramatic scene, in its picturesque surroundings, was unforgettable. The day was bright and beautiful, and the Bosphorus wore its most attractive coloring. Turkish functions, whether official or ceremonial, are always arranged with quiet dignity and precision.

Among the pleasant things during this sojourn in Constantinople was a trip to Cairo to meet Roosevelt. On New Year's Day, 1910, I received a note from him scribbled off in pencil, asking that I meet him if possible about March 22d at Cairo; he would wire me later from the upper Nile a more exact date. He could not come to Constantinople because he had to include Christiania in his itinerary, which made it a little difficult to carry out his plans.

In due time I received a telegram from him from Gondokoro, on the lower Nile, to meet him on March 23d. Accordingly Mrs. Straus and I started from Constantinople on March 7th in the embassy dispatch boat, Scorpion, a ship of about seven hundred and fifty tons, manned by a crew of seventy-five or eighty bluejackets. We left a little early in order to be able to make stops at several ports on the way, notably Salonica, which in many respects was the most advanced city of the empire. It had about 135,000 inhabitants, of whom some 20,000 were Greek, 15,000 Bulgarian and other Balkan peoples, and the rest chiefly Jews. The ancestors of many of the latter had settled there centuries before as refugees from Spain at the time of the Inquisition. As was the case with many of the other Jews of Turkey their language was Ladino, a Spanish dialect.

We stayed at Salonica three days and visited the principal institutions of the city, and the Jewish hospitals and schools, all of which I found superior to any I had seen in Turkey proper. They were conducted on modern scientific lines. The leaders of finance and industry were the Jews and the Greeks, while at the same time the hewers of wood and the drawers of water, those who loaded the ships and did the hauling, were also principally Jews.

Next we stopped at Athens, where we met my brother

Isidor and his wife, who were making a tour of the Orient. Our six-days' stay in Athens was made delightful for us by the courtesies of our minister, George H. Moses, now and for some years past United States Senator from New Hampshire. We visited the Boulé, or Greek Chamber, one afternoon. What mainly impressed one was the lack of decorum and dignity. The Minister of War, who also represented the military league, was the dominating power. I thought then how unfortunate it was for a country to be ruled by the sabered politician. Then truly does the army become a curse to the Government, as well as inefficient for the protection it is supposed to give. When the army enters politics, then politics also enters the army, a double calamity for any state. But that seemed to be the lamentable condition of Greece as I saw it at that time.

We were received in audience by King George, who spoke perfect English. I had met him before, on my visit to Athens in 1888. He conversed freely and with the objectiveness of an outsider about the disturbed political conditions of Greece, which was at the time dominated by a military league, a secret organization of army officers. Referring to this league, the King said that outsiders probably regarded him as weak in giving way to its demands, but that they did not appreciate conditions; he did it to prevent a revolution, and he hoped that unity among the people might be promoted by the approaching meeting of the Assembly for the revision of the constitution.

He seemed remarkably well informed regarding our system of government and American affairs generally. He said that Greece needed a council of state with coördinate legislative power, rather than a senate. He appeared to favor a small appointed body rather than an elective senate. He said he had been in Greece for fifty years; he had come there when he was eighteen and was educated for the navy. He added drily that it might have been better if he had stuck to the profession of his training.

He knew I was on my way to Egypt to meet Roosevelt for whom he expressed the greatest admiration. He said he had read several of Roosevelt's books and had always had a desire to meet him.

We went on to Alexandria by the Roumanian boat. The sea seemed rough, so we thought best to send the Scorpion on ahead so that we might make the trip leisurely, and on March 21st we arrived in Cairo, where Consul-General Iddings had reserved rooms for us at the Shepheard Hotel, adjoining the suite reserved for the Roosevelts.

The Roosevelt party arrived from Luxor at about nine o'clock on the morning of March 24th. We went to the station to meet the train, and there was quite a gathering, including the consul-general and his wife, an aide of the Khedive, an aide of the Sirdar, a number of American missionaries, and several others. Cairo was astir. American flags were flying on many buildings, and at the hotel a great crowd cheered as Roosevelt entered.

After breakfast the first morning, Roosevelt wanted me to read several letters he had dictated, among others a reply to the invitation that had been extended by the Kaiser asking Roosevelt to be his guest in the palace in Berlin. The invitation did not include Mrs. Roosevelt, and this he resented. He therefore dictated a letter to Ambassador David J. Hill saying he would be pleased to call on the Emperor on the day designated, but could not accept the invitation to be his guest, as he did not purpose to separate from Mrs. Roosevelt. He asked Ambassador Hill to be sure to submit the message to the Emperor's

chamberlain in such a way that it could not be construed
as a hint for an invitation for Mrs. Roosevelt. I advised
against sending this letter and asked him to let me handle
the matter. This I did, and Ambassador Hill soon discovered, what I had suspected, that the Emperor was
not aware at the time the invitation was sent that Mrs.
Roosevelt was with her husband. The omission was immediately corrected.

Roosevelt was, of course, anxious for news from home.
He spoke again of Taft's having told him he would retain
Garfield and myself, and said Taft was aware that he
(Roosevelt) was specially attached to us both. I showed
him an article in a current "North American Review,"
entitled "The First Year of Taft's Administration,"
which plainly showed that much ground had been
lost.

Roosevelt was to deliver an address before the Egyptian National University. He handed me the draft of it
and asked me to criticize it freely. I suggested a number of
changes, which he promptly adopted. He had been asked
not to refer to the recent assassination of the Premier of
Egypt, Budros Pasha — a deed that had probably been
inspired by the Nationalists, a party composed chiefly of
young students, half-educated theorists, and a few others
whose shibboleth was "Egypt for the Egyptians." Roosevelt considered that it would be cowardly and evasive to
avoid this subject, and that usually the subjects one is
asked not to refer to are the ones uppermost in the minds
of the people. Besides, if he did not openly condemn such
an act, his silence might be interpreted as an approval.
In view of all the circumstances I fully agreed with him.
The speech was delivered in a large hall filled to capacity;
the consular body and many Egyptian ministers were
present. About one third of the audience understood

English, and the address was enthusiastically received, and had an excellent effect, as I afterward learned, upon law and order in Egypt.

Roosevelt gave a luncheon at the hotel to Sir Gaston Maspero and Professor Sayce, the eminent Egyptologists, which we attended. There were about fifteen people present, among them Mr. Lawrence F. Abbott, of "The Outlook," who had joined the Roosevelt party at Khartum. It was a delightful occasion and reminded us of the old days at the White House. Roosevelt always had the faculty of surrounding himself with people who, whether from prominent or humble walks of life, were worth while. There were so many facets to his nature that he could make interesting contacts with all sorts of folk, those of the forest as well as those of the closet.

From Gondokoro, Roosevelt had written Ambassador Leishman at Rome saying he would be glad of the honor of presentation to His Holiness Pope Pius X. At Cairo he received the following cable reply from Ambassador Leishman:

The Rector of the American Catholic College, Monsignor Kennedy, in reply to inquiry which I caused to be made requests that the following communication be transmitted to you: "The Holy Father will be delighted to grant audience to Mr. Roosevelt on April 5, and hopes nothing will arise to prevent it, such as the much-regretted incident which made the reception of Mr. Fairbanks impossible."

I merely transmit this communication without having committed you in any way to accept the conditions imposed, as the form appears objectionable, clearly indicating that an audience would be canceled in case you should take any action while here that might be construed as countenancing the Methodist mission work here. . . .

Mr. Fairbanks, it may be remembered, was granted an audience with His Holiness, but on the same day accepted an invitation to lecture before the Methodist body in Rome whose propaganda was inimical to the Vatican. This displeased His Holiness and the audience was thereupon canceled.

Roosevelt answered Leishman's cable to the effect that while he fully recognized the right of the Holy Father to receive or not to receive whomsoever he chose, he could not submit to conditions which would in any way limit his freedom of conduct. But the Vatican stood firm on the conditions set forth:

His Holiness will be much pleased to grant an audience to Mr. Roosevelt, for whom he entertains great esteem, both personally and as President of the United States. His Holiness quite recognizes Mr. Roosevelt's entire right to freedom of conduct. On the other hand, in view of the circumstances, for which neither His Holiness nor Mr. Roosevelt is responsible, an audience could not occur except on the understanding expressed in the former message.

Consequently, while Roosevelt did not go to the Vatican, he was received with great cordiality at the Quirinal by King Victor Emmanuel III. In order not to have the Vatican incident misunderstood at home, Roosevelt sent a message regarding it to the American people, through the pages of "The Outlook" of April 9, 1910. Mr. Abbott makes detailed mention of the episode in his "Impressions of Theodore Roosevelt."

Mrs. Straus and I were invited to luncheon with Sir Eldon and Lady Gorst, British consul-general at Cairo, where we met Professor Oscar Browning, of Cambridge, among others. Sir Eldon was the successor of Lord Cromer, and had had many years of experience in Egypt in official capacities. He spoke of the unrest among the natives, especially those who had lived abroad as university students. These were in fact the leaders of the Nationalist Party, a movement stimulated by the establishment of the new régime in Turkey and the parliamentary form of government in Persia. Some of the Arabic papers were encouraging, if not actually inciting, opposition to the British protectorate. He said the British policy was to grant by degrees an always larger share of local self-government, but it was feared that if the national spirit was too much encouraged there would be a reversion to conditions that prevailed prior to the British occupation of the country. He explained that Lord Cromer's administration covered the period of national improvements, such as the reform of taxes, and the building of railways and irrigation works; and that now had come the desire for political changes.

I have referred to that part of Roosevelt's speech at the National University in which he condemned the assassination of the premier. Sir Eldon said he had been consulted in regard to the speech before its delivery, and that if he had expressed any objection he was sure Mr. Roosevelt would either have omitted that part of the address or declined to speak altogether, for he knew Mr. Roosevelt would not do anything to embarrass British interests. He had had no objection, and made this clear to Mr. Iddings, who made the inquiry.

We were all invited to a tea at the German Diplomatic Agency, to meet the Prince and Princess Eitel Friedrich, who were on a visit to Egypt. Eitel Friedrich is the second son of William II of Germany. I had little opportunity to speak with him because he and Roosevelt were engaged almost the entire time in an animated conversation, during which both remained standing. My impression of the Prince was that he seemed tremendously impressed with his own importance. I had a pleasant chat with the Princess, whom I found very charming. She seemed to me of a type more Austrian than German.

On March 30th we left Cairo, going with the Roosevelt party as far as Alexandria, where they boarded a ship for Naples, and we went aboard the Scorpion. Our little ship was dressed in its complimentary flags, the band was playing, and the commander had drawn up the blue-jackets on the main deck to present arms, so that the Roosevelt party was being saluted with all the form, splendor, and dignity that our ship could muster. The sea was much calmer than when we came, and we reached Constantinople in a little less than three days. I had intended stopping at several other ports to confer with our consuls, and to visit Jerusalem, Beirut, and Smyrna; but as my instructions were to hasten my return I did so.

During my third mission in Turkey I saw quite a good deal of Mahmoud Chevket Pasha, the generalissimo of the Turkish army, who was at the same time Minister of War. He was fifty-two years old, of spare frame, medium height, with a full beard that was turning gray. He was an Arab, born in Bagdad. He told me that, when he was a younger man and a major in the army, he spent ten years in Germany studying the German military system and training. It was evident to every observer that under his generalship the Turkish army had vastly improved both in appearance and in discipline.

I found him a well-educated, modern man. At that time he enjoyed a world-wide reputation as the most important and dominating official in the empire, because, as general of the Third Army Corps, stationed at Salonica, he had marched his men to Constantinople, dethroned the late Sultan, and established the new régime. Within a few months he had made visits to Austria,

France, and Germany, and was received with great honors. In the leading cities of these countries he made addresses that were statesmanlike and internationally tactful. Throughout he represented his country with admirable tact and judgment.

During one of our conversations the generalissimo told me that the only cloud on the horizon was the effort of the Greeks to make the Island of Crete a part of their country. He thought the general conditions in Turkey were good and that there was no danger of internal troubles, because the Government had things well in hand. Should Greece make any hostile move, he knew Turkey could easily defeat her. He did not think that any of the Balkan Powers would join Greece, since they could not do so without drawing in some of the big Powers, and the latter would not, as a matter of self-interest, allow the Balkan States to join Greece in a war.

We were speaking rather frankly, and I asked him whether he thought Russia desired the advancement of Turkey and its steady growth under the new régime. He realized that Russia was then entirely friendly, but said it was not because she favored a progressive Turkey, but because since her war with Japan she was in no position to take advantage of the misfortunes of Turkey. I asked him what he thought of the real attitude of Germany. He answered that he thought Germany entirely friendly; that her desire was, of course, to advance her commercial interests in the Ottoman Empire, but that in this respect she was perhaps not different from other nations who regarded Turkey as a good field for commercial operations.

Shortly thereafter the political atmosphere was considerably disturbed by the Crete affair, just as Chevket Pasha had foreseen. The Greek army had entered politics and dominated the Government. It caused several changes of ministers and forced the King to consent to the summoning of a National Assembly consisting of twice as many delegates as there were members in Parliament. Crete also insisted upon sending delegates, which would have been tantamount to incorporating itself as part of Greece politically.

The Minister of Foreign Affairs frankly told the ambassadors of all the leading Powers, as well as the Greek minister, that if the Greek National Assembly admitted delegates from Crete, Turkey would regard that as a *casus belli*. There was a rumor at the same time that Bulgaria was preparing to take advantage of the crisis to make war on Turkey, either by uniting with Greece or in conjunction with some of the other Balkan States. The Minister of Foreign Affairs had managed well, and the four big Powers, England, Russia, France, and Italy, bestirred themselves and the situation was allayed for the time.

Greece had purchased from Italy a man-of-war of about ten thousand tons, which was being fitted and armored for delivery within six months. To offset this augmentation of the Greek navy, already stronger than the Turkish, Turkey wanted to purchase a man-of-war of sufficient size to outclass the one being fitted for Greece. The Minister of Foreign Affairs called on me with a memorandum of the size of the ship and the strength of the armament desired, together with a statement that the object of the Ottoman Government in the purchase of it was not to make war, but to safeguard the peace of Turkey and possibly of Europe. It was thought that the moral effect upon Greece of such a purchase would prevent her from taking any action that would cause war.

I cabled this proposal in detail to Secretary Knox, and requested a reply by cable. I knew that we had several ships that would probably answer the requirements of Turkey, and I thought that, aside from the moral effect this might have in preventing a war between Turkey and Greece, it would enable us to substitute a new ship of our own for an old one. It was not a question of price, as Turkey had put aside sufficient money to pay for such a ship.

A few days later Chevket Pasha also called on me, and again assured me that the purchase was designed to have an immediate effect upon the maintenance of peace, and that the people of Turkey would be forever grateful to the United States if we should sell them the ship.

But after the lapse of a week or more, I finally received a negative answer from the State Department, saying that such a sale could not be made without the authority of Congress. This, of course, I knew; but since the transaction would have given us the opportunity to add a new ship to replace the other, I thought such legislation might readily have been obtained. The Turkish Government then made application to Germany, and that country seized the opportunity further to cement its friendly relations with the Ottoman Empire, which later had such an important bearing in the World War.

About a year after this Crete affair, Chevket Pasha was assassinated as he was coming out of the Sublime Porte. No greater loss could have befallen Turkey than the removal at that time of her greatest general and most enlightened statesman. He was the best-informed Turkish statesman I have ever known, with a clear and correct view of the entire European situation. What the conspiracy was behind this shooting was never brought to light.

The affairs of Crete at that time were in the hands of

the energetic and brilliant leader who has since come to
be regarded as one of the foremost statesmen of all Europe, Eleutherios Venizelos. At the Paris Peace Conference his recognition was complete. The Greeks, however, have always shown themselves to be a fickle and
ungrateful people, and from the time of Socrates have
turned against their foremost philosophers and statesmen, and their attitude toward Venizelos is the most
recent illustration of those traits. Venizelos is practically
a refugee from his own country and at this writing is
visiting our country to study American institutions.

The main reason I accepted the post at Turkey for the
third time was to secure the legal status and rights of
American institutions under definite laws in the new
régime. The Turks had promulgated a law, known as the
"Law of Associations," under the ingenious restrictions
of which they sought to place all foreign institutions.
That would have given the Ottoman authorities, both
civil and judicial, the power so to impede the work of
these institutions as to prevent them from functioning.
I pointed out to the Grand Vizier that the Law of Associations was contrary to the acquired rights of the institutions, which had been legally recognized for many years,
and taking section by section I showed him the inap-
plicability of it to these institutions. After months of
negotiations, as usual in Turkey, I succeeded in getting
a decision from the Council of Ministers exempting foreign institutions of a religious, educational, or benevolent
character.

There were three or four other matters that I succeeded
in bringing to a successful close. Contrary to the real-
property laws of 1868, our institutions were being denied
the right to hold in their names real property necessary

for their operation, and this right I was able to secure for them. Among other things I obtained a charter for the Syrian Protestant College at Beirut, and I got an iradé or permit for the construction of new buildings for Robert College. The American College for Girls, at Scutari on the Asiatic side of the Bosphorus, wanted to transfer the institution over to Arnaoutkeui on the European side, its present location, and I secured permission for this transfer and for the construction of its buildings.

While these various negotiations were in progress, I received an instruction from Secretary Knox at which I took umbrage. It contained the following paragraph: "If I am correct in understanding that American educational and missionary interests in Turkey are in fact receiving treatment in substance entirely satisfactory, I conclude that the chief influence should at present be centered upon a substantial advancement of our prestige and commerce."

This had no other meaning than that instead of vigorous effort for the protection of American colleges, schools, and hospitals, whose rights under the new régime were being seriously threatened by new laws and regulations, I was to transfer my efforts to securing shipbuilding and railway concessions. I promptly advised the Department that this understanding was not correct, that the interests of our institutions were being seriously threatened, and that the proper protection of these interests in no way conflicted with the advancement of our commercial interests.

I continued to push the negotiations on behalf of our institutions, for I knew that a let-up at that time would, instead of benefiting our commercial interests, convey the impression of weakness on the part of our Government in looking out for American interests. In several dis-

patches I pointed out to the Department that to exert
official pressure for railway concessions in Turkey would
likewise require the protection of such concessions, when
obtained, by strenuous official action which might at
some time even involve the use of force, and could not fail
to enmesh us in the intricate political problems of the
Near East. I asked the Department to weigh carefully
the possible advantage of concessions to a few American
exploiters, against the serious disadvantages that the
protection of these concessions would impose. I pointed
out that invariably the Turkish Government, of its own
accord or through outside pressure, failed to live up to its
contracts if not compelled to do so, and that the situation would be further complicated by the conflicting
interests of the other Powers whose commercial dealings
were subordinate to their political strategy. To ordinary
commercial transactions, such as export and import,
these risks did not, of course, apply; but they were particularly troublesome with regard to the building and
running of railways on Turkish territory.

Among our distinguished visitors during this mission
were former Vice-President and Mrs. Fairbanks, who
were on their tour round the world. They were our guests
for a week, and we gave a series of dinners to have them
meet the leading diplomatic and Turkish officials. Among
the latter was Ahmed Riza Bey, president of the Chamber
of Deputies, who had for twenty years been a refugee in
Paris, where he edited a Turkish paper. He spoke French
fluently. He was said to be practically the head of the
Young Turks Party. He was blue-eyed, handsome, and
thoroughly modern. His father was one of the chamber-
lains of Sultan Abdul Aziz, and his mother, an Austrian,
once told Mrs. Straus that she had almost forgotten the

German language because she had not used it in so long
a time, for she was only seventeen when she was married.

Riza Bey was very much interested to learn from Mr.
Fairbanks the rules of parliamentary procedure. The
Chamber of Deputies had not as yet adopted any such
rules and its proceedings lacked system and order.

A few days later, while the president of the Chamber
was calling on me, the palace of the Chamber of Deputies,
Tcheragan on the Bosphorus, burned to the ground, — an
unfortunate occurrence not only because of the material
loss, but because it was looked upon by the populace as a
visitation from God against the new régime.

Judge and Mrs. Alton B. Parker and the widow of
Daniel Manning, Secretary of the Treasury in Cleve-
land's second Cabinet, also gave us the pleasure of a visit.
And a little later Cleveland H. Dodge arrived in his yacht.
He was heartily welcomed by all the missionaries, for he
was prominently connected with Robert College and was
chairman of the board of trustees of the College at Beirut.
In his party was Mrs. Grover Cleveland.

After we had moved to our summer quarters at Yenikeui, Kermit Roosevelt and his classmate, John Heard,
came to spend about ten days with us. My son Roger,
then a student at Princeton, was spending his vacation
with us and was glad to have the company of two young
men of about his own age.

At this time we saw much of Sir William Willcocks, the
eminent British engineer, who had just returned from
Bagdad where he was employed by the Turkish Government in the construction and supervision of irrigation
works in Mesopotamia. It was he who projected and
designed the Assuan Dam across the Nile. He told me he
was born to his work, as his father, Captain W. Willcocks,
was engaged in it in India.

In June I wrote the Department of State requesting a leave of absence toward the end of September or beginning of October, with permission to return home. In answer I received a cable from the assistant secretary to the effect that the railway concessions of the Ottoman American Development Company were to come up in Parliament in November, and asking if it would be convenient for me to take my leave earlier so as to be back in Turkey by November 1st. I replied in a confidential letter that it was my intention, upon my return to America, to confer with the President and the Secretary of State regarding my release from this post, in accordance with my understanding when I accepted the appointment. I decided to wait until the arrival of the new secretary of the embassy, Mr. Hoffman Philip, and before leaving I took pains to make him thoroughly familiar with the work of the embassy so that no ground might be lost pending my resignation.

On leaving Constantinople we desired a few days' rest in the mountains. At the suggestion, therefore, of our minister to Roumania, J. Ridgely Carter, we planned to go to Sinaia, the Roumanian summer capital, which he thought we should find agreeable in every way, so on September 3d we left Turkey for Roumania.

Sinaia we found not only very beautiful, but most enjoyable. We were invited to the Palace a number of times. The Court being in mourning, all entertaining was informal and more intimate. The King reminded me of the late Edmund Clarence Stedman in general appearance. The Queen, known to all the world as "Carmen Sylva," was a striking personality, tall, rather heavily built, with silver gray hair and a high complexion, strong, mobile features, and a very spiritual expression. She spoke English, French, and German with equal fluency, so that it was difficult to tell which was the most natural to her.

The Queen told me how she happened to choose Carmen Sylva for a pen-name: The woods always appealed to her; their stillness and beauty inspired her. When she began to publish her work, at the age of thirty-five, she asked a certain German writer to tell her the Latin word for "woods"; that gave her "sylva." Next she asked the Latin word for "bird," but that did not suit her. Then the word for "song" suggested itself, "carmen." The combination appealed to her poetic sense, and she adopted it.

At luncheon one day our conversation drifted to poetry and American poets. The Queen seemed to know all our bards, even the minor ones, several of whom I had not heard of myself. I happened to quote, as near as I could recall it, a couplet from a little poem that Joaquin Miller wrote when Peter Cooper died:

> All one can hold in his cold right hand
> Is what he has given away.

She was most enthusiastic about that sentiment and said she considered it real poetry. She repeated it several times so as to remember it.

"Whenever any one gives me a beautiful thought, I never forget him," she said, turning to me in her unaffected manner. I appreciated her delicate compliment.

After luncheon she invited me to the floor above to see her study. She explained that she did her best work in a little cell-like room in the monastery below the hill near the Palace, which we had visited the day before. There she was most free from disturbance of any kind. Her study in the Palace was comfortable and attractively furnished; not large, but cozy. Looking out of the windows, one saw the terraced Italian gardens and the wooded peaks of the Carpathian Mountains beyond. The low bookcases which lined the four walls contained English, French, and German books in exquisite bindings. At her desk were three typewriters, respectively from England, France, and Germany, for use in writing the languages of those countries. She used them herself, according to the language in which the inspiration of the moment had come. She presented me with a volume of poems and one of essays, both in German, "Meine Ruhe" and "Mein Penatenwinkel," which she inscribed for me.

We went through the Palace that afternoon. It is modern and very beautiful, furnished in excellent taste, and not cold and uncomfortable, sacrificed to grandeur, as most palaces seem to be. Then the King and Queen invited us to return the next morning at eleven, to a musicale and luncheon.

Next day after luncheon the King left the other guests and took me into a small adjoining room where we smoked and had coffee. Knowing that I had been Secretary of Commerce and Labor, he led the conversation to economic questions, which he said interested him most. He expressed surprise that we had not come to state ownership of railways, which he believed was the only way to regulate them. I explained our method of regulating them, but he thought that method more socialistic and arbitrary than in his own country. We talked of the Roosevelt policies and their general aim at social justice. He said he regretted very much that Roosevelt had not visited Roumania, for he had the greatest admiration for him, both as man and as statesman.

Our conversation ran on to the Jewish question, and the King spoke most sympathetically of the Jews, saying that they were patriotic subjects and good soldiers, that there was no religious prejudice against them, and that the Jewish question in Roumania was purely economic. The Jews who came in from Russia and Poland constituted separate communities in the country, with foreign methods of living, foreign language, and foreign views. I told him that in the most enlightened countries there was an absence of the Jewish problem because no problem was created by treating the Jews as separate groups with restricted rights. He saw that point, but explained that Roumania was right next to Russia where the Jews were most oppressed. If, therefore, Roumania accorded them full rights, there would be a flood of immigration much larger than they were then getting. I pointed out that it would be much better to restrict immigration than to restrict the natural rights of the Jews of Roumania. That thought impressed him, and he said he realized that, under the system they then had, much injustice was done which brought disgrace to the kingdom, but he hoped a remedy would be worked out.

We spoke of the United States Postal Savings legislation, of which he requested an outline, and thought it could be adopted by Roumania with advantage.

A few days later we again lunched with the King and Queen. The Queen mentioned the bit of poetry I had given her a few days before and asked whether I could give her another. Something had been said about Hay's Roumanian note that brought to mind the last stanza of Hay's hymn:

> Wherever man oppresses man,
>   Beneath the setting sun,
> O Lord, be there, thine arm make bare,
>   Thy righteous will be done.

The Queen admired these lines and begged me to write them out, which I did on the back of one of my visiting-cards. She put the card in her reticule, saying that the lines would inspire a poem some day, and that she would then send it to me.

Referring to her work generally, she spoke of her indebtedness to Professor Michael Bernays, the distinguished Jewish scholar, who was a frequent and welcome visitor at the home of her parents. She said he was the most modest and intellectual person she had ever known, and his conversations and teachings had greatly influenced her intellectual and spiritual life. She asked me to read her estimate of this wonderful man in her book of essays that she had given me. I have since read it several times, and it would surprise many to read such a eulogy and vindication of the Jews and Judaism by the Queen of a country where the Jews were so sorely oppressed by drastic discrimination.

Before we left Sinaia, the Queen sent me a large photograph of herself, inscribed: "Never mind deep waters, there are pearls to be found. Elizabeth. Sinaia, September, 1910."

In Vienna, we were guests at a tea given by Dr. Sigmund Münz, of "Die Neue Freie Presse." Among those present was Baroness Bertha von Suttner, the great peace advocate and authoress of "Down With Your Arms," who had received the Nobel Peace Prize the previous year. I had met her before in the United States, where we spoke from the same platform during the sessions of the Interparliamentary Union and the International Peace Societies.

Next we went to London, where we enjoyed the pleasant hospitalities of our ambassador, Whitelaw Reid. At one of the luncheons at the embassy I was pleased to make the acquaintance of Dr. Luis M. Drago, the Argentine international jurist and author of the Drago Doctrine, who had just returned from the Anglo-American Fisheries Arbitration at The Hague.

We dined one evening with the Right Honorable Sir Ernest Cassel at his charming home, Brooke House, and afterward went with him to the theater. Sir Ernest, one of England's leading financiers, was constantly being referred to in the press in connection with the negotiations pending in Paris for a new loan to the Turks. He told us that these international financial negotiations, because of their international importance, did not appeal to him, for he had no ambition to be in the limelight or to become a conspicuous international personage. He preferred quiet and obscurity, for constant publicity disturbed his peace of mind. This attitude was not one of assumed modesty; he really said what he meant and felt.

On another evening we dined with Postmaster-General Herbert Samuel and his wife. Mr. Samuel was only thirty-nine years old and gave every promise of the distinction which he has since attained in the service of his country. At this writing he is British High Commissioner in Palestine.

Lord Rothschild had written me to call on him when in London; and I went to the banking house to see him. In speaking of the Triple Entente of Great Britain, France, and Russia, I told him I thought that, from a British point of view, it was unwise. He, on the other hand, regarded it as good because it offered the best security for peace. A few days thereafter I mentioned the subject to his brother, Alfred. The latter said that he and his brother usually agreed, but in this matter they took opposite views. Alfred considered it a great mistake, from the point of view of civilization, for England to be aligned with Russia, and beyond that he considered it detrimental to the relationship between England and

Germany, which was none too friendly. In the light of all that has since taken place, it is interesting to note how the international alignment of 1910 was reflected in the minds of these big international financiers.

On September 8th we boarded the Lusitania at Liverpool, reaching New York on the 13th. My brother Isidor and our children met us, and we were made to appreciate the real truth of the bull that "the greatest pleasure in going abroad is returning home."

Soon afterward I went to Washington. First I called at the State Department and had an informal talk with Secretary Knox. I told him I did not wish to return to Turkey. The important negotiations had been brought to a favorable conclusion, and I felt that I had spent enough of my time there. He referred to the understanding with which I had accepted the post, that when I desired to be relieved, another post that might be available and acceptable to me would be tendered me. However, I purposely did not comment on this understanding. I simply said that I did not wish to cause the Administration any embarrassment, and was content to stay at home. He said he would have a talk with the President and confer with me later.

When I called on the President, I told him that since all the questions for which I went to Turkey had been adjusted, I did not wish to return. Subsequently I received a very cordial and complimentary letter from him, but, as it contained no intimation of his earlier promise to transfer me to a post more to my liking, I did not refer to it. The rift between the Roosevelt policies and the Taft Administration had by this time grown considerably, and I was known to be in thorough accord with Roosevelt and his policies.

CHAPTER XII

THE PROGRESSIVES

The Progressive spirit is kindled and shaped into a cause — My speech at the banquet of the New York Chamber of Commerce in 1910 — Roosevelt's hostility to boss rule — Liberals impatient with Taft Administration — Governors demand Roosevelt — He advocates recall of judicial decisions — This stand believed to have caused his defeat — New York State Progressive Convention is deadlocked — "Suspender Jack" nominates me for Governor and stampedes convention — I decline to consider Republican nomination — Sulzer's "non-Jewish but pro-Jewish" slogan — I stump the State — Bainbridge Colby "impersonates" me — Roosevelt, shot by a lunatic, heroically addresses Milwaukee mass meeting — I am needed in national campaign — The dramatic Roosevelt speech in Madison Square Garden — His tribute to me — Election returns — Progressives poorly organized — Their cause a crusade.

In the torrential flood of American politics, two main currents are continuously perceptible. There are, of course, innumerable permanent and temporary cross-currents, eddies, and other variations, but the two main currents are ever present. One may be generally described as professional, mechanical, and ruled by the accomplished and consummate selfishness of invisible forces. The other, while more genuine in spirit, is often amateurish in effort; it is more spontaneous; it is kindled by emotions of revolt; it sees mankind not as masses to be exploited, and profited by, but as individuals to be set freer to express themselves socially and economically. It strives to restate the better aspirations of men generally, and to mitigate some of the pressure that civilization imposes upon them.

It is not the province of the historian to moralize. It is his business to trace the changing currents of human thought and to produce accurate pictures of men in action. And so, in touching on the Progressives, I shall endeavor to give some indication of the mental processes that shaped their cause, and to depict some of the dramatic scenes that carried their cause into action. Many of these scenes I was able to observe closely. In a sense, I may have figured more definitely than I realized at the time, in kindling their cause into smoke and flame.

On November 17, 1910, the New York Chamber of Commerce held its one hundred and forty-second annual banquet at the Waldorf-Astoria Hotel. The speakers were Senator Henry Cabot Lodge, of Massachusetts; Governor Horace White, of New York; Mayor William J. Gaynor, of New York City; and myself. The president of the Chamber, the late A. Barton Hepburn, presided. My subject was "American Prestige," and I could not refrain from referring to the great extent to which American influence and prestige had been advanced by Roosevelt, both as President and during his tour through Europe. There was instant and prolonged applause at the mention of Roosevelt's name, clearly showing that his political influence was not dead, contrary to the ideas of many who thought so because the election of a few days before had shown sweeping Democratic gains and the defeat of Roosevelt's candidate for Governor, Henry L. Stimson. When the banquet was over, Senator Lodge said to me that if the political opponents of Roosevelt could have seen the enthusiasm with which his name was applauded, they would realize that even in New York he was as much alive as ever.

When I had met Roosevelt in Cairo on his way back from Africa, we had talked frequently about politics at home. It was clear to me from his conversation that he did not propose to be enticed or forced into accepting any nomination, although there was talk, yes, I may say a demand, that he reënter public life as either Governor of New York or United States Senator.

Roosevelt was so loyal a Republican that his opponents constantly chided him for going along with the bosses, like Senator Platt, for instance, and at the same time advocating reforms. He used to reply that he did and would continue to coöperate with the bosses so long as they went his way. His aim from the time he entered public life as a member of the New York State Assembly was to make the party always more responsive to its highest ideals; and from the beginning he worked against the "invisible powers" or boss rule. By word and deed all through his life he showed an independence and moral courage that careless observers might often have mistaken for headlong impetuosity. No one could know him without recognizing that he was broad-minded, liberal, and inherently progressive.

When he arrived home from abroad in June, 1910, he found the Republican Party disrupted. The dissatisfaction and impatience of the liberals was distinctly evident. By 1912 Taft had allowed himself to become so thoroughly identified with the reactionaries that the large independent element had not only become unenthusiastic, but decidedly hostile to the Administration. In his Winona speech President Taft had ranked himself on the side of those leaders in the party who opposed real tariff reform. In his famous Norton letter he had even gone so far as to imply, if not to expressly admit, that federal Patronage had been used against the Progressives in Congress.

The Progressive element both in and out of Congress was therefore casting about for a candidate who represented the liberal wing of the party, for nomination at the National Republican Convention at Chicago in June.

Roosevelt's office at "The Outlook" was daily crowded
with liberal leaders who had come to consult with him
and to urge him to "throw his hat in the ring," to use one
of Roosevelt's own picturesque expressions. This demand
grew and spread until finally came the following appeal
from the Governors of the States of Kansas, Michigan,
Missouri, Nebraska, New Hampshire, West Virginia, and
Wyoming:

We feel that you will be unresponsive to a plain public duty
if you decline to accept the nomination coming as the voluntary
expression of the wishes of a majority of the Republican voters
of the United States through the action of their delegates in the
next National Convention.

To this message Roosevelt replied:

One of the chief principles for which I have stood and for
which I now stand, and which I have always endeavoured and
always shall endeavour to reduce to action, is the genuine rule
of the people; and, therefore, I hope that so far as possible the
people may be given the chance, through direct primaries, to
express their preference as to who shall be the nominee of the
Republican Presidential Convention.

During this period I called on Roosevelt one day at the
offices of "The Outlook," and he handed me the galley-
proof of a speech he was to make before the Constitutional Convention at Columbus, Ohio. He called it "The
Charter of Democracy." His room was full of callers, so
I went into Dr. Abbott's office and there carefully read
the speech. In it Roosevelt advocated, among other
reforms such as the short ballot and the initiative and
referendum, the recall of judicial decisions. When I came
to that subject I confess I was shocked, and so expressed
myself to one of the editors of "The Outlook"; as I
remember it, it was Dr. Abbott himself. Compelled to
keep another appointment, I left the office when I had

finished reading the speech, saying that I should return later.

Upon my return I met Roosevelt just as he was going out to keep an engagement.

"I hear you don't like my speech," he said to me.

"I like your speech; I think it is fine; all but that portion of it which refers to the recall of judicial decisions," I answered. I started to give my reasons, but seeing that he was pressed for time, I said: "I should like to discuss that matter with you, provided your mind is open on the subject." To my great surprise he said that he had thought the subject over very carefully, and frankly told me that he had come to a definite decision on it.

That was so unlike the Roosevelt I knew in the many discussions I had had with him, when invariably I found his mind responsive, that I was quite disappointed and somewhat taken back. But I did not want him to feel that I had joined the ranks of the many who had parted political company with him because he had made it known that he would accept another nomination for President, and so, on reaching my office, I wrote him a letter, briefly explaining why I objected to his statements regarding the recall of judicial decisions. I assured him that on that account I did not part from him politically, for after all I agreed with him more than with any other candidate who might possibly be named.

The birth and development of the Progressive Party is, of course, an element of national history that has often been detailed. William Draper Lewis, in his "Life of Theodore Roosevelt," and Lawrence F. Abbott, in his "Impressions of Theodore Roosevelt," both give clear accounts of it. Roosevelt's candidacy and defeat have been variously analyzed, but I believe now, as I believed in 1912, that but for this unfortunate statement regard-

ing judicial decisions, Roosevelt would have been re-
elected President in 1912. It is true that he afterwards
clarified the meaning of his use of the word "recall";
that its application was limited to such decisions as held
legislative acts unconstitutional, and that such decisions
might at the following election be submitted to popular
vote, in accordance with the method employed by a
State for the adoption of its constitution. But his clarification never overcame the effects of the Columbus
speech. William Draper Lewis, who was one of Roosevelt's closest advisers at the time, says in his biography:

Looking back now over the events leading up to the Republican National Convention of 1912, it would appear almost
certain that had he, in his address before the Ohio Convention,
either refrained from making the proposal or had he called it
a new method of amending the constitution, and carefully
explained it so that it could not have been misunderstood, it is
most probable that he would have been nominated at Chicago,
and that the whole course of the recent history of the United
States would have been other than it has been.

Shortly after the Columbus speech, Roosevelt delivered, on March 20, 1912, at Carnegie Hall, New York,
what was in many respects the most forceful and eloquent address I ever heard him make. He graphically
described his dedication to his ideals of democracy:

Our task as Americans is to strive for social and industrial
justice, achieved through the genuine rule of the people. This
is our end, our purpose. The methods for achieving the end are
merely expedients, to be finally accepted or rejected according
as actual experience shows that they work well or ill. But in
our hearts we must have this lofty purpose, and we must strive
for it in all earnestness and sincerity, or our work will come
to nothing. In order to succeed, we need leaders of inspired
idealism, leaders to whom are granted great visions, who dream
greatly and strive to make their dreams come true; who can
kindle the people with the fire from their own burning souls.

NATHAN, OSCAR, AND ISIDOR STRAUS
1912

The leader for the time being, whoever he may be, is but an instrument, to be used until broken and then to be cast aside; and if he is worth his salt, he will care no more when he is broken than a soldier cares when he is sent where his life is forfeit in order that the victory may be won.

If on this new continent we merely build another country of great but unjustly divided material prosperity, we shall have done nothing; and we shall do as little if we merely set the greed of envy against the greed of arrogance, and thereby destroy the material well-being of all of us. To turn this government into government by plutocracy or government by a mob would be to repeat on a larger scale the lamentable failures of the world that is dead. We stand against all tyranny, by the few or by the many. We stand for the rule of the many in the interest of all of us, for the rule of the many in the spirit of courage, of common sense, of high purpose, above all, in a spirit of kindly justice towards every man and every woman.

A month after the meeting of the National Convention of the Progressive Party, popularly called the "Bull Moose Convention," which nominated Theodore Roosevelt for President and Hiram W. Johnson for Vice-President, the New York State Convention of the Progressive Party met at Syracuse, in the Arena. The convention met on September 5th.

All during the first day and night, amid lively discussion as to the selection of candidates for Governor, committees urged me for permission to present my name as a candidate; but I steadfastly declined, since the governorship, being so largely a political office, did not appeal to me. I was neither by training nor by temperament a politician, although I had taken active part in campaigns for many years, both local and national. The next day I was asked to take the permanent chairmanship of the convention. This I was willing and glad to do; I wanted to be of service to the party; also it was a foregone conclusion that acceptance of the chairmanship would preclude my being considered a candidate for the nomination for Governor.

The Arena was filled with about seven thousand delegates and members of the new Progressive Party. The air was surcharged with the spirit of the new movement — the genuine enthusiasm of men and women of character and standing from every county in the State, and among them a great many ministers, professors, reformers, and leaders of benevolent and charitable movements. There was a conspicuous absence of the professional politician. Indeed, that convention had more the character of a town meeting than of a cut-and-dried political convention. Instead of having decisions made for them, this great body of enthusiasts were called upon to make their own. The candidates had not even been agreed upon.

On September 6th I took my gavel in hand and called the meeting to order. The first business before the convention was the nomination of a candidate for Governor. The secretary called the counties of the State in alphabetical order, and the chairman of each delegation made his nomination. The outstanding candidates for nomination were William H. Hotchkiss, one of the organizers of the Progressive Party and chairman of the National Committee, and William A. Prendergast, comptroller of the City of New York, who had made the speech nominating Roosevelt for President at the Chicago Convention. A deadlock between these two candidates ensued.

After Yates County had been heard from, a tall, gaunt young man towered to his feet and asked to be heard; he was from the Fifteenth Manhattan District, and he had a nomination to make. It was not quite in order, though the spirit of the convention was to give each man a chance. While I was hesitating about recognizing him, there seemed to be a general desire that he be given an opportunity to speak, so I gave him five minutes.

He looked fantastic as he strode to the platform and faced the audience. His manner was somewhat bizarre. He burst forth in dramatic fashion as follows:

Fellow citizens, ladies and gentlemen: I have just come down from Vermont. I ask you people at this convention to make no mistake.

We want to put a man up for Governor that no man will be afraid to cast his vote for, against whom there can be no charge leveled of misconduct of any kind, one who can sweep the State from Montauk Point to Lake Erie, and carry every man of every race, religion, and creed; a man whose name is known throughout the civilized world; a man the mention of whose name brings a tear of sympathy to the eye of almost every man and woman in the civilized land; a man whose name, wherever men are found with red blood in their veins, irrespective of race, religion, and creed, will be carried thundering throughout the State to victory.

There is no chance for defeat with this man at the head of the ticket —

"Who is your candidate?" cried impatient listeners.

"What's his name?"

"Name your candidate!"

In sudden answer to these cries from the convention, the speaker exclaimed:

I nominate the illustrious and honorable Oscar S. Straus.

During the long, terrific applause that followed, the delegate stood awkwardly waiting for a chance to finish. Finally he went on:

We should take no chances in this fight. I could not say one undeserved word if I used the entire dictionary in praise of the other nominees, Mr. Hotchkiss and Mr. Prendergast; but, gentlemen, Mr. Prendergast or Mr. Hotchkiss would cause friction in the State. We want no friction in this election. We want success and victory.

Gentlemen, there is not a newspaper editor in the State of New York that would any more assassinate the character of Oscar S. Straus than he would assassinate the character of his own mother.

Gentlemen, remember! Remember that Rome was saved by the cackle of geese. I have no political prestige, but I warn and charge you, put up a man for candidate for governor who cannot and will not be defeated.

Gentlemen, gentlemen, heed me! Make no mistake about Oscar S. Straus. You will make no mistake in putting him up as your candidate, and you will capture victory and success. No man has had better distinction at home and abroad than Mr. Straus. I ask you to vote for him.

The moment he finished, a stampede started. The entire hall assumed the aspect of a good-natured bedlam. There was cheering and applause, and many of the delegates began marching round that big auditorium, brandishing the banners of their counties, singing "The Battle Hymn of the Republic" and "Onward, Christian Soldiers," and breaking out in the end with "Straus! Straus! We want Straus!"

I pounded the desk with the gavel, I shook my head in the negative, but to no avail. The noise lasted fully twenty minutes.

The picturesque young man who had precipitated this scene was John G. McGee, known among his colleagues as "Suspender Jack." He had been a member of the mounted police of New York City.

Meanwhile Mr. Hotchkiss and several other leaders came to the platform and insisted upon my accepting. They even brought Mrs. Straus up with the hope of getting her to exert her persuasive powers. There was no alternative; I had to accept.

Mr. Hotchkiss announced my acceptance, and immediately former Lieutenant-Governor Timothy L.

Woodruff announced the withdrawal of Mr. Prendergast and moved to make the nomination unanimous by acclamation. That produced more shouting and cheering, accompanied by much applause and the waving of banners. It was a touching manifestation and an unexpected honor. I made a brief speech of acceptance, during which I found it difficult to hide the effect of all this demonstration. And with more applause and cheering, the session closed with the singing of "The Star-Spangled Banner."

The next morning the convention named for Lieutenant-Governor Frederick M. Davenport, who was Professor of Law and Politics at Hamilton College and had made an admirable record in the State Legislature. The ticket was then quickly completed and the convention closed.

The nominations were received with great favor all through the State and in the press. Roosevelt at the time was in the Far West conducting his own campaign, and wrote me from Spokane as follows:

THE SPOKANE
SPOKANE, WASHINGTON
September 8, 1912

DEAR STRAUS:

When I left New York I had expected Prendergast to be nominated and there were certain reasons, which I think you know, why I felt that, as a matter of principle, his nomination should be made.

But there was a still further principle involved, and that was that in this Convention the people should have their own way; and, upon my word, I am inclined to think that it was a new illustration of the fact that the wisdom of *all* of us is better than the wisdom of any of us. Having in view the effect, not only in New York but the country at large, I think that your nomination stands second only to that of Hiram Johnson as Vice-President, from the standpoint of strengthening the ticket. If the only result of the next election were to place you in as Governor of New York, I should be inclined to think that the Progressive Party had justified itself.

My dear fellow, I am overjoyed; I congratulate you with all my heart. Give my love to dear Mrs. Straus and to Roger and your two daughters and all the grandchildren.

Ever yours
THEODORE ROOSEVELT

A few days thereafter he gave out the following interview:

Next in importance to the nomination of the Vice-President is the nomination for Governor of New York. And it seems to me that Hiram Johnson and Oscar Straus symbolize what this movement stands for. One is an ex-Republican, the other an ex-Democrat; they both stand for what is highest in American citizenship.

Mr. Straus is not merely a high-minded and able man, a man of incorruptible integrity and great ability, but also a man who has kept abreast of the great movement from which sprang the Progressive Party. He is eminently fitted to be one of the leaders in this movement. On every point of our platform he represents an intense earnestness of conviction for all the things for which we stand. His attitude toward business, his attitude toward the complicated, and the vitally important social and economic problems which are dealt with in our plank concerning social and industrial justice; in short, his whole position on governmental matters has been such as to warrant our saying that he is already in practice applying the very principles which we preach.

New York State has a right to be proud of the fact that in this first State Convention of the people themselves Mr. Straus's nomination was, in the most emphatic sense, a nomination by the people themselves, a nomination representing the desire of the people to have the very best man take the office, although that man was himself sincerely desirous to escape having to take it.

I have known Mr. Straus intimately ever since I was Governor of New York. When he was in my Cabinet I leaned much upon him, and a more loyal and disinterested friend no man could have, and, what is more important, no man could have a more loyal, disinterested, and sanely zealous supporter. As head of the Department of Commerce and Labor Mr. Straus himself, by study and administration of the law, was one of those who reached conclusions as to the needs of our handling of the anti-trust and interstate commerce and similar laws, which I set forth in message after message to Congress, and which were substantially embodied in the Progressive platform; and in his attitude toward labor, toward immigration, toward the duty both of public and private employees, he foreshadowed that part of the Progressive platform which has dealt with these same matters.

Moreover, by his disinterestedness, his unselfish devotion to the cause of good government and of sound progressive doctrine for economic and social reform, and by his willingness personally to sacrifice his own interests to those of the cause he espouses, he is, I am happy to say, typical of all men who are in the new movement.

Exactly as it is a real sacrifice for Hiram Johnson to accept the nomination for Vice-President, so it is a real sacrifice for Oscar Straus to accept the nomination for Governor of New York. Each has accepted because he is not thinking of himself. He is thinking of his duty to the people as a whole; of his duty to the great Nation to which he belongs. Oscar Straus's nomination is not only a most fortunate thing for the New York Progressives, but it is also a piece of real good fortune for the Progressive movement throughout this Nation.

When the Republicans had their convention at Saratoga a short while after my nomination at Syracuse, several of their prominent State leaders telegraphed me to inquire whether I would accept the Republican nomination. They feared that with three candidates in the field the State would go Democratic. One of my managers favored my acceptance, which would without doubt have meant election. But my chief adviser, Chairman Hotchkiss, agreed with me that my accepting the Republican nomination, without the endorsement by the Republicans of the Progressive platform, would destroy the Progressive Party in the State, if not throughout the country. I therefore sent an immediate reply that while I should welcome the support of any group or party that chose to give it, I could not accept a nomination that did not mean an endorsement and acceptance of the platform on which I stood. On hearing of this, Roosevelt telegraphed me from Memphis: "Three cheers for you. You are a perfect trump and you always do the right thing."

The Republican candidate was Job E. Hedges, a brilliant member of the New York Bar. The Democrats nominated William Sulzer, and Tammany Hall sanctioned the selection because he was considered a good opponent who would attract the Jewish vote. But our politicians make no greater mistake than to believe that there is such a thing as a Jewish group vote. Of course, a candidate who by word or action has shown prejudice against or hostility toward the Jews could not expect their suffrage; but beyond that the Jews are not controllable as a group at the polls. However, as chairman of the Committee on Foreign Affairs of the House, Sulzer had taken a prominent part in the abrogation of our treaty with Russia, and during the campaign the slogan, "non-Jewish but pro-Jewish," was designed to bring him the support of the mass of Jewish voters in addition to the regular Democratic vote.

On the whole the campaign was conducted with dignity on all sides. There was a noticeable absence of vilification of candidates and general mud-slinging between the camps, as is too often the case in keenly contested elections. My campaign managers arranged for me to make addresses in every county and almost every city throughout the State. I had a special car in which traveled, besides Mr. Davenport, my wife and me, and several other speakers, a dozen or more reporters from the leading papers.

I made my first speech in Getty Square, Yonkers, and from there I traveled for seven weeks, making ten to fifteen speeches every day except Sundays, including short talks at stations and from the rear platform of my car. Sometimes I made speeches before breakfast, to crowds that had gathered at the station, and there were always two or three, and often more, formal addresses a day in some public hall, to which I would be escorted from the train with a band of music, and sometimes with a fife and drum corps, invariably playing "Onward, Christian Soldiers." So many clergymen took part in the campaign that frequently the meetings were opened with a prayer. Many of the meetings were spontaneous, emphasizing the crusading spirit which was so characteristic of the campaign.

One of my slogans was that I was the "unbossed candidate of the unbossed people." One day up in the northern part of the State I was speaking on a raised platform in the open, and, as usual, my time was limited by the train schedule. A member of the committee told my wife, who was sitting behind me, that the train would leave in a few minutes, and that it was time for me to stop, and just as I got to the middle of the phrase, "unbossed candidate—" she pulled my coat-tail as a signal for me to stop. At that moment I was quite evidently not the "unbossed candidate" that I professed to be, and the audience laughed and cheered with amusement. I think that bit of bossing, however, did not cost me any votes.

Mr. Davenport proved himself a most effective campaign speaker. Another effective orator in our party for a short time was Bainbridge Colby, who discharged with

great distinction the important duties of Secretary of
State during the last year of the Wilson Administration.
At Oneonta and at one or two other places, while I was
taking a much-needed rest, the crowds had gathered and
were calling for me. Mr. Colby, without being introduced, responded for me, and the audiences were left with
the impression that they had listened to me. My cause
certainly did not suffer by my being so admirably represented, or perhaps I should say advantageously misrepre-
sented.

Roosevelt in the meantime had flung himself into the
campaign with all the force of his tremendous vigor and
energy, and gave to it a dynamic impulse that grew in
intensity as he progressed through the country. He went
out to the Pacific Coast, returned through the Southern
States to New York City, speaking at every important
center. In September he went through New England.
In October he started on his final tour through the
Middle West, and it was while on this trip that he was
shot by a lunatic just as he was leaving his hotel to make
a speech in the Auditorium in Milwaukee. The incident,
tragic in itself, was made dramatic by his heroism. With
the bullet in his breast and his clothes soaked with blood,
disregarding the entreaties of his companions, he went
on to the Auditorium and spoke for more than an hour.
To him nothing counted except the triumph of the principles for which he was fighting.

In consequence of this accident the national managers
had me leave the State of New York and take up the
national campaign, which I did cheerfully. No one, of
course, could fill Roosevelt's engagements, but the plan
was to rescue the cause so far as possible, and I spoke in
several of the larger cities where meetings had been
scheduled for Roosevelt, principally Chicago, Cincinnati,

and Cleveland. My intense anxiety regarding the condition of my chief during this time was greatly relieved by assuring telegrams from Mrs. Roosevelt and his nephew, George Emlen Roosevelt, who were both at his side.

Two final rallies were arranged in Madison Square Garden, New York — one on Wednesday, October 30th, for the national ticket, and the second on Friday, November 1st, for the State ticket. Roosevelt, though not well, considered himself sufficiently recovered to appear. His physicians, Doctors Lambert and Brewer, had prescribed no more campaign speeches, in fact, did not want him to go to these meetings; but he brushed aside their injunctions and left Oyster Bay for Madison Square.

His presence at the national rally was his first public appearance since the shooting, and keyed-up the meeting to a high dramatic pitch. Fully eighteen thousand persons were in the auditorium and a few thousand more were outside clamoring for admission. When Roosevelt appeared on the platform, a roar of applause broke loose and continued for forty-five minutes.

Roosevelt's speech, characteristically, was confined to a plea for the Progressive cause and for the State ticket; no word for himself. He appeared in good form and to possess his usual vigor, although it was observed that he did not use his right arm. His speech was earnest, calm, and exalted, closing with what he called his political creed:

I am glad beyond measure that I am one of the many who in this fight have stood ready to spend and be spent, pledged to fight while life lasts the great fight for righteousness and for brotherhood and for the welfare of mankind.

At the rally for the State ticket two nights later the crowd inside the Garden was as large as at the national rally, though there were fewer people outside. The enthusiasm was at the same high pitch. When I arose to speak, the cheering began and lasted twenty-seven minutes before it could be checked. Roosevelt was expected during the evening. His physicians had reminded him when he started from home that he had promised not to speak any more in the campaign, to which he humorously replied that he had promised not to speak for himself, but that this time he would talk for Oscar Straus and Fred Davenport and the candidates on the judiciary ticket!

At the close of my thirty-minute address, Roosevelt appeared. The crowd went wild, and stopped cheering only when Mr. Hotchkiss, who was presiding, besought them to stop out of consideration for the Colonel. Roosevelt spoke for an hour and held that vast audience in rapt attention. He devoted the first half of his speech to outlining the Progressive cause, its meaning and purpose, and the second half to advocating the State ticket. He referred to my public career in terms of unmeasured praise, beginning with my first mission to Turkey. He told the crowd that everywhere he spoke, from the Great Lakes to the Gulf and from the Atlantic to the Pacific, he had "found that the name of Oscar Straus was a name with which to conjure," and that it "helped the Progressive cause in California and in New Mexico, in Illinois and in Kansas, that we here in New York had named such a man as our candidate for Governor." He then gave accounts of the personal services and qualifications of the other members of the ticket, and with this meeting the Progressive campaign of 1912 closed with a blaze of unforgettable enthusiasm.

On election day I received the following letter from Roosevelt:

OYSTER BAY
November 5, 1912

DEAR OSCAR:

I count myself fortunate in having run upon the same ticket with you and in having had the privilege of supporting you. You are the kind of American who makes one proud of being an American; and I wish also to say that I feel just the same way about all your family, your dear wife, your two daughters and son. It is just such a family, and just such a family life, as I like to think of as typical of our citizenship at its best.

With affectionate regard and esteem

Faithfully yours

THEODORE ROOSEVELT

The Progressives, as might have been expected, had been poorly organized. The time had been too short for intensive development of our forces. We had no machine, and in a number of the counties there was scarcely a skeleton of an organization. It was, in fact, not a party in the ordinary sense of the word at all, but rather a crusade, and what we lacked in organization we made up by an abundance of spontaneous ardor. We did not really expect victory, although Roosevelt several times said that while he knew he would be defeated, he thought I would be elected. As a matter of fact, I believe I was the only candidate of the Progressive cause for Governor in any State who ran ahead of Roosevelt. In New York State he got 389,000 votes, in round numbers, while I had 393,000.

I knew from observations during my campaign from one end of the State to the other, how poorly, from a political standpoint, the Progressives were organized, and I confess I did not see the slightest chance of being elected. I was not disappointed, and I think that the men generally who ran for offices on the Progressive ticket were not disappointed. They realized that their

contest was waged for a cause and not for office, and from
an educational point of view the campaign was eminently
successful.

Considering the vastness of the undertaking and the
shortness of the time, we did as well as any of us could
have anticipated, if not better. We were confident that
the cause would triumph, in a degree at least, no matter
what party was in power, and I think the facts amply
justify our belief that the Progressive ideals made a
definite impression upon the country, and have given
strength, if not dominant influence, to Progressive principles in both of the old parties.

CHAPTER XIII

THREATENING CLOUDS OF WAR

Sinister tension in the international air — The Hague Treaties — Germany's opposition to satisfactory understandings — New spirit of international good-will gains popular momentum — A conference with Secretary Hay — The Senate jealous of its authority; the treaties are not submitted — My address before the New York Peace Society — Other addresses on world peace — Carnegie's notable efforts — My lectures at the United States Naval War College at Newport — Conflicts of sovereignty respecting naturalized citizens — The Lake Mohonk Conferences — The American Society of International Law is founded — Distinguished speakers at first annual meeting — The Society's growth and permanence — Roosevelt astounds the world by sending the fleet around the world — The homecoming of the fleet — Opposition to free tolls for American ships in coastwise trade — The Mexican problem and my suggestions to the President as to how to meet it — Italy makes war on Turkey for Tripoli — Other Powers fail to grasp their opportunity to effect peaceful adjustment — My protests and warnings are published by "The Outlook" — The outburst of wars in the Balkans — Germany's ruthless aggressive policy is disclosed.

THE ominous clouds, visible from time to time on the diplomatic horizon during my last mission to Turkey, had latterly expanded from only local significance into implications of greater and more sinister magnitude. It had accordingly grown more and more apparent to me that the tinder box of Europe, the Eastern Question, was likely to burst into flames at almost any moment; and, in common with other close observers, I was not unaware of an inscrutable and widespread tension in the international air.

It seemed to many of us that America, which had so long remained wrapped rather complacently in its cloak of isolation, might have a stern duty to perform, not only to itself, but to the rest of the world. That duty seemed to us to involve the immediate need of a more vigorous promotion of world peace and of the specific and definite designing and constructing of a proper machinery of enforcement.

In 1899, and again in 1907, to be sure, we had taken a leading part in the two Hague Peace Conferences, at the first of which twenty-six, and in the second of which forty-four, nations participated. These nations had signed and ratified the various treaties formulated by the two conferences. The first conference was called by the Emperor of Russia. Its main purpose, as stated in the Russian note proposing the conference, was by means of international discussion and agreement to provide the most effective means for ensuring to all peoples the benefits of a real and lasting peace, and, above all, to limit the progressive development of armaments.

Soon after the conference assembled, it was found that no agreement could be reached respecting the limitation of armaments, whereupon the attention of the delegates was chiefly directed to formulating plans for the peaceful settlement of international disputes. This resulted in the adoption of a treaty of arbitration entitled: "Convention for the Pacific Settlement of International Disputes." The American, the British, and the delegates of several other leading Powers favored an agreement for compulsory arbitration of all matters of a juridical nature; but this was opposed at the first conference by Germany,[1] and again at the second conference. The treaty, however,

---

[1] Andrew D. White, chairman of the American delegation, states in his diary: "It now appears (June 9, 1899) that the German Emperor is determined to oppose the whole scheme of arbitration, and will have nothing to do with any plan for a regular tribunal whether as given in the British or the American scheme. This news comes from various sources and is confirmed by the fact that in the sub-committee one of the German delegates, Professor Zorn of Königsberg, who had become very earnest in behalf of arbitration, now says that he may not be able to vote for it. There are also signs that the German Emperor is influencing the minds of his allies, the sovereigns of Austria, Italy, Turkey, and Roumania, leading them to oppose it." (*Autobiography of Andrew Dickson White*, vol. II, pp. 293-94.)

in a modified and purely optional form, was adopted, though it fell short, by reason of Germany's opposition, of much that it was hoped to attain; yet it was a distinct gain in providing definite machinery for the maintenance of peace and the adjustment of international differences by peaceful means.

In the development of international relations, in case of the threat of war or of actual war, it was regarded as an unfriendly act for outside Powers to tender good offices or to mediate in the cause of peace. This unfortunate and unrighteous condition was radically changed and indeed reversed by the treaty; the signatories agreed not only to have recourse to the good offices or mediation of friendly Powers, but agreed also that such Powers should on their own initiative tender such good offices to the States at variance, and that such overtures should never be regarded as an unfriendly act by either of the parties in dispute. Especially in our country and in Great Britain, these treaties awakened anew the spirit of international justice and good-will, and there ensued many meetings designed to inform and stimulate popular interest in the cause of world peace.

John W. Foster, former Secretary of State, who had been in New York a short time before as a member of a committee to provide for a public meeting urging the ratification of the arbitration treaties, had made an appointment for me to meet Secretary Hay for a conference regarding them. I met Mr. Foster at the Cosmos Club and went with him to meet Mr. Hay at the latter's residence. Hay, as usual, met us in his gracious way and we discussed the subject from all sides. My main concern was that these little arbitration treaties, which excepted questions of "vital interest and national honor," should not have the effect of abridging the broader provisions of the Hague Treaty. I had brought with me a draft of a treaty which guarded against such contingencies, with which Mr. Foster seemed to be in agreement.

Hay said he fully caught my idea, but that it had been desired to make all of these treaties alike and to conform with the one between France and Great Britain. He said it would be difficult enough, as it was, to get these treaties through the Senate, as there was considerable opposition, and therefore it was advisable to have these treaties with the several Powers identical; otherwise separate arguments would be made against each of the treaties. The Secretary asked me, however, to leave with him the draft I had prepared, saying that it might prove very useful to him.

The final upshot was that these treaties, to which Hay had devoted so much care and thought during his last months in Washington, and by which he hoped to lessen the likelihood of war throughout the world, were violently opposed in the Senate on the ground that they deprived it of its constitutional rights. Senators Knox and Spooner and their followers took the view that every separate agreement to arbitrate under these treaties must be submitted to the Senate. An amendment to this effect emasculated the main purposes of the treaty and left the subject of arbitration substantially as it would be without any treaties. As Hay stated, Roosevelt saw the situation plainly enough and decided not to submit the treaties for ratification by the other Powers.

On my return home from Turkey, the New York Peace Society, of which I had been the president until I entered the Cabinet in 1906, and whose membership and activities had been very much enlarged under my successor,

Andrew Carnegie, gave me a reception on January 7, 1910, at the Hotel Plaza, in New York. Mr. Carnegie, who was earnestly and intensely devoted to the cause of international peace, and who had donated the necessary money for the construction of the Peace Palace at The Hague, presided at this reception, and made one of his characteristic addresses. The subject of my talk was "The Threatening Clouds of War," as they appeared to me to be gathering in the Near East and in the Balkans.

It seemed to me that the most timely public service I could possibly render during this period was to help arouse public opinion to a sense of the imperative need of a newer view of world relations, and a genuine public demand for an international understanding and machinery with which peace might be maintained.

"World Peace" was therefore my subject when, on April 13th of the same year, the Authors' Club tendered me a dinner " in recognition of my public services at home and abroad." It was presided over by the veteran author and publisher, Henry Holt, who nominated Mr. Carnegie as toastmaster. Speeches were made by our ambassador to Berlin, David Jayne Hill, by Rev. Dr. Thomas R. Slicer, Edward M. Shepard, Professor William P. Trent, of Columbia University, and several others.

Though the Authors' Club has a comparatively small membership, limited to members of the craft, yet there have sprung from its ranks a number of our most eminent diplomatists, such as John Hay, Andrew D. White, General Horace Porter, David Jayne Hill, Dr. Henry van Dyke, Seth Low, and Frederick W. Holls. The last two were delegates to the First Hague Peace Conference.

Determined to make the most of the growing popular agitation for the promotion of international arbitration and peace, Mr. Carnegie soon afterwards organized a great peace meeting which was held in Carnegie Hall, New York City. The big hall was packed from pit to dome, and thousands were unable to gain admission. The meeting was opened by Mr. Carnegie, as presiding officer, and he was followed by Baron d'Estournelles de Constant. In my address I specially emphasized neutral duties in time of war and the inhibition upon neutrals to lend money to belligerents pending war as being quite as much an unneutral act as the selling of ships of war and armaments, as had been usually the case in the past when money thus borrowed was used for that very purpose.

During the years 1903, 1904, and 1905, I devoted much attention to questions affecting international relations. I was invited by Admiral Chadwick, president of the United States Naval War College at Newport, to deliver several lectures during the summer of 1903, and took for my subject the protection of our citizens abroad, and surveyed the entire subject of citizenship, native-born and naturalized. I pointed out that by the law of July 27, 1868, it was specifically provided that naturalized citizens while in foreign states shall receive from our Government the same protection as to their persons and property that is accorded to native-born citizens in like circumstances. All the European countries denied the right of expatriation, while America from the beginning had insisted upon that right as one of its basic elements of liberty.

In several notable instances, our Navy had taken prompt action to uphold American rights. One such case was that of Martin Coszta, a Hungarian insurgent in the revolution of 1848–49, who escaped to Turkey and from there came to the United States and made the usual declaration preparatory to being naturalized under our laws. He returned to Turkey in 1854, and at

Smyrna he was seized while on shore and taken up by the crew of an Austrian frigate and put in irons. Before the boat got under way, an American frigate arrived and threatened to sink the Austrian vessel unless Coszta was released. This led to an agreement under which he was put in the custody of the French consul-general.

It is of the highest importance that the men of our Navy, especially those in command of ships, should be conversant with the principles of international law, as they are frequently called upon to act promptly. This conflict of sovereignty respecting naturalized citizens caused the war between us and Great Britain in 1812. Beginning with 1868, we concluded treaties of naturalization with the German States and Austria-Hungary, and subsequently with most of the other States.

My address was subsequently published in the quarterly proceedings of the College of March, 1904. The following year I delivered another address before the College on international relations specifically with reference to Russia and the United States. This address was likewise published in the proceedings of the Naval War College, and with some modifications appeared in the "North American Review" of August, 1905.

For a number of years many of the leading men of the country who were interested in international relations were annually, at the beginning of the summer, the guests of Messrs. Smiley at their noted hotel at Lake Mohonk. These gatherings were known as the Lake Mohonk Conferences on International Arbitration, lasted several days, and addresses were made upon various international subjects.

At the conference of 1905, it occurred to some of the

members who were in attendance, who had long entertained the idea that an American society devoted exclusively to the interests of international law should be
formed, that, in view of the large attendance that year of
many prominent men interested in the subject, it would
be a propitious time to organize. James Brown Scott,
Professor of International Law at Columbia University,
and Professor George W. Kirchwey, Dean of the Law
School of the University, were most active in promoting
the idea. A preliminary meeting was called, and about
fifty of the gentlemen in attendance at the conference
took part. They elected me as chairman, Professor James
Brown Scott as secretary, and appointed a committee of
twenty-one to effect a permanent organization. The com-
mittee so appointed consisted of the following: Chandler
P. Anderson, James B. Angell, Professor Joseph H. Beale,
Jr., David J. Brewer, Charles Henry Butler, J. M. Dickin-
son, John W. Foster, George Gray, Professor Charles
Noble Gregory, John W. Griggs, Professor George W.
Kirchwey, Robert Lansing, Professor John Bassett
Moore, W. W. Morrow, Professor Leo S. Rowe, Professor
James B. Scott, Oscar S. Straus, Everett P. Wheeler,
Andrew D. White, Professor George G. Wilson, and
Theodore S. Woolsey.

The American Society of International Law was formally organized on January 12, 1906. Back of its founding was the firm belief that the influence of an association
of publicists and others, organized along the lines indicated, would count for much in the formation of a sound
and rational body of doctrine concerning the true principles of international relations.

The following editorial comment regarding this organization is quoted from the January, 1907, issue of "The
American Journal of International Law":

While the necessity of such a society was felt by many, no serious steps were taken until the summer of 1905. It occurred to some of the members of the Mohonk Lake conference on international arbitration, that a society devoted exclusively to the interests of international law as distinct from international arbitration might be formed and that the members of the Mohonk Conference would supply a nucleus membership. Accordingly a call was issued to the members present at the conference, and as the result of the call and meeting of those interested a committee was appointed with Oscar S. Straus as chairman and James B. Scott as secretary, to consider plans for a definite organization and for the publication of a journal exclusively devoted to international law as the organ of the Society. On December 9th, 1905, a meeting of the committee was held at the residence of Oscar S. Straus in New York City, and as the result of favorable reports of the members present it appeared feasible to proceed immediately to the definitive organization of the Society. Accordingly a call was issued by the chairman for a meeting of those interested in international law and its popularization, to be held at the New York Bar Association, on Friday, January 12th, 1906.

At this meeting it was decided to organize upon a permanent basis a society of those interested in the spread of international law with its ideals of justice and therefore of peace; a constitution was adopted; officers were elected and the Society took its place, it is hoped, permanently among the learned and influential societies of the world.

On April 19 and 20, 1907, was held the first annual meeting of the American Society of International Law, at Washington, which was attended by an unexpectedly large number of members. The society had grown, in the short time since its organization, to a membership of over five hundred. The various sessions were devoted to discussions of international topics, and closed with a banquet presided over by Secretary Root, and addresses were made by several speakers, including two former Secretaries of State, namely, Richard Olney and John W

Foster, as well as by James Bryce, General Horace Porter, and the writer.

To-day the society has more than twelve hundred members, and since 1907 it has regularly held annual meetings and issued its quarterly publication, "The American Journal of International Law." Since the beginning, Elihu Root has been the president, with whom are associated as vice-presidents and members of the executive council more than forty of the leading writers and authorities, Senators and judges, including the Chief Justice of the United States. I still am the chairman of the executive committee, of which Professor Scott has from the beginning been the recording secretary, as well as the editor-in-chief of the "Journal." An analytical index of the fourteen volumes of the "Journal" (1907–20) has recently been prepared by George A. Finch, secretary of the board of editors.

While these various groups were pressing forward on their respective avenues of approach to a better understanding between nations, President Roosevelt was applying his energies to the problem in his own way. His method was in this instance characterized by a strikingly objective and dramatic treatment. He firmly believed that the greater power a peaceful nation has to make war in a world threatened by war, the greater becomes its power to command peace. The peace societies will not endorse this contention; but the history of international relations gives force to that proposition. Such are international amenities, paradoxical as it may appear.

Roosevelt's terse message to a world threatened by war was to send a great fleet of battleships on a voyage round the world.

The fleet was scheduled to return to Hampton Roads

on Washington's birthday, February 22, 1908. It was to
be reviewed on its arrival by the President. Admiral
Adolph Marix, the chairman of the Lighthouse Board in
my Department, in the tender Maple took my wife and
me, Mr. and Mrs. Leonard Hockstader, my son-in-law
and daughter, and several officials of the Department
to Hampton Roads, and we steamed out to the tail of the
Horse Shoe some ten miles from Old Point Comfort. At
the appointed time, eleven o'clock that day, Admiral
Sperry in his flagship Connecticut passed in review before
the President, and following him came the twenty-four
battleships consisting of the sixteen ships that went around
the Horn, and eight additional ones, most of which had
been completed since the squadron had left the Atlantic
on this voyage sixteen months before. These ships had
steamed 42,000 miles without any hitch or any casualty,
or any untoward circumstance.

When the President first decided that this trip should
be made, all kinds of hostile criticism bristled in the press
of the country. But the President, with his usual alert-
ness, had several far-sighted purposes in view. He says
in his "Autobiography": "At that time, as I happened
to know neither the English nor the German authorities
believed it possible to take a fleet of great battleships
around the world, I made up my mind that it was time
to have a show-down in the matter; because if it was
really true that our fleet could not get from the Atlantic
to the Pacific, it was much better to know it and be able
to shape our policy in view of the knowledge."

The great show of naval strength on the part of the
United States that this voyage illustrated naturally had
its effect throughout the world. A strength that is not
menacing tends to allay menace. And in this instance
the visit of the fleet to Japan was promptly interpreted

by the Japanese as one of courtesy and good-will. The President, again and again in his public utterances, as well as in his private statements at Cabinet meetings, had emphasized his view that a strong navy makes for peace. And toasting the admirals and captains in the cabin of the Mayflower, he exclaimed:

"Is n't it magnificent? Nobody after this will forget that the American coast is on the Pacific as well as on the Atlantic!"

The home-coming of the fleet was a most imposing sight. The weather was beautiful, and altogether the function appeared as calm and peaceful as if it had been a magnificent pleasure excursion, which indeed it had proved to be.

On my return to America in the fall of 1913, there were two notable questions that occupied the attention of President Wilson and Congress, in which as a private citizen I had taken some part. I was soon invited by the National Republican Club to take part in a luncheon discussion of "Present World Problems," and this enabled me to discuss a subject that had resulted in a plank in the National Platform of the Progressive Party, "that American ships engaged in coastwise trade shall pay no tolls." As this question did not arise in the New York State campaign, I had had no occasion to discuss it except on one occasion when I was asked what my stand was upon that subject, and I plainly stated that I did not favor the remission of tolls, as it conflicted with the spirit, if not with the express wording, of the Hay-Pauncefote Treaty, and that I would only favor it in the event the question were left to arbitration and decided in our favor. In this discussion I went somewhat fully into the subject, making it clear why I was not in favor of free tolls, and why I supported the President in the stand that he had taken for repeal of the act that freed our coastwise ships from such tolls.

Others who spoke at this luncheon on various phases of the general problem were William L. Mackenzie King, at this writing the Premier of Canada, and Miss Mabel T. Boardman, representing the American Red Cross.

In April the Senate Committee on Interoceanic Canals held hearings upon an act to amend the Panama Canal Act repealing the provision providing for freeing coast-wise American ships from tolls. Upon invitation I appeared before this committee and supported the position that the President had taken, in opposition to the provisions of the platform of his party, for the repeal of the free tolls clause. Upon the urgent request of the President, the repealing act was passed. Some of our ablest Senators, regardless of party, took opposing sides upon this question. Elihu Root, who was then Senator, presented, in my judgment, the most convincing argument and the ablest speech of his distinguished career in the Senate, advocating the repeal of the free tolls clause.

Another international subject which I was carefully studying at this time was our relations with Mexico. I felt then, as I do now, that our Government has often been badly served and wrongly advised in regard to affairs in Mexico. I suggested to the President that he should send to Mexico a commission of experienced men who could in a comparatively short time lay before him the true conditions as a guide for our governmental action. I pointed out that under circumstances different, but no less perplexing, this plan had been adopted by Cleveland during the Venezuela trouble, and that the appointment of that commission, of which Justice Brewer of the Su-

preme Court was chairman, had hastened the solution.
When the idea of the United States sending a commission such as I recommended became publicly known, it
was favorably received by General Huerta, the then President of Mexico, as well as by Carranza. The appointment of such a commission would have had the additional
effect of offsetting the pressure in Congress for inter-
vention, and several of the leading Senators expressed
themselves as favoring it.

When storm clouds are rushing across the sky, it is very
difficult to foretell where the lightning will strike. It is
needless here to discuss the professed but spurious reasons
why Italy declared war upon Turkey in 1911. It was
evident that no *casus belli* existed in any international
sense. The naked fact was that Italy determined to have
a slice of northern Africa, and was favored in that craving by several of the Great Powers, chiefly to prevent
Germany from getting a foothold on the Mediterranean.
I knew from my observations in Turkey that this aggressive action on the part of Italy would far transcend the
interest of either Italy or Turkey, and would inevitably
arouse the restless Balkan Powers to action.

In a communication that I sent to Secretary of State
Knox on September 29, 1911, attention was directed to
what would probably be the outcome of this action on the
part of Italy; also that the Hague Treaty not only sanctioned, but made it morally incumbent upon Powers that
were strangers to the dispute, to tender their good offices
for the purpose of a peaceful adjustment. Just because
the United States could not be accused of having any
direct interest, such an offer could have been made with
best grace by our country. If ever there had been a war
of conquest, that was one. One of the London papers had

frankly criticized Italy's precipitous act as that of "pirate, brigand, and buccaneer."

In an article written for "The Outlook" following a number of public addresses upon the same subject, I pointed out that Turkey, both immediately before and since hostilities began, had appealed to the Christian nations of the world, who were co-signatories with her of the Hague Treaty, to use their good offices for peace, but the Christian nations had declined to act. In this article I stated:

So far as it opens an era possibly of the gravest menace to Europe, it is primarily of European concern; but in so far as the provisions of the Peace Treaty are disregarded by neutral Powers, this is a grave moral loss no less for us than for all nations, the magnitude of which is not lessened, but increased by the fact that Christian Italy is making an unprovoked war upon a Mohammedan Power. The efforts to bring about a peaceful adjustment under the circumstances is not only a moral right, but a right under the Convention in which Turkey, Italy, and the United States are equally signatories with the other forty-one nations.

The international moral damage this war entails is the concern of all nations. The manner in which it was precipitated without first having recourse to the enlightened methods of peaceful adjustment, combined with the concerted refusal of European Powers to attempt mediation, will make peace treaties waste paper, and peace professions of civilized nations sham and hypocrisy.

In quick succession this war was followed in 1912 by the first Balkan war against Turkey, and then in 1913 by the second Balkan war, between the Balkan nations themselves to divide the spoils. For thirty years the Treaty of Berlin (1878) had served to maintain European peace. The first breach was the annexation of Bosnia and Herzegovina by Austria. The second was the Italian-Turkish war, followed by the Balkan wars. The toll of these latter wars entailed a sacrifice of 300,000 dead or permanently disabled on the field of battle; and the immediate consequence was to upset "the balance of power" so that the Great Powers at once heavily extended their armies and navies, and their budgets ran wild.

Probably the most illuminating document concerning the conditions that led up to the World War is the Lichnowsky Memorandum which is entitled: "My London Mission, 1912–1914." I had known Prince Lichnowsky when he was one of the secretaries of the German Embassy during my first mission to Turkey. He was appointed ambassador to England after the death of Baron Marschall in September, 1912. This memorandum was prepared as a personal record during the second year of the war, and, after being privately circulated, was, by design or otherwise, published. It is the most convincing indictment of Germany's ruthless aggressive policy, and it naturally brought down upon its author the severest condemnation of the Emperor and the militarists. Germany's reiterated claim that Great Britain, having designed Germany's destruction, sought to justify the large increase of her navy, was disproved by her own ambassador.

The events that resolved themselves into the World War, as well as the World War itself, are most convincing proofs that the preservation of peace is a matter of common interest to the entire family of nations, and that it must not be left to a single member of this group to disturb the world's peace at will.

CHAPTER XIV

PERSONAL VIGNETTES

We motor through northern Africa — The King of Italy discusses world politics — Exploring historical ruins with the Mayor of Rome and Georg Brandes — Two Cardinals — David Lubin, international genius — In London — William Watson, the British poet, considers residing in America and asks about cost of living — Lloyd George curious about Progressives — He guarantees a one-pound note — John Burns discourses on British history — The notable housing experiment at Hampstead Garden Suburb — Earl and Lady Grey — At Skibo Castle with Andrew Carnegie — Indifferent golf, but fine trout fishing — At The Hague Peace Palace — Some eminent Hollanders — Turning the laugh on the cartoonists — Rudyard Kipling on having a daughter in society — An evening with Israel Zangwill — Henri Bergson in an argument with Roosevelt, with Rodin, the sculptor, a bored listener — To Spain to attend Kermit Roosevelt's wedding — Spanish politics — A protégé of Bismarck — Recollections of Disraeli — Evidence of Spanish and Jewish origin of Christopher Columbus.

MOTORING leisurely through Algiers and Tunis with Mrs. Straus, I was now enjoying a delightful holiday, free from cares and responsibility. The drowsy tropical air invited complete relaxation, and the lazy African days ushered us into a world unbelievably remote from that of American politics. Graceful, luminous Algiers, with its brilliant European hotels, charming cafés, veiled women, and swarthy men, etched lasting impressions upon our minds. My defeat in the tense Progressive contest for the governorship of New York had afforded me this opportunity for another taste of freedom. It was in the spring of the year 1913, and the mountains through which we toured were full of unexpected and beguiling scenes. This region is not only rich in historic associations, but the engineering skill of the French has in turn modernized it with excellent motor roads. From Tunis we crossed to Sicily, where we visited the Carthaginian, Greek, and Roman remains of columns and temples that still bear tragic

witness to the conflict between the armies of Hannibal
and Scipio, and between the transplanted Asiatic and
European civilizations.

We made our way to Rome, where Ambassador
Thomas J. O'Brien showed us many attentions, and
arranged for an audience on April 28th with Victor
Emmanuel III. The King was most affable and agreeable, and spoke perfect English. He referred to my several missions to Turkey, and said he, too, was there frequently when he was in the navy. He spoke with an
intimate knowledge of the men and affairs in the Near
East that surprised me. We discussed Arabia and the
unrest there due to the incompetency of the Sultan's
Government, and soon the conversation turned to the
Balkan situation. I said I feared that as soon as the
treaty then being negotiated, which was to end the first
Balkan War against Turkey, was signed, a fresh war
would break out among the five Balkan Powers. That
would not surprise him, he said, but considered that it
might be best to let them fight it out. I answered that
the trouble with that course was that the fight would
involve the Great Powers, as the several Balkan States
were attached to strings that led directly into the chan-
celleries of the Great Powers — with which the King did
not disagree.

We talked of the Jews, and he said in Italy they were
not made a separate element in the population. "We
neither know nor care whether a man is a Jew or not," he
remarked, adding that the only persons who took special
notice of the subject at all were occasional clericals. Personally he was very fond of the Jews; nearly every ministry had contained one or more; and General Ottolenghi,
a Jew who had been Minister of War a few years before,
had been one of his most favored instructors. Altogether

we had a fine talk of over an hour. The King's quick and vigorous mind, his clearness of vision and breadth of intellectual grasp I found very refreshing. Unlike some of the monarchs, he did not seem detached and weighted down by a sense of his own importance.

From my friend Isaac N. Seligman, since deceased, of New York, I had received a letter of introduction to Ernesto Nathan, Mayor of Rome, of whom I had heard much and whom I was therefore anxious to meet. I sent Mr. Seligman's letter, together with my card, to the Mayor. The next morning, when Mrs. Straus and I were leaving our hotel for a motor ride, a tall, prepossessing gentleman, who impressed me somewhat as a typical Englishman, came toward me with a look of recognition which I instinctively answered.

"Is this Mr. Straus? I am Mr. Nathan," he said, in perfect English.

His brother was with him, and we were glad to return to the hotel with them for a chat. We arranged for a little excursion the next day to the ancient Roman commercial city of Ostia, whose ruins were being excavated. In the midst of these plans the Mayor remarked that a friend of his, Georg Brandes, the Danish savant and critic, was in Rome, and if agreeable to us he would like to have him join us. Of course it was agreeable, and in our little party next day were Mayor Nathan, his brother, his daughter, Georg Brandes, a Signor Cena, editor of a leading Italian review, and ourselves. The Mayor acted as guide and showed an astonishing familiarity with things archæological in a most delightful way; even the occasional spells of rain in no way dampened our enjoyment of the trip. Upon our return, the Mayor took us to lunch in a typical Italian restaurant, where we spent two hours at a sociable repast.

My introduction to Mayor Ernesto Nathan led to a friendship which I prized highly and enjoyed until his death in April, 1921. He was born in England of Jewish parents. His father was a banker and a descendant of the Frankfort family of Nathans, a collateral branch of the Mayer family from whom is descended the great banking family of Rothschild. After his father died, his mother took the family to Pisa to live. Here their home became a refuge for Italian patriots, as it had been in London. At twenty-five Signor Nathan became business manager of "La Roma del Popolo," a paper started by Giuseppe Mazzini, a friend of the family, whose works he later edited. Nathan remained an editor and publisher until he entered politics. He became Mayor of Rome in 1907, elected by the anti-clerical party, and during the six years he remained Mayor he did much to modernize Rome, especially in the improvement of its street-car service and its sanitation, so that the city's death-rate became one of the lowest in Europe. He was highly esteemed, and even the clericals respected his uprightness and efficiency.

Brandes, when I met him, was nearly seventy years old, but intellectually vigorous and brilliant, although cynical, even if at times humorously and delightfully so.

Through David Lubin, American delegate to the International Institute of Agriculture, whom I had known for many years, we met Professor Luigi Luzzatti, Professor of International Law at the University of Rome, a leading member of the Italian Chamber, and a convincing orator and publicist. He was then in his seventies, a large, statesmanlike figure of distinguished appearance. We spent a pleasant hour in his apartment on the Via Veneto opposite our hotel. He said he was gratified to

find my views, as expressed in my "Roger Williams" and
in my chapter on the development of religious liberty in
my "American Spirit," so much in accord with his own.
He told me about his brochure, "Liberta di Consciensa
e di Sciensa," which had been translated into German
under the title "Freiheit des Gewissens und Wissens."
In it he makes considerable reference to Roger Williams,
and pays me the compliment of saying that he derived
the inspiration for his book from mine. He also quotes
extensively from Roosevelt's letter on religious liberty,
which I have embodied in Chapter X of this volume.

I called on Professor Luzzatti a number of times thereafter, which in his charming way he had begged me to do
because he was confined to the house with a cold and
therefore could not call on me. In one of his notes he
wrote that we were friends because our ideas and ideals
were the same, and he wanted to be sure to see me again
before I left Rome. He confirmed what the King had
told me, that there was no anti-Semitic spirit in Italy.
He said he was a Jew, but was not brought up religiously
as such, although he was known to be ready on all necessary occasions to stand up for his people.

Professor Luzzatti was largely responsible for improv-
ing Italy's financial system, and in the establishment of
the Banca Popolari, or People's Banks. He was also
influential in the negotiation of Italy's commercial
treaties.

Through the offices of P. R. Mackenzie, who for a
number of years had been Rome correspondent of the
"New York Sun," I met Cardinals Rampolla and Falconio. We called first on the latter, who knew our country
well. For nine years he had been papal legate at Washington, during which time he became a naturalized citizen. As we entered his reception room, I observed two

little American flags attached to an ornament on the
center table. He informed me as he greeted me that His
Holiness was quite ill, otherwise he would have advised
me to allow Cardinal Rampolla and himself to arrange
for an audience.

Mr. Mackenzie informed the Cardinal that I had been
a member of the Roosevelt Cabinet, which recalled
Roosevelt's visit to Rome in 1910. Of course, I was
anxious to learn how both these prelates regarded that
incident. Cardinal Falconio said that the Holy Father
had made no conditions as to the visit, but had merely
expressed the hope that there might be no repetition of
the Fairbanks incident; the Holy Father knew how
broad-minded and well-disposed Roosevelt was toward
all creeds and had really wanted very much to meet him.
The Cardinal said that of course Roosevelt could not
be blamed; the matter should not have been handled
through the embassy. His remarks implied that the mis-
management had been there.

We now went within the Vatican district, under the
arch on the side, to the palatial residence of Cardinal
Rampolla. On entering, we were led to the Cardinal's
private room next to the formal reception chamber,
where the Cardinal greeted us warmly. He has great
charm of manner and is most gracious; withal he impressed one as a keen, learned, and shrewd prelate. He
was regarded as the ablest and most distinguished of the
cardinals eligible to the Holy See, and it may be remembered that he was considered the logical successor of
Leo XIII, and it was said he would probably have been
elected Pope but for the opposition of the Emperor of
Austria.

In referring to the Roosevelt incident, he too held
Roosevelt entirely blameless, and added that both he and

Brother Falconio knew how kindly Roosevelt felt toward Catholics and the Holy See, and that there should have been nothing official about that message; if he had been in Merry Del Val's place, the regrettable misunderstanding would not have happened. Evidently he blamed the papal secretary.

David Lubin gave a dinner at the Hôtel de Russie to Mrs. Straus and me on May 1st. Among the guests were Mayor Nathan and Marquis Sapelli, president of the International Institute of Agriculture, and the Marchioness. Professor Luzzatti had accepted, but his cold still prevented his going out. Lubin was a rough diamond, so to speak: a man of vision, unlimited energy and enthusiasm. It was he who induced the Italian Government to recognize the International Institute of Agriculture, and he was regarded by that Government as its founder. Indeed, he was better understood in Rome than in Washington. He knew nothing and cared less about diplomatic amenities. When I was in the Cabinet our ambassador at Rome had made an unfavorable report about him because of some supposed tactless move which was objected to by our ambassador. This report displeased Secretary Root, and the result would have been Lubin's recall as our delegate to the Institute, had I not interceded for him with the President, explaining what manner of man Lubin was, that he had no manners but genius, and that I felt sure the King of Italy himself would intercede for him.

As a matter of fact about a year after that there was some question of appointing another person as American delegate, and the King did intercede for Lubin. For the help and encouragement that I gave this worthy man he was always thereafter most grateful to me. It was David Lubin, too, who first aroused interest in America in the establishment of an agricultural credit system, as well as in the coöperative banks.

From Rome we went direct to London, where I shortly got in touch with William Watson, the poet. I had met him the year before in the United States. I was chairman of the executive committee of the Authors' Club at the time, and as such its president; the Club gave him a reception; also he was at my house several times. It was said of him that he was better known than Robert Bridges and would have been selected as poet laureate in preference to Bridges had he not written a poem called "The Woman with the Serpent's Tongue," referring to Margot Asquith, wife of the Premier, which spoiled his chances for official recognition. He appeared somewhat disappointed and to be considering permanent residence in America. He asked me about the cost of living in cities other than New York, which he considered too extravagant.

Watson gave me a luncheon at the British Empire Club, where I met a number of his friends — Sir Sidney Lee, editor of the "Dictionary of National Biography"; Sir William Robertson Nicoll, editor of the "Bookman" and of the "British Weekly"; H. W. Massingham, editor of the "Nation"; and a few others. Watson told me that Sir Sidney Lee's biography of Shakespeare was considered the best extant from an historical and critical point of view, and that his biography of King Edward had created a sensation in England, but that its aim was to portray the human side of King Edward. He told me also that Sir Sidney was an Israelite. My own conversation with Sir Sidney was very general. He is a mild man with a reserved manner.

Sir Charles and Lady Henry invited us to luncheon at

their beautiful town house in Carlton Gardens, to meet Lloyd George, who was then Chancellor of the Exchequer. The other guests were: Sir Alexander Ure, solicitor-general for Scotland; Dr. Thomas J. MacNamara, parliamentary secretary to the Admiralty; Robert Donald, editor of the "Daily Chronicle," a leading labor daily.

Lloyd George explained the important Liberal measures to me, particularly the National Insurance Act of 1911, amendments to which were then being considered in the House. He declared that it was necessary to curb or reform the House of Lords before social justice measures, such as this insurance act, legislation for old age pensions, etc., could be put through. He asked about Roosevelt and the status of the Progressive Party, and whether the newspapers were favorable to the cause; it seems that the newspapers did not give him adequate information regarding the Progressives. I had to tell him that many of our leading dailies were not with us. I explained to him that I thought the Progressive movement could hardly be regarded as a party, but that I believed its influence in liberalizing both of the old parties would be considerable.

When I was in London shortly after the outbreak of the World War, I remember a humorous incident at another meeting with Lloyd George, at a small dinner. For emergency use there had been issued one-pound treasury notes that looked more like a "shinplaster" of our Civil War days than like a dignified British pound. One of the guests brought in a number of these, for which some of us exchanged gold. As I took one up I remarked about the appearance of it and added that before I accepted it I would require the endorsement of the Chancellor of the Exchequer. Lloyd George quickly answered, "That can be done," and promptly took the note and wrote his name on the back of it. It remains in my possession as a souvenir.

The following Sunday, Sir Charles and Lady Henry again invited us to luncheon, this time to their country home near Maidenhead, to meet Sir Rufus and Lady Isaacs. Sir Rufus is now Lord Reading, and it was then quite well understood that he would be appointed Lord Chief Justice. He expressed great interest in our parliamentary system as compared with that of Great Britain, but thought the British method had an advantage over ours in that members of the Cabinet were at the same time members of Parliament and could advocate their own measures, and that in England a Cabinet member must be not only an administrator, but a parliamentarian as well. He was very anxious to know how administrative measures in our country are brought forward and enacted into laws. I explained our system to him and told him I thought the system of questioning in Parliament members of the Cabinet left very little opportunity for the Cabinet members to devote themselves to the administrative work of their departments.

During this stay in London, I again had several pleasant meetings with Postmaster-General Herbert Samuel, whom I had visited when I passed through London on my return from Constantinople in 1910. He informed me that within a month he intended visiting Canada and then the United States. Later in the year I met him in my own country, where he delivered several public addresses and made a fine impression.

While we were at tea one afternoon on the terrace of the House of Commons with Mr. and Mrs. Samuel, the Right Honorable John Burns, president of the Local Government Board, joined us. He knew both my brothers and was pleased to meet me. He asked me to ac-

company him to his department, which is only a short
distance from Westminster Hall.   As we passed the entrance to Westminster, he said to me:

"Let us stop here and let me give you a graphic page
of British history."

So we halted for about ten minutes under the scaffold-
ing of the men who were doing some repair work on the
edifice, while Burns discoursed eloquently on the well-
known facts of British history. I was as much interested
in the man as in the great Gothic structure, and my mind
went on to review the march of democracy from the
booted and spurred Cromwell to the radical labor leader
John Burns. The radicalism of Burns was at one time
considered dangerous, but on entering the Cabinet he
became conservative and reliable, proving the effect of
responsibility upon even the more radical minds when in
office.

Across the Thames Burns pointed to some factories,
saying: "There is where my father worked as a day
laborer, and where I worked." And I was indeed impressed with the democracy of Great Britain in our day.

We spent a charming evening with Mr. and Mrs.
Harry Brittain, now Sir Harry and Lady Brittain, in
their cozy home on Cowley Street. The only other guest
was Earl Grey, former Governor-General of Canada.
Earlier in the year I had met both Sir Harry Brittain and
Earl Grey in New York, when they came over respectively
as chairman and secretary of the British committee for
the Celebration of One Hundred Years of Peace.

A few days thereafter Earl Grey invited Mrs. Brittain,
Mrs. Straus, and me to breakfast with him and then to
accompany him to the now famous Hampstead Garden
Suburb. I was glad of this opportunity to see that experiment, because the subject of housing workers in whole-

some homes and surroundings at a moderate cost was one that interested me very much.

Hampstead is only about five or six miles from the heart of London. In this beautiful suburb, every house has a garden, and the architecture of the houses is varied and attractive. Earl Grey knew several of the tenants, and took us into a number of the houses. At that time the rental of an entire house per week was six and a half shillings and upward; and there were large single rooms with cooking facilities for three and a half shillings a week. The population was almost seven thousand, and the suburb was being extended. There was an air of contentment about the place, and the children looked robust and happy. The wonder of it all was that the plan was on an economically sound basis and was paying four and a half per cent annually on the capital invested. The Earl had much to do with the development of this suburb and, if I mistake not, was chairman of the board at the time.

Mrs. Straus and I were also invited to spend a week-end with Earl and Lady Grey at Howick, their Northumberland estate. Mrs. Straus, however, had planned to take a cure at a German health resort, so my son Roger was invited in her stead. The only other visitor was Henry Vivian, M.P., who was associated with Earl Grey in both the Hampstead Garden Suburb and the organization of the coöperative societies, of which latter Earl Grey was chairman. I participated in a meeting of the Coöperative Society of Northern England and saw how practical and inexpensively conducted they were, cheapening merchandise of all kinds by eliminating the profits of middlemen and the cost of distribution, and to that extent lowering the cost of living. Along these lines we have much to learn in our own country.

Roger and I spent a delightful few days with Earl and

Lady Grey. The Earl represented the finest type of English nobleman. He was a man of the highest ideals, even regarded by some as rather visionary in his various plans for the betterment of economic conditions; a man who recognized, as do so many of the British titled people, the patriotic responsibilities attached to their position.

I now proceeded to the northern part of Scotland to spend a few days with Andrew Carnegie at Skibo Castle in Sutherland. It was what Andrew Carnegie called "university week" at Skibo, for in accordance with an annual custom he had as his guests the provosts of the several Scotch universities.

Every morning we were awakened by the music of several Scotch highlanders dressed in their kilts and playing old native tunes on their bagpipes. Those were unique and memorable awakenings in the steel-master's castle; the bagpipes attuned the mind instantly to the Scotch atmosphere and Scotch tradition. We started our day invariably with a game of golf, at which we helped each other out as caddies, for all of us, Mr. Carnegie included, were indifferent players (beyond which stage I have not even since progressed), so that we all felt quite at home with one another on the links.

We had hoped to test Carnegie's much-lauded and far-famed salmon pond, but that season the fish were late in coming up the run, so we were deprived of that pleasure and had to console ourselves with a little trout fishing. Two or three were put into each of our baskets for breakfast, and the remainder were religiously restored to the pond.

At that time Skibo Castle had but recently been built, but already it was noted for its generous hospitality, which both the British and American friends of Mr. Carnegie so much enjoyed.

I had promised Mr. Carnegie that I would attend the ceremonies opening the Peace Palace at The Hague, to which all the members of the Hague Tribunal had been specially invited. From Skibo, therefore, I returned to London, to meet my old friend Hakki Pasha, who was one of the Turkish members of the Tribunal, and together we went on to The Hague.

A word about the origin of the Peace Palace may not prove tedious. Shortly after the close of the first Hague Conference in 1899 the late Professor Martens, distinguished Russian international jurist, had a talk with our ambassador at Berlin, Andrew D. White, who had been chairman of the American delegation at that conference. Together they discussed the desirability of a building at The Hague which should serve as a "palace of justice" for the Permanent Court and as a place of meetings for international conferences. Subsequently Ambassador White presented the idea to Andrew Carnegie, and Carnegie invited him to come to Skibo to discuss it. Ambassador White records in his "Autobiography":

The original idea had developed into something far greater. The Peace Palace at The Hague began to reappear in a new glory — as a pledge and sign of a better future for the world. Then there came from Carnegie the words which assured his great gift to the nations — the creation of a center as a symbol of a world's desire for peace and of good will to man.

The programme for the dedication was in keeping with the occasion. The city itself was decorated with festive drapery and floral arches. It was a beautiful day and great crowds of people had gathered. The great conference hall and the galleries of the Palace were filled with representatives of the nations: the diplomatic corps; about forty members of the Permanent Court; members of the States General of Holland; the Queen; Prince

Henry; the Queen Mother, and many ladies; altogether an imposing assembly.

The ceremony opened with the singing of anthems by the choir from Amsterdam. An historical address was made by the former Minister of Foreign Affairs, Jonkheer van Karnebeek, president of the Carnegie Building Foundation. His son, by the way, is Minister of Foreign Affairs at this writing and was Holland's chief representative at the Washington Conference of 1921. Mr. Van Swinderen, the retiring Minister of Foreign Affairs, made the address accepting the custody of the building.

In the evening a banquet to Mr. Carnegie was given in the Hall of Knights at Binnenhof by the Minister of Foreign Affairs in the name of the Government, to which were invited the nobility and all the high officials who had attended the ceremony, and who thereafter were received in audience by the Queen at the Royal Palace.

The greatest possible distinction was shown to both Mr. and Mrs. Carnegie, who were brimming over with gratification. Well known as Carnegie was as one of the greatest captains of industry, he is even better known, and will be longer remembered throughout the world, by the extent of his benefactions, in the distribution of which he found his supreme happiness in the last two decades of his life.

When the World War began, the cartoonists made much sport of the Peace Palace as the outstanding embodiment of the irony of fate, and with the peace advocates for the failure of their vision. But evidence is not entirely lacking that the peace advocates may yet be able to turn the laugh on the cartoonists. Some of the most constructive features of the League of Nations were formulated by commissions working under the roof of the Peace Palace. The International Court of Justice, organized under the provisions of the covenant of the League of Nations, has its seat within the Palace and will soon be ready to commence its constructive work. The Palace is a contribution whose worth to civilization can hardly be measured in a single generation.

In the fall of that year we returned to New York, but only for a few months. When Kermit Roosevelt became engaged to Miss Willard, charming daughter of our ambassador to Spain, my wife promised him that unless we were unavoidably prevented, we should be present at his marriage in Madrid early in the following June. We had become very much attached to our young friend, whom we got to know so well during his stay with us at Constantinople.

On May 19, 1914, we returned to Europe on the S.S. Lusitania. On board we were agreeably surprised to find our long-time friend, Mrs. T. J. Preston, Jr., formerly Mrs. Grover Cleveland, seated at our table in the dining-saloon. She was traveling alone and was to meet her husband and daughter in London. Naturally we spoke of Cleveland and of his qualities as they had revealed themselves to her and to his more intimate friends. When a man is President and always in the limelight, people get a perverted impression of him, a fact true more or less since Washington's day, but perhaps to a greater degree in the case of Cleveland. Mrs. Preston referred to many incidents that illustrated his gentleness and consideration, and she gave credit to his advice and guidance for much of the tact she displayed as mistress of the White House, for she was scarcely out of her teens when she occupied that important post.

In London I received a letter from Roosevelt saying he would meet us in Paris on June 7th, and suggesting that

I keep in touch with our embassy there. Miss Catherine Page also was going to the wedding to be one of the bridesmaids, and Ambassador Page asked us to take her with us, which of course we were glad to do.

We stayed in London for several days, and soon after our arrival, there was a young people's dance at the embassy to which the ambassador asked us to come if only for a short stay. There we met Mr. and Mrs. Rudyard Kipling. In the course of a pleasant chat, I asked Kipling in what work he was then engaged.

Kipling pointed to the next room at the dancing, and said: "Sitting up late nights as I have a daughter in society, which is my principal occupation at present."

I spent an evening with Israel Zangwill, during which he unfolded to me a plan he was formulating to call a conference of representative Jews from various countries to form a central committee which was to be more internationally representative than the Alliance Israélite of Paris, which is in reality dominantly French and therefore does not represent the world of Israel in an international sense. Such a body was to protect, defend, and plead for the cause of the Jews wherever necessary and to speak in behalf of the Jewry of the world. He said he had talked it over with his colleagues and they wanted me to take the presidency of such a body because of my experience in statesmanship and world diplomacy. I took care not to discourage him, but told him I should have to consider the matter, because with me personality sank out of sight when an important cause was to be carried forward.

When we arrived in Paris, a note awaited us from Ambassador Herrick asking us to come to the embassy, and informing us that Roosevelt was there. When I arrived I found Roosevelt in the smoking-room engaged in an animated conversation with ex-Premier Hanotaux regarding the physical characteristics of the races of Europe, in which Henri Bergson also participated, and to which the sculptor Rodin appeared to be a bored listener. Roosevelt was talking French, and when he could not find the word he wanted, he used an English term for which Bergson would then give him the French equivalent.

The next day our party left for Madrid — Roosevelt, his daughter Alice, their cousin Philip, son of William Emlen Roosevelt, Miss Page, Mrs. Straus, and myself. We were a jolly party.

Roosevelt and I, of course, talked politics, especially the future of the Progressive Party. The State campaign for Governor and United States Senator was being discussed when Roosevelt left home, and he had given out an interview before sailing regarding the sort of men that should be chosen, in which he had kindly referred to me as the standard of nominee for Senator. The press had commented extensively and favorably upon such a choice and there had appeared many articles and editorials giving consideration to my name. Roosevelt had, of course, referred to me only as the type of man to be chosen, and believed that if the nominee for Governor were chosen from New York City, it might be well to choose the candidate for Senator from up-State. I told him I had no personal vanity in the matter, that what we wanted was the candidates that would best embody the cause. He answered that he knew me well enough for that, but that every one agreed that next to him I was the most prominent Progressive, and in New York State even stronger than he, as shown by the election of 1912. Of course I did not agree with this generous statement, which was another proof that figures do sometimes lie.

He expressed the hope that the Progressives and the liberal wing of the Republicans might unite. He lamented the difficulties for the party in the coming election, and said he was reluctant to enter the campaign, but, he added: "I must stand by the men who stood by me." If Johnson was again to be the candidate of the party for Governor of California and needed his help, he would have to go there, though he could not overtax his throat, which had been weakened by his fever in the jungles of Brazil. He said if that fever had overtaken him two weeks earlier, he would not have pulled through; as it was, he had had a narrow escape.

At Irun, the Spanish border, King Alphonso's private car was hitched on to our train. From there on to the King's summer palace, where he left the train, a small guard of honor was drawn up at every stopping-place and the chief officials of the district came to pay their respects to their sovereign. The King was only twenty-eight years old, but was generally conceded to be a man of ability, with enlightened views, and highly regarded by his subjects. However, among the random notes that I made at the end of this visit to Spain, I wrote:

I very much doubt if monarchy will last another score of years in Spain unless the King takes a lesson from Great Britain and is content to have Parliament govern the country. The democratic spirit is rapidly growing, but I very much doubt if the people with their long traditions of monarchical government, will be prepared for many years for a democratic form of government.

The most powerful man in Parliament, though out of the Ministry at the time, was the late Premier Maurer. The Conservatives were in power, but their tenure was precarious. It was said that Maurer's ancestors several generations ago were Jews, which is also true of several members of the nobility, whose ancestors were converted during the period of the Inquisition.

Our ambassador and his staff of secretaries were at the station in Madrid to meet us. The Roosevelts went to the embassy and we went to the Ritz Hotel. At eleven o'clock on the morning of June 10th, the civil marriage took place in the Prefecture of Police before a district judge. It was a simple proceeding, attended only by the immediate family and a few intimate friends, perhaps a dozen in all. The ceremony was read from a book in which was included the marriage contract. The bride and groom and four witnesses then signed the contract, the witnesses on this occasion being the father of the bride, the father of the groom, and two Spanish noblemen.

The following day at high noon the religious ceremony was performed in the chapel of the British embassy. There were about seventy-five persons present: the diplomatic corps, the Minister of Foreign Affairs and several other Spanish officials, and some friends. After the ceremony, there was a wedding breakfast at the embassy. The Roosevelts left that same evening for Paris, and I did not see them again in Europe.

This was our second visit to Spain. In 1897 my wife and I had been there for about a week, and many of the men with whom we had spent pleasant hours at that time were now no longer living. Chief among these were Sir Henry Drummond Wolff and Signor Castelar. Sir Henry, who was British ambassador to Spain at the time, I had not seen since he was special envoy to Turkey in 1888, and I remember how delighted he was to see us again and how very much at home he made us feel. We also met Lady Wolff then, who, however, was not well. She told us of some of her experiences in Persia; also that

Sir Henry was very ill there, having been poisoned at a dinner given by the Shah.

Another colleague of my first Turkish mission whom I had found at Madrid in 1897 was Herr von Radowitz, German ambassador. He invited us to dine one evening at the embassy, and after dinner showed us the throne room in which hung a picture of the Kaiser. Radowitz explained that it was painted by a friend of the Emperor, "somewhat theatrical, you see, but he is fond of appearing grandiose." He started to tell me how he came into possession of the painting, that he had told the Emperor that the embassy had no likeness of him, but he corrected himself by saying: "No, I did not ask for the picture, my wife did." He displayed rather a slighting estimate of his sovereign. The fact was that he was a protégé of Bismarck, and after the latter's retirement Radowitz was transferred from Constantinople to Madrid, which was regarded in the nature of a demotion, and that perhaps largely accounted for his attitude.

As we conversed after dinner, Radowitz made the remark that in 1878 he was one of the secretaries to the Berlin Congress and that there he met Disraeli. Disraeli always made specially prepared speeches in English, which Radowitz took down in French. Then Disraeli would compliment him and say, "Did I really speak in this nice way or did you only write me down so elegantly?" When Radowitz replied, "Yes, this is what you said," Disraeli would say, "So let it stand."

This led me to draw out Sir Henry, who was also present, regarding Disraeli. He had known Disraeli very well. He told me that at the age of twelve he had met Disraeli and had always had access to him. I asked Sir Henry whether he had not kept a diary. He said he had not, but wished that he had. "Dizzy," he said, was not a compromiser; if he had opponents, he recognized them as such and never sought to placate them. When he first entered Parliament he was a brilliant, flowery speaker, so much so that his party, the Conservative, was afraid of him. Afterward, when he became a member of the Ministry, he had trained himself down to a rather prosy level, yet now and again his speech would glow with brilliant passages excoriating his opponent. He was quick at repartee and often held up the other side to ridicule in telling metaphor.

I asked Sir Henry about Dizzy's loyalty to Judaism. He said Dizzy never denied it, holding up especially the race idea. I remarked that in reading such of Disraeli's novels as "Coningsby" and "Tancred," and in the Proceedings of the Berlin Congress, I was impressed with his race loyalty and his purpose to secure equal political rights for the oppressed members of his race in the newly constituted Balkan States.

Sir Henry answered me: "I don't recall the novels, but what you say was true, although of course his loyalty was to England first. Dizzy's idea was that the race should amalgamate."

I wanted to know whether he recollected when Disraeli's novels first came out. He said he remembered all but "Vivian Grey," which Dizzy wrote when he was quite young. He added that Disraeli's writings made him quite a lion among the literary set, but did not help him politically. He wanted to count among the best socially, and ever pointed his political guns toward that target.

When I asked Sir Henry about Disraeli's personal appearance, he said: "Lord Dufferin (Frederic Blackwood) looked very much like him; so much so that he might have been taken for Disraeli's son. Dizzy and Mrs. Blackwood were said to be very good friends. He met her on many of his frequent visits to the home of Lady Blessington, during the period when he was beginning to gain popularity."

Sir Henry had been rather critical of Disraeli, but he ended by saying: "Taking Dizzy all in all, he was the greatest English statesman I have ever known." And to me Disraeli had always been a fascinating subject, so much so, indeed, that at one time I had the intention to write a biography of him.

With Emilio Castelar I had come into correspondence following the publication of the French edition of my "Origin of the Republican Form of Government in the United States," in which he was much interested. He expressed the hope that the next time I came to Europe we might meet, and when I came to Madrid, Mr. Reed, for many years secretary of our legation there, made an appointment for me, and accompanied Mrs. Straus and me to his home.

He was a short, rather stout man of sixty-five, bald, with dark skin and sparkling brown eyes, and a gray moustache. He was a bachelor. We spoke French, and though it was an ordinary conversation he was quite oratorical. He said he was a republican and believed thoroughly in conservative republicanism such as we had in the United States, but that Spain was not ripe for republicanism, and that he had parted company with the Spanish republicans because he could not endure their principles; they were ready to pull down, but not to build up; they were anarchists, and not republicans.

He presented Mrs. Straus with his photograph, and when she asked him to autograph it, he returned to his study and wrote in Spanish on the back of it a charming sentiment regarding us and our country. He was anxious to have us come and take Spanish dinner with him, but unfortunately we were leaving that evening for Seville.

I was interested in some articles Castelar had written for the "Century Magazine" in 1892–93 regarding Columbus, and especially in those of the articles in which he referred to the expulsion of the Jews from Spain. I asked him whether he had finished the work, and he told me he had brought it out complete in book form in Spanish, in which he had dwelt more fully on the Jewish expulsion and had published a number of facts from original research made for the work, though not by himself. He went to his study to give me a copy of the book, but found that he had none on hand. He promised to send me one in a few days through Mr. Reed, which he did.

The expulsion of the Spanish Jews was of great interest to me, and on this second visit to Madrid I took advantage of the opportunity to see some of the historical relics from that period. I got in touch with Dr. Angel Pulido, life senator of Spain, and together with Professor A. S. Yahuda, we visited the historic city of Toledo, about two and a half hours by rail out of Madrid. Dr. Pulido had for years advocated measures to induce Jews to return to Spain, especially those who still retained the Spanish language, as do many in Turkey and nearly all those in Morocco who are the descendants of those driven out of Spain.

Toledo is one of the most ancient cities of Spain. It was once the residence of the kings of Castile, and under the Moors had a population of some two hundred thousand, of whom seventy-five thousand were estimated to have been Jews. The population now is about twenty thousand, and the city is but the bedraggled remains of its former grandeur. In its ancient glory it was noted for its silk and woolen industries and for the manufacture of the famous Toledo steel from which were made swords and other weapons that rivaled those of Damascus; and it was the home of a number of Jewish scholars and noted men, Eben Ezra (1119–74), for instance.

There are two old synagogues in the city which I was anxious to see. One was erected at the end of the twelfth or beginning of the thirteenth century, and was converted into a church in 1405. It is called Santa Maria la Blanca. Its architecture is of the best Moorish style; the interior has twenty-eight horseshoe arches borne by thirty-two octagonal piers, and the elaborate capitals are ornamented with pine cones.

In the same district, near by, is the Sinagoga del Transito, of similar style, erected about 1360. It was built at the expense of one Samuel Levy, treasurer of Peter the Cruel, who was afterward executed by order of his king. The walls of the interior were decorated with Hebrew writing, mainly passages from the Psalms. In 1492 this synagogue was turned over to the Calatrava Order of Knights, and many members of this order lie buried in the body of the building. Later the synagogue was consecrated to the death of the virgin.

Near these synagogues also was the Casa del Greco (House of the Greek), so called because the famous Greek painter, Dominico Theotogopuli, forerunner of the impressionists, lived there. Among his pictures is a large one of an "auto da fé" which took place in the main square of the city, and the square when I saw it still looked much the same as in the painting. The picture shows the balconies of the houses surrounding the square filled with eager and gay spectators who had come to witness and enjoy the burning of Jewish heretics. They must have assembled in about the same spirit as fashionable people of a later day came to the bull fights. In the picture the procession is entering the enclosure where are seated the members of the Holy Office, or inquisitors, at whose side stand the officers holding torches with which to light the pyre on which the condemned victims were bound. As I gazed at the square, I could graphically visualize the scene portrayed in the picture. Such cruelty and perversion inevitably presaged the spiritual as well as the material decadence of the inhabitants of the Iberian Peninsula.

By the courtesy of Senator Pulido, I met and had several conferences with the Marqués de Dosfuentes, who several years before, as Fernando de Antón del Olmet, had written an article entitled "La verdadera patrio de Cristóbal Colón," which was published in "La España Moderna," a leading monthly of Spain.

I was very much interested in the data that several of the historians of Spain had unearthed regarding the ancestry and place of origin of Columbus. The article by the Marquis just mentioned was based on the research made by Celso Garcia de la Riega, and both Olmet and Riega came to the conclusion, based upon their examination of records, that Columbus was not an Italian, but a Spaniard, and that he was born in Pontevedra, Galicia, in the northern part of Spain; that his father's name was Colón (the Spanish for Columbus), and his mother's name Fonterosa; and that he was of Jewish ancestry.

In his article Olmet says, after going into detail regarding the nationality of Columbus according to the documents which he was able to examine:

Nothing seems more logical than the preceding reasoning, and, moreover, this is the simplest method of explaining that the Admiral's parents were a Colón and a Fonterosa, which gives us a clue to the mystery of his life. From the document under notice it is to be inferred that Domingo de Colón named was a modest trader. If the admiral was his son, it would not be absurd to suppose that, given the social prejudices of the times, this should have been a sufficient motive for hiding his origin and country. But there is still another reason that fully justifies his secrecy and clears up all mystery. The patronymic "Fonterosa" appears in the Province of Pontevedra connected with the names of Jacob the elder, another Jacob, and Benjamin; Colón's mother was called Susana. "If the admiral belonged to this family, doubtless Jewish," says Sg. La Riega, "since we may draw this inference from the Biblical names, or if he belonged to a family of new Christians, should we not forgive his action in the matter and declare him fully justified in his resolution not to reveal such antecedents? We must bear in mind the then existing hatred toward the Hebrew race and the merciless fury let loose against it in the latter half of the fifteenth century."

In another part of the article Olmet says:

Colón never mentioned any relative, paternal or maternal. Even when Colón was at the zenith of his fame no one in Italy came forward to claim relationship with him, although he was the most famous personage of that time. Thus everything goes to corroborate Don Fernando Colón's affirmation in his "Life of the Admiral" that his father wished his origin and birthplace to remain unknown.

The research of La Riega was continued to 1914 and published in that year. The author died early in the year, shortly before I arrived in Madrid. Other Spanish historians also have published conclusions similar to those of La Riega. There was, for instance, a brochure by Enrique de Arribas Y. Turull, entitled "Cristóbal Colón, Natural de Pontevedra," which was originally delivered as a lecture before the Madrid Historical Society. This also sums up, in nineteen points, the reasons for the conclusion that Columbus was a Spaniard, and of Jewish ancestry.

CHAPTER XV

THE WORLD WAR

TOURING through Normandy late in July, 1914, we met some friends who had just come from Paris who told us that war was imminent and from best reports would break out within a very few days. Accordingly we hurried to Paris and in the course of twenty-four hours the whole aspect of the city had changed. From the windows of our hotel on the Place Vendôme and on the principal boulevards of the city we saw youths of military age marching to headquarters. The air throbbed with the *Marseillaise*. Everywhere there were crowds, but they were neither boisterous nor hilarious. Everywhere there was an air of tension and determination, vastly unlike the usual mood of jovial, happy Paris.

Starting at once for London, we found the trains so overcrowded that it was impossible to get accommodations, so we motored to Dieppe and reached there in time to take the boat that left at three o'clock in the morning for Newhaven. The ordinary capacity of the boat was five hundred passengers, but it was packed from stem to stern with some two thousand persons on this voyage, mainly Americans. The Calais–Dover crossing of the Channel had already been suspended.

On board the train from Newhaven to London, a curious incident occurred that indicated the derangement of things. I had four fares to pay, amounting to about three pounds. I handed the conductor a five-pound Bank of England note. He took it, but shortly returned with it, saying he could accept nothing but gold. I expostulated with him, told him I had no gold, and since a bank note was valid tender I insisted upon its acceptance. But the upshot was that he preferred to take my card with my London address!

It would appear that my credit at that moment was better than that of the Bank of England.

We arrived in London on Sunday, August 2d. At the Hyde Park Hotel, to which we went, a typewritten notice was posted announcing a meeting on the following day at the Waldorf Hotel on the Strand. The persons who signed the notice were unknown to me, and at first I was inclined to pay no attention to it. However, I did go, and found gathered inside and in front of the hotel several thousand stranded Americans. The main hall and all approaches to it were packed. Several persons in the crowd recognized me and made a passageway so that I could get into the room where the meeting was being held. Upon my entrance I was lifted upon a table that served as a platform, and was asked to speak. I made a short address to the panic-stricken assembly, assured them they had nothing to fear and were as safe in London as if they were in New York, and that our committee would remain with them and help them get suitable transportation as early as practicable. There was loud cheering and my words seemed to have a comforting effect.

Immediately thereafter a group of us came together and organized a special committee for the aid of Americans in Europe. There were Frederick I. Kent, one of the vice-presidents of the Bankers' Trust Company; W. N. Duane, another vice-president of the Bankers' Trust Company; Theodore Hetzler, a vice-president of the Fifth Avenue Bank; Joseph P. Day, a prominent real estate auctioneer of New York City; William C. Breed, an officer of the Merchants' Association; Chandler P. Anderson and James Byrne, prominent American lawyers, several others, and myself. We arranged for headquarters at the Hotel Savoy, where several of the largest salons were placed at our disposal so that we had room for the various departments that needed to be formed to attend to the wants of the many terrified Americans who were pouring into London from all over the Continent. Mr. Hetzler was chairman of the general committee, Mr. Duane secretary, and Robert W. DeForest, vice-president of the American Red Cross, was member *ex-officio.* I was made chairman of the embassy committee of which Ambassador Page was honorary chairman, and the American ambassadors to France, Germany, Austria, and the ministers to Holland and Belgium were made advisory members. We found many willing helpers, including a number of professors from American universities and other public-spirited men and women.

The necessary sub-committees were speedily formed: Mr. Day was made chairman of the transportation committee and got in touch with the managers of all the transatlantic steamship companies. Mr. Kent was chairman of the finance committee, and through his banking connections was able to get a limited amount of gold to advance to those who could not convert their foreign money, notwithstanding the moratorium that had been declared which made it impossible for several days to get ready money; foreign bills were not being accepted by the banks. With the declaration of the moratorium we at once called a meeting of the managers of the hotels where most of the Americans were stopping, and without exception these men were very accommodating. They agreed not to require payment from their American guests for the time being, and as far as possible to advance them a little money to meet their immediate requirements.

Our embassy was crowded from morning to night with hundreds of citizens, most of whom wanted to make application for passports, for the steamship companies required the exhibition of passports before arranging for transportation. The rooms at the embassy were not large enough to accommodate the crowds that filled them, so we transferred the passport division to the Hotel Savoy, and Ambassador Page assigned to me several clerks to facilitate the handling of our business. I am sorry to say there was a tendency on the part of many American travelers to find fault with our ambassador and the embassy. This was not at all justified, and I took every occasion to assure them that the ambassador was doing all in his power with his limited staff, and that our committee had his fullest coöperation and was getting his aid in every possible way. I consulted with Ambassador Page almost every day, and together we planned for arranging for money and the many other requirements of our citizens.

In those first hectic days, some of us worked all day and far into the night, or rather into the next morning. Many British friends who visited our rooms marveled at the promptness and efficiency with which we dispatched business under the circumstances, and were solicitous for the health of "the unofficial ambassador," as I was being called, and his staff.

After the committee had been going a few days, it secured the coöperation of Mr. and Mrs. Herbert C. Hoover. He was chairman of an American benevolent society, of the woman's committee of which Mrs. Hoover was at the head. As the members of our relief committee returned home, the work was by degrees turned over to Mr. and Mrs. Hoover and their associates, until by August 27th we put all of the remaining work and funds into the hands of their society.

One day Earl Grey paid me a visit at our headquarters, and with him was Mrs. Waldorf Astor, now Viscountess Astor, who reminded me that "all work and no play makes Jack a dull boy," and insisted that Mrs. Straus and I spend the week-end at Cliveden, their residence, a short distance by rail out of London. Other guests were Earl Grey, Geoffrey Robinson, editor of the London "Times," and several others connected with the editorship of "The Round Table," a political quarterly.

Mr. Waldorf Astor was an earnest, modest young man, then about thirty-four years old, unspoiled by his enormous wealth. On the contrary, he was and still is devoting much of his wealth as well as his parliamentary activities to philanthropic work, including the treatment and prevention of tuberculosis, and in this connection had been in touch with my brother Nathan in regard to milk pasteurization.

There were several subsequent week-ends at Cliveden. On one of these visits, a dozen or more young men were there, members of England's foremost families. They enjoyed themselves at tennis and other games and on Monday were to join the colors. It is sad to record that most of these fine fellows, with the exception of two or three, were killed or seriously wounded within the next few months.

When England entered the war, the diplomatic correspondence was published in what was called the British "White Paper." Sir Edward Grey, now Viscount Grey, had made a speech in Parliament, of which I read the published version in this "White Paper." It happened that on that very day Earl Grey, cousin to Sir Edward, was lunching with me at my hotel, and I took the occasion to point out to him the necessity of making clear, especially for the American public, that the reason England had joined the Allies was not only on Belgium's account, but to uphold the sanctity of international obligations. This concerned not alone the belligerent nations, but all the nations. Without the sanctity of international obligations the war, no matter how it ended, would cause a reversion to a state of international barbarity. Earl Grey suggested that I discuss the subject with his cousin, and arranged for a meeting. A few days later we three sat down to a simple and informal luncheon at Earl Grey's home on South Street, in Park Lane.

Sir Edward Grey spoke earnestly and frankly. He felt the great responsibility of the decision that brought England into the war, and said he had often asked himself whether he could have done otherwise. There was nothing chauvinistic in either his attitude or his arguments. It was plain that he had weighed the entire issue carefully. His open-mindedness, his simplicity and straightforwardness of manner, his great ability and humanitarian zeal, impressed me very much.

I called his attention to the importance of having Russia grant civil and religious rights to her subject nationalities; the failure of such action would weaken the moral cause of the Allies, and also from an American point of view it was important that Russia give some evidence of a liberal spirit, otherwise it might be feared that victory for the Allies would redound mainly to the advantage of autocracy in Russia. I contended that it was not a question of humanity, but plain state policy, and that it was important that the Governments of Great Britain and France bring Russia, as their ally, into line. I had received several cables from prominent men in New York and Boston who had thus expressed the American point of view.

The conversation ran on for an hour and a half in a very informal way. Earl Grey then made the suggestion, in accordance with my remarks of a few days before about the necessity of making clear England's position in entering the war, that I give out an interview to the American press covering the substance of our conversation. I demurred. Naturally I hesitated to state publicly the delicate and critical questions that the British Minister of Foreign Affairs had so frankly discussed with me. However, Sir Edward himself said he would appreciate my doing so, for he had perfect confidence in my doing it without embarrassment to his country. I therefore agreed to it, with the proviso that he approve the interview before it was released for publication.

I got in touch with the representatives of the American papers in London and that evening gave out the interview. The next morning I sent a copy to Sir Edward, who returned it to me without a single change, saying he approved both its form and content. The matter was then cabled to America, published in our leading papers on August 15th, and cabled back for republication in the British papers.

Thereafter the London papers came to me for further interviews, and in a subsequent statement I dwelt more specifically on the importance of Russia's fair treatment of her subject nationalities, particularly the Jews, who had suffered most. The press representatives asked whether they might show my interview to Lord Weardale and if possible get his comment, to which I gladly consented.

Lord Weardale had been head of the Parliamentary deputation that visited Russia the year before and had an intimate knowledge of Russian conditions. He told me later that he had already written the Russian Minister of Foreign Affairs, Sazonoff, along the identical lines of my interview. He supplemented what I had stated, with an interview, saying, among other things:

It would be an immense step in the path of progress of Russia herself and would create a profound sentiment of satisfaction in the civilized world if the Tsar at such a juncture were to give emphatic endorsement to his already declared intention to give full religious liberty to all his peoples. It is not enough to be powerful in the battlefield; it is even more important to conquer the approval of the human conscience.

The Government and people of Great Britain were very solicitous at that time regarding public opinion in America and the probable attitude of our Government. In many quarters there was a feeling of uncertainty and even of misgiving toward the statement by President Wilson respecting an offer of mediation at the opportune moment, in accordance with the provisions of the Hague Treaty. Because of this and other considerations, Sir Edward Grey and others recognized the importance of having Russia give evidence of a more enlightened spirit.

We left London at the end of August, and upon arrival home went up to Hartsdale, a short distance out of New

York, to visit with our son. A few days afterward Mr. James Speyer, whose summer home was but a few miles distant, at Scarboro, telephoned, inviting Mrs. Straus and myself to dine with him. Mrs. Speyer had not returned from abroad; the guests were Mr. and Mrs. Frank A. Vanderlip and Count von Bernstorff. As Mrs. Straus was rather worn out by her London experience, I went alone. There were several other neighbors, Mr. Frank H. Platt and Mr. Frank Trumbull and perhaps one other, about eight of us, of whom Mrs. Vanderlip was the only lady.

Bernstorff I had known for a number of years. I had first met him in 1888 when I was on my first mission to Turkey and he was attaché of the German embassy. Later he came to Washington as ambassador when I was in the Cabinet, and we met frequently there.

The conversation at dinner was general, although it was inevitable that we discuss the war. Bernstorff voiced the usual claim of the Germans, that they did not want war, and that the Kaiser and the German Government stood for peace. When he had dilated upon that theme I asked him:

"Is that the present sentiment and attitude of your country?"

He replied that it certainly was when he left Berlin only two weeks before, on returning to America from his leave of absence.

Knowing how anxious President Wilson was to use any proper opportunity that might present itself for ending the war, I asked Bernstorff whether his Government would entertain a proposition for mediation.

He answered me promptly: "Speaking for myself, I certainly would entertain such a proposition." But he added that he could not speak officially, since cable communication with his Government had been cut off for a week or more.

I asked him whether in his opinion his Government would give favorable consideration to such a proposal. He said that before leaving Berlin he had discussed with the Chancellor the possibility of mediation, following the report of President Wilson's statement that he was ready to offer his services as mediator to both parties, and the Chancellor had said that the war had but begun and it was too early to instruct regarding mediation until the offer was presented. On my questioning him further, the ambassador said his personal opinion was that his Government would accept an offer of mediation. I remarked that I could not but regard his statement as significant, and asked him if I might use it in such a manner as I saw fit. He replied that he had no objection.

As we rose from the table, I made sure of my understanding of his statements, and then the thought occurred to me that the best thing to do was to report the conversation to Secretary of State Bryan, so that he might, if he saw fit, bring it before the President. I so informed Bernstorff, and again he told me he had no objection.

I looked at my watch. It was ten-fifteen. I announced that I would go to Washington on the midnight train. My host suggested that I "sleep on it and don't hurry"; but I concluded that if there was anything I could do to shorten the war by even a few hours I would have to charge myself with neglect of duty if on account of personal convenience I had refrained from doing so. The next day was Sunday; the day after was Labor Day; and all the while thousands were falling on the battlefield. Several of the guests agreed with my decision, so I bade them good-night, called my motor, and caught the midnight train for Washington.

Sunday morning I telephoned to Mr. Bryan at once and made an appointment to meet him at his home. I repeated my conversation with Bernstorff precisely as it had occurred, and Bryan believed, as I did, that it might pave the way to mediation. I suggested that he have the German ambassador come to Washington and speak with him. He communicated with the German embassy, and Bernstorff arrived the following morning.

Bryan presented the subject to the President, who expressed himself as pleased with the possibility of a favorable outcome. The Secretary advised me to have a conference with the British ambassador, Sir Cecil Spring-Rice, and with the French ambassador, M. Jusserand. He had already informed them what had taken place and of my presence in Washington. Sir Cecil asked whether I would kindly come to the embassy, and I replied I would do so, and suggested that he arrange to have the French ambassador also present. This he did.

When I reached the embassy, M. Jusserand had not yet arrived, and Sir Cecil and I indulged in reminiscences. He too had been in Constantinople during my first mission, as secretary of the British embassy. Soon we were joined by M. Jusserand, whom also I had known well for many years, for he had been in Washington since 1902, and I had seen much of him during my Cabinet days.

When we took up the proposal regarding which we had come together, both of these gentlemen agreed that it was deserving of serious attention, but Sir Cecil had little confidence in Bernstorff, who had been his colleague at Cairo, where they had represented their respective Governments. He asked whether I thought an ambassador would make such a statement as Bernstorff's without authority from his Government. I replied that both he and M. Jusserand were better qualified to answer that question, upon which M. Jusserand said that he knew that no ambassador under the German system would dare make such remarks without previous authority from his Government.

"That is so much the better," I commented.

Sir Cecil declared that German diplomacy was peculiar and that the Foreign Office had no conscience in disavowing statements by its ambassadors if it suited Germany's purpose.

After we had gone over the whole subject, both ambassadors stated that if it held one chance in a hundred of shortening the war, it was their duty to entertain it. I replied that I hoped they would entertain it cordially.

Jusserand in his usual happy manner said, "'Cordially,' that is a little too strong."

"Well, sympathetically, then," I said.

"Yes, sympathetically, yes." And with that we parted, both ambassadors expressing their thanks and appreciation of my services.

I had been scrupulously careful to be absolutely accurate in all my statements, and it was therefore gratifying, after the Bryan-Bernstorff conference, to have the Secretary tell me that the ambassador's report of the Scarboro incident was in every detail in accord with mine, and to have the ambassador also confirm the correctness of Mr. Bryan's understanding from my report. Naturally I was anxious to avoid misunderstandings or misconceptions of any kind. The issue was too important.

Both Secretary Bryan and Ambassador Bernstorff cabled to Berlin, and for the time the subject rested there. My remaining in Washington was unnecessary, and I returned to New York. But before leaving, I called by appointment at both the French and British embassies, which also had communicated events in detail to their

Governments. Both ambassadors expressed their high appreciation for my services and hoped I would keep in close touch with them regarding the matter, both for their sake and for the sake of our respective Governments. I told them I would regard myself as "messenger boy" for mediation. Sir Cecil replied, "Ambassador extraordinary." He promised to keep me informed, and two days later wrote me:

I have not yet received any intimation from my Government, nor do I expect one unless something definite is before them. But I need not tell you how heartily my sympathy is with your humanitarian efforts, and you know Grey well enough to be sure that, while scrupulously faithful to all his engagements, he will do everything possible in the cause of peace.

Throughout these negotiations we took great care to keep the matter secret. Despite that fact it leaked out in some way, and the correspondent of the London "Times" reported it in such a way as to give the impression that I had been duped by the wily German ambassador; and there were one or two other papers which took that view. Sir Cecil Spring-Rice was incensed at this interpretation and wrote me on October 3d:

I am sure no one who knows you and knows the facts would ever think that you were either duped or the secret agent of Germany. I am quite positive that Sir Edward Grey would never have such an idea. What you did — and what I hope you will continue to do — is a work of pure philanthropy.

On October 15th he wrote me again on this subject, saying that when the London "Times" representative returned to Washington from New York, he would set him right as to the facts with a view to having the report corrected, and adding:

We used to say at school, "Blessed are the peace makers, for they get more kicks than half-pence!" It represents a melancholy truth, but, however, I am sure every well-thinking person must appreciate your beneficent efforts.

But in general the press of Great Britain expressed its appreciation of the services I had rendered in lifting the latch of the door to mediation.

A letter from Earl Grey concerning the negotiations sheds important light upon the British attitude:

FOREIGN OFFICE, LONDON, S.W.
Saturday, 26 September, 1914

DEAR MR. STRAUS:

Thank you for your letter of the 9th. I am so busy that I have not time to write at any length; but do not let that make you suppose that I am out of sympathy with what you say.

First of all, however, we must save ourselves and the West of Europe, before we can exercise any influence elsewhere. The Prussian military caste has dominated Germany, and the whole of the West of Europe is in danger of being dominated by it. The German Government, in the hands of this military caste, prepared this war, planned it, and chose the time for it. We know now that the war has revealed how thoroughly the German preparations had been made beforehand: with an organization and forethought which is wonderful, and would have been admirable had it been devoted to a praiseworthy purpose. Not one of the other nations now fighting against Germany is prepared in the same way.

Now, we wish to have three things: Firstly, to secure our own liberty as independent States, who will live and let live on equal terms; secondly, the establishment somehow of a Germany not dominated by a military caste; a nation who will look at liberty and politics from the same point of view as we do, and who will deal with us on equal terms and in good faith; thirdly, reparation for the cruel wrongs done to Belgium; to get that is a matter of honour and justice and right.

The statements made by Wolff's Bureau in Europe deny that Germany is yet ready for peace. If she is ready for peace, then I think that her ambassador in Washington ought not to beat

about the bush. He ought to make it clear to President Wilson
that he is authorized to speak on behalf of his Government; and
state to the President that Germany does wish to make peace.
In that case, President Wilson could approach all the others
who are engaged in this war and bring them into consultation
with one another and with him. But at present we have no
indication that Germany wishes to have peace, and no indication that she would agree to any terms that would give reparation to Belgium and security to the rest of Europe that the
peace would be durable.

Yours very truly

E. GREY

The history of those negotiations is presented somewhat at length because my friend of many years, the late
Ambassador Page, in his recently published letters also
expressed the feeling that I had been used as a dupe to
throw the blame for continuing the war upon Great
Britain, though he expressed great confidence in me and
friendship for me. I may say I was not unmindful of
this contingency; but I felt that if the negotiations did
not result as we hoped, they would serve to expose the in-
sincerity of the German Government with regard to its
peace professions. And this is precisely what happened,
as the answer of the German Chancellor, received by the
State Department on September 22d, confirms:

The Imperial Chancellor is much obliged for America's
offer. Germany did not want war, it was forced upon her.
Even after we shall have defeated France we shall still have to
face England and Russia. England, France, and Russia have
signed a convention to make peace solely in mutual agreement
with each other. England, that is, Mr. Asquith, the London
Times, and English diplomatic officers, have on various occasions . . . [sic] that England is determined to conduct the war
to the utmost and that she expects success from it lasting a long
time. It is therefore up to the United States to get our enemies
to make peace proposals. Germany can only accept the peace

which promises to be a real and lasting peace and will protect her against any new attacks from her enemies. If we accepted America's offer of mediation now our enemies would interpret it as a sign of weakness and the German people would not understand it. For the nation which has been willing to make such sacrifices has a right to demand that there shall be guarantees of rest and security.

Secretary Bryan, in his instruction to Ambassador Page on September 8th, had anticipated Germany's refusal to accept mediation. The instruction concluded:

We do not know, of course, what reply the German Emperor will make, but this war is so horrible from every aspect that no one can afford to take the responsibility for continuing it implacably. The British and French ambassadors fear that Germany will not accept any reasonable terms, but even a failure to agree will not rob an attempt at mediation of all its advantages because the different nations would be able to explain to the world their attitude, the reasons for continuing the war, the end to be hoped for and the terms upon which peace is possible. This would locate the responsibility for the continuance of the war and help to mould public opinion. Will notify you as soon as answer is received from Bernstorff.

On September 29th all the British papers served by the Central News War Service carried a cable from New York detailing the negotiations, which ended:

It is believed by those concerned that an important step has been taken to pave the way for mediation, when the opportune moment arrives. In other words, the bolt on the door of mediation has been thrown back so that it will be possible for the door to be opened without either side being forced to take the initiative. Time will doubtless show that the initiative so fortuitously taken by Mr. Straus will prove of real service in the interests of ultimate peace negotiations, and any endeavors to deprecate those services as having been made in Germany's interests are not only contrary to all the facts, but are most unfortunate.

Note: The censor does not object to the publication of the foregoing details, but insists that publication should be accompanied by a footnote pointing out that since these occurrences took place the German Government have disavowed their ambassador.

Had Germany's oft-reiterated peace professions been sincere, she would have accepted this offer for mediation. By her refusal the falsity of her professions was exposed not only in Great Britain and in our own country, but in all the neutral countries; and the *exposé* served as added proof to all peace-loving and neutrally-minded persons that the responsibility for the war and its continuance rested upon the German Government.

In America many of us continued to hope that some way might be found to bring the representatives of the warring nations into a conference, thereby removing misunderstanding and misconception and paving the way for an early peace. On December 31st the New York representative of the Central News of London asked several Americans to write New Year's messages to the warring nations of Europe, to be cabled to all the chief newspapers of the continent. Messages were given by Dr. Nicholas Murray Butler, Andrew Carnegie, Bishop David Greer, and myself, and they were all substantially of the same tenor, as a passage from each will show:

Bishop Greer: It is the earnest hope and prayer of all Christian people in America that the awful and deplorable war now raging may soon reach an end which will insure lasting peace and one satisfactory in character to all the nations involved.

Andrew Carnegie: I am convinced that the next effort of lovers of peace should be to concentrate the world over in demanding that this unparalleled slaughter of man by man shall be the last war waged by civilized nations for the settlement of international disputes. War dethroned — Peace enthroned.

President Butler: May it be in America's fortunate lot to bind up the wounds of the war and to set the feet of her sister nations once more in the paths of peace, international good-will and constructive statesmanship.

I said: For the past five months each of the nations has been seeking victory in the trenches of death; but it has not been found there. Only through wise counsels can the victory of permanent peace be obtained. President Wilson and His Holiness the Pope have offered their offices to open the door of mediation. Will not the Kaiser and King George give the mandate so that the door may be opened and this delusion be dispelled, thereby earning the blessings of a bleeding and suffering world?

These statements are cited as evidence of how slowly we in America came to realize the ruthless designs for conquest which the German militarists had prepared and fostered for forty years, not only strategically, but even in shaping the psychology of the child in school and the man in the street to conform to their design.

For a year or more events marched on, tragically, like a malignant disease. On February 2, 1917, I lunched with Roosevelt at the Hotel Langdon, on Fifth Avenue and Fifty-Sixth Street, where Roosevelt was in the habit of stopping when in New York. The German Government two days before had announced her submarine blockade of the British, French, and Dutch coasts, and our own entrance into the war seemed likely.

We were discussing the crisis, and Roosevelt said he did not think we should be involved; the President would probably find some way out and arrange to have Germany's pledge, not to destroy merchant ships of neutrals or belligerents without warning, whittled down so as to apply only to ships flying the American flag. He told us that he had engaged passage on one of the United Fruit Company steamers to Jamaica for Mrs. Roosevelt and himself. Mrs. Roosevelt needed a change, and they would start in a few days. Regarding the war, he could do noth-

ing more. He had done all he could. He had made an offer
to the Secretary of War to raise a division, and had a
whole card catalogue of names of men who had volun-
teered to serve in it.

His relations with the President were far from friendly.
He had violently criticized him in articles contributed to
the "Metropolitan Magazine" and in several public addresses had urged preparedness and compulsory military
training. I asked him, in view of the German blockade,
what he would do if he were President. He said he would
promptly assemble our fleet, put marines on the interned
German ships, and show Germany that we were in dead
earnest; that unless she recalled her decision to sink
merchant ships without observing the rules of modern
warfare we should take immediate steps to protect our
rights.

"If we continue to back down we will become China-
fied, without any rights that other nations will respect,"
said Roosevelt emphatically.

In such critical times, personal differences might be
laid aside, I suggested, and I wanted him to write the
President and let him have the benefit of his views. I
went further: I suggested that I could write the President
about it. But in Roosevelt's opinion, Wilson would conclude that Roosevelt had himself urged me to do this
because of my close association with Roosevelt.

My own relations with the President were always agreeable, I might even say most friendly. He had written me
sometime before, that he would consider it a favor if I
would keep him informed of developments that came
under my observation regarding important matters. It
occurred to me that on the eve of war it would be a fine
thing if he consulted with his two surviving predecessors, as Monroe had done in consulting with Jefferson

and Madison before issuing the doctrine which bears his name. In the crisis we were facing such a step would allay partisan differences and serve to solidify the Nation. With these ideas in mind I sent the President the following telegram:

Every patriotic American should support you in this great crisis in the history of our country. May I suggest the course followed by Monroe under a crisis involving many of the same principles, to confer with the two surviving ex-Presidents, whose advice, I feel sure, will be most helpful and serve to patriotically solidify the country behind you?

I informed Roosevelt of my action. He felt sure the President wanted neither advice nor coöperation, though he himself was ready to give him the fullest coöperation should Wilson desire it. He thought the same was true on the part of Mr. Taft. The telegram, to my surprise, was given out at Washington to the press a day or two later, but nothing ever came of it.

On February 7th the country was more or less agreeably surprised by the fact that Count von Bernstorff had been given his passports and Ambassador Gerard at Berlin had been instructed to demand his. I say the country was surprised because the President had so long delayed and avoided such a step — even after the sinking of the Lusitania and the Sussex following his "strict accountability" and other strong statements — that it was generally believed he did not mean to take it.

Roosevelt, of course, thought that we should have taken such action long before. His contention was always that had we taken prompt and decisive steps after the Lusitania tragedy, we should have been spared the submarine invasions. In fact, he thought we should have acted when Germany announced her submarine blockade and possibly saved ourselves from the Lusitania horror.

Now that diplomatic relations were broken off, he canceled his trip to Jamaica, not wishing to be out of the country when war was likely to be declared at any moment.

At about this time the impression was current that the Jews of America were anti-Ally, a fact that had a prejudicial effect in France and England. It probably grew out of the fact that three of the largest Jewish banking houses of the country were of German origin, and further that the Yiddish press was anti-Russian in its sympathies as a result of the treatment of Jews in Russia.

After a careful investigation of these reports, a group of us met at the home of Eugene Meyer, Jr., later chairman of the War Finance Corporation. Among those I recall at this meeting were: Fabian Franklin, of the "New York Evening Post"; George L. Beer, the historian; Rabbi Stephen S. Wise; Professor Richard Gottheil, of Columbia University. M. Stephane Lauzanne, editor of "Le Matin" of Paris, and Professor Henri Bergson, both of whom were then in New York, had also been consulted. It was decided that the most practical way of correcting this erroneous impression was for me to write to the French and British ambassadors at Washington.

Accordingly I wrote to Ambassadors Spring-Rice and Jusserand that the impression was unfounded, that our investigations and observations showed a large preponderance of pro-Ally sympathy among the Jews, and I cited a number of leading citizens in business and the various professions, who were representative of their class, whom I knew personally to be pro-Ally. I stated further that in one of the largest Jewish clubs, whose membership consisted almost entirely of Jews of German origin, the pro-Ally sentiment was so strong as to be practically unanimous.

The ambassadors were grateful for this information, which they communicated to their Governments; and through the agency of M. Lauzanne and with the consent of the ambassadors, the letters were given in full to the French and British press.

On the very day that Congress declared war against Germany, April 6, 1917, we were giving a dinner at our home to Professor Henri Bergson. Among our guests were James M. Beck, author of "The Evidence in the Case" and "The War and Humanity"; ex-Senator Burton of Ohio; former Governor and Mrs. John M. Slaton, of Georgia; Adolph S. Ochs, of the "New York Times," and Mrs. Ochs. Bergson was regarded as the unofficial representative of France in our country at the time. Of course, our thoughts and conversation were dominated by the great event of the day. Professor Bergson and Mr. Beck drank and responded to toasts with eloquent fervor. It was felt by all that the entrance into the war of the United States would prove a decided factor in winning it for democracy and constitutional liberty.

Just before Christmas, 1918 — to be specific, on December 22d — I called on Roosevelt at the Roosevelt Hospital, where he was convalescing from his seven weeks' illness, believed to have been inflammatory rheumatism. He was dressed in his *robe de chambre* and was seated in an armchair with a pile of books before him. He looked neither enfeebled nor emaciated, though he showed signs of illness. When I asked him how he had been since my last visit, for I had called on him frequently during his illness, he told me that he had had an attack of embolism — I think that was the ailment — which showed in his wrists, and that his fever had gone up to 104. But that was all gone and he was again feeling fine. He was planning to return to Sagamore Hill to spend Christmas, which he subsequently did.

He inquired particularly about my son Roger, of whom he was very fond, and who was then in Siberia, where he had served for some months as captain and assistant intelligence officer on the staff of General William S. Graves, in command of the American Expeditionary Forces. I told him we had had a cable from Roger from Blagoveschensk that he was well. In his last letter he had expressed a desire to come home, since the war was over. Roosevelt agreed that that was right. He would not want his own sons to endanger their lives in the civil war raging in Russia, and he would not have Roger do so. "Let the Russians settle their own internal affairs; that is not our business," he added.

By way of amusing and interesting Roosevelt, I told him of a curious incident narrated in one of Roger's letters. He had been sent as the official representative of the army into the Amur Province, of which the governor was Alexandre Alexiefsky, who had been a member of the Constitutional Assembly of the Kerensky Government. When Roger called, the governor repeated his name familiarly and then asked: "Are you related to His Excellency by that name in the Cabinet of President Roosevelt?" When Roger told him he was my son, the governor immediately expressed a readiness to help him in every possible way, because as the latter said he owed his life to me. As Roger expressed it, "He was courteous before, but after that he was ready to give me his undershirt."

Alexiefsky had told Roger the story of his case. In the autumn of 1908, several Russians whom the Czar had exiled to Siberia as political prisoners made their escape and came to the United States. The Russian Government discovered this and engaged one of the leading New

ROGER W. STRAUS

First Lieutenant, afterwards Captain, on the Staff of General W. S.
Graves, American Expeditionary Force in Siberia. Now Major in the
Reserve Corps, U. S. A.

York law firms to secure the extradition of the refugees, which was demanded on the specious charge of murder. Secretary Root, in the midst of his many important duties, favored the extradition, and the papers were referred by the State Department to Attorney-General Bonaparte. Application for deportation was also made to me under the immigration laws.

Meanwhile several prominent men and women interested in the case — Miss Lillian Wald, of the Henry Street Settlement House, New York, and James Bronson Reynolds, chairman of the American Society for Russian Freedom, foremost among these — supplied the intelligence and the proof that these men were not criminals in any sense, but political refugees. When Roosevelt spoke to me about them, I told him that I had declined to deport them because it was clear to me that they were political refugees. At that moment Bonaparte joined us. Roosevelt requested him to return the papers in the case, and shortly directed that the men were not to be deported.

Roosevelt said he vividly recalled all this. His face beamed as he said: "Is n't that fine! Very fine! I 'm delighted to hear it!"

"You did that," I said to him; "without your sustaining me these men would have been either extradited or deported, which would have meant death."

"Both of us did it; it 's fine! I 'm delighted to hear it," he commented, his face glowing with its usual vivacity.

The next day Roosevelt left the hospital to return to his home in Oyster Bay. He apparently gave every indication that soon he would be entirely well again and be with us for many years. Certainly that is what we all expected. He was only sixty.

Exactly two weeks later, on January 6, 1919, I received a telephone call at seven o'clock in the morning from Miss

Striker, secretary to Mr. Roosevelt, announcing that he had died early that morning. For thirteen years or more he had had a large and affectionate share in our lives and thoughts, and Mrs. Straus and I felt as though we had been stricken with the loss of a member of our immediate family. I can truly say that I never had a more loyal or a dearer friend. He always treated me and mine as if we were among his nearest relatives.

On January 8th my wife, my son's wife, and I motored to Oyster Bay to attend the funeral in the little Episcopal Church. It had been Roosevelt's wish that he be buried from the little church that was the place of worship of his family. The building held only about three hundred and fifty persons, so that none but his family and close friends could be present. There was a committee from the United States Senate headed by Vice-President Marshall; a committee from the House; several former members of the Cabinet — Elihu Root, Truman H. Newberry, Henry L. Stimson, James R. Garfield, Mrs. Garfield, ex-President Taft, Governor Hughes. William Loeb, Jr., and Captain Archie Roosevelt were ushers. The other sons, Theodore and Kermit, were still in France. The church was filled with a company of sincere friends and bereaved mourners. The regular Episcopal service was begun at twelve-forty-five, and lasted about twenty-five minutes, when we all accompanied the body to the little cemetery on the side of the hill half a mile away.

Hardly a day passes without its scores of pilgrims to that grave. They come from near and far. Many lay flowers on the grave. On holidays and Sundays they come by the hundreds. Two years ago the intimate friends of Roosevelt, who had been officially or personally associated with him, formed the Roosevelt Pilgrimage, an association whose purpose is to keep alive the ideals and personality of Theodore Roosevelt by an annual visit to his grave and a simple ceremony. The idea and organization originated with Mr. E. A. Van Valkenburg of the Philadelphia "North American." On January 6, 1922, some sixty persons made the pilgrimage, headed by Dr. Lyman Abbott, permanent chairman of the association. James R. Garfield read Roosevelt's Nobel Peace Prize address, delivered in Christiania in 1910, at the conclusion of which some wreaths were laid on the grave. Mrs. Roosevelt invited us all to luncheon, and the old-time hospitality and friendliness of the Roosevelt home brought many memories of our departed leader.

After luncheon the annual meeting of the Pilgrimage took place in the great North Room, where Roosevelt had so often received his friends and guests. Dr. Abbott made a brief and feeling address, and Mrs. Richard Derby (Ethel Roosevelt) read from original manuscript Roosevelt's proclamation of 1912 which called into being the Progressive Party. Hermann Hagedorn read a poem entitled "The Deacon's Prayer," by Samuel Valentine Cole, which had especially appealed to Roosevelt. The last stanza of this poem is as follows:

> "We want a man whom we can trust
>   To lead us where thy purpose leads;
> Who dares not lie, but dares be just —
>   Give us the dangerous man of deeds!"
> So prayed the deacon, letting fall
>   Each sentence from his heart; and when
> He took his seat the brethren all,
>   As by one impulse, cried, "Amen!"

CHAPTER XVI

PARIS PEACE CONFERENCE

Now that the curtain of armistice had descended upon the world's most devastating war, the League to Enforce Peace was endeavoring to coöperate in every possible way with President Wilson and the official delegates to the Peace Conference, and with similar organizations in Europe, to bring into existence a League of Nations.

I had been made chairman of the overseas committee, and on the afternoon of Theodore Roosevelt's funeral, former President Taft and I met to confer regarding the work to be done. Both of us were very much depressed by the death of our friend. Taft felt grateful that "Theodore" (as he always called Roosevelt) and he had some months earlier reëstablished their long-time former friendship, which had unhappily been interrupted by political events.

Mr. Taft courteously told me that he was glad that I was going to Paris, and that he believed I might render a great service in helping to secure an effective League of Nations. He hoped I would have conferences with Balfour, Lloyd George, and Léon Bourgeois, and that I would be able to show them what kind of a League we, and as we thought, the American public generally, wanted. At my request, Taft agreed to write me a letter, signed by himself as president of the League to Enforce Peace, and by A. Lawrence Lowell, chairman of the Executive Committee, giving me full authority to take whatever action in Europe I might consider wise. I told Taft that I wanted a letter which should expressly state, among other things, that I was to support our official delegates, as it would not do for America to show a divided front. He told me, what I also had known from conversations with Roosevelt, that Roosevelt had latterly expressed himself in favor of such a League of Nations as we stood for. I reminded Taft that Roosevelt had been the first in recent years to emphasize the subject of a League of Nations, having done so in his Nobel Peace Prize address.

The committee to represent at Paris the League to Enforce Peace consisted of myself as chairman, Hamilton Holt as vice-chairman, and such other members of the League as might be in Paris at that time. Mr. Holt, after consulting me as to methods and plan of action pending my arrival, had left New York on December 28th. I had postponed my departure for Paris until I could learn of my son Roger's departure from Siberia.

On January 25, 1919, I left New York, reaching London on February 4th, where I promptly conferred with the members of the British League of Nations Union. Sir Willoughby Dickinson, M.P., gave me full details of the meetings that had been held by the English, French, and Italian leagues in Paris, at which our League was represented by Hamilton Holt. I also had a consultation with Lord Shaw, the chairman of the conference of delegates, who gave me a copy of the resolutions that had been adopted.

We remained in London several days, and while there dined with our new ambassador, John W. Davis, formerly the Solicitor-General of the United States. Both he and Mrs. Davis, in the short time they had been in London, had won the esteem of official England. At this dinner I had a long conversation with the new Lord Chancellor, Birkenhead, formerly Sir Frederick Smith, who held a distinguished position at the British Bar, and had been Attorney-General in the last Cabinet. In the latter part of 1917 he had visited the United States, where I had met him, and where he had made a number of addresses in the leading cities, as well as in Canada. He was then only forty-seven years of age, but looked much younger, and therefore quite unlike the typical Lord Chancellor robed in venerable dignity. He told me that he was the youngest Lord Chancellor, with one exception, that had ever sat on the woolsack. He had the youthful and vivacious face of a man in the thirties. He said that nothing would please him more than, when he was no longer Lord Chancellor, to practice law in America, but he said that precedent would not permit a former Lord Chancellor to return to the bar and practice his profession.

Birkenhead was very outspoken in his opposition to a League of Nations, saying that it was a Utopian idea. He

asked whether I had seen his book which had recently
appeared, describing his visit to America. I told him I
had not, and on the next day he sent me a copy bearing
his inscription.

The following day we lunched with Mr. and Mrs. Herbert Samuel. He had held several Cabinet positions, and
had been Secretary of the Home Office in the last Cabinet. He was defeated as candidate for Parliament in the
last election. He told me he had recently returned from
Paris from a Zionist Conference where his views and
advice were desired. He stated that he was not a Zionist,
but was in full sympathy with the Balfour Declaration to
secure a homeland in Palestine with equal civil and religious rights for all nationalities. I told him that was
precisely my position. His son was present, who was
about twenty years of age, and had been in the British
army, and was later transferred to the Zionist Corps.

That evening I dined with Sir Arthur Steele-Maitland,
M.P., Under-Secretary of the Foreign Office, where I
met my old friend Viscount Bryce, who was then about
eighty-two years of age. He was still in the best of
health and his mind was as alert as ever. He brought me
a copy of his recent brochure, "Proposals for the Prevention of Future Wars." Maitland strongly favored a
League of Nations, and told me that after I arrived in
Paris, if I found it necessary for the committee of the
League of Nations Union to return there to reënforce the
official delegates, I should write or wire him, and several
of the members would go over to coöperate with our
committee; and that he would write Lord Robert Cecil
so that we might have a conference. I had similar letters
from Lord Shaw and Sir Willoughby Dickinson.

We arrived in Paris on February 9th, where our friends,
Mr. and Mrs. Edward Mamelsdorf, had generously

placed at our disposal their comfortable apartment in the rue Montaigne, which was most conveniently and centrally situated, and saved us the necessity and difficulty of securing accommodations, all the hotels being jammed full. The following morning I met Mr. Holt, who had admirably represented our committee at the several conferences that were held prior to my arrival; also Judge William H. Wadhams, Mrs. Fannie Fern Andrews, Arthur Kuhn, secretary and legal adviser of our committee, besides several other members of our League.

With Mr. Holt I went to the Crillon Hotel, headquarters of the American Delegation, and had a conference with Colonel House, with whom arrangements were made for the fullest coöperation between our League and the Official Commission. We also conferred with Mr. Gordon Auchincloss, the son-in-law and secretary of Colonel House, who, after consulting with the latter, gave me in confidence a typewritten copy of the Articles of the League entitled: "Draft as Provisionally Approved." He said that the Colonel wanted me to have this, so that I might study it. I was told at the same time that the outlook for the adoption of a League was very discouraging because the French Delegation, of which Léon Bourgeois was the head, insisted upon the inclusion of two additional clauses, (1) the control by the League of the manufacture of all armaments and of all war industries, and (2) an international military force to defend the French frontier, which, Bourgeois insisted, quoting from a former speech of President Wilson, "was the frontier of civilization."

President Wilson had emphatically objected to the proposed additions.

When I informed Colonel House that I was about to call on Léon Bourgeois at his home across the Seine, he said, "By all means, go," and added that Bourgeois's attitude "had put the League on the rocks."

Mr. Holt, Mr. Kuhn, and I proceeded to Bourgeois's house, but when we arrived there late in the afternoon, we were told that M. Bourgeois was out, that he was then in the Senate and would not return until late. While there, however, I met my friend and colleague on the Hague Tribunal, Baron d'Estournelles de Constant. He said he would see to it that we met Bourgeois that evening. Mr. Holt, Mr. Kuhn, and I then returned to my apartment, and had hardly arrived there when my telephone rang and I was informed that M. Bourgeois and Baron d'Estournelles were on their way to my residence. They arrived promptly at seven o'clock.

In the course of the discussion, Bourgeois presented the interposing difficulties to which I have referred, giving the divergence of views between him and President Wilson and Colonel House. I explained to him, more fully than he seemed to have appreciated before, that the war-making power was lodged by our Constitution exclusively in Congress, and that even if the President should agree to the additional articles, if these articles would in any way conflict with the war-making power as provided for in the Constitution, President Wilson's assent would be without effect, and would never be ratified by our Senate.

At this point in our conversation, the telephone rang and M. Bourgeois was informed that the President of the Ministry, M. Clemenceau, desired to see him at once. Bourgeois said he would shortly return and hurriedly left us. In the meantime we continued the conversation with d'Estournelles, who, being familiar with our American system, was better able to appreciate the problem. I told him plainly that Colonel House had said to me that afternoon that "the League of Nations was on the rocks."

Bourgeois returned in half an hour and we resumed the discussion. After explaining more at length our constitutional provisions, I told him that if the proposed League were made too strong it would be useless, so far as America was concerned, since it would not be ratified by the Senate. Knowing what a strong advocate he had always been of the League of Nations, as he was and had been for years past the president of the French League of Nations Society, I asked him whether he would prefer having no League rather than a League as drafted, without the two articles he had proposed.

He frankly replied that if that were the alternative, he would prefer to have the League as drafted. He then referred to the fact that at our last Congressional election, the Administration had been defeated, and therefore, as he understood it, the President represented a minority party. I told him that, while such would be the case under the European system, it was not so under our system, and then read to him from my letter of credence "to support the President," explaining that the president of our League, Mr. Taft, along with Dr. Lowell, myself, and many others, was not of the President's party, yet I was authorized and instructed to support the President.

Bourgeois replied that at the Plenary Session of the Conference, which was to be held on the Friday following, namely, on the 14th, at the Quai d'Orsay, in view of the American position which I had made clear to him, he would support the "Draft as Provisionally Approved," but that he wanted me to appreciate that they had politics in France as well as we had, and that therefore he would, at any rate, have to present at the Conference the two articles referred to, if for no other reason than for their popular effect; but that I could rely on it that his Government would in the final analysis accept the covenant or draft as provisionally presented by the representatives of the fourteen nations which had participated in its preparation and had preliminarily agreed to it.

When Bourgeois and d'Estournelles departed, which was at about ten o'clock, I called up Colonel House, and, after briefly informing him what had taken place, I told him that the League was "off the rocks." He expressed his great gratification, and on the following morning when I met him he said that he had informed the President, who desired heartily to congratulate me.

When Colonel House had informed me that "the League was on the rocks," it was more real than figurative; for at the session of the Commission on the League held the evening before, the French members having insisted among other provisions upon an international army to guard the frontier, and President Wilson having point-blank refused to agree to it, an *impasse* had been reached, since neither side would give way. The Commission thereupon adjourned, apparently without any possibility of coming to an understanding. Considerable bitterness was developed in the discussion, as I learned, between the President and M. Bourgeois. It was at this stage that I fortuitously arrived at the Crillon to report that our committee, by calling on M. Bourgeois, had been able unofficially to take up and discuss with him the situation, which officially had apparently passed beyond the stage of further discussion. Therefore it was, as Holt and I were subsequently informed, a great relief to the President and Colonel House, as well as to Clemenceau and Bourgeois, that we had been able to remove the *impasse* by inducing the French delegates to agree to support the Covenant as preliminarily drafted.

Some months before, there had been organized in Paris

a luncheon club, the Cercle Interallié, as a comfortable and convenient meeting-place for many officials and others. Immediately upon my arrival, I was introduced at the club, where I frequently took lunch and met many people, officials and delegates of the allied nations. The day following our conversation at my apartment, I met Baron d'Estournelles by appointment at lunch, and he informed me that Bourgeois had expressed himself gratified with the clarification I had given him and that I could rely upon the Covenant being adopted as we had agreed.

On the morning of the 14th, while I was at Colonel House's office, I received a copy of the Covenant which had just been put in print, as reëdited by the Sub-Committee of the League of Nations under the chairmanship of Lord Robert Cecil. While I was there, President Wilson came in to meet the representatives of the American press. When he saw me, he expressed his high appreciation for our services and helpfulness. The President made a brief address to the correspondents, beginning in a semi-humorous vein, and then giving a general description of the Covenant as finally drafted, explaining that where so many nations were involved, no one's individual ideas could be fully satisfied, and that there had to be yielding on all sides. Wilson added that he would have liked to see some definite declaration regarding the protection of religious minorities, and referred to several of the other outstanding provisions.

Colonel House asked me to see Bourgeois again before the Plenary Session which was to take place that afternoon, saying that he had heard that Bourgeois was going to oppose the Covenant. I immediately called on Bourgeois again, and told him precisely what the Colonel had said, but Bourgeois assured me that there had been no change, and that the Covenant, or as it was styled in French, *Le Pacte*, would not be opposed.

That same afternoon, I went with former Ambassador Henry White, one of our official delegates, to the Session of the Plenary Conference at the Quai d'Orsay which convened at 3.30 o'clock. I accompanied him into the Conference room, a large, vaulted, ornate chamber known as the Clock Room, where were seated, at the tables arranged along three sides of a square, with an inner row of seats arranged in the same way, the delegates of the thirty nations.

On the outside of the square were the tables for the secretaries of the several nations. At the head of the table sat M. Clemenceau; to his right was President Wilson, and on his left was to be Lloyd George, but as he was not present, Lord Robert Cecil sat in his place. Next on the right was Mr. Lansing, and next on the left was Mr. Balfour, and so on in order. In the rear of the chamber were a number of distinguished persons and other officials of the Powers. To one side was another large room with arched entrances, occupied by the correspondents of the press of the world. The proceedings began at four o'clock. The ushers closed the large entrance doors leading out into the foyer, and all was still and in expectancy when Clemenceau rose and, in his usual brusque and unceremonious manner, announced that "Monsieur Wilson" would have the "parole," meaning the floor.

President Wilson arose, calm, dignified, and entirely self-possessed, and, after a few preliminary words, stated that the representatives of the fourteen nations which composed the League of Nations Committee had unanimously agreed to the Covenant consisting of twenty-six articles to be presented to the Conference, representing, according to the estimate, 1,200,000,000 people.

He read the articles of the Covenant, one by one, interpolating here and there brief explanations. The title "Covenant" had been given the document by Wilson, a designation he had previously used in one of his speeches. This was regarded as most appropriate, since the pact was not a treaty or convention, but something higher and more sacred, hence the scriptural designation "Covenant," such as God had made with Israel.

After reading the articles, Wilson made an address of about thirty minutes. It was clear, forceful, and in his inimitable style. In closing he said: "Armed force is in the background in this programme, but it is in the background, and if the moral force of the world will not suffice, the physical force of the world shall. But that is the last resort, because this is intended as a constitution of peace, not as a League of War. Many terrible things have come out of this war, gentlemen, but some very beautiful things have come out of it. Wrong has been defeated, but the rest of the world has been more conscious than it ever was before, of the majesty of right."

Lord Robert Cecil then spoke briefly, and I will quote a single passage from his address: "Finally, we have thought that if the world is to be at peace, it is not enough to forbid war. We must do something more than that. We must try and substitute for the principle of international competition that of international coöperation."

Signor Orlando of Italy followed with a brief address, then M. Léon Bourgeois rose and spoke somewhat at length in French. He said that he proposed amendments which he thought he ought to mention; that while his country had accepted the text which had been read, the amendments were mentioned so that, as the text went before the world, the amendments might also be considered, to the effect that we ought to have a permanent organization to prepare military and naval means of execution and make them ready in case of emergency.

Baron Makino, speaking with persuasive eloquence in perfect English, maintained his previous amendments which were as follows: "The equality of nations being a basic principle of the League of Nations, the High Contracting Parties agree to accord, as soon as possible, to all aliens, nationals of States, members of the League, equal and just treatment in every respect, making no distinction either in law or in fact on account of their race or nationality." He then added: "I feel it my duty to declare clearly on this occasion that the Japanese Government and people feel poignant regret at the failure of the Commission to approve of their just demand for laying down a principle aiming at the adjustment of this long-standing grievance, the demand that is based upon a deep-rooted natural conviction. They will continue in their insistence for the adoption of this principle by the League in the future."

George Barnes, the English labor leader, then spoke, upholding the argument of Bourgeois for an international force. After him Venizelos spoke, referring to the amendments of France which had been held back because of constitutional barriers of acquiescence on the part of certain countries. He thought those countries should make an effort to remove those barriers, but that, if they could not do so, then France should recede from her position. Mr. Hughes of Australia interposed a question, demanding to know when and where the discussion of mandatories would take place, to which Clemenceau replied that the document would rest on the table and would be discussed at a distant date. Thereupon, he abruptly adjourned the session.

As the delegates moved out, I met President Wilson,

who asked me for my opinion about the Covenant. I
replied that it was much more comprehensive and forceful than I had believed it possible for the nations preliminarily to agree upon. He expressed himself as much
gratified. I believed then, and do yet, that but for Wilson's prestige and dominant leadership of the Conference, so far at least as the Covenant was concerned, it
would perhaps not have been formulated, if ever, until
after the Treaty of Peace was concluded. At any rate, I
very much doubt if an agreement could have been
arrived at.

After my conversation with Wilson, Bourgeois said to
me that he hoped I was satisfied with his remarks in support of the Covenant, that he had to refer to the amendments he presented so that they might receive consideration. I told him that he had followed the course he had
agreed to when he spoke to me two nights before, that
while he would refer to his amendments, he would nevertheless support the Covenant.

When I had returned to my apartment, I wrote in my
"Random Notes": "I regard this day and its happenings
as the golden chapter in the history of civilization."
Notwithstanding what has since happened, I have not
abandoned hope that such may yet prove true.

Two days before the meeting of the Conference, Hamilton Holt and I had tea with General Smuts, the distinguished South African delegate. He is a man of very
pleasant appearance, rather short in stature, and with his
florid complexion looks like a veritable Dutchman. He
was then apparently about fifty years of age. He would
hardly, from his appearance, be taken for a soldier, but
rather for a student. He had given much detailed study
to the subject of a League of Nations, and from his bro-

chure "The League of Nations — A Practical Suggestion" (1918) more of his suggestions as there set forth entered into the articles of the Covenant than those proposed by any other of the delegates, including Wilson. Smuts advocated in this brochure that "the League should be put in the very forefront of the programme of the Peace Conference," the same position that Wilson afterward successfully pushed forward. In the preface of his brochure, dated December 16, 1918, Smuts says:

> To my mind the world is ripe for the greatest step forward ever made in the government of man. And I hope this brief account of the League will assist the public to realize how great an advance is possible to-day as a direct result of the immeasurable sacrifices of this war. If that advance is not made, this war will, from the most essential point of view, have been fought in vain, and great calamities will follow.

Several days after the Conference, on February 17th, my wife and I, Mr. and Mrs. Holt, and Arthur Kuhn of our committee, attended the French Senate with Baron d'Estournelles, who is a member thereof. He introduced us to a number of Senators, with whom we had tea. I had a talk with the venerable Alexandre Ribot, head of the group of the Moderate Republican Party, a refined gentleman of the old school, and of thoroughly statesmanlike appearance. We also met Senator Paul Strauss, whom I had known when he and his wife visited our country some eighteen years before. He is the editor of the "Revue Philanthropique," and is a member of the Academy of Medicine. He said that he believed his family and mine were connected. This may be so, but I have no definite record.

Dining with Sir Robert Borden, then Premier of Canada and one of the British delegates, the following evening, we met several of his colleagues. Balfour was ex-

pected, but he had been compelled to return to London
that day. Sir Robert was an important member of the
British Delegation and made some very helpful suggestions. He opposed Article X of the Covenant which
provides that "the High Contracting Parties undertake
to respect and preserve as against external aggression the
territorial integrity and existing political independence of
all States, members of the League," etc., the same article
that eventually met with so much opposition in our Senate, and doubtless was the principal cause for the Senate's
failure to ratify. At that time it was generally rumored
that Borden would be selected as ambassador to the
United States to succeed Lord Reading. He would
doubtless have made a most acceptable representative
in Washington of the British Government, exceptional
as it would have been to have the British Empire represented by a colonial official. No one could have been sent
who understood our country and our people better.

Washington's Birthday was celebrated by the American
Society, which gave a luncheon at the Hôtel Quai d'Orsay,
which I attended. There were present about one hundred
and fifty Americans. It was a notable assembly, and I
had the pleasure of sitting next to General Pershing, with
whom I had a lengthy talk. We spoke, among other
things, of the proposal that our country should take a
mandate to govern the Ottoman Empire or any part of
Europe. Great propaganda had been made that we
should take a mandate for the Ottoman Empire. Pershing agreed with me that this would lead to endless complications and would not be approved at home. I also
talked with Colonel House upon the subject, who was of
the same opinion. Pershing was evidently quite nervous,
for he was expected to speak, and he was making some

notes. It appeared to me he was more disturbed than if he were about to enter into a serious military engagement.

I had lunch the next day with Boris Bakhmeteff, the Russian ambassador to the United States, at which I met Sazonoff, former Minister for Foreign Affairs under the Czar's régime. We naturally spoke about affairs in Russia and the possibility of reconstruction. I was told that the late Czar was kindly and humane, but that he had been completely misled and dominated by crafty ministers who were plotting and intriguing one against another; that Russia was not, by reason of the ignorance of its people, fitted to become a republic, but that it must have a government powerfully centralized, and that its best hope would be the restoration of the monarchy under Grand Duke Nicholas as constitutional ruler. Sazonoff said it was a pity that Petrograd was not taken by the Allied fleet. I am told that, under the Czar, Sazonoff was the leader of the liberal wing.

A few days later I gave a little dinner at my apartment to enable Mr. Vance McCormick, chairman of the War Trade Board, to meet several prominent Russians, including Ambassador Bakhmeteff and Sazonoff. Mr. Hoover was also present. We discussed the rehabilitation of commerce with Russia.

On the 26th of February the Union of Associations for the Society of Nations, together with the European Bureau of the Carnegie Peace Foundation, gave a luncheon in honor of Ambassador Sharp and myself at the Cercle Interallié, at which M. Léon Bourgeois presided. There were present some seventy-five guests, mostly delegates and French officials, including Sir Robert Borden; Venizelos, the Greek delegate; the Roumanian minister; M. Vesnitch, the Serbian minister; and the Brazilian ambassador. At the conclusion, M. Bourgeois arose, and, although there were to be no set speeches, he expressed the regret of the French nation that Ambassador Sharp would in the near future relinquish his post, and complimented his Administration upon its work of the past four trying years. He praised my effective helpfulness in regard to the League of Nations, and stated that he not only greeted me as a twin, because he was born in the same year as I was, but also as a Frenchman, since my father, who was born in 1809, was a Frenchman by birth, and because my great-grandfather was a delegate to the Conference which was summoned by Napoleon during the first decade of the past century.

In reply, I stated that an American, to be truly patriotic, should understand our early history, and that no American with this knowledge could fail to have a love and sense of gratitude for France, our ally in the establishment of democracy, as we had so recently been her ally for the liberation of the world.

My various conferences regarding the League of Nations, while it was under discussion and formulation by the Committee of the Conference having charge of that subject, were held with Colonel House and his secretary, Mr. Auchincloss. On February 27th, I had lunch with Secretary Lansing. It had been quite obvious to me that even before this he had been practically side-tracked, and that Colonel House had replaced him from the beginning, doubtless by direction of the President. This was very evident so far as the League of Nations was concerned. Mr. Lansing informed me that he had pointed out a number of technical objections to the Covenant as formulated, which, he was sure, would prove a fruitful source of difference and would make trouble. It seemed to me that he was evidently not conversant with the various stages of discussion regarding the articles of the

Covenant. I referred to the entire omission in the second draft of the section respecting civil and religious liberty and the protection of minorities, which was contained in the tentative draft, but was finally omitted because Japan had insisted that the equality of races be included, where-upon the whole subject had been omitted. I suggested that the entire subject, which was in fact a Bill of Rights, now that it had been excluded from the Covenant, should be incorporated in the treaties to be made with each of the new nations. Lansing agreed with me that that should be done and would under the circumstances be the best plan.

At this time, during February and March, 1919, the League to Enforce Peace had organized numerous meet-ings throughout the country from New York to San Francisco, advocating a League of Nations. Mr. Taft had spoken at many of these meetings for months past, traveling untiringly and making most effective addresses. At these meetings the Covenant was approved and resolu-tions to that effect were passed. On February 25th and 28th I received cables briefly describing such meetings and the substance of the resolutions passed. I received cables to the same effect from Salt Lake City, from San Francisco, and from New York. These I gave to Colonel House, who in turn gave them to the press, and some-times they were cabled back through the Associated Press to American newspapers.

From time to time a number of the representatives of the Balkan and East European nations came to my apartment to confer with me, doubtless because of my diplomatic experiences in that part of the world, and because of my relationship with Colonel House and our official Commission. Among others who conferred with me was M. Venizelos, who came to discuss the claims of Greece to additional territory to the north, and on the western littoral of Asia Minor, and to the islands adjacent. He explained, as an ethnological basis for such a claim, that the Greek race was purer and less mixed in that part of Asia Minor and in the islands than in Greece proper. He placed before me several brochures containing studies of these points and sent me maps illustrating those claims, also a document in English entitled: "Greece Before the Peace Congress." He told me that, unless his presence was imperatively demanded in Paris, he would attend with me the London Conference of the Peace Societies of the various nations which was to be held there March 11th.

On March 7th M. Vesnitch, the chief delegate of Serbia, came to see me about Serbia's claims to two towns, Verschatz and Weisskirchen, which the sub-committee of ten, under the chairmanship of M. Tardieu, had awarded to Roumania. He claimed they were predominantly Serbian as to sympathies and population, and that because they happened to be on the railroad running through Roumania was no valid reason for transferring them under Roumanian sovereignty. He said Serbia could never consent to such transfer, which would cause not only dissatisfaction, but constant trouble.

The day after the Plenary Session of the Conference and the preliminary adoption of the Covenant, President Wilson returned to America. I talked with M. Bourgeois, M. Vesnitch, M. Venizelos, and several of the chairmen of the allied societies for a League of Nations, and we agreed to hold a conference of the delegates of the various societies. Chiefly because of our desire of having with us

Sir Edward Grey, who was the chairman of the British Society, and Lord Bryce, both of whom at that time were not entirely well, we decided to hold the conference in London instead of in Paris. It was subsequently decided to hold it March 11th–13th for the purpose of discussing the draft of the Covenant as preliminarily adopted, and to consider such changes and amendments as might be deemed advisable, which when acted upon and adopted were to be presented to our respective official delegates prior to the next meeting of the Plenary Conference, to be held after President Wilson's return.

Accordingly, on March 11th, the delegates representing America, Great Britain, France, Greece, China, Jugo-Slavia, and Roumania assembled in London, in all about fifty in number. Besides myself as chairman, there attended, from America, Hamilton Holt, Arthur Kuhn, Dr. Henry Churchill King, Mrs. Fannie Fern Andrews, Raymond V. Ingersoll, Dr. Frederick Lynch, and Edward Harding. Great Britain was represented by Lord Shaw of Dunfermline, Sir W. H. Dickinson, Major David Davies, M.P.; J. H. Thomas, M.P.; J. R. Clynes, M.P.; Sir A. Shirley Benn, M.P.; Sir Arthur Steele-Maitland, M.P.; Professor Gilbert Murray; Aneurin Williams, M.P.; H. Wickham Steed, and others. From France came M. Léon Bourgeois, Vice-Admiral Fournier, General Léon Durand, Baron d'Estournelles de Constant, and others. Greece was represented by M. Venizelos and Professor Andreades. China was represented by Mr. Chang and Mr. Cheng; Jugo-Slavia by M. Yovanovitch; and Roumania by Professor E. Pangrati, Professor Negulesco, and Miss Helene Vacaresco.

A preliminary consultation was held on the 10th, with Professor Gilbert Murray in the chair, and next morning the first meeting of the conference was held at Caxton

Hall, Westminster. Lord Shaw was elected chairman, and W. J. T. Griffith, secretary. The various articles of the Covenant were discussed, together with the amendments and changes proposed by the delegates from the several countries. On behalf of our delegation, I offered a resolution regarding the free exercise of religion as well as freedom from civil and political discrimination because of religion, which resolution after discussion was unanimously adopted. Nine separate resolutions were offered by the British delegates, some ten resolutions by the French delegates, and others by the Roumanian and the Chinese delegates. In all, there were three sessions, and the resolutions that were adopted M. Bourgeois was authorized to present to the allied prime ministers.

On the evening of the 12th, Major David Davies, on behalf of the League of Nations Union, gave a dinner at the Criterion Restaurant to M. Bourgeois, Dr. Nansen, M. Vandervelde, M. Venizelos, and me. Right Hon. H. A. L. Fisher, Secretary for Education, was toastmaster. Besides the delegates, a number of other prominent men were present. Several speeches were made laudatory of the Covenant and expressing high hopes for the new world order. Emphasis was laid upon the necessity of building up a body of opinion throughout the world to support the ideals of the League and of international peace.

After adjournment, I returned to Paris, and on March 24th made a report to President Wilson, who, a few days before, had returned from America, and sent him the resolution proposed by the American delegates, namely, to add a new article to the Covenant as follows:

The High Contracting Parties, realizing that religious discriminations give rise to internal dissatisfaction and unrest which militate against international concord, agree to secure and maintain in their respective countries, as well as in states and territories under the tutelage of other states acting as mandatories on behalf of the League, the free exercise of religion as well as freedom from civil and political discrimination because of adherence to any creed, religion or belief not inconsistent with public order or with public morals.

To this proposal President Wilson replied, saying: "I am indeed interested in a religious liberty article in the Covenant, but am trying to reach the matter in another way." He doubtless had in mind to cover it in treaties with the new nations for the protection of minorities, as was subsequently provided in the treaty with Poland and with the Balkan States.

At a luncheon on April 6th with the Russian group of refugee statesmen in Paris, I again met M. Sazonoff; M. de Giers, formerly ambassador at Constantinople; M. Bark, formerly Minister of Finance under the Government of the late Czar; and M. Boris Bakhmeteff, the Russian ambassador to the United States. They all spoke most disparagingly of Russian conditions at the time. M. Sazonoff criticized and complained of the Peace Conference, which, as he stated, had in no way condemned Russian Bolshevism, and its failure in so doing had encouraged the Bolsheviki. He said that had the Allies taken Petrograd, which could have been done with very little sacrifice, that would have been the beginning of the end of Bolshevism and would have rallied the Russian people, who would themselves have destroyed the Bolsheviki. He added that Russia's cruel treatment of the Jews under the Czar's Government was an indefensible wrong, and doubtless contributed to driving some of those who had suffered most into the ranks of the Bolsheviki.

While Sazonoff was talking, I wondered why he and

some of his colleagues in the Ministry had not prevented the outrages against defenseless Jews, which resulted in the horrible pogroms which shocked the moral sensibility of the world.

It is true that Sazonoff belonged to the so-called liberals of Russia, and they did not have the courage to stand up for the basic principles of humanity when in office, which they now, doubtless, sincerely proclaim. Such is the withering and dispiriting effect of autocratic government upon its own highest officials, who often lack the courage, even if they have the vision, to correct abuses; and because of this moral cowardice they prepare the way and supply the motive that sooner or later expresses itself in revolution. Napoleon is reputed to have said that the treatment of the Jews in every country is the thermometer of that country's civilization.

Several times a week, during this period, conferences occurred in my apartment with representatives of the Eastern and Balkan States. Information had reached Paris that serious persecution of Jews was threatened in Prague and throughout Tchecko-Slovakia; and on March 25th a conference was arranged between M. Edouard Benès, Minister of Foreign Affairs of the Tchecko-Slovak Republic, and several gentlemen representing the American Jewish Committee and the American Jewish and Zionist Committee, consisting of Julian W. Mack, Judge of the United States Circuit Court; Professor Felix Frankfurter, of Harvard University; Aaron Aaronson, head of the Agricultural Experiment Station of Palestine; Lewis L. Strauss, the assistant of Herbert Hoover; and myself. Letters from Prague from two of the Food Administration officials reported that a press propaganda was carried on against Jews, and that several attacks upon them had been made; that a movement was on foot to deport a number of them to Pressburg, the hot-bed of Bolshevism.

M. Benès pointed out that if any pogroms occurred, which these reports foreshadowed, it would seriously prejudice his country and would alienate American sympathy, which in turn might result in discontinuing food shipments to his country. He stated that he was a disciple of President Masaryk and always shared his liberal social and political views; he said he would at once telegraph President Masaryk, who he knew would do everything in his power to suppress the anti-Semitic agitation. We were very much impressed with the enlightened statesmanship of M. Benès, who, since then, has shown himself to be one of the foremost statesmen in middle Europe. He assured us at the time that any persecution of minorities in his country would be contrary to its organic laws, and in direct violation of the principles and policies upon which it had been determined to organize the State, and that we could rely on it that no efforts would be spared in securing equal justice for all without regard to race or religion.

From Sir Robert L. Borden, the Premier of Canada and one of the delegates of the British Empire to the Peace Conference, I received on March 21st a copy of his memorandum on the several articles of the Covenant. I found them well conceived and in the main admirable. He opposed Article X as drafted. He wanted it either stricken out or clarified. I sent him a copy of a speech of Mr. Taft's of March 5th referring to the same subject.

At the request of Colonel House, on April 11th, I had another conference with M. Bourgeois. The Commission on the League of Nations of the fourteen nations, under the chairmanship of President Wilson, had the night before held a protracted session discussing the revision of the Covenant, at which President Wilson offered the revised Article XXI containing the special provision regarding the Monroe Doctrine, as follows:

ARTICLE XXI

Nothing in this Covenant shall be deemed to affect the validity of international engagements such as treaties of arbitration or regional understandings like the Monroe Doctrine for securing the maintenance of peace.

M. Larnaud and M. Bourgeois, the French representatives, both objected to specific reference to the Monroe Doctrine, and made long speeches in support of such objection. Colonel House desired me to impress upon M. Bourgeois the reasons for this amendment and why it was necessary specifically to mention the Monroe Doctrine, because, without it, it would not be possible to have the Covenant confirmed by the Senate. As I did not know M. Larnaud, I thought it best to discuss the subject with M. Bourgeois so that he might confer with his colleague. In company with Baron d'Estournelles de Constant, I called on M. Bourgeois at his residence. I soon learned that M. Bourgeois did not object to specific reference to the Monroe Doctrine, but he desired, in return for his assent, to obtain President Wilson's assent to the amendments Bourgeois had offered respecting a general staff and control or supervision of the military force that each of the States was to supply to support the League. As the Commission was to meet again to finish the consideration of the Covenant, he agreed to confer with M. Clemenceau, saying he would have to learn the other's views. He further said it must be determined how best to formulate the article especially referring to the Monroe Doctrine so as not to conflict with the general provisions.

At the session of the Commission that evening at the

Crillon Hotel, which lasted until after midnight, the article as quoted above, specifically mentioning the Monroe Doctrine, was adopted. Colonel House gave me the exact wording of the article, which I at once cabled to the League to Enforce Peace in New York, with the request that Mr. Taft be informed. The same day I received a cable from Mr. Taft and Dr. Lowell, forwarded by Acting Secretary of State Frank L. Polk, to the effect that, in the opinion of the Executive Committee of the League, specific reference to the exclusion of the Monroe Doctrine from the jurisdiction of the Covenant of the League was absolutely necessary to secure confirmation by the Senate. On the following day Taft cabled me that the Monroe Doctrine amendment was "eminently satisfactory."

I immediately advised President Wilson, sending him a copy of the cable. The following day, I received the following letter from him:

18 *April*, 1919

MY DEAR MR. STRAUS:

I have been very much cheered by your kind letter of yesterday, with the message which it quotes from the League to Enforce Peace and from Mr. Taft personally, and I want to thank you very warmly for your own kind personal assurances of satisfaction with the results of our work on the Covenant.

Cordially and sincerely yours

WOODROW WILSON

On April 23d, on the invitation of Professor Stephen Hayes Bush, of the State University of Iowa, who was in charge of the Free Lecture Course of the American Expeditionary Force, I delivered an address in the Grand Amphitheatre of the Sorbonne. The great hall was filled with about one thousand of our officers and men who were taking courses at this ancient institution of learning. There were two lectures that afternoon, the other by M. Ferdinand Buisson, the noted educator. His subject

was "The Educational System of France," which he had
done so much to develop since the educational system had
been secularized by the separation of Church and State
in France. He described why education had been taken
from the control of the Catholic clergy, not out of hostility to the Church, but in order not to prejudice the
religious scruples of non-clericals and non-Catholics.

I took as my subject "America and the League of
Nations," and showed in what respect the Covenant provided definite sanctions to make peace decisions effective. I pointed out that following the war, for the first
time in history, the dominant power of the world rested in
democratically governed nations, and that theirs was the
opportunity and the responsibility to make provisions
that such a war shall never be waged again; and that now
it was the duty of statesmanship to translate the victory
won in war into greater security for the future peace and
happiness of the world. I quoted from the speech of
President Poincaré in welcoming the Peace Delegates,
in which he had described the reasons why America entered the World War. He had said: "It was a supreme
judgment passed at the bar of history by the lofty conscience of a free people to rescue her mother from the
humiliation of thralldom and to save civilization."

That same evening, M. Nicolas W. Tchaikovsky, president of the Archangel Government of Northern Russia,
called at my apartment to discuss with me conditions in
Russia. I had met him before when he was in Washington in 1907, after his escape from prison in Siberia. During several periods before that time he had lived in
western United States, where he had engaged in farming.
He had formerly belonged to the group of social revolu-
tionists. I spoke with him about the Hoover plan of
sending food into Russia, to which he replied that if an

armed force could be sent there it would be better, but that without an armed force the Bolsheviki would use the provisions for their own red guard. I explained to him that that could not be done, since the agents of the Food Administration would themselves supervise the distribution, just as was done in Belgium during the German occupation. He did not seem to think well of the whole plan and considered that it would be of advantage to the Bolsheviki politically, and would make their people believe it was a recognition of their régime. He seemed to think that the Bolsheviki authorities could not stop fighting in Russia even if they wanted to, as their several generals acted independently.

He spoke of Lenin as an honest, strong-headed, misguided fanatic, who he believed would in time discover his error and would have the moral courage and honesty to throw up his hands. Trotsky, he said, was quite another sort — an ambitious adventurer.

The Plenary Session of the Conference was called to order at the Quai d'Orsay on April 28th, at 3 P.M. I again attended with our official delegate, former Ambassador Henry White. The representatives of the thirty nations were seated as before. I was given a seat just behind the American Commission. The Session was presided over by M. Clemenceau, who showed no signs of the effects of his recent wound by an assassin's bullet. He opened the session with a few words, then called on President Wilson, who declared in a matter-of-fact way that, since he had read the articles of the Covenant to the Conference at the previous session (February 14th), and since all the delegates had the Covenant as amended before them, he would confine himself to pointing out the amendments and the reasons therefor.

The immense hall was packed as on previous occasions. After President Wilson had made his statement, which was rendered into French by the official interpreter, he moved several resolutions, one nominating Sir James Eric Drummond as Secretary-General of the League, and one that Belgium, Brazil, Greece, and Spain should be members of the Council pending the selection of the four additional States by the Assembly of the League.

As chairman of the League to Enforce Peace, I wrote a letter to the President on the following day offering my congratulations upon the adoption of the Covenant. To this I received the following reply:

PARIS, 1 *May*, 1919

MY DEAR MR. STRAUS:

Thank you with all my heart for your generous letter of the 29th. It has given me the greatest pleasure and encouragement, and I want to take the opportunity to say how valuable in every way your own support of and enthusiasm for the League of Nations has been. It is a real pleasure to receive your unqualified approbation.

Cordially and sincerely yours

WOODROW WILSON

After the Plenary Session on April 28th and the adoption of the Covenant of the League of Nations, I felt that my duties in Paris were at an end. The winter had been very strenuous, and the weather had been very inclement — much rain and very little sunshine. I decided to take a rest, and was advised, because of some slight ailment in my left leg due to impeded circulation, to take the baths at Bagnoles de l'Orne. The usual régime there is to take twenty-one baths. After I had taken eight, I received a letter from Colonel House saying that he would regard it most helpful if I would return to America at as early a date as possible. He informed me that the counsel for the American Commission, David Hunter Miller, was also returning; that passage had been secured for both of us on the U.S.S. Mount Vernon which was sailing from Brest on June 2d. He stated that it would be rendering a valuable service if I would confer with some of the Senators, so that they might be fully informed regarding the discussions and details of the negotiations as they progressed.

I accordingly returned to Paris, and on May 27th had a conference with Colonel House, who again impressed upon me the services I might render in returning to the United States, since no one was more familiar than Mr. Miller and I with the meaning and significance of the articles of the Covenant; no one, therefore, was better qualified to answer the criticisms and objections that had been made.

In the course of conversation, he said that in his opinion Woodrow Wilson would not become a candidate again for President unless the treaty were rejected, which might force him to run against his will in order to save the treaty; should the treaty, however, be ratified, there would be no occasion for him to become a candidate.

The day before this, while I was paying a visit at the Hotel Continental, I met Jane Addams and Lillian Wald, and with them was Alexander Kerensky, the former Premier of Russia. They asked me to meet Kerensky, which I did. He proved to be not at all the kind of man in appearance that I had pictured. He did not resemble the Russian type. He was clean-shaven, rather spare, a little above medium height, and seemed about forty years of age. He looked more like a student than like a leader who had stood in the storm-center of political turmoil.

Kerensky told me that he did not believe in Kolschak, principally because he regarded him as a tool of the British and Russian nobility. Kerensky expressed himself as opposed to having the Allies recognize Kolschak unless it was conditioned on definite guarantees that a free democratic election be held so that the people might decide what form of government they desired.

The following day, Dr. Dluski, the Polish peace delegate, together with M. Lieberman, a Jewish member of the Polish Diet, called upon me to explain, if not justify, the Polish pogroms, evidently because of the great publicity that had been given thereto by the mass meeting in New York. The resolutions passed by that meeting, and presented to the President, had appeared in dispatches to European papers.

We left Paris for Brest on May 30th. The Mount Vernon, which was scheduled to sail on the following day, had postponed sailing until June 3d. It carried some five thousand officers and men of the Sixth Division. Dr. Mezes and his wife were also on board. Dr. Mezes, who is a brother-in-law of Colonel House, organized the group of experts, of which he was chairman, which had rendered such valuable service to the Commission. We were all very comfortably provided for on the ship, and it was most interesting to observe the system and order with which the five thousand officers and men were taken care of. They were a jolly lot, happy to return home, and without exception conducted themselves in a correct and orderly manner. We had a delightful crossing; the weather was fine and the sea was calm.

Shortly after my return to the United States, the League to Enforce Peace called a meeting of the Executive Council to determine what action it could best take to further the ratification of the treaty which was now being vigorously debated in the Senate. It was decided that

Mr. Vance McCormick and I should be a committee to confer with the President. We subsequently desired to add Dr. A. Lawrence Lowell, president of Harvard University, to our number, provided it would be agreeable to the President, which Mr. McCormick was to ascertain when arranging for the appointment. The President designated August 6th as the day on which he would see us, and accordingly Dr. Lowell, Mr. McCormick, the Secretary of the League, Dr. Short, and I went to the White House.

President Wilson assured us that, while he was somewhat tired, he felt in good condition. He said he had had a number of conferences with individual Senators who had objected to the ratification of the treaty, and that he had given them explanations regarding the main points in dispute, namely, Article X, guaranteeing against external aggression; Article XXI, providing that nothing in the Covenant should be deemed to affect the validity of the Monroe Doctrine; and Article I, providing that any member of the League may, after two years' notice, withdraw from the League. These were the main subjects covered by the reservations formulated by the moderate group headed by Senators Kellogg and McCumber.

We suggested that it might be of good result if the President could in some public and formal way make his explanations and interpretations regarding these points. The question was how this could best be done. The President believed it would be preferable if one of the Senators of the opposition addressed to him a letter of inquiry, so framed as to enable the President to give his views. It was then understood that Dr. Lowell, Mr. McCormick, and I should confer with Senator Hitchcock, the Democratic leader of the minority of the Committee on Foreign Relations, who could advise us as to what

member of the Republican majority on the committee it
would be best for us to confer with.

After our conference with the President, we went to the
Senate and found the Committee on Foreign Relations in
session, examining Secretary of State Lansing. Senator
Hitchcock suggested that we call on Senator McCumber,
but as he was not then in Washington, Dr. Lowell and
I called on Senator Kellogg. The latter told us what we
already knew, namely, that he was in favor of the League
and was scheduled to make his speech in the Senate advocating the ratification of the treaty with the reservations his group had formulated, which reservations he
felt confident were not in the nature of amendments, but
interpretative only, and therefore would not require re-
submission either to the Plenary Session or to Germany.
Dr. Lowell and I outlined our plan regarding the letter
to the President, asking for his interpretation of the articles above referred to. While Senator Kellogg personally
favored this plan, he said he would first have to confer
with the members of his group, and he believed they
would be favorably inclined. We then inquired whether
the President's interpretations and clarifications might
not serve the purpose of making the reservations unnecessary. The Senator said "no," but that the reservations could recite the fact that they were based upon the
President's interpretations. We arranged that Senators
Kellogg and Hitchcock should confer upon the subject
with a view of preparing such a tentative letter of inquiry
which might be shown to the President in advance, and
to which the President could reply, giving his interpretations.

After leaving Senator Kellogg, we again called on
Senator Hitchcock. In all of these conferences between
the Senators of the various groups, we acted as the "hon-

est brokers" for the League. Senator Hitchcock thought
very favorably of our plan and believed it would work
out advantageously. Dr. Lowell and I felt gratified with
our day's work, though, as matters developed, nothing
came of this plan.

In this connection I cannot refrain from quoting a story
which Dr. Lowell told apropos of the problem. The story,
as I recall it, was that a noted colored preacher was holding a service in which he read a chapter from Isaiah referring to the Seraphim. After the service one of the colored
brethren asked the preacher what was "the difference between a Seraphim and a terrapin." The latter, rubbing his
head, replied: "My son, I grant you there is a difference,
but they have made it up."

Unfortunately, while there was, in words at least, if not
in context, a difference between the reservations offered
by the Administration group, the group of mild reserva-
tionists, and the majority group, yet, for reasons that I
need not enter into here, they did not "make it up."

In concluding this chapter and in closing these memoirs, I cannot resist reflecting how much wiser the Allied
Powers and America were in the conduct of the war than
in the making of peace, and afterwards. In war they
finally pooled their strength and won; in the peace terms
they again drew measurably apart. The men who framed
the peace terms subordinated world policies to home politics. The United States, by reason of a contest between
the Administration and the majority group in the Senate,
allowed its sense of world responsibility to be negated
by partisan differences. Reconstruction is being halted.
And why? Because the leading statesmen of the Entente
Powers still lack the economic wisdom, or, what is the
equivalent, the courage, to shape their international pol-

icies along world economic lines. My own country, in withholding its coöperation, is equally culpable. The result is tension and derangement in the relationship of nations.

As the malady from which this and other countries are suffering is world-wide, so must the remedy be world-wide. And America cannot free herself from the responsibility by isolating herself and refusing to do her part in applying the remedial measures necessary to restore normal conditions. The remedy does not consist in the lessening or weakening of sovereignty by individual states. It consists in the enlargement of their sovereign functions in concert with and in just relations to other states for the administration of common interests. It requires no surrender of sovereignty for individual states to conform their policies to the world's common needs.

THE END

Index

INDEX

Throughout the index, *S.* stands for the author.